WE ARE AIMING,

THEN, TO INQUIRE, IN A

RATIONAL WAY, INTO

THE THINGS HUMAN

REASON CAN DISCLOSE

CONCERNING GOD

St. THOMAS AQUINAS,
Summa Contra Gentiles, 1, 9, n. 4

PHILOSOPHICAL THEOLOGY by

James F. Ross

HACKETT PUBLISHING COMPANY, INC.
Indianapolis • Cambridge

To Kathleen

Cover design by Laszlo J. Balogh

For further information, please address the publisher,
  P.O. Box 55573, Indianapolis, Indiana 46205

Library of Congress Cataloging in Publication Date

Ross, James F 1931–
    Philosophical Theology.

    Includes index.
    1. Philosophical theology. I. Title.
BT40.R6 1981   231   80–22024
ISBN 0-915144-67-0
ISBN 0-915144-68-9 (pbk.)

Contents

Preface to the Second Printing

Certain objections, questions, and comparisons proposed since the first printing deserve replies. In addition, some widespread misconceptions of the arguments and strategies of the book are worth correcting.

My comments follow the general order of the book: (i) proofs; (ii) modal arguments for the existence of God; (iii) omnipotence and divine personality; (iv) dealing with the problem of evil; and (v) refuting the principle of sufficient reason.

Besides rejoinders to particular objections, e.g., by Rowe, Plantinga, and Mavrodes, I respond to the broader interpretations of the book offered by Donnelley and Lyons ("Recent Problems in Metaphysics," *New Scholasticism*, vol. 45, 1971, pp. 291–323) and E.M. Curley ("Spinoza and Recent Philosophy of Religion," *Spinoza: New Perspectives*, edited by Robert W. Shahan and J.I. Biro, University of Oklahoma Press, Norman, 1978).

(1) *Concerning Proof*. George I. Mavrodes, in "Some Recent Philosophical Theology," (*Review of Metaphysics* XXIV, No. 1, 1970, pp. 82–111) criticizes the conditions I state to be necessary if *any* argument (no matter what its subject matter) is to be a good argument which shows or establishes its conclusion. Good arguments for the existence of God, on my view, are to be demonstrative; that is, they are *to show*, in a theoretically satisfactory way, that God exists. And any good argument needs at least three things: it must be *sound*, and its premises must be both *accessible* and methodically *assessable*.

Mavrodes does not like my condition that contingent premises of good arguments have to be *assessable*; that is, that the interested observer must be able to confirm them for himself or replace them with premises which he has confirmed for himself. Proofs in physics, Mavrodes points out, often fail to satisfy this condition. I agree. Many arguments in physics do have premises which the interested observer cannot confirm for himself because they require special equipment and trained observers. But *functionally equivalent* conditions for direct reconfirmation are acceptable in the sciences. That is to say, even when the interested observer can't check out the premises for himself, if there are properly skilled people who can, and if the observer's faith in them is well-based, then the premises are assessable for him. In effect, a network of *testimonial* knowledge (see my "Testimonial Evidence" in K. Lehrer, ed., *Analysis and Metaphysics*, Reidel, Holland, 1975) can function equivalently to one's own inquiry. In the arguments we deal with, however, no functional equivalences are acceptable.

As I have defined "accessibility," the accessibility of an argument may be lost for a time and then return. Mavrodes wants to know why this sort of *time-relativity* with arguments is desirable, while what we both call "person-relativity" is not. If we say that a good argument is one which is *good for,* or convincing to, someone, then we have made our notion of the goodness of arguments *person-relative.* But this, I argue, is something that we want to avoid, while the characterization of good arguments as having accessible premises, and therefore being epoch-variant, is not.

For an argument to be *accessible,* it must (in principle) be *practically* possible for someone other than the one who proposes the argument to determine for himself by observation or the application of philosophical method whether the premises of the argument are true. Since, however, the observations and philosophical methods available to us vary with time, it is a simple fact that the accessibility of premises can wax and wane. Habits of *construing* our experience, for instance, may change so that whether experience confirms a claim (e.g., "All human thought occurs in a medium, either feeling, emotion, visual symbols, auditory symbols, actions, gestures, and so forth, with which it is identical") will vary. The consequence of my accessibility condition for good arguments, then, merely mirrors what is obviously true: what is a good argument at one historical period or in one culture may not be in another.

But while this sort of relativity is acceptable, and even desirable, in the specification of what a good argument is, person-relativity is not. For to make it a condition that a good argument must convince someone, as

Mavrodes wants to do, is to confuse one of the various *purposes* for which a good argument may be *employed* with the *function* of a good argument. The function of good arguments is not to make people know what they did not know before. Even if an argument failed to convince anyone—say, because everyone who ever saw it *already* knew its conclusion to be true, the argument might still be a good argument, being sound, non-circular, and having assessable and accessible premises. Good arguments, I acknowledge, may be employed for various purposes. Indeed, I state (*PT,* p. 10) that I employ certain arguments to make people know what they did not know before. But one should not misconstrue that such an employment of a good argument is instrumental and not definitive.

Mavrodes also finds disconcerting two other aspects of the conditions that I offer. First, my account of what a good argument is offers no criterion by which to tell, with doubtful cases, whether we have a good scientific or a good philosophical argument before us. But it's no fault of my account of proof that we have no yardstick by which to measure the border between philosophy and science; this lack is not a consequence of my account of proof but is an independently evident fact. And, secondly, it is true that my account may lead us to admit that perhaps every truth decidable by any method at all is decidable by some philosophical method. But our not knowing just how far we can go while still recognizably practicing philosophy and employing a method that allows us to decide reliably what is true, is again not a consequence of this theory; it is, as is the difficulty with establishing the border between science and philosophy, an independently evident fact.

The analysis of "good argument" in Chapter 1 is made against a limited background of contrasting views and may need supplementation later on. It was intended to provide reasons for approaching natural theology in a quasi-scientific spirit reminiscent of Aristotle, Aquinas, and Scotus, rather than within the apologetic "rationality of belief" approach of Plantinga (see *God and Other Minds,* Cornell University Press, Oxford, 1974) or a person-relative evangelical approach in which a good argument must *convince* someone on the evidence (see Mavrodes' *Belief in God,* Random House, New York, 1970).

(2) *Modal Arguments for the existence of God.*

(a) *Central Idea.* The elaborate articulation of a modal proof for God's existence (Part 2 of Chapter 3) still turns upon this simple consideration: that

God could not (consistently with our conception of what we are talking about) *exist in some possible worlds and not in others.* That's true for a number of reasons that different authors employe variously.

Because God cannot just happen to exist or happen not to exist, He must either exist under all possible conditions or under none. But things that exist under no conditions at all are inconsistent. And 'God exists' is not inconsistent. Therefore, God exists in all possible worlds, and therefore, exists actually.

A divine being has an infinity of attributes that entail that such a being is not a contingent thing. I chose to consider "self-explanatory" in Chapter 3 and "uncausable and unpreventable" in Chapter 4 because I regard the absolute independence of God to be a religiously relevant identifier of the divine being and, at the same time, central in a metaphysical story about what *accounts* for the being of all things.

Nevertheless, there is nothing wrong with one's selecting any other property that only God could have, provided it also excludes contingency—for instance, "perfection" (Hartshorne, *The Logic of Perfection* and *Anselm's Discovery*, LaSalle, Open Court, 1965), or "maximal greatness" (Plantinga, *The Nature of Necessity*, 1974).

For the heart of the strategy is still the same two steps: (i) to show or display that there is some possible world in which such a being would exist—that's the same as showing (urging or motivating, as the case may be) that it is possible that there is such a thing; and (ii), to show that such a thing couldn't exist only under *some* conditions or only in some possible worlds and not others, by deducing an explicit contradiction from that assumption. That shows that if such a being were to exist under any circumstances, it would exist no matter what, and, so, exists actually.

Since philosophy demands the disciplined articulation of what we discover about the ultimate nature of things, different *versions* of the modal argument involve different conceptual and logical decompositions, each with certain theoretical expenses attached. I consider the expense of my Chapter 3 proof to be modest because it commits us only to real possibility and necessity and to real *explanatory, accounting,* relations that hold among states of affairs and between things (e.g., uncausable and unpreventable things) and the states of affairs involving their existence. But we are *not* committed to the *existence* of possible worlds other than the actual but only to saying things might have been different from the ways they are. (See Robert W. Stalnaker, "Possible Worlds," pp. 454–465, *Philosophy As It Is,* Penguin Books, 1979.)

Alvin Plantinga, however (*The Nature of Necessity*), follows the two steps I outlined above by means of a "possible worlds" metaphysics claiming that the actual world is distinguished from all other possible worlds by a *property*, 'being actual'. I doubt that 'being actual' is a real property of anything and prefer ontologies of possible worlds which do not distinguish worlds from one another qualitatively. (See S. Kripke, "Naming and Necessity," Harvard University Press, 1980.) I also share Peter Geach's view ("What Actually Exists" in *God and the Soul*, Schocken Books, N.Y., 1969) that actuality, real being, belongs not to states of affairs but only to real objects. In fact, this possible world is not a real and substantial thing but only the logical consequence of real relationships among real substances. This possible world is the actual world because, and only because, it is the logical consequence of what is substantially real (what has being, "esse").

If one or other of the elaborated versions has to be abandoned because of anomalies or emerging falsity in its presuppositions about the metaphysics of possible worlds, that will not show that the modal argument is defective. It would still be true that God cannot exist contingently, and if God can exist at all, He must exist under all possible conditions and, therefore, must exist actually. And it would still be true that under some religiously acceptable descriptions of God, the consistency, the possibility, of such a being is *transparent*.

To dethrone the modal argument, one must show that *every* articulation that preserves its validity will (i) require an inconsistent logic of necessity and possibility; or (ii) require an inconsistent metaphysics of possible worlds; or (iii) involve, as essential premises, statements that are false, epistemically inaccessible or, for one reason or another, not methodically decidable; or (iv) involve descriptions that are religiously unacceptable as God-descriptions.

If it cannot be proved that there is *no* logically consistent God-description that is religiously acceptable and that excludes God's existing contingently, then there is no way to establish that God is not possible.

When one considers what a powerful counterargument it takes to refute the modal argument, one can see the extraordinary force behind the idea that *any being that is possible but not contingent must have that status because of what kind of thing it is, and must actually exist*. And *if there is a consistent and quiddidative God-description that entails non-contingency, a being satisfying that description must actually exist*.

(b) *Unpreventability.* Professor Curley (op. cit., p. 163) wants to know more about unpreventability, one of the attributes I appeal to to show that

God cannot exist contingently. Some being, some substance, is unpreventable just in case it is logically contradictory (inconsistent) to say of it that there is some other thing that prevents it from existing. Again, to say something is unpreventable is to say that there is no possible world in which any other thing, or logically independent state of affairs, accounts for that thing's not existing. And that's about the same as saying "it is false in all possible worlds that something else *causes* or otherwise really *explains* the thing's not existing." I show in Chapter 4 that every contingent state of affairs can be prevented and conclude from God's independence that God's existence cannot be contingent because it cannot be prevented causally.

The religiously relevant "absolute independence of the being of God" is thus cashed out metaphysically into the *impossibility* of any other thing's accounting either for the being or for the non-being of God. That's what uncausability and unpreventability come to.

Alvin Plantinga (in a Review of *Philosophical Theology* in *Philosophical Review,* 1972, pp. 509–511) misunderstood my use of "causally necessary." He treated "causally necessary" as a *predicate* of propositions, whereas I employed it as a *propositional operator.* Causal necessitation is elegantly explained by Arthur W. Burks (*Chance, Cause, Reason,* University of Chicago Press, 1977, Sec. 7. 2.2. Causal Laws, pp. 426–435).

In particular, to say of something that it is causally necessary is *not* to imply that it true. Rather, it is to imply that *if* the causal antecendents were to obtain actually, it is a logical consequence of the obtaining laws of nature and antecedent conditions that the consequent would obtain actually as well. Put simply, to be causally necessary is to be hypothetically logically *necessitated* under the causal laws (if any) and antecedent conditions obtaining in a given possible world.

Thus Plantinga's "proof" that if there are any unexplained states of affairs there are some inexplicable ones (in Ross's sense) is based upon a misconception (esp. p. 138) and seems "to have been written with undue haste" (see Plantinga, p. 510).

Further, Plantinga thought that because 7+5=12 is self-explanatory under my definition (see Chapter 3) while Paul's favorite proposition (which happens to be that equation) is not, some difficulty is created. If "Paul's favorite proposition" is a proper name rigidly designating the relevant equation, the proposition is self-explanatory on my definition. If "Paul's favorite proposition" functions as a mere description which could have had varying designata, then the *stated* proposition is not self-explanatory even though the subject term designates (refers to) a self-explanatory state of affairs. In view of his publishing so much similar material a few years later, it is to be wondered that Plantinga's review and later work did not mention the bright future of the modal argument he encountered here and of other matters of substantial agreement.

(c) *The Structure of the Argument.* Mavrodes, who acknowledged that the existence of a self-explanatory being follows logically from its possibility (p. 96), thought my elaborate versions involving production and principle E were unnecessary. That is, if there is a possible world in which there is a thing that has the property of existing in every possible world, then there is a thing that exists in every possible world. (I use terminology that became current later than Mavrodes' paper, to say the same thing.) That is true, but it does not render the rest of my arguments unnecessary, as Mavrodes thought. The machinery functions, in effect, to establish that there is such a possible world or at least to make it obvious that there is and to relate such necessary beings to what religious believers call "God." I was much too modest about what can be shown about possibility in the text of Chapter 3. For the possible-world quantificational understanding of possibility makes it practicable to produce a *transparently* consistent description of a possible world containing God.

There are two ways to approach this matter. One is to start with obvious divine attributes such as "total independence" and provide an articulated correlate such as "self-explaining" or "uncausable and unpreventable," then to seek out an argument that shows that such a being *could not* exist contingently because an explicit contradiction would result, and then to motivate that such a being is possible. That is the route I most often follow.

But there is another route as well. That is to find some attribute which it is obvious, *transparent,* that some substance *could* have; e.g., being perfect, or having all pure perfections, or super-excellence or being *self-accounting;* and then to show that such a being could not exist contingently and, so, must exist necessarily and, therefore, actually. I follow that route too in Chapters 3 and 4.

Some people misunderstand the function of the *parallel* argument in Chapter 3 from the supposed possibility of God's *not* existing to the impossibility of God's existing. Its function is to show that if you start either from "possibly God exists" or "possibly God does not exist" you get (by parallel reasoning that God's existence is not contingent) the conclusions, respectively, that God exists necessarily and that God cannot exist. Because the considerations against contingency can be applied to both the existence and to the nonexistence of God, *whether* God exists is an a priori matter, not a matter of mere a posteriori causal reasoning. The believer must, therefore, not accept that "possibly God does not exist" because it leads to the contradiction that God cannot exist. I particularly remind readers that no distinction is made in the book between "a priori" and "either necessarily so or necessarily not so". This is purely a matter of convention adopted for this book and *not* a doctrine about a priori knowledge or the nature of necessity.

The logical structure of the argument is also simpler than most critics suppose. It is:

1. Possibly-p (possibly God exists).
2. Whatever is possible is either contingent or necessary.
3. p can't be contingent (sub-proof that God can't exist contingently).
4. So, p is necessary.
5. Therefore p is true; God exists (because whatever is necessary is actually so).

And there are endless variations and sub-arguments that can be used to show that neither "God exists" nor "God does not exist" can be contingent. One way, like Plantinga's, is to *devise* a predicate that if a being has it in any possible world it must have it in all, a predicate that has that very structure in its definition, instead of merely implicity in its logical consequences, as is the case with the predicates I use and Hartshorne uses.

There are three limitations upon the predicates one might use in a modal argument. First, such a predicate must be easily recognized as part of or closely related to an orthodox religious conception of God, so as to assure the reader that it *is* God we are talking about. Second, it must make perspicuous and transparently obvious the sub-proof that such a being cannot exist contingently. And third, it must facilitate our providing direct proof or endless reinforcements of the claim that such a being is possible.

Some objections to these arguments, such as Purtill's "Three Ontological Arguments" *(International Journal for Philosophy of Religion*, Vol. 6, No. 2, 1975) are explicitly contradictory. Purtill, discussing the then unpublished form of Plantinga's argument, grants that there is a way to put the reasoning so that "If God exists in any possible world, He exists in all." He then says the objector "will be forced to deny that God exists in any possible world just as the critic of the first ontological argument denied that the term 'God' had any referent"... (p. 105) "Both denials free us from any self-contradiction and both seem *prima facie* tenable" (p. 106). (Discussing my own arguments, Purtill raises the same issue.)

Well, the *only* condition under which "God" would, in the relevant sense, have no referent at all is that no possible world contains anything named by it. That can happen only if it is *inconsistent* to say that such a being exists. And thus the whole objection comes down to saying, without any offer of proof, "But it is inconsistent to say God exists."

Furthermore, it is naive to think denying that "God" has any referent in any possible world avoids contradiction. If it is not inconsistent to say God exists, then it *is* inconsistent to say God does not exist. And it is also inconsistent to say *"possibly* God does not exist." And it is further inconsistent to say that there is nothing in any possible world that is referred to by the word "God." Purtill is quite evidently in error when he says "But if we deny that the term 'God' refers to *anything* existent or non-existent, we do not contradict ourselves."

John Hick (*Arguments for the Existence of God*, N.Y., MacMillan, 1970, pp. 97–100) transcended reason when he regarded one version (below in Ch. 4, p. 174) as involving a disjunctive first premise that is not exhaustive and found the argument, therefore, invalid. For the first premise I employed stated (without expressing the overall modal operator, "Necessarily") that whatever is *not* the case is either self-explanatory or heteroexplicable. Hick thought some alternative had been ignored. But there are only two candidates, the unexplained and the inexplicable. All unexplained situations are either explicable or inexplicable, and the former have already been provided for, so what is left out can only be the inexplicable situations. Moreover, Hick forgets that the basic principle under which these arguments are presented is the Principle of Explicability: that *every* state of affairs is explicable, that there are, and can be, *no* inexplicable situations. So unless Hick is prepared to *prove* that the Principle of Explicability is false (because inconsistent), his argument that some possibility has been ignored in the first premise simply begs the question.

It is just *because* there cannot be any metaphysically inexplicable states of affairs that God must exist in all possible worlds and, consequently, in the actual world. Why is God's *not* existing not a possible state of affairs? Because every possible state of affairs is *explicable,* and whatever is explicable is either self-explanatory or heteroexplicable. But God's not existing is not self-explanatory (because its opposite is not self-contradictory) and it is not hetero-explicable because God is uncausable and unpreventable. So it is not *possible* that God does not exist. Hick confused "explic*able*" with "explain*ed*"!

(d) *On showing that God is possible.* This book is too cautious. *Demonstrations* of the consistency of complete descriptions of God are, as I point out (p. 139), endless. But articulated descriptions whose consistency is transparent because the component conceptual relations are as clear as the facets of a crystal, can be devised, as is illustrated by Plantinga's explanation of "has maximal excellence in every possible world" and by my discussion of pure perfections, which follows.

What the believers *mean* to talk about is something that is both possible and non-contingent. *So the only way to kill the basic consideration underlying all this reasoning is to show that nothing can be both possible and non-contingent, not any substance, anyway.* The very implausibility of such a position is strong reinforcement that God is possible.

· (e) *The Consequences of the Modal Proof.* Mavrodes' appraisals of the consequences of the modal proof are typical and represent mistakes that I, too, was making at the time. He conceded (p. 97) that the argument I gave had true premises and a true conclusion that followed validly, but complained that "not only is there a self-explanatory being; there are plenty of them." That was thought to be a defect because the argument did not pick any one such being out and say that it was God nor did it have another stage that identified one such being as God. If numbers are beings, as he and I think they are, there are *many* self-explanatory beings! But there are not so many self-explanatory *substances* and there are even fewer self-explanatory substances that are omnipotent, omniscient, and so forth. What is the mistake we were making?

I begin with a principle I did not state in this book: if 'F' is the predicate in virtue of which something that is F exists in all possible worlds, then *everything* that has F exists in all possible worlds provided only that the set of all its attributes is consistent.

And so, what Mavrodes calls the "Gaunilo strategy"—namely, "conjoining this property to others which it is supposed God does not possess—and then rejecting the argument" creates no problem whatever. Does a self-explanatory, self-existent substance, that is omnipotent, omniscient, and *evil* exist? That depends *entirely* upon whether such a being is possible, and possibility is entirely determined by the internal consistency of the attributes.

For any beings thus described, all and only those whose quidditative descriptions are consistent will exist, the rest are impossible. (Someone wants to know how I know that all those whose quidditative descriptions are consistent are compossible? Each is to exist in all possible worlds and thus must be compossible with *every* consistent thing. I'll explain that below).

One can *make* the argument into an identifying argument for the existence of God by adding to the basic property F, "self-explanatory substance", whatever attributes are needed. The more you add, the more questions one may have to answer about consistency. But the *fact* remains the same: if the description *is* consistent, there *is* such a being. And so, this argument proves the existence of the divine substance just as well as it proves the existence of any self-explanatory being.

John Donnelly and L. S. Lyons ("Recent Problems in Metaphysics," *New Scholasticism*, Vol. 45, pp. 291–323, 1971) patiently and most sympathetically restated the main thrust of my reasoning and then considered the same objection: that "the argument established the existence of God *qua* uncausable and unpreventable thing, but it fails to answer satisfactorily whether the additional signification of the term "God" (e.g., his omnipotence, benevolence, and so forth) has been instantiated *in re*." That puts the matter clearly. They go on to extract an elaborate and convincing reply from my proof that the clearly divine attributes of omnipotence and omniscience, as I define them, entail necessity on the part of the thing.

But there is a simpler, more general and equally effective answer, one that I should have included in this book: No matter *what* attributes you conjoin to "is an unpreventable and uncausable being", *if* the conjunction is logically consistent, then there is actually something that satisfies that description.

Thus, if there is a consistent quidditative thing–description that is religiously adequate as a God–description and involves as essential predicates the uncausability and unpreventability of the thing or the omnipotence and omniscience of the thing (as I have defined those attributes), then it follows logically that the "the additional signification of the word "God" has been instantiated in *re*."

Professor Curley took that objection even more seriously than Donnelly and Lyons. Curley states the main point of the argument for the existence of God succinctly (p. 162) and recognizes that the principle, "any state of affairs is explicable either per se or per aliud," is the rationale by which I pass from the claim that God is possible to the claim that God is necessary (because 'God does not exist' is inexplicable). But I mislead him into thinking (p. 165) that "unless there is some necessary connection among the various attributes, there is no reason to say that the argument has proved the existence of the being possessing the full set of attributes in the definition, i.e., no reason to say it has proved the existence of God (as understood in the tradition)." Curley notes, "Ross allows that this objection is sound, and that the argument I have sketched out does not, without further ado, prove God's existence. But he thinks the required necessary connections exist." And they do. But that misses the point; for the arguments, "without further ado," *do* prove God's existence.

Simply conjoin "uncausable and unpreventable" with any and all religiously essential attributes, such as "omnipotent," "omniscient," "benevolent," "eternal," "loving," "all good," "perfect," into what is obviously a God-description. If such a description is logically consistent then something exists that satisfies such a description.

It is an underestimate to say the argument as presented does not prove the existence of God as traditionally conceived; it most certainly does.

These are the only published objections to my modal argument that I have seen. I conclude that it remains unscathed.

(3) *The Conception of Omnipotence.* In Chapter 5 I explain that S is omnipotent just in case, for any contingent state of affairs, p, p obtains just in case S *effectively* wills that p (and I add this qualification below: where p is not identical with a state of S's willing).

(a) *Effective Willing.* Professor Curley (pp. 166–170) takes two principles to apply to willing in general that I apply only to *effective* choice, choice that is productively sufficient, in every possible world in which it occurs, for what is elected. Only the divine will is effective over the entire range of its external choices. Those principles are:

(1) whatever an effective chooser brings about by choice is also something it could have effectively chosen not to obtain, (p) $(SWp \longrightarrow \Diamond SW\bar{p})$; and (2) for any contingent state of affairs (not a state of S's willing), its being false that S willed p is logically equivalent to S's having willed that not-p, (p) $(\overline{SWp} \longleftrightarrow SW\bar{p})$.

(b) *Necessary Existing.* An obvious consequence of my definition is that nothing omnipotent exists contingently (see pp. 213, 214). The same thing is true of anything that satisfies the conditions for omniscience. An omnipotent being's contingently *not* existing would have its *existing* as a necessary condition; such a situation is impossible. Thus we have another a priori proof that an omnipotent being exists. (See Chapter 4, below, for a critique of the notion of "a priori" proof.)

(c) *Concurrent Willing.* A second consequence of the definitions is that God's choosing that I freely do x is logically sufficient and necessary for everything that I freely choose to do. That provides a strong version of divine governance, divine providence, and even divine predestination.

God *effectively* chooses each state of affairs that belongs to the actual world and is not part of all possible worlds—that's a consequence of the account of creating in which God determines which possible world is actual. That so crucial a determination could be left to creatures and outside God's power, as in Plantinga's free will defense (*God, Freedom and Evil,* Harper and Row, 1974, and also *God and Other Minds: A Study of the Rational Justification of Belief in God,* Cornell University Press, 1967), would have the consequence that God does not know timelessly and determine by His election alone what possible world is actual.

That the concurrent will of God should be both necessary and logically sufficient for me to do what I do freely is no new doctrine and it lies in the heartland of religious orthodoxy. Nor is it paradoxical. For one thing, the object of the divine will as thus described is the *state of affairs* that I freely choose to write these pages, whereas, the object of my choice is an *action,* to do x, to write the pages. (See my "Creation," Jrl. of Philosophy, Oct. 1980.)

In a neat metaphysics, the categorial differences in the objects of the will and thus the differences in scope of the divine and human wills would be conspicious, evaporating what has been claimed to be, but has never been shown to be, a problem concerning the consistency between such causation and freedom of choice.

And what is the matter with the account of levels of reality in Chapter 6 (pp. 254–256 below) that makes clear the categorial differences in the objects of divine and human choice and the existence of two kinds of causation?

(d) *Surviving the Paradoxes.* Mavrodes ("Defining Omnipotence," *Philosophical Studies* 32, 1977); Richard Swinburne ("Omnipotence," *American Philosophical Quarterly* 10, 1973), Richard LaCroix ("The Impossibility of Defining Omnipotence," *Philosophical Studies* 32, 1977), J. L. Cowan ("The Paradox of Omnipotence Revisited," *Canadian Journal of Philosophy,* vol. 3, 1974), Douglas Walton ("The Omnipotence Paradox," *Canadian Journal of Philosophy,* vol. v, 1975), and Peter Geach ("Omnipotence," *Philosophy* 48, pp. 327–333, 1973) have all bypassed my analysis of omnipotence despite its obvious orthodoxy, its continuity with the views of Aquinas, Scotus, and Maimonides, and its ability to dispose, as Chapter 5 concludes, of the so-called paradoxes that the above cited papers still contend with. Of course God cannot make a stone that He cannot lift because God's power extends only to the contingent. If the state of affairs to be realized is in fact inconsistent or necessary, it does not fall within the divine will. That's all there is to it. The "paradoxes" consist only in confusions about what kind of a task is being proposed and whether some inconsistent description applies to it.

In this respect Donnelly and Lyons (op. cit., p. 298) concede too much to what they call "the paradox of the stone" and to Ockham's problem about God's ability to bring about immediately whatever he can bring about through secondary causes (a problem I think Scotus initiated by characterizing that ability as the "Catholic" conception of omnipotence, a power not demonstrable of God by human reason (*God and Creatures, Quodlibetal Questions,* trans. Alluntis and Wolter, Question 7.29–34, Princeton University Press, 1975).

God can produce Beethoven-Fifth-Symphony-sound-waves so that Jones hears that very symphony (say on a desert island in 1989) even though no broadcast of that symphony by humans was ever directed over that island. If in some possible world there is a tenth Beethoven Symphony—one he would have composed after the Ninth had matters been suitably otherwise—God can bring it about that someone's radio picks up sound waves electronically indistinguishable from what would have been produced had matters been otherwise, as above supposed. Thus the hearer would listen to what would have been Beethoven's tenth symphony had another world been the actual world.

(e) *How Many Omnipotent Beings?* Curley's problems are different. He wants to know whether "omnipotence entails omniscience, and conversely." He puts the question, "Does the one conception involve the other?" But another way to put it is, "Is there a possible world in which there is an omnipotent being that is not omniscient or an omniscient being that is not omnipotent?" The latter permits a swift answer: No. For if it is possible that an omnipotent and omniscient being should exist at all, then it is true in all possible worlds that such a being exists. So no world contains the one and not the other.

Further, in any possible world in which there is an omnipotent and omniscient being, there is no *other* being which is either omnipotent and not omniscient or omniscient and not omnipotent, Why? Because there is no possible world in which there are distinct omniscient or distinct omnipotent beings, that is, beings whose first-level properties (attributes) are different.

The reason comes to this: neither omnipotent nor omniscient beings can exist contingently. That's because, as defined, those attributes require that the being exist in all possible worlds (as the explicit definitions of Chapter 5 entail and the commentators have acknowledged). But a substance that exists in all possible worlds has all the pure perfections (see "pure perfections," following). Therefore, these beings cannot differ from one another in any first-level property, properties *constitutive of the kind* of substance, e.g., as to whether they are substances that live, think, choose, and so forth. If they cannot differ in kind, they cannot differ in number. Therefore, all necessary beings that are substances are identical.

(f) *Pure Perfections.* The argument, more elaborately expressed in my "On Proofs for the Existence of God" (*Monist,* vol. 54, No. 2, 1970) comes to this. The attribute by which some substance exists in all possible worlds and is constituted to be the *kind* of thing that it is, is a "pure perfection," an attribute which does not entail any unfulfilled capacity (as does "infant"), any unexercised potentiality (as does "waiting") or any kind of incompletion, composition, or dependence upon external causes. Omnipotence and omniscience, although pure perfections, are not "first level" attributes because they do not constitute a *kind* of thing. It is always appropriate to ask, "An omnipotent and omniscient *what?*"

Further, a being that exists in all possible worlds must have no attributes that are *not* pure perfections. And no pure perfection is incompatible with any other. So, there is a possible world in which there is a being that has all pure perfections (to be, to live, to know, to love, and so forth) and that includes the attribute of existing in all possible worlds (which is one of the pure perfections). So, the actual world contains such a being.

Any *other* being that exists in all possible worlds (as all omnipotent and omniscient beings must, on my definitions) must *differ* from the first either by *lacking* some pure perfection or by having some *limited* perfection. But every limited perfection entails the lack of some pure perfection, so the latter difference boils down to the former. But lacking some pure perfection in all possible worlds is the same as not being capable of such a perfection in any world. Yet, there can be no explanation of that incapacity because all the being's other attributes are pure perfections and they never exclude one another. So there is no possible world in which there is an explanation of why the other omnipotent and omniscient being would *lack* some pure perfection by which it is distinguished from the first. Thus, applying principle E, no possible world contains an omnipotent and omniscient being that lacks some pure perfection. Therefore, in no possible world are there different omnipotent and omniscient beings.

Thus my argument at the bottom of *PT*, p. 215, is erroneous in two respects. First, one *can* demonstrate the uniqueness of the omnipotent being as I have, above. Second, there cannot be two things so related that one can effectively will that the other effectively will something (where both are omnipotent and free). That could happen only if the one were metaphysically dependent upon the other. But metaphysical dependence is an asymmetrical relation, while the conditions stated on p. 215 require that the relation of equivalence of choices be symmetrical. This time, caution caused a contradiction. There cannot be a plurality of omnipotent beings because the difference that would make them two *cannot* be explained. Thus the hypothesis would violate principle E.

On the same subject Curley (p. 167) urges Spinoza's reflection that it is not enough to show that "each of the divine attributes is separately capable of exemplification" . . . "we must have some argument tending to show that it is logically possible for the traditional attributes to be combined in one being." Curley concludes that "Ross' program is incompletely carried out" in this book.

But the general method, sketched above, shows (a) that each divine attribute is a "pure perfection" and (b) that no pure perfection can be incompatible with any other and, therefore, that *all* pure perfections can be instantiated in the same being. It further shows that there can be no substance that has some but not all of the divine attributes and, yet, exists in all possible worlds, because its lacking some pure perfection would be an *inexplicable* state of affairs.

(4) *Divine Personality.* Professor Curley observes,

When contemporary philosophers of religion . . . turn to the question of whether that being has the attributes traditional Christian theology ascribes to God, they may find it difficult to resist Spinozistic conclusions (p. 171). . . . The analysis of the way in which God has the properties of intellect and will, i.e., the analysis of his omnipotence and omniscience, is incompatible with the ascription of personality to him in any sense which would require having intellect and will as we do (p. 169).

I agree that the ascription of personality to God is, within the philosophical theory, based chiefly upon the ascription of reason and choice to God.

But within the *religion,* personhood is ascribed on the basis of the religion-originators' reported experiences. Although the personhood of God is not investigated in this book, I acknowledge that God's having joy, sadness, and desires, as understood in the Biblical tradition (see Curley, p. 171) should be accomodated by a philosophical account of God's personhood. But that will and intellect in God are named by *mere equivocation* on the names of the corresponding faculties in man (as Spinoza states, I *Ethics,* prop. 17), I deny and rebut on philosophical, linguistic, and the very scriptural grounds that Curley appeals to to create the issue.

These powers of God are named by *analogy* to the powers of man, just as the medievals believed and as I think I have adequately explained in *Portraying Analogy,* (Cambridge University Press, 1981, forthcoming). I can state this much succinctly: even if both x and y are called "intelligent" and even if some necessary condition for anything's bearing the predicate "is intelligent" in sense #1 (in which it applies to x) is *not* a necessary condition of anything's bearing the predicate "is intelligent" in sense #2 (in which it applies to y), that does *not* establish that "intelligent" is used *merely* equivocally (like "bank/bank") in the two cases. A difference of truth-conditions may (but does not always) represent some difference of meaning but does not, by itself, guarantee *unrelatedness* of meaning. Hence Spinoza's and Curley's arguments conceal a crucial premise, and one that is false, too.

To say "All humans are *intelligent"* and also "John is not an *intelligent* human" is, of course, to equivocate on "is intelligent," but it is *not* to employ the word *merely* equivocally. The two senses of "intelligent" are not *un*related in meaning as are "charge (an account) and "charge" (a criminal).

Because a difference in *some* truth conditions cannot show that divine knowing and willing "differ entirely" from human knowing and willing and do not satisfy *related significations* (cf. C. I. Lewis, *AKV*) of common predicates ("knows" and "wills"), the argument that attributing personhood to God is inconsistent with my analyses of divine knowing and divine willing is simply a non sequitur.

Curley asks whether "S wills p at t" can have different truth values for different times if "God" is substituted for "S". If not, he says, "it would be one more indication of a radical difference in meaning between properties ascribed to God and those ascribed to men" (p. 170). Well, it would indicate no such thing. As I already said, a difference of truth conditions may reflect *some* difference of meaning but it does not guarantee mere equivocation. Furthermore, the fact that the truth conditions for a sentence-frame instantiated with "God" are different from the truth conditions for the same frame instantiated with "Curley" does not *assure* us of a difference of *meaning* in any *common* term. Example: a frame instantiated for a man and then for a woman. The one resulting sentence has the necessary condition for truth: that some man did x; the other, that some woman did x. No meaning difference in a *common* word is required. I stop to point this out because the error here, like the previous one, is not merely Curley's, but Spinoza's. And it is a very common error in thinking about these matters.

A personality that consists in "willing" and "knowing" alone would be, as Curley says, "thin." But I can go further, saying that God experiences joy as well as happiness, that God understands sorrow and loss, that God has compassion for His children, but not as someone *made* sorry or having lost some good.

God understands and experiences some feelings by *expressing* them in His creation and not as perturbations caused in His life. Similarly, Shakespeare experienced, explained, and understood the rage, jealousy, and pride of the hunchbacked king Richard, by *creating* such a character, not by becoming enraged, jealous, and proud himself. There is no Spinozistic reason to think that an adequate account of God's personhood would be incompatible with the positions developed in this book.

I do not address Hartshorne's position that personality requires that a being be self-surpassing, and, therefore, be passible, in process, and changing in some respects. The attributes of power and knowledge I have defined exclude such self-surpassing and, therefore, *are* inconsistent with Hartshorne's requirements for God's being personal. I deal with that matter in "An Impasse Concerning Competing Conceptions of God" (*International Journal for the Philosophy of Religion,* vol. III, No. 4, 1977, pp. 233–249).

(5) *Purposive Action and Personality.* Curley says (a) omnipotence, as I define it, conflicts with the conditions for purposive action that are required for personality (p. 171–173), and (b) both omnipotence and personality are incompatible with eternity (as timelessness) (p. 171). The second point is merely a conjecture with a reference to N. Pike's *God and Timelessness* (London: Routledge and Kegan Paul, 1970, pp. 176–179, 189–190). If one regards eternity, as did Boethius, as "the simultaneous enjoyment of perfect life" and involving no time relationships to objects created, the range of problems is vastly restricted. Of course, there are

issues not settled here about what the content of God's knowledge is when He knows what I know when I know I have a pain. And there are difficulties over the fact that God has attributes that He might not have had, had He decided otherwise, and, yet, not in any time.

The dispute about purposive action is more important. According to Curley,

> . . . it would make no sense to say I do these things ["things as a means to an end which is both contingent in itself and contingent in relation to the means I employ," p. 172] . . . to achieve this end, if I were omnipotent.
>
> If I am omnipotent (as Ross defines the notion, at any rate) and I choose some contingent end (e.g. that this water shall boil, that I should know the answer to some question), then my choosing that end is logically sufficient for its occurrence, and it is not necessary that any other condition be satisfied to achieve this result. And if that is the case, it cannot be said that my doing anything else is instrumental to achieving the result (p. 173).

Yet, for action to be purposive it must involve doing things as means to an end. So Curley concludes that, conceived of as I propose, God cannot act purposively and so cannot be personal. But that is a mistake. Curley concludes from the fact that God *need* not act purposively that He *cannot*. Besides metaphysical causation, natural agency is possible for God.

Curley tells us that purposive action involves production of an outcome (e.g., the rolling back of the Red Sea) through an *intermediate* (the wind's blowing all night) which is neither logically necessary nor logically sufficient but which is a cause (though contingently). And he suggests a version of Ockham's principle, that whatever God can produce through intermediate causes, He can produce directly, that I too share: where God produces an effect through intermediate causes, contingently related to the event as described, God can produce the event without those intermediates. Simply, whatever is causally (but not logically) necessary for an event E is such that in some possible world E occurs when that condition does not occur or is not causally related to E.

But notice what Curley suggests about the Red Sea case:

> Here God is pictured as causing one event in order to bring about another, where the first event is causally related to the other. But if God is omnipotent, he could have produced the second event immediately. Indeed his willing that the event occur was logically sufficient for its occurrence. And the question is, how can we understand the suggestion that the first event was instrumental to the second when it was

neither logically nor causally necessary to the occurrence of the other? (p. 173).

There are multiple confusions. On one level Curley confuses the or-dained power of God with God's absolute power: anything E, which has a causally necessary condition c in this world cannot, the causal necessity re-maining, be produced by God *in accordance* with the laws of nature without that condition's obtaining. Nevertheless, E, no matter what it is, oc-curs in some other possible world *without* that condition (c's) obtaining. That follows from the fact that the condition is *causal* and, therefore, con-tingent. So, in His absolute power God can produce *any* effect without its natural causes. Of course, I am premising that all the natural causes of things are logically independent of their effects, a condition Kripke sug-gests is not satisfied in the relation of human parents to their offspring (S. Kripke, *Naming and Necessity*, Harvard University Press, 1980). That point need not be resolved here because when I say God does not need to pursue ends through their natural causes, I condition that reply upon the logical independence of the causes and effects.

So for Curley to say, about Spinoza's example of the Red Sea miracle, that "the strong east wind was neither logically nor causally necessary to the occurrence" is confusing. It does not follow from the fact that God could, had the world been otherwise, have accomplished the result without the wind or, even, by a simple act of will, that the wind had no causal role, no necessity in the event. It had *hypothetical* necessity, necessity under the laws of nature. In a word, Curley thinks the one event was not instrumental to the other because it was not causally necessary to the other (in the sense that the other was not impossible without the wind). And he thinks it was not causally necessary because God could have produced the outcome without the intermediate.

Indeed God· could; but not under the laws that were involved in *that* event. Not only the wind, but the system of physical laws functioned in-strumentally in God's purposes. Further, it is surely a mistake to assume that no event is an instrument toward another unless the end is impossible, either logically or causally, without the former. Your sending me a letter explaining my mistakes might be instrumental to my correcting them, even though you could have telephoned the explanations. Either would be in-strumental, though neither is necessary.

(6) *Sufficient Reason.* Curley (p. 170–171) uncovered·an inconsistency. I claim to show that the Principle of Sufficient Reason (hereafter, PSR) is false

because some actual state of affairs lacks an explanation. And yet I so define omnipotence that every contingent state of affairs *has* an explanation, namely, that God effectively wills it (Curley, p. 171). Moreover, on that definition of omnipotence, PSR would be true in every possible world.

There are three steps to a reply. First, I have to provide an explicit qualification of the range of contingent states of affairs that fall within the *effective* choice of an omnipotent being: that is, every contingent state of affairs that is not *identical* with some state of S's effective willing. Second, insofar as there is a regress of divine willing, it is not a regress of *effective explanatory* choices. And third, despite the appearance in Chapter 5 to the contrary, effective choices cannot be explained by effective choices unless the beings involved are not identical and are of different levels of reality. That's the basis for the first and second steps.

I had thought earlier that a regress of divine willing was harmless, like the sequence Leibniz postulated, because there would still be one thing to be explained: *that* that sequence was in the actual rather than merely in a possible world.

Nevertheless, the regress is not harmless. For if it is an explanatory regress, then *every* contingent state of affairs is embraced by it and has an explanation in God's choice. That conflicts with our saying that the fact that God chose this world is not explained; for the definition entails that God willed to will, and so forth, an infinite regress. It also conflicts with the proof, at p. 308, that there *must* be unaccounted states of affairs but there cannot be any unaccountable ones.

Further, the regress is vicious. To the question, why *that* sequence of choices rather than some other that was possible, the answer again has to be that the sequence itself is the product of an infinite sequence of choices; and so we get infinite sequences "at right angles to one another" in an infinite sequence, the whole of which is *still* contingent and, therefore, unexplained, requiring a further "right angled" sequence. It's like explaining why there is an infinitely long string of dominos, rather than some other, by saying there is an explaining string outside it, at right angles, and then explaining the second by a third, and so forth.

That warns us not to phrase the definition of omnipotence as if God's choices were infinitely self-including and by their sheer number could run after, overtake, and get ahead of the repeated question "Why?" Even if every effective divine choice were, logically, preceded by an effective divine choice to make that choice, still that sequence, no matter what it contains, might not have happened. That follows from the fact that the final events, the objects of God's choices, might not have happened. And, so, it is obvious that any attempt to explain why what happened (as a whole) happened, will fail. For as long as it did not *have* to happen, there is no place to seek an explanation. (See p. 301, bottom.) Thus it is obvious that a definition of omnipotence that provides an explanation for every contingent state of affairs is mistaken and must be qualified.

The relevant range of omnipotent power is effective choice over every contingent state of affairs *that is not identical* with one of the agent's states of will. That is not a merely an *ad hoc* amendment to escape inconsistency with the denial of the Principle of Sufficient Reason. It is also motivated by the fact that for the choices of one being to be included within its own effective choices is to create an inconsistency.

An effective choice is one such that the object chosen occurs in every possible world in which the choice is made. That is, it is not possible that the choice be made and what is chosen not happen. Now, one's own choosing cannot be the object of an *effective* prior choice. For the prior choice will either be a *natural* or a *metaphysical* cause of the latter. But if the prior choice is a natural cause of the latter, then the later choosing is not free. But if the prior choice is a metaphysical cause of the latter then the subjects (makers) of the choices cannot be the same being. For metaphysical dependence is an assymetrical, alio-relative relation and, hence, nothing has it to itself. (See Ch. 6.)

I do not use arguments based on the premise that if choices could be included within effective choices, the included choices could not have been otherwise than as they are, given the prior effective choice. The reason is that I do not think it is always a necessary condition for one's choice to be free that there should be a possible world in which *all* the circumstances "up to" the choice are the same but the choice is different. For a person in the presence of the beatific vision worships God willingly and freely and yet there is no possible world in which in that beatific presence he chooses otherwise; and God acts rightly and justly from His free will, even though there is no possible world in which He does what is wrong.

That allows me to digress briefly to explain again how God's effective choosing that I *freely* do X is compatible with my freedom, even though there is no possible world in which He chooses that I freely do X and I freely choose to do Y. I act freely when I act willingly (in accord with inclination), in the absence of violence and defeating ignorance, and from that ability by which I act rightly (e.g., Anselm: "from that ability by which I can keep uprightness of the will for its own sake"; and Augustine: "the capacity to act rightly"). In such a case God is not a *natural* cause of my acting because He is neither the *agent* of my acting (*I* am) nor is any divine *event* related by some contingent causal law to the event of my acting. God's effective choice is over the actuality of the state of affairs; mine is over the action. His concurrent will is a *sine qua non* of my acting at all and is sufficient for it's being the case that I am free, but is not *constitutive* of it.

So, the Leibnizian infinite regress of explanatory choices is a delusion; it does not explain every contingent state of affairs and it lines up divine choices in impossible ways, particularly, as if they were metaphysically dependent upon one another.

Charles J. Kelly, "Some Arguments Concerning the Principle of Sufficient Reason and Cosmological Proofs" (*The Thomist,* vol. 40, No. 2, April 1976, pp. 258–293) says I am attacking such principles as "Everything is ex-plain*able*" (italics mine) and "Every fact is explain*able*" (italics mine), op. cit., p. 263. I argue, on the contrary, that whatever *might* have been so (and that includes whatever actually is so) might have had an explanation. But in no possible world is there a sufficient reason for everything that would be contingently so if that world were actual.

Nevertheless, Kelly (p. 269) quotes an interesting argument from Jacques Maritain (*A Preface to Metaphysics,* Mentor, Omega Books, 1962, pp. 99–100) that, in effect, defines a sufficient reason for a thing as the totality of its necessary conditions. Thus, Maritain argues, if you say that something exists without a sufficient reason, you say something exists without one of its necessary conditions, and that is self-contradictory.

Further, Maritain argues, a contingent state of affairs is, logically, insuffi-cient to account for its own being. It has not, "in itself" that "in virtue of which" it exists. Now, Maritain says, "that in virtue of which something ex-ists" is the *same* as "that without which an object is not". And so, if a thing not having *in itself* "that without which it is not" does not have it in some-thing else, then it does not exist. So whatever exists has either in itself or in another "that without which it is not", a sufficient reason, the totality of its necessary conditions.

What's the matter here? The *what* of a contingent thing is not sufficient to account for its existence. But whether having an extrinsic sufficient cause of being is a *logically* necessary condition for the thing's existing is just what the defender of PSR is supposed to prove. Maritain's argument *supposes* it. For, of course, if there is any possible world in which the contingent thing exists without an extrinsic cause, then having such a cause is *not* logically necessary and, therefore, is not one of the necessary conditions for its being. So Maritain's argument begs the question.

William Rowe, *The Cosmological Argument* (Princeton University Press, 1975), preceded by "The Cosmological argument and the Principle of Sufficient Reason" (*Man and World*, 1, 1968, pp. 278–292) and "The Cosmological Argument" (*Nous* 5, 1971, pp. 49–61), does not consider that my arguments against what might be called Spinozistic formulations of PSR (e.g., "whatever is the case has a sufficient reason either in itself or in something else") also refute Samuel Clarke's more modest formulations that Aquinas might also have held: PSR 1, "Every existing thing has a sufficient reason for its existence", and PSR $_2$, "Whatever comes into existence must have an explanation for its coming to be". If PSR 1 is taken, almost as Maritain does, to be "every existing thing satisfies every necessary condition for existence" it is tautological and says nothing about whether there have to be actual extrinsic causes of contingent existents. But if PSR 1 is taken to mean that all contingent existents have extrinsic causes, (i) no contradiction can be deduced from its denial and (ii) no amount of induction will establish it.

(7) *Evil.* My basic strategy concerning the problem of evil has been misunderstood. First, I regard any answer such as the Free Will Defense, that resolves the problem by saying "Maybe the evil was unavoidable even by an omnipotent being," as inherently unsatisfactory. The reason is that evil is a mystery; its challenge to the understanding *cannot* be talked away.

It is insufficient to say that evil came about because the omnipotent being *could* not guarantee its absence from a world of free creatures, consistently with preserving their freedom. A sensitive historical understanding of genocide, of the Holocaust, of the religious truth that God was no more absent from the death camps than He was from Calvary, tells us God *must* have been able to prevent or avert the evils; that is a precondition of the *mystery*.

Similarly, solutions that say God "need not" have avoided the evils because they are "justified" by a greater good, the "tapestry" views discussed in Chapter 6, even when most ably expounded as by R. M. Chisholm in "The Defeat of Good and Evil" (*Proceedings of the American Philosophical Association*, vol. XLII, 1968–79, reprinted in John E. Smith (ed.), *Contemporary American Philosophy: Second Series*, George Allen Unwin, London, 1970, pp. 152–167), simply miss the point. "Justification" is probably not even an appropriate thought-category for talking of human wrong-doing of plague-like proportions.

So, eschewing as basically inappropriate to our experience of evil, both the defense that God could not effectively prevent the evil and that greater goods justify the evils, I adopt the *negative* strategy of showing that the rational creature, no matter what the events of the actual world were like, would never be justified evidentially in concluding that God is morally imperfect.

If we are guided by Augustine's *City of God* and sensitive to human atrocities, "God couldn't have effectively avoided it" and "It is justified by a greater good" make recent history *meaningless* to us. What kind of God couldn't have avoided the death camps? And what *conceivable* greater good would justify such injustice? No, the reality of evil must remain a mystery and God be *vindicated* (not "justified") by the fact that every world is within His power to create and the proportions of evil therein can not impugn the perfection of the creator.

The argument of Chapter 6, that one cannot determine that God is *not* morally perfect from the evil in the world (or any world) is *not,* I emphasize, *is not* an argument by analogy from the relationship of an author to his characters. There is no suggestion that humans are related to God as Hamlet to Shakespeare, without any further qualification, so that the reality of humans is somehow compromised or the fictional being of characters is somehow converted into thin real being. (See my "Creation," Jrl. of Philosophy, Oct. 1980.)

Nevertheless, with respect to the defined relationship of *metaphysical dependence,* humans are metaphysically dependent upon God and Hamlet is metaphysically dependent upon Shakespeare. That does not imply that humans are literally characters in relationship to God, their author, but rather that both the creation of real beings and the creation of fictional beings involve metaphysical dependence.

One cannot determine that God is *not* good, no matter how bad the world might be, because there is something else you'd need to know and can't know. You'd need to know something of which God is the only *possible* instance, something which we do not know a priori or through any relevant experience. And if you do not know that missing thing, your reasoning from the condition of the world would be missing a premise.

The thing you'd need to know is this: Any *real* being which could, without cost or moral defect, preclude or avoid the evil acts and sufferings of other *real beings which are metaphysically dependent upon it* and fails to do so is morally imperfect. (See p. 269.) The argument proceeds to show that the Principle of Limited Inference (in effect, the principle that you are not permitted to infer properties from lower to higher reality levels unless the lower beings would be impossible if the higher beings lacked those properties), and the fact that the missing premise is not true by virtue of its meaning, make the missing premise epistemically inaccessible. For the premise "applies to only one case and that is the case that is in doubt." (cf. Mavrodes, op. cit., p. 110.)

Because my reasoning seems to lead to the consequence that "*nothing which God did with His creatures could reflect upon His character*" (Mavrodes, p. 110), Mavrodes finds the underlying reasoning incredible, particularly suggesting that perhaps there are other ways in which we know premises like the missing one I claimed to be inaccessible. But I do not say that "nothing which God did with His creatures" could reflect against God (although that is true). Rather, *no matter what evil there is in the created world, it cannot logically imply that God is morally defective.* So you can't *infer*, from the condition of the world, a denial of the good moral character of God. If we can know about God's character in some other way than inference or induction, it is up to Mavrodes and the others to show it.

In addition to Mavrodes, some distinguished philosophers, such as Charles Hartshorne and Peter Geach, apparently think you can infer, from the prevalence or absence of evil in the world, to the moral character of God.

Maybe there can be such knowledge, though not of scientific standard because it is neither deductively nor inductively related to the evidence. But if there can be, it is knowledge that God is *good*. No matter *what* the pattern of evil, even if the world were suffused with evil and suffering for millenia or epochs, that would not provide *knowledge* of any kind that God is not morally good. There simply are no conditions under which we *would* know what *could not* be so.

If it is really true that all genuine evil comes from the free wills of men and angels, why would a world literally blackened with evil show more than the need for divine justice to evildoers and the fittingness of some kind of redemption? Such a world cannot be "less possible" than any other possible world and, thus, *cannot* manifest that God is not morally perfect; for such a condition cannot *be*.

(8) *Getting Really Mixed Up.* David R. Griffin ("Divine Causality, Evil and Philosophical Theology: A Critique of James Ross," *International Journal for*

the *Philosophy of Religion,* 1973, and *God, Power and Evil,* Westminster Press, 1976) actually takes me to be arguing by analogy, when I use the author–character counter-examples, to certain principles to justify my *demanding* more restrictive principles applying only to *real* beings, and, then, applying only to *real* beings *metaphysically dependent* upon a real being.

So Griffin concludes that "the implications in regard to the reality of the world are unacceptable" (op. cit., p. 172). How, he asks, "does it express the *intention* of orthodoxy to suggest that the world has no more reality in relation to God than an idea in a mind?" (p. 173).

Well. I *did* say that the creature is to God, as thought to thinker, dream to dreamer, and character to author, in these respects: (i) the one *could not be* at all without the other; (ii) the one has all its attributes *causally dependent* upon the other; (iii) the one is *conserved in being* by the other, as long as it has being; and (iv) all possible things of the same kinds are similarly dependent upon the same sorts of originating and conserving causes.

Which of these conditions is not satisfied by any of the pairs mentioned?

Does that reduce the being of creatures, in relation to God, to the wraith of reality that dreams have? To the relative unreality of fictions? To the status of mere thoughts? Not at all.

Nevertheless, it is still true, as Robert Oakes pointed out ("Classical Theism and Pantheism: A Victory for Process Theism," *Religious Studies* 13, 1977, pp. 167–173), creation is *essentially dependent* upon God. To use my own words, there is no possible world in which the present created substances are to be found and God is not; nor is there one in which both are to be found but the creation is not dependent upon God. Moreover, all finite things (things that exist only under some conditions and not all) are essentially dependent upon God: there is no possible world in which there is *anything* other than God, whether substance or things as evanescent as numbers, when God does not exist.

Those facts tempt Oakes to add that the only mode of such metaphysical dependence is *esse est percipi.* And Griffin, in his own way, rushes into the same intellectual trainwreck. Phillip L. Quinn ("Divine Conservation and Spinozistic Pantheism," *Religious Studies,* vol. 15, 1979, pp. 289–302), after pointing out the implausibility of various notions by which one might say that the world is "included in the being of God," asks whether the *esse est percipi* understanding of metaphysical dependence means that the world is an "ontological parasite" of God (as that notion is defined by R.

Chisholm, *Person and Object: A Metaphysical Study,* LaSalle, Open Court, 1976). And Quinn points out that while being dependent upon a given being (even upon the same being in every world in which the object exists) is necessary for being an "ontological parasite," it is not sufficient, chiefly because "not all truths which ostensibly refer" to the world "can be analyzed into truths which refer only to" God.

Furthermore, it is evidently erroneous to infer, from the fact that several classes of things satisfy certain parallel conditions for dependence upon other things of other kinds, that *they* are all of the same kind and that the dependence in question is dependence *of the same kinds of beings.* In a word, categorially distinct things can be in the same kind of dependence without ceasing to be categorially distinct. (Otherwise, Griffin's belief that both substances and accidents can be *caused* would result in the obliteration of any categorial distinction between substances, accidents, events, beliefs, and all the other things that can be caused.)

Metaphysical dependence (like life, material life, and immaterial life) may be a transcategorial relation, an analogical relation, that obtains among categorially diverse things.

A rare metaphysical obtuseness construes my words as Griffin has: "there is no essential difference between the thought-thinker relation and the creature-creator relation" (op. cit., p. 173). There are undeniable essential differences among the kinds of things that are metaphysically dependent and among the kinds of things they are dependent upon.

Griffin says "Given Shakespeare's decision that Othello kill Desdemona, Othello could do no other. Likewise, given God's decision that Jones kill Smith, Jones could do no other" (p. 173). But he leaves out *my* explicit assumption that Shakespeare decided that Othello would *freely* kill Desdemona and that God decided that Jones would *freely* kill Smith. And, of course, given *those* decisions, it could not be otherwise than that Jones *freely* killed Smith.

Furthermore, Griffin falsely supposes that for an act to be free there must be some possible world where *all* conditions not logically equivalent to that act obtain, when the act is not performed. But, the very definition of omnipotence points out that God's choice *is* equivalent to the state chosen; hence, on Griffin's own assumptions, there is no possible world in which Jones acts otherwise, given God's choice that he will freely kill. Yet that does not weaken Jones's freedom because it is only under all conditions that are neither logically equivalent nor logically entail the action, that one must be able to do otherwise than one does. And that is satisfied in the cases at hand.

Anyway, I don't think it *is* a necessary condition for free action that one should be able to do otherwise, *all* other conditions remaining the same or even, all *prior* and logically independent conditions remaining the same. (See the discussion above in Section 6.) Furthermore, when Griffin says, "If God be the sufficient cause of our acts, then we do not really act freely", he simply *ignores* the serious and substantive issue of whether there are two kinds of *causation,* two kinds of real explanation, one of which is a pre-requisite for natural causation and natural agency. Yet that's what the metaphysical issue of Chapter 6 is all about.

Critics such as Griffin, and to a lesser extent Oakes, have not formulated a religiously orthodox and philosophically articulated analysis of the essential dependence of all created substances and all states of affairs involving the existence of such substances upon the concurrent will of God. If they suppose God's willing is only necessary, not sufficient, so that there is a possible world in which God wills things to happen that do not happen, it must be explained how, despite God's willing, those things do not happen. To reply that it is because of the free wills of creatures is simply to sidestep what is at issue: the nature of the dependence of the *being* of whatever is actual upon the will of the creator. Griffin's "argument" is merely a repetition of the equivocation on "cause" that Chapter 6 already exposes.

"Two relations that were essentially different would be classified as the same type of relations" (op. cit., p. 175), says Griffin, urging that I have to regard the world in relation to God as "not really real" the way an image is to the mind that imagines. I skip his confusion over imagining. Of course, the image is as real as is the imagining mind; it is the state merely imagined that is imaginary. And, as I have already illustrated, the same relation can obtain analagously among objects that are categorially different.

Further, at p. 176, Griffin misconstrues the "facile amendment" criticism (see p. 264 below), thinking I regard the difference between "all beings" and "*real* beings" as "trivial." That misses the point. Amending the principles is a fallacy of facile amendment because by amending *exactly* to avoid the counterexamples that instantiate the first approximations, the *resulting* principles either beg the original question by assuming we have already answered it or make claims that are in principle inaccessible to a decision that is "of scientific standard." As I point out (Chapter 6), the amendments make both mistakes.

Griffin's paper, clearly written as it is, is a model of miscontrual, making an excellent teaching device for students to compare with the text interpreted. Finally, Griffin observes:

Either one must speak meaningfully of God's causality and admit that such essentials of theism as freedom, sin, and even a real world can be affirmed only in some Pickwickian sense. Or, if one wishes to hold these latter elements of orthodoxy, then God's "omnipotence" can be spoken of for its orthodox ring and emotional impact, but it should then be pointed out that we have no idea at all what the word means (op cit., p. 181).

That's direct enough and to the point. It lets the reader know where, once the existence of God is established, the serious problems lie and why my discussions of power, goodness, freedom, sufficient reason, selection of possible worlds, and metaphysical dependence are so central to philosophical theology.

JAMES F. ROSS
1980

Preface to the First Printing

For discussing words with words is as entangled and
interlocking as rubbing the fingers with the fingers,
in which case it may scarcely be distinguished
except by the one himself who does it, which fingers
itch and which remedy the itching.

ST. AUGUSTINE, *De Magistro*, Chapter V.

The elaboration of analytic philosophy through the English-speaking world has distinguished the twentieth century. Yet it has not been adequately tested whether this method of philosophy will aid the justification or uncover the futility of the distinctively scholastic positions in philosophical theology.

The beginnings of an analytic reconstruction of scholastic natural theology are what will be found in this book, where I address myself with particular and sympathetic attention to three characteristically scholastic doctrines: (a) that one can establish the existence of a being which could (and perhaps does) have the attributes orthodox Christians attribute to God; (b) that it is consistent and intelligible to conceive of God's power as limited only to the logically possible; (c) that there is no theoretical conflict between the universal causality and absolute entitative and moral perfection of God, on the one hand, and the admitted reality of the evils of the world and the premised freedom of man, on the other.

From among a perhaps limitless array of problems (logical, epistemological, metaphysical and ethical) which involve, or are involved in, those key topics, I have extensively considered some questions concerning proper names and logical modalities; some questions (which recur as themes in almost every chapter) concerning the nature of good arguments and the processes by which philosophical controversy is to be concluded; and some questions concerning the neutrality of philosophical analyses of religious claims. Moreover, I have debated the substantively religious question of whether God had a reason for creating the world, a question which is rendered fundamental by our discovery (see the first part of Chapter III) that it is false that every contingent fact has an explanation (and, therefore, that the very strict and characteristically neo-scholastic interpretations of the principle of sufficient reason are false) even though God, a universal cause, may exist. This makes it evident that analytic reconstruction of scholastic natural theology demands that we jettison some of its most familiar elements and that we redesign as well as rebuild.

With gratitude I acknowledge the magic by which Miss J. Harriet Dietz transformed my illegible notes into a manageable typescript.

James F. Ross

April 1967

Philosophical theology

1 ✐ Arguments

and proof in philosophical

theology

Summary: The abstractness and impersonalness which
characterize good arguments in philosophical theology
remove them as far from the commerce of religion-getting
and religion-dropping as are good arguments on the
subject of other minds from the taxpayer's abandonment
or continuance in such a belief with regard to his wife.

This meta-philosophical chapter is not characteristic of those which
follow it. The main problems here are transitory, and the purposes
are largely negative: to eliminate certain conceptions of our objectives and of our initial materials which would hamstring our activities later.

There has been great confusion and equivocation among philosophical theologians over the place and function of specific arguments, especially arguments concerning the existence of God. For
instance, some recent theologians have no respect for "proofs" of
the existence of God (or for rational argumentation of any sort), and
say not only that the existence of God *cannot* be "proved," but that
such an enterprise is blasphemous. At the antipode, we find those

zealous neo-scholastics who have married Pius IX's overconcretiza-tion[1] of the first Vatican Council (which merely claimed that a man could come to know that God exists through the exercise of human reason[2]) and have claimed that the existence of God can be *demonstrated*, and furthermore that it can be demonstrated to any intelligent and unprejudiced man—and even more, that such demonstrations are based on self-evident truths!

These are only the extremes. Between them, opinion ranges from the belief that the construction of arguments is primarily to serve the purposes of the religious apologists, to the belief that the arguments primarily fulfill a testimonial role as a recitation of one's own reasons for one's belief.

In this chapter I shall, by undertaking a short inquiry into the nature of a good argument in philosophy, offer considerations which eliminate all the views mentioned, and some others besides. The moment when we have to choose between what may be called the "person-relative" concept of a good argument and the "impersonal-objective" concept thereof is a crucial one; for this decision in behalf of "objective" concepts is of the greatest importance for the kind of reasoning to be found elsewhere in this book (a kind of reasoning which does not stress what is obvious to everyone, or even what is widely acknowledged or is thought to be widely persuasive); the decision, although supported by some explanation, nevertheless appeals to concepts like 'accessibility', 'assessability according to scientific method', etc., which provide very little in the way of a recipe for one's accepting or rejecting any given argument. Our criteria of what constitutes a good argument demand assessability through philosophical analysis; but they do not even pretend to be rules by which one might identify the individual arguments which will survive such assessment. That is too bad. But let it be remembered from the outset that the primary objective here is to display the unintelligibility, the implausibility, the falsehood, or the strategic absurdity of the doctrines referred to above and to protect the arguments that will be given later from the artificial demands that those objectives would have imposed upon them. Clarification and development beyond

---

[1] See Henricus Denziger, *Enchiridion Symbolorum* (Fribourg: Herder & Co., 1937), ¶ 2145.

[2] *Ibid.*, ¶¶ 1785, 1806.

what we now generally possess concerning the nature of "good arguments" is only incidental. And hence our failure to provide criteria or recipes for the identification of good arguments is not a failure at something that we set out to do.

The reader who is not interested in meta-philosophical detail may profitably turn ahead to the conclusion of this chapter, where he will find a description of our steps and their applications.

A good argument proves something: it shows that its conclusion is so. This is its function.

Yet sometimes we say someone gave us a good argument for a certain conclusion even though what he claimed to show was not so or was not shown to be so. In such cases we are applying a *relative* standard of goodness, as when we say such things about the work of a student, when it is measured not against the objective optimal but against the *attainable*, given the student's training and resources.

So too, some arguments are found to have greater significance when viewed in historical perspective and in the light of their influence upon the course of scientific development than they could possibly have, viewed solely in terms of their intrinsic merits. Such appraisal of arguments in terms of their environmental effects indicates the employment of another *relative* standard of goodness.

We shall not be concerned with discovering relative standards but seek an objective standard by which to measure our work and that of our predecessors. We shall try to decide what we have to do to "prove" or "show" that something is so and shall assign meaning to the tasks of proving the existence of God and proving that God has the attributes ascribed to Him by the faithful in terms of the general concepts of 'good argument', 'proving', and 'establishing'. Hence, when we later claim to have shown that something is so, the arguments must not be required to meet standards not entailed by those we set up here.

The standards our arguments must meet are in part imposed by the objectives the arguments are expected to serve and in part independent of the *uses* to which they are put. Yet sometimes (as we shall illustrate) the objectives and the standards that are allowed are found to be at cross purposes.

In the first section we examine certain conceptions of the function that one might expect his arguments to serve and, by indicating facts which require us to eschew these functions and the allied standards, we uncover some principles by which the standards we suggest in Section 2 will be supported.

SECTION 1: THE DEFECTIVE STANDARDS AND CHIMERICAL PURPOSES

(1) Suppose it were said that the function of a good argument is to convince *everyone who is acquainted* with the argument of the truth of the conclusion. (This is the way some lovers of "demonstration" have talked about showing the existence of God.) Then theologians and philosophers would have a singularly poor record as producers of good arguments: no one of their products has fulfilled its purpose. Moreover, there is no reason to think any argument for any conclusion whatever has ever satisfied this objective. Even if we mitigated the conditions, saying that the purpose of a good argument is to convince *most* of those who study it, the theologians and philosophers would have a lamentable record.

Moreover, if "to convince X" meant only "to bring it about that X believes the conclusion because he believes it is entailed by premises he believes," then an unsound[3] argument could be imagined which would convince many who study it; for valid arguments with true conclusions can have false premises, and it is possible that many people should hold these false beliefs. On the other hand, if "to convince X" meant something much stronger, namely, "to bring it about that X *knows* the conclusion is true because he sees that it follows from premises which he *knows* to be true (without having as his reason for believing the premises his belief that the conclusion is true)," the philosophers certainly cannot claim to have convinced many or even a significant number of those who have considered their arguments (on any subject at all). For the very best arguments are often without appeal to anyone who does not already know the conclusion to be true. (Consider the scientist's establishment of a

---

[3] An argument is unsound either if it is invalid or if it has a false premise.

conclusion long known by his colleagues but not hitherto proved.)

The moral: When one determines the function of his arguments, he must do so without *forcing* himself into a failure to produce good arguments (because the conditions cannot be satisfied) or into the correlative failure, where countless arguments that even a child can construct will qualify as good (because the conditions for "showing" or "establishing" are too weak).

Most of the objectives envisioned (usually implicitly) by thinkers in the past involve one of these two poles; either they are objectives which almost any argument (or at least an infinite number of trivially easy-to-construct arguments) will fulfill, or they are objectives which no imaginable argument can achieve. Requiring that the argument convince everyone is a case of the latter; a case of the former follows.

(2) Suppose it is said: The objective of the philosophical theologian, like that of any other philosopher, is to present true premises which entail true conclusions: *sound* arguments. What is wrong with that?

Let us suppose "God exists" is true, and let us assume statement (2), below, is true. The following argument fulfills the objective described above:

A. 1: *If Adam was created by God, God exists.*

   2: *Adam was created by God.*

   3: *God exists.*

This argument is a good argument under this criterion, being sound, given our assumptions about (2) and (3). Moreover, there is an *infinite* number of such arguments which are readily constructed. If *this* is the purpose of the natural theologian's efforts, to provide sound arguments, it is hard to imagine why he would perspire so in searching for arguments.

No doubt the person who holds that God does not exist will dispute the decisiveness of this example. Before he departs in outrage, let us construct an argument for him:

B. 1: *If Adam was not created by God, God does not exist.*

2: Adam was not created by God.

3: Therefore God does not exist.[4]

Now, some non-theists will claim that (1), (2), and (3) are true; they will see that (3) follows from (1) and (2) by *modus ponens;* and they will see that there is an infinite number of substitutions for "Adam" in (1) and (2) and hence an infinite number of examples of this kind of argument.

Since either the conclusion of this argument or the conclusion of the previous example must be true, and since most philosophers will agree that either (A2) or (B2) is a true statement, there is an infinite number of sound (valid with true premises) arguments for *some* true proposition, e.g., either for "God exists" or for "God does not exist." Hence, if all we need in order to have good arguments is sound arguments, we have shown that either the theist or the atheist has an unlimited supply at hand. This constitutes a *reductio* which shows that a sound argument is not *eo ipso* a good argument. Hence that philosopher whose objective is to present *good* arguments, arguments which *function* as proofs, will not fulfill his program by the mere production of sound arguments.

Even if it be granted, as I think it must be, that *one,* and only one, of the arguments (A and B) is sound, it will surely be agreed that neither is a *good* argument for its conclusion (though both serve a worthwhile purpose). But why are they not good?

(3) Perhaps it will be said that these arguments fail because their major premises are not proved (i.e., are not themselves backed by

---

[4] This reasoning is to be found (for the first time, I think) in *The Concept of a Direct Experience of God,* by George Ion Mavrodes (a University of Michigan Ph.D. thesis, 1961; Microfilm-Xerox by University Microfilms, Inc., Ann Arbor, Michigan, 1962), pp. 50–52. Chapters II and III of Mavrodes' thesis, concerned with the nature of proof and argument, are in my opinion an excellent analysis of the conditions for 'proving something to someone'. Moreover, many general principles fundamental to the analysis of 'argument' are carefully stated, including the proofs used here that neither validity nor soundness is a sufficient condition for 'being a good argument'. Several of the other important contentions of the first part of the present discussion are to be found in Mavrodes' thesis: (a) that for every true proposition a sound argument is available; (b) that, as Aristotle said, you cannot prove every premise of every argument (p. 88); (c) that one's emotional attachment to the denial of a conclusion may cause one to become more ignorant in the presence of a sound argument. The main difference between Mavrodes' ingenious doctrine and the one proposed here is that he thinks an argument is not good unless it is *good for* someone, convincing to someone; that is, he makes 'being a good argument' a "person-relative" characteristic. I do not. I agree with the general outline of conditions Mavrodes gives for 'being a good argument for S', but wish to describe a non–person-relative property of arguments, 'goodness', which may obtain independently of whether the argument is good *for* anyone.

good arguments offered). But *that* objection cannot stand, since it would vitiate the first argument (or the last) that any philosopher gives for any conclusion whatever. The fact that one's premises are not proved cannot *by itself* be a legitimate ground for our criticizing any argument; otherwise any finite chain of philosophical argument is useless: any chain of arguments which is finite in length will begin with an unproved premise. See Aristotle: "They seek a reason for things for which no reason can be given; for the starting point of demonstration is not demonstration."[5] This point has the important dialectical consequence that for you to say (rightly), "You haven't proved your premises," is by itself *wholly irrelevant* to the value of an argument which confronts you.

Perhaps you will propose that a good argument must have true premises which entail the conclusion, *and* that it must convince anyone who comes to understand that it is valid and what its premises mean. Arguments A and B are unconvincing, and hence not good.

This might appear to be a more reasonable objective. But its advantages are superficial. Will everyone who does not become *convinced* (in the stronger sense indicated in subsection 1, above) be said to have failed to understand the premises? Can one understand a sound argument without *seeing* that it is sound? If one says no, then either I misunderstand the atheist's simple argument (B) quoted above (subsection 2) or he misunderstands mine (A), since neither of us *sees* that the other's is sound although we both see that *one* of the two is sound. Yet, surely, each of us understands both his own and the other's argument (which differs from his own only by the addition or absence of some negations). Therefore, it must be possible to understand a sound argument without seeing that it is sound.

Yet one cannot be convinced (as this notion is explained in subsection 1, above) by the argument unless he knows that it is sound.[6] Is there a class of sound arguments such that one cannot *understand* them without seeing that they are sound? What property must they have, in addition to being sound? There is no property that any argument could have, if it does not have premises which everyone *knows*

---

[5] *Metaphysics* IV. 6, 1011a13; see also 1011a6–10, 1006a8–12.

[6] But someone may feel convinced because he thinks it is sound when it is not, or because he thinks he sees that it is sound when he does not (even though it is).

(or will come to know) to be true, which would bring all who understand it (and see its validity) to see that it is sound. If there are any premises which everyone knows or which everyone can come to know merely by understanding their terms, then perhaps it would be possible to construct such ideal arguments as this criterion of good arguments requires. We shall consider this apparent possibility, noting first that even if there were such arguments, it is highly doubtful that their conclusions would be philosophically significant.

Those philosophers who thought arguments should begin from *self-evident* premises (among whom we find many scholastics and a host of neo-scholastics) sought premises which needed only to be understood in order to be found true. The consensus of the philosophers who have examined arguments alleged to contain such premises has been that self-evidence in the premises, along with validity in the form, has not been achieved except in those cases where simple tautological premises are employed and where no conclusion with existential import is involved; wherever significant existential conclusions have followed validly from the argument, *additional* non-self-evident premises have been found. This matter of self-evidence will arise again. For the moment it need only be observed that if it is necessary that *all* the premises of good arguments should be self-evident or deduced from such premises, the philosophers have failed utterly and without exception to produce good arguments for any significant conclusion.

It should be obvious that not all our arguments will serve the same immediate purpose. For example, the argument I am developing to show that there *is* a problem about the purpose of arguments in philosophy of religion is supposed to bring it about that those who understand what I say and who did not know that such a problem existed will come to *know* (via the conceptual relations it exposes) that there is such a problem and know precisely what it is; moreover, it is supposed to pass muster, for those who already know that such a problem exists, as a statement of what the problem is and of why one should find the matter problematical.

The two arguments A and B of subsection 2, above, were not intended to convince anyone of their respective conclusions but were instead intended to supply evidence, in conjunction, for the claim that not all sound arguments are good arguments and, later on, for the claim that one can understand a sound argument without seeing that it is sound. They served the purpose of proof by standing as part of a larger argument. This shows that a sound argument (or an unsound one) may function in a worthwhile way without convincing anyone of its conclusion and that an argument may serve a worthwhile function without being a good argument. But no one of these things in any way detracts from the main principle that the function of a good argument is to establish its conclusion. And while we might want our good argument to have the *additional* merits of convincing many of those who read it and of being worthwhile, nothing has been discovered yet which *requires* that a good argument be actually convincing to anyone.

There are at least two reasons for thinking that arguments for specifically theological propositions (for which class I can give no satisfactory definition, although I have no trouble deciding upon the status of most candidates for the title "theological proposition") *ought* not to be offered in the hope of convincing everyone who understands what is asserted by their premises. We consider the first such reason now and another in subsection 4, below.

Not everyone who understands what is claimed in one's premises can be assumed to have an equal amount of knowledge about the world or about our conceptual scheme by which to see that one's premises are true. Hence, it would be foolish to hope to convince all those who do not know the conclusions are true by a few abbreviated chains of reasoning which would be offered by one supposing what is manifestly false: that all the understanders have the requisite knowledge to know that the premises are·true. For instance, consider the following argument with a truth-functional major premise:

If the square root of 256 is 16, God exists.

The square root of 256 is 16.

Therefore God exists.

Many who know the minor premise to be true are ignorant of whether the major is true. (And think of the billion persons who know nothing of either premise!) In fact, it is probably (but not necessarily) the case that only those who know the conclusion to be true know both premises to be true: this particular argument will convince no one where convincing someone involves bringing him to know the conclusion which he did not know before. Yet this is a most simple case of an argument where different people have different amounts of knowledge which will allow the argument to *appear sound* to the one and doubtful to the other. The point is too elementary to require a more elaborate proof. There is no reason whatever to think there is any argument which will in the same form convince everyone who understands its premises and grasps its validity; knowledge and the ability to manipulate our knowledge vary too much among human beings, with the result that what appears most obvious to one person may seem utterly unfounded to another. Hence, the neo-scholastics, who expected to convince every fair-minded person, were blindly optimistic.

(4) It cannot be a necessary condition for an argument's being a good argument that it should convert *anyone* (not identical with the author) to belief in the conclusion. While we may very much want to change the belief of someone to whom we present our arguments, and while it may be necessary that our argument convince Jones if it is to be a good argument *for Jones,* converting people cannot be the purpose that our arguments must serve in order to be good philo-sophical arguments. I have never known of a person, whether con-temporary or in history, whose coming to believe in the existence of God or in the fact that God has a plan for the world or in the fact that God has decreed a moral law for the world, or, for that matter, in any important proposition, has been entirely or even largely the result of an argument. It seems to be on empirical grounds false that men come to know these basic truths via arguments, even though there may be arguments which do establish (in the sense to be explained) such truths.

This, of course, does not mean that arguments have not served an important function in the conversion of unbelievers, or that there may not have been *some* person who was convinced of an important conclusion by an argument. It merely means that an argument can be good and yet not serve this function.

Arguments, both good and bad, have served several purposes in the conversion of persons to religious belief. For instance, in some cases they have drawn the person's attention to certain features of the world in such a way that the person has an experience which he takes to be a perception of the indwelling presence of God, and through such an experience, the person comes to *know* these conclusions.[7] In such a case the argument functions as a psychological catalyst, ordering one's past experience, conditioning one's present and future experience, and making a new and unique perception occur. It makes a person look at the world in a new way and sometimes the person *sees* things he did not see before.

In other cases, the arguments assign some rational or logical coherence to a belief which other forces are driving the believer to accept. When the proselyte is before his preacher demanding an argument, he is often asking for *reasons* for what he already (perhaps without attending to what philosophers call "reasons") knows to be true. The arguments then seem to supply status to the private belief of the proselyte, by supplying him with reasons which depend not upon his *personal* insight into the universe, but upon general features available to a large community of men. He is asking for arguments which have the impersonal and publicly assessable character of "scientific" truth; these serve in his eyes to raise his conviction from the realm of personal opinion to established truth. The believer does not need to understand the arguments as much as he needs to know that there *are* such arguments.

In still other cases, the first two functions may be combined; a person may be on personal reasons inclined to belief that God exists, for which he wants confirmation by means of a more formal and "scientific" (and therefore definite and assessable) chain of reasoning. When one of the old stand-bys like the argument from design is given him, he is satisfied that his personal reasons have not misled him and accepts *their* force, in turn accepting the force of the design argument. The fact that there is no *logical* sense in which the "scientific" argument confirms his own reasons (especially since it is not a sound argument as it is usually stated) does not affect the person, who is unlikely to notice this; in fact, the so-called "objective" argument probably derives most of its force from the personal conviction which *precedes* it, so that the "private opinion" is not replaced with new status as established fact, but is *veneered* with status which the argument offered cannot properly confer.

[7] See Mavrodes, p. 228.

Arguments do function importantly in some conversions, but they do not convert anyone, even the unresisting, on the more important matters discussed by natural theologians.

These two points have this effect: (a) We ought not to hope to convince *everyone* by any one argument (or dozen arguments) in philosophy of religion, since not everyone should be thought to possess equal knowledge or possess the knowledge equally, which is supposed for any argument on these points. (b) We ought not to hope to convert, by argument, *anyone* to religious belief, or belief in the existence of God, since there is very little reason to hope, especially in the case of those thinking persons who respond to arguments with the critical assessment arguments deserve, that arguments will bring about knowledge on such important points; in fact, when we take emotional factors into account, good arguments often make people more ignorant than they were before, as will be explained a few pages hence. Therefore, we ought not to require of a good argument that it convince any of those who are not already attached to the conclusion. This means that a *good philosophical argument need not convince anyone who does not already accept the conclusion.*[8] Furthermore, if our object were to convince people of religious truths, there are many better ways to employ our time than in complicated philosophical analyses which very few human beings could ever hope to grasp and whose very complexity may obstruct conviction in the inexpert. Religious convictions have been brought about much more successfully by prayer, fasting, good works, good example, and preaching of the gospel, and sometimes even by persuasions which have neither the merits of soundness nor those of validity. Nor can it be said that such methods do not bring knowledge; for they may conceivably do so by putting a person into the *position* of having those personal experiences which provide him with the knowledge, although they may not by themselves communicate the grounds for his new knowledge to him.

It is easy to imagine a world of fully rational men possessing equal knowledge, all of whom could be convinced by one and the same sound argument because they possess common and extensive intel-

---

[8] Of course, the argument will not be a good argument *for* the person who does not already accept the conclusion and is not convinced by it; thus a good philosophical argument may be good *for* no one. But that does *not* make it "good for nothing."

lectual equipment and an integral human nature in which the emotions are controlled by the intellect. It is also possible to imagine a race of men none of whom has a great stake emotionally or intellectually in the falsity of the religious hypotheses of Christianity. These people could in principle be convinced by one or another sound argument, arguments far less complex than those we now employ. Yet the more *expensive*, emotionally or intellectually, the hypothesis that God exists (or any other hypothesis for that matter) is for a man, the less likely he is to be convinced by a sound argument for it. For consider a sound argument of the form: *a, b,* therefore *c.* If a man for whom *c* is extremely expensive (i.e., who thinks belief in *c* would require a massive alteration in his conceptual scheme and his way of life) sees that given what he already claims to know (and in fact does know), both *a* and *b* must be considered true and entail *c,* he will very probably abandon some of his former claims to know (and in doing so, end by knowing *less* than he did before) in order to avoid accepting the conclusion he dislikes and whose falsity he has privileged as more evident than his beliefs, *a* and *b.*

Nevertheless, we can imagine a world where the psychological laws are such that no one ever knows less at a later time than he knew at an earlier time. In such a world it would be possible, were someone ingenious enough to constuct a sound argument related correctly to what a person already knows, to convince him of a true proposition, even if it be very important. But the regularity of that world is not to be found in ours.

These considerations show that the ineffectiveness of arguments in bringing about such basic convictions is not a logical function of the structure of reasoning. The hopelessness of attempting to convince people of the truth of basic religious hypotheses by argument alone derives from the unequal ignorance of men and from the fact that if a man sees that what he claimed to know leads to an important proposition which he thinks is false, he may abandon his former claim (and often his former knowledge) to avoid the consequence. Every person, even the most learned, has implicit privilege scales by which to determine which beliefs are expendable and which counter-evidence is to be rejected. I have met philosophers who have said that if I could show them that the existence of God followed from the fact that contradictions are always false, they would abandon their belief that the latter is a fact. What is the value of arguments in such a case?

Besides the increased *ignorance* that a sound argument may bring to a man who privileges the negation of its conclusion over his belief in the premises, there is a possibility that one man may know, on the whole, more than another but not enough to see that the argument he is given is sound, even though a more ignorant man may know this.

A man, A, who does not know as much as a man, B, may have before him an argument the premises of which he knows are true and the structure of which he knows to be valid. Hence, A may have an argument which entails a certain conclusion and which, for him, is a good argument. And yet B may know on the whole *more* than A and not know that the premises A believes are true. For B may know just enough more than A to notice objections which cast the premises into doubt but not know enough to resolve those doubts even though they are resolvable. Hence the argument, really sound in itself and a proof for A, is not a proof for B, since the latter does not know what A knows—namely, that the premises are true—even though on the whole he knows more than A; for it is certainly not a condition upon A's knowing the premises to be true that he should be aware of all objections to the premises *and* of their answers. Hence both A and B may possess the same good argument, but only the more ignorant, A, derives a cognitive benefit from his possession. (Does this suggest a plausible interpretation of the "ordinary" man's reasonings about God on the basis of the "design" and "purpose" in nature?)

Now let us suppose that A does not know the premises are true when in fact they are. For A, the argument does not serve as a good argument for its conclusion since he does not know the premises to be true, though he may see the validity of the argument. No argument is good *for* the man who does not know that it is sound; this is obvious since it cannot serve to show him its conclusion. Yet an argument can be a good philosophical argument even though at some particular time it is not good *for* anyone (in the sense that there is no one who *sees* that it is sound), although in fact it is sound. Thus, we can speak of good arguments that we have not discovered and good arguments that no one noticed.

We do not need a precise criterion of "philosophical argument." An argument is "philosophical" if someone calls it philosophical or employs it for philosophical purposes (i.e., the theoretical pursuit of wisdom). Thus "God revealed that man is immortal; what God reveals is true; therefore man is immortal" is a philosophical argument if someone thinks it is; but it is not a *good* philosophical argument, even though it be sound.

Just as an argument may be poor yet sound, so too, an argument may be worthwhile, but *not* sound. Hume's arguments to establish his philosophical skepticism are generally thought to be unsound; yet the person who considered such arguments worthless would be barren of philosophical sensitivity. We are not primarily concerned to explain what makes arguments worthwhile or significant, but only what is needed for them to be *good*. Hence, we can conclude for now: (a) that a good argument need actually convince no one; (b) that a sound argument is not *eo ipso* a good one; (c) that a worthwhile argument is not *eo ipso* good; (d) that a good argument need not be worthwhile or significant.

(5) The purpose of philosophical argument in behalf of religious claims is not to supply missionaries with persuasive devices. Philosophical investigation into religious truth is a theoretical enterprise, having its *raison d'être* quite independently of the existence or activity of missionaries; philosophical arguments are never rendered "good arguments" by fulfilling some extrinsic purpose for some agent. This is not to deny that a philosopher might appropriately and usefully write a handbook of information for missionaries, as it is sometimes thought St. Thomas Aquinas did (*Summa Contra Gentiles*). A philosopher *can* be practical; but to be justified and to have a worthwhile objective he need not be, nor need he produce arguments which will have the slightest utility for agents of the gospel. Whatever purpose the philosopher has must be self-justifying; otherwise his work will fall victim to the considerations I raised against setting oneself the objective of converting anyone, even the most learned, much less the primitive and logically unsophisticated, who are more likely to become ensnared and confused than to become educated. A good argument has its *own* function (to "show" or "establish"), a function which is distinct from the achievement of a pragmatic purpose by those who employ such arguments.

(6) Neither should it be the philosopher's purpose to supply a recital of his own reasons for having accepted the religious beliefs he has,

for he may have had very poor reasons when he accepted his beliefs, or he may not know what his reasons were. In any case, the mere fact that they *were* his reasons is of no import philosophically, and endows them with no evidential relation to what was believed.

(7) Neither can it be the purpose of philosophical arguments to supply additional evidence for those who are already committed to the conclusion the philosopher supports. If their reasons are good, no others are needed. Moreover, philosophy as a theoretical endeavor is not at all concerned with whether or not a particular person possesses a good reason for a given belief. Philosophy is concerned solely with producing a good argument for a given conclusion without concern for whether or not anyone employs this reason in selecting his beliefs.

SECTION 2: IMPERSONALNESS, INDEPENDENT ASSESSABILITY, ESTABLISHMENT

Philosophers usually try to answer two types of questions: (1) the "big" questions about immortality, freedom of the will, the origin of the world, the nature of time and space, etc. In their attempts to decide these matters they are put into positions which require them to show (2) *how* we know many of the other things that we *do* know; e.g., how we know that bodies continue to exist when no one sees them; that there are other minds than our own; that certain regularities in nature will continue into the future, etc.

When we demand people's reasons for these obviously true beliefs, we discover that the reasons they *give* are not adequate bases for such claims at all. Attempts by philosophers to provide reasons for such beliefs often fail, too. In our century the attempt to provide philosophical arguments for the existence of other minds has been widely recognized as a failure. Since the skepticism of David Hume was rejected, our failure to discover such sufficient reasons has not led us to say that no one *knows* those things about the world; rather, most human beings do know that there are other minds than their own, that bodies do continue to exist when unperceived, and that certain regularities observed in nature will continue into the future. But we now realize that the way in which we come to know these things and the reasons we have which are in fact good reasons for these beliefs are, or at least have so far been, in some sense inaccessible to philosophical analysis.

When philosophers propose arguments that are said to establish such beliefs as we already possess and perhaps even know to be true, they are not claiming to provide *new* reasons for these beliefs under circumstances where the ordinary man might be said to have been previously *unjustified* in belief, as a man who accidentally comes upon a true belief may be said to lack justification. These arguments (if sound) might indeed provide the ordinary man with good reasons for his beliefs, if he understood and accepted the arguments; but that is not the purpose of our constructing such arguments. Rather, the purpose of the argument is to establish such beliefs as part of a theoretical and explanatory picture of the world; to provide a set of arguments, based on *publicly accessible information*, that would justify these beliefs and also admit of integration into a general body of knowledge which will eventually provide us with the materials for a satisfactory reply to those "big" questions whose answers some men may quite rightly profess not to know.

The philosopher investigating religious truth need not deny that many religious people know things about God and His plans for the world that some others do not know. In fact, many philosophers, being themselves religious believers, cannot consistently deny this. But this does not preclude philosophical investigation of the truth of such beliefs. For the philosopher of religion his own religious beliefs and knowledge may function in the same harmless way that a philosopher's belief in the existence of other minds functions when he seeks an establishment of that truth.

As soon as we understand that we really don't expect anyone to give up or take up religious belief on the basis of our arguments (any more than we expect a person to give up or take up belief in other minds, the regularity of nature, or the subsistence of things unperceived on the basis of our arguments), we can free ourselves from the mistaken belief that a previously held conviction about one's conclusion prejudices the argument and somehow infects it, and we can settle upon conditions for *showing* or *establishing* a conclusion which will apply to good arguments regardless of the subject matter we treat.

Thus the question of what *showing, proving, demonstrating,* or *establishing* consists in is not confined to the area of philosophy of religion; it applies to the whole of philosophical endeavor, and, moreover, touches our whole concept of science. Take any true proposition whatever and ask: what constitutes a proof of this? A *sound* argument (one that is both valid and has true premises) is necessary but is certainly not sufficient, as should be obvious. What more is necessary?

At least two things: *Accessibility or impersonalness*, and *methodical assessability* in the premises.

A: Accessibility

If the premises of some argument for c are such that I alone can determine whether or not they are true, those premises may be a means of *my* coming to know that the conclusion is true, but they cannot function significantly in anyone else's discovery of the conclusion.

Personal premises, premises where knowledge originates in me alone, will vitiate an argument because the method of the philosopher will not be applicable by all philosophers alike to determine its soundness. Thus, if I employ the argument: "If I see the chair, therefore . . ." and make the "I" essential to the premises in such a way that *no one else* can substitute himself as referent of "I," then the second premise vitiates the argument; we do not have a good philosophical argument to establish the existence of the chair in question—even if the argument be valid and have true premises, and even if I *know* it is valid and has true premises. It must be at least in principle practically (rather than merely logically) possible for someone other than the one who proposes the argument to determine for himself by observation or the application of philosophical method whether or not the premises (as given in the argument) are true; and, certainly, "taking *my* word for it" is not part of philosophical method. While a philosopher is not prohibited from selecting a premise because he has "taken someone's word for it" (after all, this is oftentimes a way to find out whether something is true), he is prohibited from taking as a premise anything which one can come to know *only* in this way; for this runs contrary to the independence of observation and impersonalness of proof which are required in science. In this context the phrase "one can come to know only in this way" is taken to involve practical and not merely logical possibility. It is logically possible that I can discover the truth-value of *any* contingent proposition merely by asking God, in prayer, to reveal it to me. In fact, however, I am not able to do this. If we were concerned only with logical possibility in this case, no true premise at all, provided it be known to *someone*, would be excluded from the class of acceptable true premises for good arguments.

Yet since our methods for determining the truth or falsity of premises may change in such a way that things not now accessible to independent observers may someday be accessible, there is, perhaps, a transitoriness to being a poor argument. Some arguments which are *now* not good because their premises are not accessible may someday become good because their premises do become impersonally accessible while they continue to fulfill the other requirements. Such relativity in the status "being a good argument" is not vicious; it is desirable.

B: Methodical assessability

From some of the things said so far it might appear that a good philosophical argument is merely a sound argument with impersonal or accessible premises. But this is not satisfactory. For philosophy is, at least in its hopes if not in its accomplishments, a science, employing scientific methods (primarily those of the pure, non-empirical sciences). Proof must accord with this method.

Although it is practically impossible to specify just what the elements of this method are, approximations sufficient to establish another condition upon our proofs can be made. Suppose I, by some special means like telepathy or a vision of God, have discovered that a proposition *p* (for example, "Jones murdered his wife") is true, and then argue that since murdering one's wife is breaking the law, Jones has broken the law. This sound argument cannot be considered a good philosophical argument since (in addition to the fact that the premise is not practically accessible to someone else, even though anyone else *might*, had things been otherwise, have telepathically or directly observed the event), it is not generally known to be true and is not such that thinkers generally who might be puzzled about whether or not it is true could settle that question by the scientific methods available. When one wants to establish a conclusion in a science, he must seek sound arguments whose premises are generally known to be true or else, if not generally acknowledged, are *decidable for those who do not then hold them by some method which is generally followed in the science*. This is assessability. It seems to follow from this that the only contingent truths with which we are justified in beginning our arguments are those that each interested observer can confirm for himself *or* can replace with truths he has confirmed for himself. (This does not mean that the methods of assessment may not alter with time, or that one may not sometimes rightly follow some method not generally accepted; these are matters peripheral to the main point here.)

It is a fact that a thinker may have "right at hand," so to speak, the reasons for some claim but not know what these reasons are. It is perfectly appropriate for one to use an argument whose premises are claims about which knowledge is thought to be available, should the search be undertaken, even though one does not at the time know what the reasons are; it is equally *in*appropriate for one to use arguments with premises not generally acknowledged in one's time, if reasons for these premises are not thought to be available to other inquirers using the approved methods of investigation and for which there is no process of decision available to a person who doubts the claims.

Thus, it is a complete misconception of the kind of starting point from which philosophy should proceed to argue for the existence of God, as many neo-scholastics proposed, from some metaphysical axiom which one "knows" to be true but which is not generally acknowledged to be true, and, by treating it as an axiom, to *suppose* that there are no premises which anyone knows or experiences available from which, were he in ignorance, one might proceed to discover the truth or falsity of this axiom. Usually philosophers who suppose that for their axioms no true premises are possible are assuming (1) that there is nothing better known (nothing more obvious on the basis of which a man who did not know this axiom might discover it) and (2) that each axiom is self-evident in the sense that a man once understanding it cannot fail to see its truth.

Both these assumptions are demonstrably false for any proposition whatever. The first is false because for a given individual such a premise as the principle of non-contradiction in its general form may not be obvious. He can by a consideration of the falsehood of particular contradictions proceed by induction to accept the principle in its general form. If it were objected that inductive considerations are logically posterior to the principle in the sense that they would have no validity if it were false, one would reply that although that is true, *logical* priority has nothing to do with whether or not something is more obvious to someone than something else; for the only sense we can assign to "*a* is more obvious than *b* for *S*" is in terms of *S*'s epistemic states,[9] and, as philosophers have long known, the order of logic and that of knowledge will not coincide. Hence, no matter what proposition you may have, there may be some other that *S* knows, from which he can come to know the one in question. Since the order of knowing need not follow the logical order among propositions, it may vary significantly from one person to another with the result that there is no proposition which *no one* could come to know as a result of knowing something else.

The second assumption fails also. The concept of self-evidence, on shaky footing when one attempts to analyze it, is in any case of no use when we are confronted with the bleak fact that there is no proposition whatever that someone might not be *prevented* from knowing just because he sees it leads to some consequence which he thinks he knows to be false; his reasons for holding the negation of the consequent seem to him more basic and significant truths than any others. Suppose I present the Principle of Sufficient Reason to some confirmed atheist along with a valid argument from it, entailing the existence of God, assuring him that the Principle of Sufficient Reason is self-evident. He proceeds to understand it, but denies that it is true *on the ground that* it leads to a false proposition. If I wished to maintain my doctrine that there are self-evident truths, I should have to abandon the conviction that he understood the principle, but at the *same* time I should have to maintain that it is possible for a man who, with respect to a proposition *p*, knows what the terms mean and knows what would have to be so if *p* were true and what would falsify *p* if *p* were false, might *still* not understand *p*. This seems entirely unfruitful since it puts a fog of mystery around the notion of

---

[9] For instance, *S* knows *a* and does not know *b* to be true; or *S* knows both but can give his reasons for *a* and not for *b*; or *S* knows both and, while he is unable to give reasons for either, sees that all reasons for *b* will be reasons for *a*, but not vice versa, etc. This is, of course, not a complete analysis of the expression in question, but is enough to indicate that what is in question is epistemic priority for someone, not logical priority.

"understanding a proposition," with the result that one has no idea what is required in order for it to be true that one cannot understand a self-evident proposition without seeing that it is true.

If, on the other hand, we do not abandon the conviction that the atheist understood the proposition, then we must take the fact that he does not concede its truth, and furthermore that he has committed no demonstrable logical blunder, as a falsification of the hypothesis that this principle (of sufficient reason) is self-evident. Since for any general principle one chooses, it is logically possible to find someone who rejects it because it leads to some consequence he considers false, it follows either that there are no self-evident propositions *or* that a proposition may be self-evident without being believed by everyone who understands it. Neither consequence should comfort the proponents of the "self-evidence" theory. In either case, it seems that there can be a premise from which someone might come to know any true proposition whatever, and that there are in principle no ultimate truths epistemically (although there may be in fact and for given persons). Therefore, to begin philosophy from "self-evident" axioms and to claim that nothing is cognitively prior to these axioms is to begin with a false conception of one's materials. This conclusion should lay the ghost of "self-evidence" which has haunted neo-scholastics for generations.

Having dismissed the claim that there are some propositions which are epistemically primary for everyone (in that there is no one who can use something else he knows as a means of coming to know these propositions) and the claim that there are self-evident propositions (in the usual way this claim is understood), I conclude that arguments which are claimed to stem from primary axioms of human thought are arguments presented under false assumptions.

Thus, suppose I argue as follows:

1: *If Christ was bodily removed from the earth, God loves the world.*

2: *Christ was bodily removed from the earth.*

3: *Therefore God loves the world.*

Let us assume that this is a sound argument; still, it is a flagrantly poor one. It is not logically circular; nor is it epistemically circular, since a person could come to know premise (1) without knowing the truth value of either (2) or (3) and might come to know (2) by the communication of an angel, or by some theosophic sense or some other weird power, without knowing that God loves the world. Moreover (2) is possible (logically) even if (3) were false (at least in the sense that it is intrinsically consistent). What is important here is that if a person wanted to find out whether or not (2) is true, he would have no way of doing so which is provided for in the accepted methods of philosophy.

Since many philosophers would be dissatisfied with my reasons why this argument falls short of a good argument because they cannot feel comfortable in assuming that it is sound, let us consider another:

1: *If Christ raised a dead man, God loves the world.*

2: *Christ raised a dead man.*

3: *Therefore God loves the world.*

A few more philosophers will think that this is sound and will agree that it is the unavailability of a means within philosophical method for deciding upon premise (2) which makes it poor. Yet some may say that what is peculiar to this and the preceding argument is that most of us could not come to discover the truth of the second premise without first having accepted the conclusion; as a matter of psychological fact, this may be correct. But it is not part of the *logical* structure of the argument, because I can imagine ways of discovering the truth of one or the other of the premises which do not presuppose either the knowledge of the conclusion or even the fact that it is true; therefore, it is not epistemic circularity which makes this a poor philosophical argument; it is the unassessability of the premises.

A decisive establishment for every philosopher that there are sound arguments whose premises cannot be assessed within the framework of philosophical method is not possible. For note: Suppose I want to establish the point that some sound arguments are not good arguments because they have premises which, for those philosophers who do not know them, are practically undecidable either because it is a contingent psychological fact that only those who accept the conclusion accept the premises, or because the source of the information would not be normal (angelic visitations, paranormal perception, etc.) or because of other conditions, not specified, which render knowledge of the premises unavailable to some philosophers. What must I do? I must present arguments which are sound and which each philosopher knows to be sound. How then can I claim that there is a premise in the argument the *knowledge* of which is not available to all investigators alike? Any argument which I know to be sound but which some philosophers do not know to be sound and whose premises I know to be unavailable for decision by these philosophers will fail to be a convincing example to *them* of a sound but not good argument—just because these philosophers will doubt its soundness.

For all those who do have knowledge from some source not accessible to everyone, it should be evident that an argument employing such knowledge in its premises is deficient in one of the prerequisites of a natural science: that its claims should be assessable through the normal and natural procedures of the science.

We have sufficiently argued that good arguments in philosophical theology must be sound and non-circular, and must contain only premises which are generally known in one's time or which are decidable through investigation conducted according to the methods of philosophers. It is not necessary that the philosopher succeed in beginning from generally acknowledged premises. Nor, to *give* a good argument, is it necessary to *show* that it is good; it need only be endowed with validity and with true premises whose truth is discoverable through observation or the employment of philosophical method. This condition of *methodical decidability* of the premises applies to all arguments which are intended to be part of the body of scientific truth, but does not apply to arguments which are produced to aid the conversion of some individual or for rhetorical or persuasive purposes, unless their *function* is to serve as philosophical-scientific support for faith. Since natural theology is a science, at least in its objectives, the arguments to establish its propositions must accord with the standards of pure science, in particular, independent methodical decidability of the truth-value of the premises (at least in principle) for the interested investigator: *assessability*.

The purpose of philosophical investigation is not just to *discover* the truth or falsity of some proposition. Often we know very well whether the claim we investigate is true or false before we begin. The purpose of scientific arguments in general is to *establish*, or confer scientific status upon, our conclusions by incorporating them into a body of truth (a science), entrance into which is governed by "knowledge standards." This is also what good arguments in philosophical theology are designed to do; they must settle objectively the truth-value of certain religious and para-religious claims according to methods of decision and on the basis of principles widely acknowledged among philosophers, and do this without regard to or concern for the conversion, reinforcement, or refutation of the religious convictions of anyone.

It is simply false that in constructing a good philosophical argument a person may employ as premises anything he knows to be true. This is why we first exclude all premises which are not independently *accessible* to the interested investigator regardless of who he is. Secondly, we permit only those premises whose truth or falsity can probably be *settled* by the application of the method of the philosopher (or by direct observation).[10]

We must, after all, be able to distinguish what Jones knows from what Jones has *established*, just as we do in the physical sciences. Jones may know from the boiling of his liver, the belching of his wife, or the psychic power of foreknowledge that his hypothesis is true; but if he has not submitted it to the tests and standards of his science, he has not *established* it. Assessability according to philosophical method is thus indispensable for the good argument.

Some philosophers are sure that no such "establishment" exists in philosophy; hence they say our "necessary" conditions are pointless. They do feel that such a status does exist in the "sciences"; in fact, it is because they believe philosophy lacks such a status that they withhold the term "science" from philosophy; they say that once we have a reliable decision procedure for a class of claims, we have formed a new and non-philosophical science.

I do not agree with this. Establishment is to a theoretical pursuit what winning is to a game. If there is no establishment, there is no point in the pursuit; in fact, there is properly speaking nothing pursued. Even if philosophers substitute 'clarification' for 'demonstration', there is a state of "establishment" to be sought.

If these philosophers reply that they are not seeking to establish the truth or falsity of particular claims but are seeking to discover

---

[10] We will briefly consider, below, the difficulties surrounding the attempt to rule out "theological" truths as premises for good philosophical arguments. These difficulties disclose the fact that our stated conditions for a good philosophical argument are not sufficiently precise.

methods of decision for families of claims,[11] I counter with the suggestion that they will not claim success until they have established that there is a method and that it is reliable. Hence their disagreement with me is only with respect to what *sorts* of truths they seek to establish, not with the claim that often the objective of the investigation is to *show* that certain claims are true (or false) by arguments which conform to the accepted method of philosophy.

Other philosophers, much more formidably, are more sympathetic but just as pessimistic, saying that they understand that certain truths have "scientific" status as parts of an organized body of knowledge, and that philosophers like Aristotle, Averroes, Avicenna, and Aquinas set themselves the objective of answering their philosophical questions in a manner which was *of knowledge standard* and which would confer the status of "scientific truth" upon their hypotheses; but, given this as understood, they then say: (1) no concept of "integration" or "organization" of knowledge has been given which cannot be *trivially* satisfied by all our knowledge, so that it makes no sense to talk of a science as an organized body of established truths (especially since not *every* "scientific" truth could actually be established); (2) no description of the method of philosophy has been given which shows (a) that its products are any different from any other thing we come to know to be the case (except insofar as the reasoning must be impersonal and independent of the experiences of a unique individual); or (b) that everything "established" by this method will in fact be a truth.

Point 2(b) must be distinguished. While no *description* of philosophical method has been given here and while no attempt at such a description has ever been more than a scandalous failure, we need not concede that such a description is needed. A proposition *p* is established in a science *S* if and only if:

p is the conclusion of some argument, A, which fulfills these conditions:

a: A is sound.

b: A is not epistemically circular for everyone.

c: A has publicly accessible premises.

d: The truth of the premises of A is discernible for someone by assessment according to the method of the science S.

---

[11] See Waismann, *Principles of Linguistic Philosophy* (New York: St. Martin's Press, 1965), pp. 32–33.

Nothing can be established according to the method of philosophy or of any other science unless it is a truth; see condition (a). Hence we need not show that philosophical method will always lead us to the truth.

Secondly, with respect to point 2(a), we need not claim that there *is* anything about the truths established according to philosophical method which makes them distinct from any other things we come to know that can be known independently of the experience of any unique individual. In fact sometimes the truths we establish by philosophical investigations are the same truths we knew prior to those investigations. There is no need at all to claim that the truths established by philosophers are different *in content* from those we know in other ways. Hence, the supposition of this point (2a) is quite mistaken.

The first criticism—that no principle of *organization* or rule of *integration* can be given which will distinguish a science from an encyclopedia of truths or even a random collection of true propositions or a set of truths related deductively by material implication—is quite well taken. There is no such principle, despite what Aristotle and Aquinas thought. That philosophy was to be organized in the way axiomatic-deductive formal theories may be organized was believed by many eminent philosophers who thought that self-evident truths functioned in place of axioms and that their *organizing* relation was that of *strict deducibility*. As a matter of fact, we can indicate no such principle of organization even for our most highly developed physical sciences. That philosophy lacks such organization should not be allowed to stand in the way of its being considered a science; this would be imposing a condition upon philosophy which is not imposed upon other candidates for the title "science." Rather, the existence of standards for the establishment of conclusions and of a *method* for the investigation of the truth of premises, the linguistic and logical analytical method as well as the phenomenological method, is what renders philosophy a science. For it is generally held that by beginning with the knowledge available to a sensible and prudent person we may determine the truth or falsity of the premises of philosophical arguments through logical, linguistic, and phenomenological analysis and through tests not unlike those applied in other sciences. Philosophy does not have a method of *discovery*; it has methods of *assessment*. And while we cannot decribe its methods in detail, we can see that its applications have increased in rigor over the centuries; that it does provide a measure of objective agreement about the value of particular arguments; and that, in view of the method of assessment rather than in view of the ancient principle of organization, philosophy is to be considered a science.

That we cannot say (in theoretically general form) just what makes a good *philosophical* argument, as distinct from a good legal or good theological argument, is indeed to be regretted; but we must not forget that the converse holds too. That we cannot say just what principle of organization distinguishes a science from a mere collection of true propositions about a given subject is the more to be regretted, although it is the presence of an interpersonal and generally acknowledged decision method or assessment method which more probably constitutes the *scientific* character of our enterprise. But that these defects should lead one to think that the arguments of the philosopher of religion must be directed *not* to developing an abstract science but to the acquisition or deposition of religious belief by some unnamed individual or group would be a disaster. It would suggest that we apply rhetoric, persuasion, salesmanship, showmanship, and literary ingenuity where we intend, instead, to employ the Spartan diet of analysis.

Lest anyone overestimate the set of conditions we have provided above or underestimate the pragmatic importance of the points at issue, let us briefly apply these considerations to the centuries-old dispute over the distinction of philosophy from theology.

When St. Anselm wrote his *Cur Deus Homo*, he presented arguments designed to show that it was a matter of *fact* that God became man. He offered no *principle* by which one should class these arguments as "theological" while classifying the arguments of the *Monologion* and *Proslogion* as "philosophical." Moreover, the premises of all three sets of arguments were such that he could reasonably expect that any interested investigator in the community of theoreticians to which he addressed himself could *methodically* determine their truth or falsity, merely by consulting the other things they, in common, held themselves to know; e.g., that man had sinned, that God intended to bring good out of evil, etc.

It does not seem to me that the Christian theologian who (a) holds those premises along with Anselm, and (b) thinks he knows them to be true, can without *further* justification say that despite their admitted (for the sake of argument) soundness, the arguments of *Cur Deus Homo* are not good philosophical arguments. If he admits that he knows the premises to be true and the form to be valid, and admits the structure is not circular, how can he deny that they are *good* philosophical arguments? He cannot do so by saying that the premises must be truths the philosopher has *found out for himself*. This is surely too strong. But if he says they must be such as one *could* find out for himself, then any truth will qualify. If this is restricted to truths such that one is actually able to *find* out for oneself, it will again become too strong because we do use premises we are at the time in no position to decide independently for ourselves.

It was just this dilemma which St. Thomas tried to escape through his distinction between knowledge acquired by faith and knowledge acquired by scientific investigation. But St. Thomas failed to address the problem head on. The acquisition of knowledge through scientific investigation does not *begin* with this kind of knowledge, but rather begins with a combination of what is known through faith (trust in others) and direct perception. The very structure of our perceptual experience is dependent upon our faith in others. Naturally, that body of knowledge which results from faith in God, religious faith, is a sub-set of the knowledge acquired through faith in others. "Faith is that habit by which we acquire knowledge of things unseen." In what ways does this sub-set of knowledge differ from the rest of the knowledge acquired through faith? Primarily through the superiority of its witness, who could not have deceived or have erred. Why is a person not justified in beginning a philosophical argument with what he knows to be true as a result of his religious faith? Why may a person not use everything he knows as a starting point?

It would only be avoiding the issue for us to say that no one does have such knowledge. And it would be wholly irrelevant for us to say that we do not know whether anyone has such knowledge; what has our ignorance of whether another has knowledge of his premises got to do with whether he is justified in using such premises (especially if he, like Anselm, is not particularly concerned with convincing us)?

This problem is especially acute for those Christians who wish to do responsible philosophy and who think they do have knowledge (through the habit of divine faith) of certain creedal truths. Why does their employing such premises vitiate their arguments?

To say that their premises would not be accessible and methodically assessable would not be unequivocally true. Such premises were accessible to the entire community of believers to whom Anselm spoke; and they were decidable by a standard method of decision available to that community of scholars. That we do not generally accept the testimony of scripture or theological tradition as decisive nowadays is merely incidental.

This shows us that the conditions we have given are not adequate because they do not create the fundamental distinction of philosophy from theology and do not provide grounds for ruling the whole family or arguments in *Cur Deus Homo* (an "obviously" theological work) "defective" as philosophical arguments. We cannot say such premises are not objects of knowledge for those who employ them. We cannot say that the epistemological status of faith (as trust in others) is such that faith cannot be just as effective a means for acquiring knowledge as one's investigation for oneself. The theoretical grounds actually given by St. Thomas Aquinas for his generous exclusion of "revealed truths" from the class of suitable philosophical premises are actually insufficient to support his distinction. This does not mean that his distinction between philosophy and theology (whereby there is a body of premises legitimately employed in the latter but not in the former science) is misguided; it is merely inadequately founded. Unfortunately, I presently see nothing which can be cited as a matter of principle by which to re-establish his distinction, though I acknowledge its necessity. We must content ourselves for now with the sober realization that the set of conditions for a "good" argument that we have cited are not explicit enough to distinguish good arguments in one science from those in another, and that we do not have at hand any good reason why a person may not use any accessible and assessable premise he knows to be true. That it may sometimes turn out that what is considered accessible and methodically assessable at one time is not so considered at another is evident and inconvenient. We must, therefore, expect no more than what has been claimed for the analyses I have offered: they are designed to show that certain widespread expectations of the kinds of results we should achieve are inappropriate; they are not designed to provide a full analysis of the concept 'good argument' or to draw any useful distinction between philosophy and theology or between philosophy and any other purely theoretical science. Above all, it is to be insisted that to be good, our arguments need not convert, convince, or comfort anyone.

CONCLUSION

In this chapter we have asked the question: What are some of the central conditions a philosopher's argument must meet in order to be a *good* argument, one that establishes its conclusion? In particular we have been concerned with the requirements to be met by arguments put forward in the philosophical investigation of religion. Yet it must be remembered that nowhere has it been assumed that philosophy consists entirely of arguments. Rather, every philosopher has required more than the most obvious of truths for his premises and has employed various devices for causing us to see the truth of such additional premises without arguments. The analytical and phenomenological methods of philosophy are often used to disclose such truths.

Our arguments are definitely intended to serve the purpose of showing that their conclusions are true. This is establishment, and a sound argument which is epistemically non-circular and methodically assessable achieves that.

But what has the discussion accomplished? Surely, not significant progress in explaining what a good argument is. Is it then to "set the stage" for forthcoming arguments which are specious and which will be accompanied by a cavalier statement: "It makes no difference whether they convince you or not, since good arguments need convince no one"? Not at all, although it should have disclosed itself that the mere fact that an argument fails to convince you is, by itself, irrelevant to its intrinsic merits.

No. The purpose of this discussion has been to set our later discussions in unambiguous perspective with respect to whole classes of views on what we ought to be trying to achieve and how we ought to be approaching our objectives.

First, I wanted to restate the truths which show that certain theologians (Ballie, Barth, Tillich, etc.), who say or imply that the existence (or reality) of God cannot be proved and yet hold that God does exist (or does have reality), are either holding an inconsistent position or fail to understand what is involved in "proving" or "establishing" something.

Second, I wanted, with equal decisiveness, to cut the ground from under some common neo-scholastic conceptions: (a) that there is a finite set of arguments which will work to show the existence of God to all fair-minded men; (b) that fair-minded men can be expected to come to believe in the existence of God through arguments; (c) that there are epistemically ultimate (self-evident) truths from which these arguments begin or should begin; (d) that Pope Pius IX's interpretation (as found in the Oath against Modernism) of the first Vatican Council's statement on the knowledge of God, which turns it into a statement in terms of "proof" or "demonstration" rather than "discovery," and which has become a very common neo-scholastic doctrine for several generations now, is inherently absurd. Thus, the second objective of the chapter was to jettison entirely the widespread neo-scholastic conception of arguments for the existence of God as vehicles of persuasion or education which are to be applied to a wide variety of persons, and to insist upon a separation between the theoretical purposes for such arguments and their practical or apologetic employment.

Third, I want it to be clear that we need not construct our arguments with an eye for what is persuasive or likely to be believed; for we have no practical objective which demands that we bring individuals around to our view of the matter. We may become as abstract as we like.

Fourth, by insisting that the reasonings which follow be entirely divorced from the atmosphere of "religion-getting" and "religion-reinforcing," we acquire for them a purely theoretical, non-polemical context in which philosophers, despite their differences of religious conviction, can subject them to assessment according to methods and families of tests which they hold in common.

2 ✒ On how the term "God" functions in our discussions

The three sections of this chapter correspond to three questions about how the term "God" functions in our discussions of philosophical theology:

(1) Is a *petitio* the logical consequence of our employing the term "God" in proofs of God's existence, since the term appears to be a proper name whose very use involves existential import?

(2) What descriptive associations are attached to this name and by what criterion do we select one set of these associations to the exclusion of some other?

(3) How do the existential and the descriptive aspects of the term "God" interact in statements that are modally qualified?

SECTION 1: "GOD": THE EXISTENTIAL
IMPORT OF THE NAME

·It need not involve a mistake for someone who knows or believes that God exists to consider establishing that God exists.

But still, some points need clarification. Religious believers, when asked what makes them think God is omnipotent or think God is good, will more often than not reply "Of course; that's part of what I mean by 'God'." They are unaware that some philosophers think that proper names do not have meanings and that it is, for example, a synthetic matter both that "Julius Caesar" is the name of a man who crossed the Rubicon and that Julius Caesar (the man named) crossed the Rubicon. Yet, if proper names cannot have descriptive meanings, then "God" as used by Christian believers must be an equivocal term, functioning both as a proper name (for instance, when they pray) and as a common name or term with descriptive meaning (for instance, when they explain what "God" means).

Actually we need not treat "God" as equivocal, because there is no impropriety in speaking of the meaning associated with a proper name. Professor Peter Geach created confusion when he reported, without making distinctions between what we nowadays mean by "proper" and "common" names and what was the case in Aquinas' works, that *Deus* is a common name in St. Thomas' proofs for the existence of God; the notions were markedly different for St. Thomas, though closely related to our own.[1] The reasons suggesting that proper names do not have meanings were developed in the narrow context of Russell's Logical Atomism, where it was better, on heuristic grounds, to draw a line whereby many of the expressions that would ordinarily be called proper names were thrown into the class of descriptive terms. For our purposes we need draw no such line and, indeed, should avoid an arbitrary classification; otherwise we will not be able to account for various features of ordinary discourse which are to be cited below. In ordinary discourse we seldom use what is *for us* a non-connotative name, and hence we do not need Russell's narrow concept.

In order to take account of the facts at the root of Russell's idea, we must distinguish proper names from indexical variables (like "this," "that") and from indexical constants (like "*k*," "*f*"); and we hold that without exception ordinary-language proper names have de-

---

[1] Professor Geach, in his article on St. Thomas in *Three Philosophers*, constitutes an example of those otherwise excellent philosophers who fail to give Aquinas his due by making too easy an equivalence between our terms and his. It is true that St. Thomas (in *Summa Theologica*, I, q. 13, a. 3, 8, 9, and 11) uses a distinction between a "proper" and a "common" name (distinguishing among the latter those that are communicable *secundum rem* and those communicable *secundem opinionem*). But he does not mean anything like what we mean by the distinction between common and proper names. For instance, he considers "He Who Is" (*ST*, I, q. 13, a. 11, c) to be the "most proper" name for God because it signifies not a form but the very being of God. Notice the comparative language: "most proper"; and notice the intricate series of distinctions among "common" names. I think it can reasonably be claimed that St. Thomas was saying nothing very different when he said "*Deus*" is a *common name* imposed to signify the divine nature, from what I am claiming when I say (in a different scheme of classification) that "God" is a proper name which signifies the divine nature. The confusion and apparent contradiction can be cleared up only by a careful reading of St. Thomas, where one pays attention to the distinction between names imposed to signify a nature or form from those imposed to signify the very being or individuality (*suppositum*) of a thing.

scriptive meanings associated with them in their actual naming uses.[2] On the other hand, proper names must be distinguished from essentially significative or connotative expressions like "chair"; the latter, in order to *stand for* an object or group of objects unambiguously and correctly, must be modified by an article or a grammatical plural in the statements in which they occur, or by clearly implied modifiers furnished by the context. Such expressions cannot by themselves designate any thing,[3] whereas proper names have a definite designation without the addition of any grammatical modifiers.[4] Hence, we are saying that those uniquely designating terms which are not indexical symbols (because they have signification) and which are not essentially significative terms in ordinary use (because their unique designation is not to be accounted for by grammatical and logical quantifiers or their substitutes) are proper names. As we shall remark later, a proper name can be put to various *uses*; some of these are primarily designative and some are primarily significative. But the entire separation of signification and designation is abnormal for a proper name in ordinary discourse.

The descriptive meaning associated with a proper name is all-important *practically* on those occasions when, were doubt to arise as to whom one is referring or to what sort of thing one is referring, demonstrative indication would be inappropriate—for example, when we are talking about someone not present or when two people with the same name are present but out of pointing or indicating range. It is not possible to *indicate* God, should some doubt arise as to whether there is such a being; thus, the matter would have to be

---

[2] When I, as a philosopher, use "Socrates is a man" as an illustration of a simple declarative sentence, I *may* not be using "Socrates" really to name anything, and hence may have no connotations for the term in mind. That is why I distinguish actual *naming* uses of a proper name from other uses, e.g., using a simple declaratory sentence with a proper name for the subject in order to illustrate a class of expressions for some philosophical purpose. Surely no one is named, even though we use someone's name, in such a case; for we would not be talking *about* the person named at all.

[3] This, of course, applies only to normal cases. In some unusual contexts whose meaningfulness rides piggy-back upon more usual forms, we find someone saying "Chair" when he means "Take this chair." In such uses the designation of an object is achieved by means of an article-substitute (e.g., a gesture) or by means of ellipsis or context.

[4] Note that an expression may have a definite and, even, unique designation without its being the case that what it designates actually exists; for example, "the tallest man in the world" (suppose there are two who are as tall as anyone else).

decided at least in part by our saying what descriptive meaning we associate with the expression "God" and by our showing whether there is anything that satisfies the description. There can be no doubt that this proper name "God" has at least one descriptive or significative mode of meaning as well as a designative mode of meaning; these modes of meaning interact in various ways, as we shall indicate in Section 3.

In certain circumstances, one can attach a quite incorrect descriptive association to a name and yet succeed in identifying the person in question for someone else. For example, I may tell a story about a certain Jones. My auditor may ask: "Who is he?" I reply: "He's the doorman at the Ritz." This may be entirely false, either because I misstated myself or because I am misinformed. Yet I may, by accident or association, direct my auditor to think of the man who is night clerk at the Barclay, and without attempting to correct me—because he now knows whom I am referring to—he may proceed to discuss quite correctly certain antecedents or consequences of the events recounted in the story I have already told. A man who ill conceives God can have similar success in a religious discussion. Attention to our psychological vagaries will show that we are often able to communicate successfully even in circumstances where we grossly misapprehend the nature of what is discussed; but such successful communication involves the possession, by both communicating parties, of information (but not necessarily *common* information) about the individual to whom we refer.

The fact that believers refer to God, despite extensive differences of opinion about His nature, is the basis of discussion of God by those who do not think there is such a being or who are in doubt about the existence of such a being; for the unbelievers are talking about the being the believers think exists.

We cannot intelligibly discuss someone in whose existence no one believes or is thought or expected to believe; but there is no reason why we cannot discuss someone in whose existence someone believes or can be expected to believe, even though we do not share that belief. Santa Claus is one of the beings which are thought to exist by someone (certain children), but who we know do not exist; Lychurgus is the sort of person we might expect someone to believe exists, regardless of whether we believe or even know that there is no such being. Fictional and legendary characters can (reasonably, I think) be thought to fall into the class of existing beings, since this class includes existence through human thought and human interpretation of symbols—whether written, auditory, or performed (e.g., ballet characters).

The philosophical perplexities about fictional and legendary existences need not detain us here, since if someone were expected to believe fictional or legendary characters exist other than in fiction and legend, this belief makes reference, as to a real existent, appropriate; and if no one can be expected to believe this, all reference will be restricted to the context of fiction and legend.[5] Because a person who does not believe God really exists might very well think God a legendary character, his employment of "God" as a proper name need not involve a commitment to *real* existence, even if he employs the term in what we shall later call "primary reference." We must take account not only of the *kinds of reference* but also of the mode of being (real, theoretical, fictional, etc.) ascribed to what is referred to.

When the agnostic asks me whether I think God loves me, I do not presume that he agrees that God exists, but neither do I doubt that he is referring, in the context of real and not legendary or fictional existence, to the being which he knows I think exists; otherwise, how could he be asking a question relevant to me? What sense would it make for him to ask me "Does Buddha love you?" Hence, discussions which involve our using a proper name will be meaningful to both of us and will be about the self-same being even though *his reference is dependent upon my reference*, and from *his* point of view, upon what he takes to be my misplaced reference. It would be totally incorrect to say that he employs "God" as a merely descriptive term while I employ "God" as a proper name; in that case we would not contradict one another, should he say "God does not exist" and should I reply "But God does exist."

Some thinkers hold that the proper name "God" is used by them to refer to a being that they and a whole community of other believers know (or at least believe) to exist and to have certain attributes (al-

---

[5] Someone might think we do not refer to characters, but we do. Notice the great difference between referring to the actor who plays Hamlet, and referring to Hamlet; for Hamlet may (and certainly does) have characteristics that are entirely opposed to those of some actors who play that part.

though there is a broad area of variance in the sets of attributes which are attributed to that being). Other thinkers hold that there is no such being as that thought to exist by the members of the first group, and would say they use the proper name "God" to refer to what the believers think exists, but does not really exist.[6] When the positions are stated in this way, there can be no question that the two groups are at least sometimes talking about the same being even though they disagree about its existence, and may disagree in part about its attributes.

Still other philosophers will object to our stating the position of the non-believers as one of *referring* to a being which they do not think exists; they say one does not and cannot refer to a being which does not exist. This objection is unfounded; reference is an *intentional* relation. The reference of the non-believer is derivative from the reference of the believers. The objectors have assumed without adequate study of the practice of competent speakers that referring has a point only when the being referred to exists. Real and actual existence is not necessary for reference. It is essential only that the being referred to either exist, or be *thought* to exist, or be thought to be thought to exist, by someone (or be thought by someone to be something which someone might with some probability be expected to think exists or to have thought existed) in order for a person to refer to that being whether or not he believes or disbelieves in the existence of that being.

When a father talks to his child about what Santa Claus will do, he is referring to the same being which the child thinks exists (and which he thinks his child thinks exists). No such reference would be possible for the father were it not for his expectation or incitement of the child's belief in such an entity: when the child loses his belief and informs the father of this, much of the father's former talk about Santa Claus would be quite pointless were it repeated now, since

---

[6] Some thinkers—Professor Paul Ziff, for example—say that the person who denies that God exists is in effect denying that the term "God" has a referent. These speakers would use "God" as a non-referring term. Describing the situation this way would involve a set of reference concepts different from those I specify below. There may be many who would be satisfied with this alternative description. But in practice it will be difficult to account for discussions with non-believers in which they say such things as "I agree with you that God is almighty, but want to know what 'almighty' means." It would be necessary to interpret the phrase "God is almighty" as shorthand for "I agree with you that 'God' means 'almighty'." However, I doubt that this *is* what is meant in many such cases; therefore, I prefer the description to be explained here.

the father too does not believe that the entity exists. When the father is inducing the belief in the child, he speaks *as if* he were referring to something he thinks exists in order to bring it about that the child believes there is such a being. Then the father's use of "Santa Claus" may become a derived reference rather than a purported reference. A statement of sufficient conditions for the various kinds of reference will clarify the terminology I have introduced.

Kinds of reference

Primary Reference:

S makes a primary reference to x if (but not only if) S uses a proper name or definite description of x to talk about x, thinking that there is something, x, which exists and fits the description or bears the name.

One may refer to what does not exist, since primary reference by *S* is an intentional relation to something, *x*, which is such that *S* thinks it exists and either has certain properties or bears that name. Thus it makes perfect sense to say, "There is no such being as *S* refers to." But it does not make sense to say, "There is no such being as I am referring to," although it does make sense to say, "There is no such being as I *referred* to."

Secondary or Derived Reference:

S makes a secondary reference to x if (but not only if) S uses a proper name for or definite description of something, x, not thinking that there is some-thing, x, which fits the description or bears the name, but in order to talk about (or think about, etc.) something, x, which someone else, R, thinks exists or could reasonably be expected to think (or to have thought) exists.

Purported Reference:

S makes a purported reference to x if (but not only if) S uses a proper name or definite description of x thinking that no x exists (which may or may not be the case) and not referring (in primary reference) to x but intending that someone else, R, should think he, S, is referring to something, x, which really exists.

This is not a case of *S*'s talking about something *R* already thinks exists, but rather a case of *S*'s attempting to bring *R* to believe in or talk about or think about some being *R* thinks *S* thinks exists, or there-by to bring *R* to a certain belief about what *S* thinks exists. Hence, one might say: "There is no such being as the one I am purporting to refer to"—although one must not say that to R, to the person to whom the purported reference is offered, if the purported reference is to be pragmatically possible.

Intelligent discussion of the existence of God involves primary reference on the part of believers and secondary reference (derived from the reference of believers) upon the part of unbelievers. It follows from this that *not all uses of the proper name "God" have unconditional existential import.* When a believer says "If God loves me, He will give me happiness," his use usually involves the supposition on his part that God exists; that is, it commits *him* to that claim; under certain circumstances[7] what is said may entail that God exists. But when the nonbeliever says the same thing, his use of the name "God" does not presuppose the existence of the being but is a secondary reference based upon the primary reference of others; his use does not commit him to claim that "God exists" is true, or to give up his assertion if he should come to know that God does not exist. Whatever may be the existential entailment of what is said, the mere fact that a proper name is used to refer does not account for such existential entailment.

Since there is an explanation both from the believer's point of view and from the nonbeliever's point of view of how the proper name "God" functions in their statements, nothing either desirable or undesirable in the form of existential commitments follows from their use of the same proper name and there is no need for anyone to confuse the issue by denying that the unbeliever is using the *same* proper name and is, thereby, making a reference, even to the *same thing;* for this would lead to another situation where the unbeliever cannot contradict the claims of the believer without careful circumlocution —something which is obviously not so.

If a proper name appears in a good argument for the *existence* of the being I refer to by that name, the existential conclusion must follow from the descriptive associations of the name and the other premises, independently of the existential import of our having employed that name for the subject, both because it will otherwise be said that the argument begs the question (since primary reference is appropriate whenever the speaker *believes* in the existence of a referent) and be-

---

[7] See Section 3, below.

cause it is possible that the same premises could be asserted by one
for whom the proper name has only *secondary reference* and only
conditional existential import.

Being circular and begging the question are not the same defect.
Circularity is not an easy property to pin down. Some arguments are
circular for some people because those people cannot come to know
that the premises are true without employing as a reason for accepting
those premises their belief that the conclusion is true; the person
simply does not have the knowledge or means to the knowledge
required to know the premises any other way. This is a situation where
the argument exhibits epistemic circularity for certain people. Whenever you must already know the truth value of the conclusion in order
to determine the truth value of the premises, the argument is *pragmatically futile* for you, since it requires you to do with respect to the
conclusion (and independently of your knowledge of the premises)
the very operation—that of determining its truth value—which the
premises and argument form were supposed to enable you to perform on the basis of your knowledge about *them*. This is what it
means for an argument to be epistemically circular for you.

Nevertheless, arguments that are circular in these ways are often the
paradigms of *formally valid* arguments, as is obvious when we consider an argument which has its conclusion given as its premise. And
even the very best argument may be epistemically circular for someone whose psychological make-up or ignorance may preclude his
knowing that the premises are true if he does not already know the
conclusion to be true. Therefore, an argument is not necessarily defective if there is someone for whom it is epistemically circular. No
matter what argument or chain of reasoning you pick, there might be
someone somewhere in the world who would not be convinced by
it unless he could add to your premises the additional premise that
the conclusion is true. The fact that an argument is epistemically circular for someone does not guarantee that it is epistemically circular
for most people or for everyone. However—as a *philosophical* argument—an argument whose premises are such that one cannot, by
employing the methods of assessment that are permitted by philosophical method, determine their truth unless he has already determined the truth of the conclusion, begs the question at issue because
it is epistemically circular for everyone using philosophical methods

of assessment. This is just the case where a person employs an argument to show that "*K* exists" is true, where "*K*" is a proper name and where that conclusion follows from the premises *only* by virtue of the fact that we take an occurrence of "*K*" in the premises to have existential import.

Epistemic circularity is thus a person-relative characteristic of an argument. Begging-the-question is a context-relative property wherever it is not already created by the universal epistemic circularity of an argument (for example, $p/\therefore p$). Since context-dependent begging-the-question has a good deal to do with what the dialectical starting point was, it is not an "objective" property of any given (not universally epistemically circular) argument that it begs the question. But surely "trading on the existential import of the proper name" is exactly a case of creating universal epistemic circularity and hence an "objective" begging-of-the-question.

There is one situation which might seem to evade the explanations so far offered to show why trading on the existential import of the use of a name is a defect that causes the argument to beg the question. Suppose someone whom I know to be telling the truth tells me that he is going to give me an argument with true premises; if he writes the premises in some language I do not know and the existential conclusion in English, I can come to know that the premises are true independently of knowing the truth of the conclusion even though (as a matter of fact) the conclusion, as I discover when the premises are translated, is part of the conjunction given in the premises. The argument is valid; but it begs the question and would be epistemically circular for a person who knows what the premises are in addition to, or instead of, knowing merely *that* they are true. To accommodate such fringe cases as this, our concept of epistemic circularity can be extended to state that *an argument* (under given conditions) *is epistemically circular for someone if, in the absence of knowing some metalanguage statement to be true which assigns a truth-value to the premises, the person could not* (in the given circumstances) *come to know that the premises are true except by means of his knowing the conclusion to be true.* (Remember, it is not epistemic circularity for *someone* that we have said is a defect, but epistemic circularity for everyone, or in some special cases, for everyone of a certain class or everyone employing a certain method of assessment.) It is a contingent matter whether a given argument is epistemically circular at a given time for a given person; and the passage of time may change this status. It may even be a contingent matter that an argument is epistemically circular for everyone; but sometimes it is a semantical (not contingent) feature of an argument whether it begs the question by being epistemically circular for everyone (or everyone of a certain relevant group). Trading on the existential import of a proper name used as subject in the premises is just such an intrinsically vitiating feature.

All sound arguments are epistemically circular for an omniscient being (since its knowing everything is a logically necessary condition of its knowing anything); for its knowing all true conclusions is a prerequisite for its knowing any premise: that is why God cannot (and need not) use arguments or reason discursively.

We can show that an argument that employs a proper name in the premises does *not* beg the question by substituting an indefinite description for the proper name, and by showing that validity and the existential import of the conclusion are preserved after the substitution;[8] but it is not necessary that such substitution be possible in order that the employment of a proper name, even as the subject in an argument with an existential conclusion, be legitimate. Existential import is not simply a logical consequence of statements containing proper names, regardless of how they are used; every statement in which a proper name is used to indicate the subject does not logically entail an existential proposition *with the same subject*. Otherwise 'God does not exist' would be contradictory, and so would 'Job did not exist'.

In expressions of the form "The person who did such-and-such *was* So-and-So," the proper name does at least sometimes function with its existential import even though it may not be used primarily *designatively*, but only incidentally designatively. Some philosophers might say that the name is not used at all in this context but is merely mentioned. But I think this is incorrect; we are not saying merely that

[8] 'Being epistemically circular for someone' and 'begging the question' are not the same, as we have said. An argument which does not beg the question may be epistemically circular for someone. In fact, if a man privileges the negation of a given conclusion highly enough, every argument for it will be epistemically circular for him, but not every argument will beg the question. Universal epistemic circularity is a sufficient condition for begging the question, but is not necessary. Epistemic circularity for someone is neither sufficient nor necessary.

the person who ordered the killing of the Jews was *called* "A. Hitler"; we are saying that he really *was* A. Hitler (without quotes). Some of these uses of proper names are irreplaceable because the name as well as its supposit is part of what is discussed. In such cases the substitution of a common name or indefinite description does not have to be satisfiable even though it becomes difficult to decide whether the argument trades on the import of the name.

SECTION 2: "GOD": THE DESCRIPTIVE ASSOCIATION

In this section we shall consider two subjects: some difficulties concerning scientific neutrality and the possibilities of fruitful philosophical dialogue between Christians and non-Christians which arise when a philosophical theologian formally adopts "orthodox Christianity" as his guide to what he will consider the proper descriptive associations of the term "God"; and the apparent logical conflict within the tradition of orthodox Christianity, a tradition which describes the attributes of God as if they were a plurality of logically distinct characteristics but simultaneously claims that God is a simple being without real complexity or plurality.

A: Orthodox Christianity and the term "God"

We have already indicated that there are broad limits set upon the sorts of characteristics we can attribute to God within the framework of Christian orthodoxy. Thus, if someone tells me I ought not to include "omnipotence" among the attributes of God because of the difficulties that arise over the reality of evil, I shall merely reply that it is part of orthodox Christian belief that God is all-powerful; and while I will admit there is some point in disputing just what is meant by "omnipotence" and how it is related to God's goodness, I will deny that there is any justification in attributing to God a defect or deficiency in power or in anything else. Orthodoxy entirely excludes such concessions. But how do we justify our determining our concept of God by such a standard? And how will we make this standard precise enough to be helpful?

"Orthodoxy is my doxy and heterodoxy is your doxy," G. K. Chesterton observed. Who is to say, and with what justification, that F and H are parts of the orthodox Christian concept of God?[9] Actually, the problem has no practical bearing upon the subjects of this book, although it is logically complex and could eventually demand direct attention. Despite the very wide divergence in the attributes that are ascribed to God at various times, there is, for the most part, no serious dispute over which ascriptions are *orthodox*. Rather, the innovators, for instance those who say God is limited in power or in goodness, are well aware that these proposals are deviations from the received tradition of orthodox Christianity.

There is no real debate about the fact that Christian orthodoxy requires that we think of God as a perfect, personal, omnipotent, omniscient, omnipresent, immense, morally excellent being who, acting by free will, created the world, determined its course, sustains it by His will, provides for the events of each rational life with personal attention, and determines the state of reward or punishment which each person attains after his death in a manner befitting the person's moral actions during his life. Real debate may surround the literal versus the allegorical interpretation of such claims, the conditions they involve, or the source of our knowledge of their truth; but it does not center upon their orthodoxy.

There should be no real debate as to whether or not we should allow our concept of God to be determined by orthodox Christianity. The negative side in such a debate must begin from unsatisfactory premises, such as these: (a) that there is no such being as orthodox Christianity would have us imagine; (b) that God has characteristics quite in conflict with the orthodox ascriptions; (c) that philosophy should be theologically absolutely neutral; or (d) that one conception of God is as useful as another to begin an investigation.

Since one of the objectives of the investigation we have begun in this book, an objective traditionally associated with natural (philo-

[9] In this respect, philosophical investigations of religious truth are *not* religiously neutral. We select one of the several conceptual settings in which God is discussed and formulate all the claims whose truth we examine in the light of that family of concepts. The points we shall discuss in these chapters are so basic to the whole Christian tradition that we need not worry over the criteria of orthodoxy, once we have admitted that settling upon a standard of orthodox belief is *not* something we can achieve by philosophical investigation alone, and that if we pursue our analyses into enough detail, we shall eventually have to decide among competing conceptions of God which fall within the broad spectrum of orthodoxy.

sophical) theology, is to establish the existence of just such a being as the Christian Church would have us imagine, premise (a) begs the question as to whether such an investigation as we pursue will succeed. Because the long-range purpose is to decide whether the being that orthodox Christians have always thought to exist actually does exist, premise (b) also begs the question; it is not relevant that someone else has a different conception of the object of his religious worship or the object whose existence he would like to investigate, *unless* this other person wishes to contend that he can establish both the existence of the being he conceives of and calls "God" and the fact that the existence of such a being is incompatible with the existence of the being the orthodox Christians have conceived of and have called "God." In that case, the objection would be relevant but need not be addressed until apparent success in our own enterprise confronts us with two incompatible existential conclusions, *both* of which are based upon apparently good arguments.

Supposition (c), that philosophy should be theologically neutral, is also misguided. For me to inquire whether there is something which has characteristics F, G, and H is not the same as my making a theoretical *commitment* to the existence of such a being, even if I already think or know that there is such a being. One conception of God is *not* as useful as another, for some concepts of God are totally inappropriate and irrelevant to the religious environment of the western world; the kind of non-neutrality required so that our investigation will be relevant to the concerns of reflective men in our time and culture is by no means prejudicial to the scientific character of our work.

Not only does orthodox Christianity place limits upon our conception of God, but the basic elements of that concept—as we have spelled them out in this section and will further in Chapter III—are explicitly stipulated by tradition. Those points that are indefinite and in dispute (such as whether God predestines men in terms of their foreseen human actions or determines men's actions in terms of His plans of predestination) are relatively few and still fall within the general rule that no answer will be considered correct which does not accord with the other and more definitely settled elements of the concept of God and with the 'sense' of orthodoxy by which the Christian community has resolved disputes throughout its history.

Yet the Christian conception of God involves several elements which are of equal importance from a religious point of view, although from a logical point of view they have quite distinct status. Thus, it is logically necessary that the omnipotent being be omniscient; but it is logically contingent that an omnipotent being actually produced a world of dependent beings. Yet, for a religious man, the two propositions are equally important and the two concepts 'omnipotent' and 'Creator of the world' are alike signified by the term "God," despite the fact that an apparent antinomy arises: the analytic statement "God is the Creator of the world" seems to state a logically contingent truth.[10]

Is it possible that diverse significations attached by different persons (each perchance claiming to be "orthodox") to their concepts of God may make their discussions pointless by precluding their talking about the same being? Some remarks on this matter have already been offered in Section 1, but further comment may be helpful here.

Suppose there are three men called A, B, and C.

Suppose A thinks there is a being called "God" that has properties A, B, C, and D.

Suppose B thinks there is a being called "God" that has properties E, F, G, and H.

Suppose C thinks there is a being called "God" that has properties A, E, D, and H.

It seems correct to say that, although they disagree about its attributes, A and C are talking about the same being; and B and C are also talking about the same being, even though they disagree about its attributes. But it seems that A and B are not, since other than having existence and bearing the name "God" the beings they appear to be discussing are completely different. This might well happen if A were an orthodox Christian, B a Hindu, and C a "liberal Christian." It is difficult to decide what to say about such cases. The fact that several people use the name "God" in talking about

---

[10] It is obvious that we cannot let this situation go untreated; for if 'God is omnipotent' is necessarily true and 'God is Creator of the world' is analytic, then one entails the other. But if the latter states a contingent truth, then the first will entail a statement (the second) which entails a contingent truth. The result will be the paradoxical (even inconsistent) derivation of a contingent truth, necessarily, from a necessary one. Since this sort of confusion is frequent in discourse about God, we devote the whole of Section 3, below, to its consideration.

what each takes to be *the* fundamental reality and the reality related to religious experience, and the fact that each of the several people thinks there is such a being as he speaks of, suggest that they are referring to the same being even though they disagree about its attributes, especially since they undoubtedly misunderstand one another as well. The apparent truth that 'talking about the same thing as . . .' should be a transitive relation also suggests that A, B, and C are talking about the same being. On the other hand, the fact that two of these people have almost no concepts in common except the context of religious utterance and a belief in the reality of the being they discuss tends to suggest that they are not talking about the same thing. The matter can best be decided in terms of the *intentions* of the speakers: whether or not they intend, in spite of their other disagreements, to be talking about the same being.

(1) Two people may be discussing the same third person even though no such third person exists; this is especially obvious when they are mistaken in believing in the existence of the person.

(2) Two people may be talking about something, x, although they think they are talking about something else, y.

(3) If A and B are talking to each other about something each refers to as t, they can be talking about the same thing even though they ascribe (or, if we told them to tell us all their beliefs about that thing, would ascribe) markedly differing sets of attributes to what they refer to by "t."

(4) A and B are *not* talking about the same thing (even though they may *think* they are) if what A refers to actually has some property that what B refers to lacks, or vice versa. But A and B may be talking about the same thing despite the fact that B thinks the thing he is talking about has almost none of the characteristics A attributes to what he is talking about; and vice versa.

Now if the Hindu who thinks God (as *he* employs the term) exists, and the Christian who thinks God (as *he* employs the term) exists, are talking about the same thing, it would not have to be the case that one and the same thing would have incompatible attributes, since one of the two could be in error in ascribing some property to the being which is God in one or the other meaning of that term; if the discussants are aware of this and are investigating such errors, they very probably *are* talking about the same being. If the discussants are not so much in disagreement as they are baffled by what appears to be the nonsense of what the other says (as is often the case between easterner and westerner) they may still be talking of the same being.

In a situation where A and B are in dispute over what is involved in the concept 'God', A and B might be constantly shifting from *primarily designative* uses of the proper name to primarily significative uses, although both, when using the term designatively, would be making primary references. Hence, at any given stage of the dialogue, both are talking about the same being; but overall, each will have employed the term "God" primarily significatively in the discussion of attributes of the being referred to. If a non-theist were to join the dispute, all his uses of "God" would involve *derived reference*, but he too would employ the term primarily significatively as he disputes each theist's claims about the attributes to be ascribed to the entity under discussion.

This way of describing the matter is probably not the only way both to preserve the sensibleness of such disputes and to account for the fact that B can deny what A says even though when B makes a proposal about God's powers, B is using "God" with the same reference but with a signification different from A's. But it does supply *an* account of how it can be that individuals with quite different descriptive associations (significations) attached to the term "God" can still discuss the attributes of a being which is the same as that referred to by someone who attaches a quite different connotation to the term "God."

We conclude this discussion as follows: Our selecting orthodox Christianity as the general guide by which we settle upon the signification of "God" does not deprive us of the neutrality essential to a scientific investigation; nor does it preclude fruitful discussion with thinkers employing a quite different method to select the descriptive association of "God" even though the conceptual difference between the two may be enormous. Rather, a substantial respect for the tradition of Judaic-Christian orthodoxy is absolutely required if our constructive theology is to have any relevance to our time and to our western culture.

B: Order among the divine attributes

Many of the basic problems of philosophical theology are complicated by the fact that our knowledge of God is restricted to knowledge by means of what, for want of a more precise term, I call "higher-level properties." This is especially true of the two subjects we consider here: the real simplicity of God and the logical ordering among the divine attributes. The concept of a higher-level property is not rigorous enough to allow us to provide more than an approximation of some important truths; but since it is the best notion at hand, we must gain as much from its use as we can.

Let us say that a property, P, is a higher-level property if nothing can have that property which does not also have some other property that is not a determinate of P; that is, if P is a higher-level property, then "Pa" ("a has P") cannot be true unless "Fa" (a has F") is also true, where F is some property not identical with P and not a determinate form of P (as 'being red' is of 'being colored'). Among the higher-level properties there is a hierarchy, since the logical preconditions of some properties are other properties or disjunctions of properties which in turn logically presuppose still other properties or disjunctions of properties (which are not related as determinate to determinable).

It may be the case that the relationship of logical subordination to which I am calling attention may more properly be said to obtain between *classes* or sets of properties and other properties or sets of properties, and is only derivatively to be said to hold between members of sets of properties. However, we shall leave this matter unresolved here, since in dealing with God we must concentrate especially upon particular properties (such as omnipotence, goodness, intelligence, freedom) and their ordering.

Logical considerations will require us to hold that some divine attributes are logically prior to others. Yet the long, profound, and authoritative theological tradition of orthodox Christianity has taught that there is no *real* plurality of properties in God. Thus, it has been said, man's knowledge of God is derived from creatures and from manifestations of God transmitted by means of the language and symbolism available to human beings; therefore we possess it in a multiplicity of concepts and propositions which involve something of the multiplicity and compositeness of our experience. So, although man can know *that* God is simple, he cannot (in earthly life) know God *as* simple. So speak Maimonides, Aquinas, Scotus, and others.

Now the problem we face here can be stated succinctly. If the proposition "God is F" (e.g., "God is wise") is true and if the proposition "God is H" (e.g., "God is alive") is true and if $(\exists x)(Hx)$ does not entail $(\exists x)(Fx)$, then F and H cannot be the same property. Since just such conditions are fulfilled in the case of God, it seems that there are some really distinct properties in God. If there are any properties in God which are "of higher level" than others, they must be distinct; logically equivalent properties will, according to our definition, be of the same level, as will also be the determinate and determinable. But the conclusion that there is a logical plurality of attributes in God apparently conflicts with the orthodox Christian tradition which has held that the properties of God are not really distinct and are not really plural. How shall we reconcile the ineluctable consequences of logic with the authority of tradition?

The matter is complicated by the fact that a great number of expressions of the form "God is or has F" (e.g., "God is alive," "God is a spirit," "God is wise," "God has knowledge of all things") are *analytic* (when we take "God" primarily *significatively*, as we shall explain in Section 3). If we allow that any analytic statement is necessarily true, we run into the paradox encountered by C. I. Lewis: that the expressions in question (all analytic statements) are all logically equivalent; it is not possible that one be true when another is not. Yet the *predicates* are not equivalent in the sense that they are substitutible, in all contexts, without change of truth-value. This is the sense in which the various predicates ascribed to God are not equivalent (even within the class of analytic statements about God). When we speak of one property as being logically prior to another, we are prescinding from the analyticity of the statements about God and considering only the relation between the propositional functions (made up of the predicate and an individual variable) with respect to all possible substitutions for the variable. Although it seems paradoxical to talk about logical priority among predicates in statements which are in fact analytic, clarification is achieved, I hope, through our distinguishing the equivalence of particular statements from the equivalence of the propositional functions involved in them.

One way for us to dispose of a problem like this is to find an interpretation of the traditional claim which preserves the intent of that claim and at the same time accords with the things we know. When the great medieval theologians claimed that God is simple, that God does not possess plural, distinct attributes, what did they have in mind? Not, clearly, the relationships between essence and accident, for they had provided a separate discussion on that point when they insisted that there are no accidents in God. Instead, they had in mind the distinction between the various essential attributes in creatures; for all creatures have composite essences, essences at least in principle describable by means of a conjunction of attributes that are such that something may exist, or might have existed, with one or several of such attributes and yet not all. Thus, man's attributes of animality and rationality are logically separable; it is possible that something should exist which shares one but not the other. Because it is logically possible that something should exist which is rational but not an animal, it may be said that rationality and animality are really distinct attributes, even though they may be essential to and definitive of a large class of things. This interpretation accords well with traditional scholastic views which depict all creatures as having composite essences as well as a composition of essence and existence. Now it is just this composition of essence which is denied in God.

The "Real-Identity" Principle: there is no attribute, F, that God has which is related to some other attribute, H, that God has in such a way that it is possible that something should exist which has F but not H. We can be fairly sure of the orthodoxy of this denial of plurality and composition in God. But we cannot take comfort in having made progress. For notice the peculiar logical consequences of this principle. It seems to follow that every divine property is logically equivalent to every other: nothing can have *any* property of God without having every property of God. That consequence does not appear compatible with the following observations:

(a) It is obviously possible that something other than God may be one thing, be a substance, be alive, and be intelligent; all these are attributes of God, and all can be possessed by other things that do not share all the divine attributes.

(b) Is it logically impossible for something to be omniscient and yet not to be omnipotent? The Real-Identity Principle requires that it should be. Yet it may seem that it is not: for some being might know everything—and know how to do everything it is able to do and how anything else should go about doing whatever *it* is able to do—and yet, despite this, not possess the ability, the active power, to produce any distinct change in the state of affairs at all. Under these circumstances, there seems to be no limit imposed upon the being's knowledge, since it extends to everything. There is no decisive reason why such a knower must also be omnipotent; in fact it cannot be if among the things it knows is either the fact that some other being prevents it from acting and that there is no means of overcoming the obstacle, or else merely that it has no transitive or active power at all.

These considerations reveal a dilemma. On the one hand, we are not inclined to say that *all* the divine attributes (*not* the statements that God has these attributes) are logically equivalent to one another because strong empirically based arguments suggest the falsity of this hypothesis. On the other hand, we are not inclined to accept the alternative view that it would be logically possible for some being to exist which possesses some but not all of the divine attributes; for denying this is closely connected with upholding the doctrine of the simplicity of God.

The first step in an escape is to invoke the ancient distinction between an attribute and the *mode* of that attribute. We can, perhaps, maintain that while the divine attributes are not logically equivalent to one another, still, it is not possible for any being to possess one of the divine attributes in the mode in which God possesses it, and not to possess all the others. However, in explicating this suggestion we must not be subverted into making the mode of divine existence into a super-attribute which is logically equivalent to a conjunction of all the others; then the claim would become merely trivial. Neither may we make the mode into an additional attribute, a quiddity, or a "whatness"; for then, taking as analytic "Nothing can possess one of the divine attributes and this additional quiddity or whatness while not possessing the other divine attributes," we will find that this quiddity can have no definition apart from a conjunction of the divine attributes. That would not advance our explanation. We must, if possible, make sense of the quite natural assumption that a being could not be wise *as God is* and not be omnipotent, and that a being could not be omniscient *as God is* and not be perfect.

Of course, one might sneer at these claims as if they were the merest trivialities, because nothing can be anything *as God is* and not be *all* that God is. Still, we must take this, perhaps as analytic, but in any case as basic and important. For a being *can* be alive as I am and yet not have all my attributes.

It appears, then, that the only way to solve the conflict between our tendency to regard the divine attributes as non-equivalent and as logically ordered and our tendency to say that God is the only possible possessor of any attribute He has, is to introduce (as Duns Scotus did) the mode of being which God has, as a non-conceptual determinant of all the divine attributes. To do this successfully, I think we must treat the divine mode (usually called "infinity" or "*a-seity*") not as an additional quiddity, as Duns Scotus did, but as an existential mode, somewhat in the manner of Francis Suarez. Of course, as Duns Scotus would point out, to *say* anything at all about the divine mode we must treat it quidditatively, *treat* it as a conceptual object; but even if this be so, we need not (and, if we are to reconcile the apparently conflicting claims discussed here, we must not) consider it to be an entity or attribute additional to the attributes by which we describe a divine being. It is, rather, quite independent and adequate to name a divine being: namely, "a being which exists in the mode of infinity or without limitation."

In one of the later chapters we will show that to exist in that mode, a being must be such that our statements of the form "God is omnipotent" are true, rather than their contraries.

If we so treat the mode of being that is intrinsic to God, we can reconcile the fact that God's attributes, known to us by means of our extrapolations from our knowledge of creatures, are not all logically equivalent but are related in levels of logical precedence, with the traditional teaching that God does not really have a multiplicity of properties or any real distinction among His attributes at all. For we can rightly say that the divine mode of being is not really a conceptual object, but is only something approximated when we say that God is infinitely wise, infinitely good, infinitely intelligent, etc. This mode of being is approximated negatively when we dismiss from consideration the vague connotations of limit, dependence, and contingency which surround all the objects of our experience. But since we cannot have a general concept of the mode of *finiteness* that characterizes the things of ordinary experience (although we can quite easily indicate features of their behavior and existence which entail that they exist finitely), we cannot have a corresponding negative concept of the divine mode.

For the sake of clarity let it be explicitly stated that the term "concept," as it occurs in my denial that we are able to form a concept of the divine mode of being, refers to those intellectual apprehensions which admit of analysis, of decomposition into other apprehensions. But as is evident, some of our apprehensions must be primitive for a given person at a given time (although there is no reason why a person must possess the same primitive and unanalyzable apprehensions at all times; indeed, this is obviously not the case). Now the most primitive apprehensions we have—for example, 'really existing' or 'changing' (which may well be quite unanalyzable within the conceptual schemes of most people)—and the negative apprehensions by which we know their opposites are not, in the sense stated above, concepts, although they are part of and even intrinsic to our conceptualization of the universe. Further, the fact that we may be totally unable to explain through analysis what the idea 'non-existent' involves does not prove that the idea is not fundamental to our intellectualization of the world.

Since the mode of being that belongs to God will be part of the connotation of every term properly applicable to God, it will follow that every attribute of God (e.g., "wise") will be partially equivocal with respect to the consistent uses of the same term in affirmative statements about finite beings (beings of other modes of existence). To account for the fact that one can understand such terms and apply them without being driven to nonsense, we need a modern and general theory of analogy.[11] That such a theory can be constructed, I have not the least doubt; but it will require a separate volume of its own and must be treated as merely hypothetical here. An analogy theory is necessary if we are to give an account of the discourse I am here supposing to be the traditional and cognitively meaningful practice of theologians.

Suppose it be granted that in God there is something corresponding to the negation of our mode of limited, finite existence and that all God's properties are possessed in this mode, just as all of ours are

---

[11] Such as the Thomist theory that I sketched in "Analogy as a Rule of Meaning for Religious Language," *International Philosophical Quarterly*, September, 1961, pp. 468–502.

possessed in our finite mode. Does it follow that there is not a real difference between the various divine attributes, and does it follow from this that no finite being can be, for example, omniscient? In a word, how does this speculation about God's mode of being solve any of the problems it was intended to solve?

There is an analytical difference between certain divine attributes: it is not at all the same thing to say that a being is omnipotent and that it is wise. Hence, the divine attributes are logically distinct and may be logically ordered. There is no way to avoid this fact. However, the *entitative conditions* for God's possessing F (a given attribute, say, 'omnipotence') are identical with the conditions for His possessing G (some other, logically distinct attribute, say, 'wisdom'), since none of God's essential attributes is or could be contingent upon anything other than the being or existing of God;[12] moreover, it is not logically possible that the existence of something which shares the essential divine attributes should depend upon any causal conditions other than the existence of God.

This is not so in my case. I am actually animal, but my being actually an animal instead of a spirit that is potentially animal (as separated souls are said to be) is dependent entitatively or existentially upon many distinct causal conditions. It is no doubt possible for God to create a rational animal not actually dependent upon finite external causal conditions, but this would not run counter to the fact that for any rational animal it is logically *possible* that its actual animality should be conditioned, and furthermore, that it should be conditioned by factors which are entitatively distinct from those external factors upon which its rationality depends or might depend. Hence, among the attributes of finite composite beings, it is possible for there to be a divergence of the causal conditions upon which the realization of those attributes in an existing being depends; but in God, there cannot be this divergence or even such a presence of causes in God. Therefore, the logically distinct attributes of creatures may be said to

[12] This odd expression "none of God's essential attributes is or could be contingent" is just a brief way of saying that for any given attribute, F, which is essential to God, it is logically impossible that whether or not there is at least one thing that has F is a *contingent* matter causally determinable by something other than the fact that God exists. Some of the divine attributes do not follow logically from the divine nature but freely from divine choice. But even in this case it is not possible that there should have been an entitatively distinct cause of God's having these characteristics.

be distinct in a way in which the divine attributes cannot be—namely, as at least possibly having a diversity of causal conditions.

This difference between God and creatures indicates another and more fundamental difference.

As Thomas Aquinas said:

> Now existence is not included perfectly in the essential nature of any creature, for the act of existence of every creature is something other than its quiddity.[13]

He felt that it is in precisely this that God differs from any creature. Yet even if one granted that there is a quiddity which is *not* a conceptual object for us but which involves existence, how would this be helpful? Aquinas understood the present problem and treated it at length in question 7, article 6 of *De Potentia*. The answer I propose here is quite similar to that which he offers in articles 6 and 7, where he considers whether the terms applicable to God are really synonymous with one another, and whether they are used analogously.

Why is it impossible for a creature to be omniscient? In one sense it is not impossible. There is no contradiction in supposing that a creature should know every truth of fact. But, of course, this will be knowledge in the manner of a created intellect—knowledge possessed in an infinite number of discrete items. It will not be knowledge by means of direct *self*-awareness; no creature could know all things by this means, since no creature could contain within its own nature and decisions logically sufficient conditions for all that is the case and for whatever may be the explanations thereof. Hence the creature's all-encompassing knowledge of truth-values will be qualitatively different from God's knowledge, although the quantitative co-existensiveness of these two sorts of knowledge will make them markedly similar.

Once we suppose that the predicates we attribute to God are derived in meaning (by analogy) from those predicates we attribute to creatures and have, as an essential requisite for their satisfying the conditions of analogy, been logically separated from the *modus essendi* of creatures (the finitude of being in all creatures), then we cannot suppose that anything not possessing the *mode* of in-

---

[13] *De Veritate*, q. 10, a. 12, corpus; translated by James V. McGlynn, S.J., and published under the title *Truth* (Chicago: Henry Regnery, 1953).

finity could possess the property signified by the *term* "infinity," as it is applied in consistent statements about God. Put roughly, the point can be made clear: it is absurd to suppose that a creature (a finite being) could possess knowledge of all things in the manner of an infinite being; but "possession in the manner of an infinite being" is just what we attribute to God when we attribute omniscience, omnipotence, wisdom, goodness, or eternity to Him in a consistent statement. Built into the meaning of all the predicates we apply to God is a provision that the mode of being of that to which the predicate is applied must be 'infinity', 'to-be, without the *possibility* of external conditions'. Hence, if we attribute omniscience to a creature (e.g., "John is omniscient"), the signification of the term "omniscient" will be the same as in the statement "God is omniscient"; but still the predicate "omniscient" must be used by analogy in the two cases; otherwise an explicit contradiction will be derivable through the fact that the predicate would require infinity as the mode of existence while the subject would require a finite mode. Since the predicate will be used by analogy, we can say that although with respect to the quiddity we are attributing to the creature and to God, the predicates are the same, they are still not synonymous with one another. Thus in the true statement "God is omniscient" and then in the false statement "Socrates was omniscient," the two uses of "omniscient" are not synonymous even though their significations are the same, for the mode of being of a predicate is determined by that of its subject. We would have an evident impossibility with regard to Socrates if we said, "Socrates is omniscient *as* God is, or in the manner of an infinite being."

The true, negative statement "Socrates was not omniscient," where "omniscient" occurs in the sense applicable to God—that is, "omniscient in the manner of an infinite being"—will, of course, be necessarily true. Hence, it is not true to say *no* term properly applicable to God is, in the very same sense, applicable to a finite being in a true statement. Rather, no term properly applicable to God is, in the very same sense, applicable to any finite being in a true *logically contingent* statement. From these considerations, it follows that no creature can have any of the divine attributes; and this claim, if one thinks about it, is obviously analytic because a divine attribute is, by definition, an attribute possessed by something with the mode of infinite being.

Thus, to the question of whether a non-divine being can be omniscient or omnipotent, or have any of the attributes that God has, we can answer as follows: There are some attributes of God (e.g., simplicity in being) which absolutely cannot belong to a creature because neither they nor their conceptual elements admit of degrees. These can be known only negatively. To other attributes of God there correspond attributes in creatures, and these are designated by *analogous* terms—'a living existent', 'a substance', 'a being', 'an intelligence', 'a knower', 'a powerful being', 'a good being', 'a wise being', 'a beautiful being', etc., but no creature can possess any of these attributes in the mode of being in which God possesses them. Finally, there are still other attributes of God, such as 'being all-powerful', 'being omniscient', 'being unlimited', 'being absolutely independent', which are logically distinct from any attribute a creature could possess, even though there are some attributes (such as 'power', 'knowledge' and 'perfection') which a creature can possess in a limited way and which function analogously as parts of the definition of the incommunicable divine attributes. For instance, Chapter V will arrive at a definition of omnipotence which involves 'effective choice', an attribute which can be possessed contingently by some creatures; its concept, used analogously to conform to the being of God, becomes an integral part of the definition of omnipotence. And yet the resulting concept of omnipotence is one which cannot apply in a contingent true statement to any creature, or for that matter in an affirmative true predication of any creature. The intricacies of this subject fairly demand that we possess an analogy theory to justify or even explicate our claims. Hence, let us regard these conclusions as largely programmatic but apparently plausible hypotheses.

Now turning to the question of distinguishing among the divine attributes, we say that although the various predicates we attribute to God differ in signification, they are all the same in their mode of being, just as the various predicates we apply to creatures differ in signification but have a common supposition of "creatureliness." The predicates we apply correctly to God indicate perfections in being; although one perfection differs conceptually from another, a being that exists in the mode of infinity—i.e., is all-perfect—will possess them all. The predicate 'all-perfect', therefore, involves all the other divine attributes, and is not really a distinct "whatness."

Our understanding of the being of God is by way of a set of concepts we have formed, from our acquaintance with finite things, of the various possible perfections in being; we must attribute these perfections analogously to God in discrete predications (since the concepts are not synonymous with each other), even though we know that God's life and His intelligence, for instance, are not and could not be conferred through diverse principles and hence do not exist in the same sort of separation that is possible and sometimes actual in other beings. Therefore, while our statements "God is omnipotent" and "God is omniscient" are both true and are not synonymous (though they are logically equivalent), nothing in God corresponds to those actual or possible diversities of conditions which make the properties of creatures really distinct; rather, there is a mode of being which absolutely precludes all such distinctness of entitative preconditions. It is just this absence of the possibility of distinct principles to account for the fact that the being has F and the fact that it has H that makes the properties F and H really the same, even though the concepts are not synonymous.

To generalize: for two properties, A and B, in an existing being, x, to be really distinct, it is necessary (1) that the concepts 'A' and 'B' not be logically synonymous, and (2) that it be *possible* that what accounts for the fact that there is something, x, which has A should be different from that which accounts for the fact that there is something, x, which has B.

The second condition is not fulfilled in the case of God. Hence, despite the logical priority among the divine attributes and the multiplicity of logically distinct attributes, the attributes of God are not really distinct.

Having arrived at a concept of 'real distinction' consonant with the traditional claims about God that we have proposed to "save," we may also settle, as follows, the more general question of the ordering of properties into deductively arranged levels: as yet, we possess no satisfactory ordering of the divine attributes, nor any predominantly quidditative concept which is the lowest or first-level property of God.

The statement "God is an omnipotent, omniscient, eternal, benevolent, living, intelligent, free being" is not, in terms of what is sufficient and what is necessary, a complete delineation of the concept 'a divine being'. Nor will it be complete if we add everything else we know about God. For we must also say that God exists *perfectly* or *without limitation:* and this is to pass from the quidditative to the modal. As a result, a reasonably satisfactory ordering of the divine attributes can be achieved only after we have completed an analysis of individual attributes and have investigated the metaphysics of modes of being; and, even then, despite its theoretical utility, the ordering will remain largely subjective.

One practical application of these considerations is that God's possession of some of His characteristics is logically (not causally) contingent. Some distinguished philosophers, Charles Hartshorne in particular, have thought the classical theological tradition did not allow for this. But that is quite mistaken. The classical Christian tradition denied that God has any *accidental* attributes (attributes for which the activity of some distinct agent is sufficient) but definitely held that God has some attributes contingently. Hartshorne and others have reasoned that the traditional notion of divine simplicity and the doctrine that God's properties are not really distinct are incompatible with the admission that God's possession of some of His attributes is logically contingent. As a matter of fact, there is no logical conflict, as our explanation of the notion 'really distinct attributes' has shown; for the issue is not over whether or not the attributes are possessed contingently, but whether or not the attributes could have entitatively distinct conditions. Still, those attributes which God has contingently will not fit into a continuous logical ordering with the necessary properties. Hence the order within our conception of God will be discontinuous regardless of the care we devote to analysis; no a priori proof will settle the question of whether there is a being which has those contingent attributes (e.g., is creator of the world). Nevertheless, there is no inconsistency in the orthodox Christian conception of God as an entitatively simple being possessing a logical plurality of properties.

SECTION 3: PROPER NAMES AND MODALITIES

There are some arguments whose validity rests upon our taking a simple statement that involves a proper name as subject to be necessarily true (for instance, "God is omnipotent"). And who would deny that "God is a divine being" looks like a necessary truth? Nevertheless, it is rightly to be wondered whether logical modalities are applicable to such statements and on what grounds.

(1) We shall confine our attention to simple statements of subject-predicate form which employ proper names in order to indicate the subject to which the predicate is attributed. What of the strict inapplicability (at least directly) of the term "analytic" to such statements if the proper name is employed *purely designatively:* to stand for something, but without connotation or signification?

Consider the statement "God is a divine being." Let us suppose for the moment that nothing can be a divine being which is not a spirit, intelligent, eternal, perfect, etc. Now how could we determine whether or not this statement is analytic? We cannot examine the conceptual relationship between subject and predicate, despite the connotation just mentioned, because under the stipulations of the preceding paragraph there is *no concept attached* to the subject term in this use; the subject term is used designatively but *precisively* (that is, without the inclusion of connotation or signification) and is no more than an indexical constant. Hence, the characteristic "analytic" cannot be applied to the statement because the requisite conceptual relation is absent. Such a purely designative use of a proper name is deviant and artificial in comparison to ordinary language usage.

Shall we say the statement is synthetic? If we applied the rule (as we shall eventually) that those statements whose subject and predicate do not fulfill the conceptual conditions which establish analyticity are to be called "synthetic," then we would designate the statement in question "synthetic." But it could be argued that the characteristic "synthetic" is equally inapplicable. For our characterizing statements in that way presupposes that there *is* at least a pair of concepts whose relationships (or conceptual discontinuity) are the basis of the character assigned to the statement as a whole. Hence, one might reasonably conclude that simple statements of the subject-predicate form, when they employ proper names as subjects and when the name is used *purely designatively* as an indexical constant (without associated signification), must not be characterized either as analytic or as synthetic.

Since, however, competent philosophers often apply the term "analytic," as well as "synthetic," to statements of the subject-predicate form where proper names indicate the subject; and since, when we take the context of the discussions into account, such applications do not appear to be unreasonable, we conclude that in these cases the proper names do *not* occur purely designatively.[14] The proper name, even though used *primarily* (as distinct from "purely") designatively, must also be accompanied by some conceptual association, some signification of attributes; and these, together with the predicate, form the basis of the judgment of analyticity or syntheticity. This accords with the general remarks we made about proper names in Section 1, above. Most often, uses of proper names are primarily designative but do not exclude signification; occasionally, as below, uses of proper names are primarily significative but do not exclude designation.

(2) Consequently, with respect to simple statements of the subject-predicate form in which a proper name, used purely designatively, indicates the subject, neither the modalities "necessary," "possible" nor the modalities "contingent," "impossible" are strictly and directly applicable; for in such strict and direct applications the sole determinants of the modality are the conceptual relations which are expressly excluded by the purely designative use of the proper name.

But we can accommodate these relatively rare uses of a proper name by substituting a wider rule that wherever there is no conceptual relation between subject term and predicate term which requires the modality "necessary" or "impossible," both "possible" and "contingent" apply (syntactical structures permitting). Hence, every simple statement with a proper name used purely designatively (as a non-significative constant) as the subject term will have the modalities "possible" and "contingent." No great confusion need arise from this practice, provided it is not mixed up with other very common practices of ordinary language which we shall indicate below. It will have apparently, but only apparently, untoward consequences, in that "Hamlet was a prince of Denmark" and "God is an impotent being" will turn out to be possible and contingent propositions where the terms "Hamlet" and "God" are used purely designatively; but when one remembers that the names are non-significative in these uses, the apparent absurdity is dispelled.

---

[14] That is, in such a way that we could replace them with any chosen constant without loss of meaning or change in the characteristic of analyticity or syntheticity to be applied.

(3) On many occasions philosophers say that a state of affairs is necessary or impossible even though it is expressed by a simple statement of the subject-predicate form where a proper name indicates the subject term. And a significant number of these philosophers (I am not among them) hold the view that proper names do not have an attached signification, a connotative dimension of meaning. On what grounds, then, can these philosophers assign modalities to statements of the form we are considering? They do so in terms of the attributes of the *referent* of the proper name (this is possible regardless of whether the name is used in primary, purported, or secondary reference).[15] Thus a philosopher may say that "God is a divine being" is a necessary truth because he has assumed that 'being a divine being' is an essential characteristic of *what is referred to* in the statement in which the name "God" is taken purely designatively. I find the following difficulty here: it is a *contingent* fact that the term "God" names a being which has this attribute essentially (or at all), and the iterative modality of the statement "it is necessary that God is a divine being" is "contingently" in such a case. There results the paradoxical conclusion: It is a contingent fact that it is necessarily the case that God is a divine being. Now it might be contended that the paradox lies only in the fact that the quotation marks indicating the levels of discourse have been omitted. I do not think this is the only source. For consider the conclusion put in the following way: *It is not necessarily the case that "Necessarily 'God is a divine being'."* This is similar to ~□(□p). Now it is assumed throughout this book that given □p the *only* appropriate iterative modality is either □(□p) or ◇(□p), another well-respected although somewhat embattled principle of traditional modal logic. The consequence of the "purely designative approach" to proper names, when combined with the perfectly reasonable practice of assigning logical modalities to certain statements in which such names occur, is that we come upon a state of affairs which conflicts with a respectable principle of logic, a principle which functions in an important way in certain arguments to be presented later on; for this reason we consider such a "purely designative" approach to be unsatisfactory in the context we are considering, just as we rejected it for other reasons in Section 1. Consequently, we can say that it is *not* generally adequate to say that modal-

---

[15] See Section 1 of this chapter.

ities are assigned to such statements as "God is a divine being" on the basis of the attributes which are *essential to the referent* of the proper name "God" but which are not part of the signification of that name. Nevertheless, some special cases arise where this is legitimate.[16]

(4) There is another difficulty with the hypothesis that proper names are used purely designatively (non-significatively) and that modalities are assigned on the basis of the attributes essential to the referent. The difficulty is that the modalities do not always transfer from statements where the proper name occurs purely designatively and in primary reference[17] to statements which are entailed by them. Thus, let us suppose that 'x is orange' is thought to employ the term x purely designatively but is said to be necessary because it is an *essential property* of what is referred to that it be orange in color. If x occurs in primary reference, then 'x is orange' entails 'there is something orange'. If the modalities were always transferred to what is entailed (as a sensible logic of modalities would seem to require in order to maintain consistency) then 'there is something orange' would be necessarily true. But it is not.

(5) We want to make sense of our saying that 'God is a divine being' is necessary and that 'Socrates married Xanthippe' is contingent, while at the same time holding that "God" and "Socrates" are proper names and can be used in primary reference without our being led to absurd consequences with respect to the modality of derived existence-statements, or into conflict with the appropriate principles of logic concerning the transfer of modality through entailment and the iterative modalities (modalities governing modalities) which accrue to modal statements. The mere fact that a given property, F, belongs essentially to something named purely designatively by k does not make 'k is F' necessarily true.

Proper names can be used purely designatively; but, more often, their use is *primarily* designative and incidentally significative. Sometimes they are used primarily significatively and incidentally designatively, but this use appears to be relatively rare in ordinary discourse. Entirely artificial are the purely designative and the purely significative uses of proper names, although the very structure of philosophical

---

[16] See subsection 6(b), below.

[17] See the sufficient conditions given in Section 1.

analysis applied to religion requires us to employ artificial uses of the name "God" frequently. Nevertheless, one could hardly consider such uses of a term in a purely theoretical enterprise to be ordinary language. When we are speaking of statements of the simple subject-predicate form in which a so-called proper name is the subject term and is used non-significatively, we employ the practical rule given in subsection 2, above, that where no conceptual relation exists between subject term and predicate term, requiring either the modality "necessary" or the modality "impossible," both "possible" and "contingent" apply. Hence all such cases of *purely designative* uses of proper names give us *contingent* and *possible* propositions (provided only that the predicate be self-consistent), despite the apparent oddities which result, for example, "God eats onions."

Proper names such as "God" and "Socrates," when they occur with no other restrictions, in statements of the sort we are considering, will not be considered to be used purely designatively; we will assume that they have attached signification and, in the absence of contextual clues, that their occurrence is primarily designative and incidentally significative. And in the absence of any contextual restriction upon the signification, they will not be assumed to signify *only* the essential attributes of the being referred to but rather anything connoted by the term in its appropriate uses. Thus "Socrates" will signify 'philosopher' as well as 'human being', although the mere fact that we mention contextual restrictions upon the signification of such names shows that there is considerable variation in the kinds of attributes that the signification of the same name involves in varying contexts. Thus, in some contexts, 'Socrates lived in Greece' will entail 'a philosopher lived in Greece', and in other contexts will not. What proposition is stated depends upon what the terms mean for the person who makes the statement. (This is generally but not universally the case, as is evident in legalistic contexts where individuals are simply not permitted to ignore the entrenched significations of terms.)

Naturally, for every attribute, F, which is included in the signification of the proper name K, there is a statement of the form FK ("K is or has F") which, when K is used with its signification, is analytic and necessary.[18] Thus, while it may be a contingent fact that the term "K"

---

[18] We shall dispose below of the matter of analytic statements whose predicates are not essential to the subject.

signifies F, the statement "K is or has F" will be necessary, and *its* iterative modality will be "necessary" again. For if it were false that "K" signifies F, we could not make the same statement as we could above by means of the expression "K is or has F." Thus we return to the position that the modal operators of propositions are assigned on the basis of the conceptual relations between subject and predicate terms—providing, however, for the case of purely designative names with the *ad hoc* rule that the absence of such relationships always yields the modalities of possibility (if the predicate be self-consistent), and rejecting the proposal that we should appeal to the attributes of the referent unless special reference to what is *essential* is invoked.

Now we must consider the matter of transferring modalities across entailments in the context of the existential presuppositions of proper names.

Wherever the modality is not determined by the syntactical form alone, logical modalities are assigned to statements on the basis of the conceptual relations between the signification of the subject term and that of the predicate term. We do not *as such* take into account the attributes of what is referred to, but consider only the attributes signified by the subject term. An attribute 'F' is signified by a subject term "t" if and only if 'F' is one of the attributes a thing must be expected to have if it is to be *properly* denoted by "t." Thus the attribute 'being a rational animal' is signified by the term "man" so that nothing is properly denoted by the term "man" which is not expected to be a rational animal. That is, if the term "man" is applied in a statement of the form "the man has leaves," where the object referred to by the subject term is not expected to be a rational animal, then the term "man" has been misused (of course, we must allow that certain "technical" misuses are part of the practice of poets and artists and sometimes give special power to their language). Hence, "false" and "true" are not applicable to such a statement as "the man has leaves" (in non-poetic contexts), in which the signification of the subject term is expected not to be fulfilled upon the part of the thing denoted. Rather, we have a case of a pointless or nonsense utterance. Thus we do not *as such* take into account the attributes of the thing denoted by the subject term; but since the thing denoted must not be *expected* not to have the attributes signified if the utterance involving the name makes sense or has point, we are, in fact, considering attributes which belong to the thing denoted. Yet we do not consider them as belonging to what is denoted, but only as *signified* by a term which may be used to denote a given thing.

All substantival expressions, when occurring as subjects of simple subject-predicate statements, designate a thing, an event, a state of affairs, or the like. Most such expressions have signification and thus impose conditions upon the thing designated. If the speaker expects these conditions not to be fulfilled by the thing designated, they make his statement pointless or untruthful (e.g., mendacious). Thus, "These chairs are purple" is pointless when I refer to booths which I expect not to be chairs. Either substantival expressions designate something indifferently (in the sense that, without change of signification or a change in the name we employ, we could designate something else), or they designate something uniquely (in such a way that without changing the signification or the name we employ we cannot designate anything else). Proper names designate uniquely.

The logical modality of a statement is, as we have said, entirely derived from the conceptual relations of the significations of subject and predicate terms (mediated, of course, by the syntax). Now what about the existential implications of such statements as "God is a divine being"? As we made clear in Section 1, what existential commitments one incurs in saying "God is a divine being" are dependent upon the kind of reference in which the term "God" is employed; and no term used purely significatively can be used to refer. There is nothing about the occurrence of a proper name as subject of an isolated simple sentence which indicates what mode of reference has been employed; sometimes context supplies an indication; sometimes our knowledge of the speaker gives us a reliable opinion, and sometimes we have to guess. But if the term does occur in primary reference, for S to say "God is a divine being" commits S to a limited series of moves in defense of his claim, one of the most important of which is that he must (if only to himself) reject outright our criticism, "But God does not exist." This is roughly the sense in which S's statement entails 'God exists' because of his use of the term "God" in primary reference.

If the term "God" is used in purported or in secondary reference, one is not required to reject denials of the existential statement. There is no existential commitment for the user, and there is no entailment of an unconditional existential which has *that* proper name as subject. Hence we cannot say that the existential import of our using a proper name as subject is unconditional or that all designative uses of proper names entail existentials. Rather, it also depends upon what kind of reference the name occurs in, and this is not so much a characteristic of the name as it is of the utterance as a linguistic act.

But even prior to the conditioning of the statement's existential import by the *kind* of reference the name is used in, there is the conditioning according to whether the name is used designatively or not. If the name is used purely significatively, it cannot be used to refer, because it is ex *hypothesi* not used to designate anything.

The *primarily* significative uses are, ex *hypothesi*, also secondarily designative, e.g., "God is a divine being." Such statements are to be analyzed as a compound: "Anything properly called 'God' is a divine being; and there is something properly called 'God'." The use is primarily significative when the first conjunct expresses the main intention and the second conjunct is carried along by the context. The claim "there is something . . ." will have its "is" conditioned by the kind of *reference* the speaker is engaging in. Thus, if it is primary reference, as to a real existent, it means "there actually and really exists. . . ." If it is *secondary* reference, it means "there is (intentionally) something which someone thinks really exists," etc. Since the "necessary" operator belongs to the first clause (in a primarily significative use), and whatever existential import there may be because of a proper name derives from the second clause, the "necessary" operator cannot be attached to anything entailed by the second clause without a specific logical derivation of the second clause from the first (such as St. Anselm would propose to provide us).

We must grant that the primarily designative occurrence of a proper name in primary reference, in a simple subject-predicate statement, does entail a corresponding existential statement whose subject is indicated by the *same proper name*, and that it does allow existential generalization to a statement of the form $(\exists x)(\varphi x)$. Entailment *does* hold between such statements. But the transfer of the modalities between "God is a divine being" and "God exists" is still conditioned as follows: a modal operator which accrues to the first statement in virtue of our taking the proper name *significatively* cannot legitimately be transferred to an existential (the second conjunct), in which we must take the proper name to be used primarily or purely designatively.

Tokens of the same verbal type (e.g., "John") may be used purely or primarily significatively in one case, and purely or primarily designatively in another. Tokens whose occurrences differ in these two ways must be considered logically distinct terms, such that a "necessary operator" governing a statement involving the first cannot *simply* be transferred to a statement involving the second. The fact that explicit contradictions can be derived from violation of this restriction constitutes what I consider a decisive argument that these two uses of a term are logically equivalent to the use of two distinct terms. (It follows, of course, that within a valid argument with consistent premises, it is illegitimate to shift from one use to the other without an explicit premise to justify that shift.)

Two men may agree upon both the truth and the *necessity* of 'God is a divine being' (where "God" must occur purely or primarily significatively), while the one does and the other does not admit the truth of 'God exists'. Either they do not agree upon the same proposition, or else—if they agree upon the same proposition and are consistent (and are not missing any logical relations between these statements which are relevant to the present issues)—then 'God is a divine being' does not simply entail 'God exists'. It should be obvious that wherever the first statement is considered analytic, its subject term is not logically synonymous with (and therefore is not substitutable for) the subject term of the second. There is then no reason to expect an entailment. Both statements contain the same name—but this name is *used* differently.

Despite our general conclusion that there is no legitimate transfer of modalities from an analytic statement with a proper name as its subject to the corresponding existential statement with the same name as subject (because the subject term must be used purely or primarily significatively in the former and purely or primarily designatively in the latter), we still cannot simply and unqualifiedly say that there is no entailment between two such propositions; if both the former (e.g., 'God is omnipotent') and the latter ('God exists') are logically necessary truths, they will entail each other, at least by means of auxiliary premises which are logical truths. But this can happen between logically equivalent propositions that contain no synonymous terms; and if that should be the case, there will be a legitimate transfer of modalities, but it will not be based upon the conditions which we have examined and criticized. Rather, the existential import of the proper name will not be what accounts for the entailment of an existential statement; nor will the occurrence of the proper name in an analytic statement be the source of the necessity ascribed to the existential statement. Hence, the fact that "God" is a proper name will be supplementary to, and irrelevant to, the matter of the modalities.

(6) We know it to be a perfectly correct practice linguistically for a man who is mistaken in his belief that someone exists to use a proper name in primary reference to refer to that person, *as long as* he continues in his mistaken belief. Thus Jones may say, "I wonder whatever happened to Bill Smart." Black remarks, "What Bill Smart? Old John Smart never had a son." Ensuing discussion may disclose the fact that Jones was mistaken. If Jones came to see his mistake, he would make a further mistake by adding, "I misused the expression 'Bill Smart', since I used it as a proper name in primary reference when there was no such being." He did not *misuse* the expression; he *made a mistake* when he used it. The mistake was not a linguistic one at all, nor was it logical in character; it was purely a mistake in fact.[19]

Now suppose a pious Greek called Euthyphro should say "Zeus is omnipotent," and further should add that what he stated was a necessary truth. Suppose, moreover, that discussion has revealed that he is using "Zeus" in primary reference—and hence designatively—and that it is part of his religious belief that Zeus is by nature (essentially) omnipotent. We will have to concede that he is quite right in saying that "Zeus is omnipotent" is a necessary statement, even though we claim that Euthyphro is mistaken in supposing that there actually exists any thing which is properly referred to by the term "Zeus," where the term has the whole signification he gives it, i.e., 'father of the gods', 'dweller on Olympus', etc. Since there is no such being, Euthyphro is mistaken in his *reference*, although the statement he has uttered is necessarily true (assuming for the present that the set of attributes signified by "Zeus" is consistent).

We have suggested that the expressions of the form ' "N is F" is

---

[19] I am not, of course, denying that a philosopher-playwright might design a scene in which by the very same form of words a *linguistic* mistake might be made; but such possibilities are irrelevant to the much more common and important cases we are considering.

necessarily true' (where the speaker uses the name *N* primarily significatively but not *purely* significatively, and where he makes a primary reference, believing that there really is such a being as he talks about) are to be analyzed as conjunctions: e.g., 'Necessarily anything that is properly called *N* is, or has, F; and there is something properly called *N*'. The modal operator that accrues to the expression '*N* is F' in virtue of the signification of *N* does *not* extend to the second conjunct. Whenever we want to go further and claim that a "necessary" operator should precede the second conjunct as well, we must admit that such an operator cannot be derived from the first, as has already been explained. While Euthyphro's statement entails that Zeus exists (because of the complex way in which we suppose he uses the name), someone else could agree that 'Zeus is omnipotent' is necessarily true and not be committed to the existence of Zeus.

That '*N* is F' is analyzed as a conjunction is not the same as saying '*N* is F' *means* the conjunction; for a statement need not "mean" everything that is entailed by it. Moreover, the *conjunction* that is equivalent to one person's statement that *N* is F need not be the same as the conjunction equivalent to another person's statement that *N* is F, if they differ in whether they use the name primarily designatively or primarily significatively, or if they differ in mode of reference.

Let us suppose that an early Christian, Origen, says, "God created the world," and adds " 'God created the world' is necessarily true"; and suppose that he does this in a context in which we know he is making a primary reference. His claim is complex and can be interpreted in two widely different ways. Let us consider these separately.[20]

(a) Origen[21] may mean that it is part of the meaning or signification of "God," as the child and catechumen are taught the meaning of the term, that the being referred to is creator of the world as well as omnipotent, eternal, loving, etc. Hence, for people so taught, the state-

---

[20] The first of these ways, in subsection (a) immediately following, employs the distinction between what is included in the signification of a name and what is essential to the referent, and explains ambiguities which are common. The second of these ways, in section (b) beginning on page 78, is concerned with further relationships between what is said to be necessarily true and what is said to be essential to a referent. In the one case we take Origen to say that 'being creator of the world' is essential to God (the referent); in the other, to say that 'being creator of the world' is involved in the signification of the *name* "God," but not that it is essential to the referent. In part (a) the name "God" occurs primarily *significatively;* in (b), primarily *designatively.*

[21] Not the real Origen, of course.

ment "God is creator of the world" is logically necessary (if they know enough logic to see that the predicate is contained within the signification of the subject term). Having been told this, suppose we admit that for Origen "God created the world" is a necessary truth. Suppose also that we admit that there is a being properly referred to by the term "God," who is omnipotent, etc., *and* creator of the world, but that we deny that 'being creator of the world' is an essential or natural attribute of this being, although we grant that the other attributes signified are essential and natural. Suppose further that we are right in what we have denied. Then someone has made a mistake. But what mistake? Origen has made no mistake about the logical character of "God created the world"; that is, his claim " 'God created the world' is necessarily true" is true and has been granted by us. Apparently he has made a mistake of reference: there is (by hypothesis) no being that fulfills the signification of his term "God." But if we say to Origen, "My friend, you are wrong; God does not exist"— using the term "God" in secondary reference, primarily significatively and with the same signification as Origen ascribes to it—then what we say is quite literally true even though our putting it this way will cause Origen to misunderstand the point of our objection. Moreover, it will not be easy to make our point clear, since it is not a disagreement about the signification of the term "God." We granted him his signification, and, furthermore, were right in doing so, since there is plentiful historical support for the claim that that is the signification of the term "God" as it is employed in orthodox religious preaching and instruction. Neither can we say that he has *failed* to refer to any being, since we know full well that he is referring to the same being that, *ex hypothesi*, we have also conceded to exist, although there is no being which fulfills (by means of essential attributes alone) the signification of his term.

The fact is that Origen's mistake is only an apparent one, provided he does not proceed to claim that 'being creator of the world' is a necessary or essential attribute of God, the referent. We shall consider that case and its results in subsection (b) below. Here we suppose that as soon as we say that 'being creator of the world' is not an essential attribute of God, Origen agrees heartily. Where, then, is the mistake? It is on *our* part, in assuming that the proper way to interpret the statement "the signification of a name is the set of attri-

butes which a thing must be expected to have to be properly designated by that term" is as implying that the attributes must be *essential*
to the thing properly designated. All that is required is that the attributes be expected to be possessed. The "must" does not modify the
manner of possession of the attributes but indicates the inexorability
of the requirement that the being *should be expected to have* the
attributes signified in order to be properly designated—that is, designated in conformity with the usage of the term in our language.[22]
Having made this distinction between the necessity of the referent's
being expected to possess the attributes signified and its possessing
the attributes necessarily (essentially or by nature), and having indicated that the former does not entail the latter, we may now consider
some results.

First, we have accepted the statement "God is creator of the world"
as a necessary truth whose necessity is established by the fact that
the predicate is included within the signification of the subject term;
this is empirically confirmed through examination of the usage of
the term. Yet we have also taken as a hypothesis that while it is true
that God is creator of the world (i.e., that there is a being which is
properly and uniquely designated by the term "God" and which has
the attributes signified by the term), still "God is creator of the world"
is a contingent statement. For clarity let us list these statements (whose
context is indicated elsewhere).

1: *God created the world.*

2: *'God created the world' (1) is necessarily true.*

3: *God created the world.*

4: *'God created the world' (3) is contingent but true.*

Now, (1) and (3) are word for word the same expressions; yet we
have assigned to the statements differing modalities. Further, (2) is
equivalent to (5):

5: *The signification of "God" in (1) includes the attribute 'being creator of
the world', which is what is meant by the predicate in (1), and hence we have
an analytic statement.*

---

[22] This does not say that one cannot improperly use language and do so to communicate successfully,
although the success of such usage is parasitic upon proper usage.

Whereas statement 4 entails the following:

6: The being designated by the term "God" actually exists and has the attribute 'being the creator of the world', but does not have it essentially. (That this is what is meant by (4) can be seen from the context in which the claim was first introduced as an hypothesis.)[23]

We can observe that (4) and (5) are not incompatible; does it follow from this that (1) and (3) are not the same statement? While Origen and I would certainly agree in saying that God is creator of the world, we could be using the term "God" in logically distinct ways. Even though it does not in fact follow logically that (1) and (3) are not the same statement, they could be different. For (6) does not imply that 'being creator of the world' is not part of the signification of the term "God"; it merely requires that 'being creator of the world' is not an essential attribute of God (if God exists necessarily)—that it is not necessarily the case that the being referred to has the attribute mentioned. This is quite compatible with its being required that, in order for me properly to use the term "God" to refer to the being in point, that being must be expected to have the attribute mentioned. (This would be like "Socrates was a philosopher.") Still, if Origen employs his term "God" primarily significatively and I employ my term primarily designatively, then we have different statements; for what is entailed by (1) would not be the same as what is entailed by (3), even though the two would be compatible.

From this we can draw a general conclusion: that when we are dealing with an expression of the form "A is or has F," where A is a proper name (used in one of the three forms of reference indicated in Section 1) and F is some attribute, the modal statement "necessarily 'A is or has F' " is an ambiguous one. In the one case, we may merely be claiming that F is included within the signification of the name A; in the other, we may be saying that the thing designated by A has F essentially. The ambiguity between the two cases is not explained by the fact that (1) and (3) are not the same statement; for, although they

---

[23] Saying (6) is entailed by (4) is something of an oversimplification, since it supposes that "God exists" is necessarily true and not merely contingently true. Otherwise (6) would have to read "the being designated by the term 'God' actually exists and has the attribute 'being creator of the world', but it either does not exist necessarily or does not have the attribute essentially." Obviously, something which exists actually but contingently can have an attribute essentially and yet, for example, it could still be the case that 'Socrates is human' is contingent but true.

may differ, they do not need to. Rather, what accounts for this ambiguity is the fact that when we consider what has been said and assign a modality to it, we may consider the subject term "God" primarily designatively (and secondarily significatively). If we do not specify the way in which we have considered the object-language statements (1) and (3), when we produce our modal statements (which are by nature metalanguage statements), we will produce the ambiguous modal statements (2) and (4). For should we take (1) and (3) to be the same statement, either (2) and (4) would be inconsistent or else one or both would be ambiguous. Both are ambiguous anyway. In neither is it indicated whether the proper name "God" is taken primarily designatively or significatively, nor does the context provide the information. Since proper names (except for the very rare purely designative use of a name) are bivalent in that their logical force is at once designative and significative, the assignment of modalities to statements like (1) is not a simple matter of determining whether the signification of the subject term includes the predicate or is included by it (especially in these cases where signification is only incidentally involved). The signification of the subject term often includes some attributes which are not essential to the being uniquely designated. For example, 'being a Greek' is included within the signification of "Socrates." Therefore, to assign the modality "necessary" to "A is F" is to leave open whether one is saying that "A is F" is analytic significatively, or whether we are saying that whatever is properly referred to by "A" has F essentially. An example of the former is "Socrates is a philosopher"; of the latter, "Socrates is human."

It should be noticed that the latter may not be the same as saying, "What is referred to by 'A' necessarily has F"; for in that statement, which is ambiguous, I think we are claiming either that A has F essentially or that A exists necessarily and has F by nature.

(b) Now let us suppose that Origen, when he claims (2) " 'God is creator of the world' is necessarily true," is taking the term "God" primarily (but not purely) designatively, and is saying that God, the referent of his statement, is creator of the world *and* that this attribute is essential to God. He is quite wrong (by our hypothesis) that God is essentially creator of the world. Is his statement (2), thus interpreted, to be classified as false? If it is, does it follow that it is *necessarily* false? The answer to both questions is yes. God does not have the attribute essentially. Moreover, since He does not, it is impossible that He should ever have had the attribute essentially. Socrates does not have the attribute 'being a stone' essentially; nor could he have. But that is due to the fact th   Socrates has essential attributes which are *incompatible* with being a stone, and an essential change by its very nature would require that we do not have the *same* individual, nor even the same sort of individual, after as before.

Yet suppose someone says (7) "Socrates was essentially white." Now, since Socrates was white, he did not have any attribute incompatible with being white. But he was not essentially white; hence (7) is false. But *could* he have been essentially white? Apparently he was essentially indeterminate to whiteness and to non-whiteness. But by what? Was it merely because his essence did not include such a specification? Why is "white-human" not a species of the genus (for the purpose) "human"? Perhaps it is because "white" designates not a *quidditative* but a *qualitative* difference, and hence cannot be a specific difference of a thing or substance but only of a quality. If so, 'Socrates is essentially white' is contradictory because 'white' to signify in its usual way would have to be a quality but to differentiate essentially would have to be a quiddity. This is well begun. It suggests that, as they stand, essences (whatever *they* are!) are quidditatively complete and that false statements of the form "*A* is essentially F" (where there is an *A* which is F) are false because they are impossible. In a way that answers our question. Such states of affairs are impossible because every essence contains notes which are incompatible with every other quiddity, and no quality can serve to differentiate things or substances essentially, simply because qualities cannot be quiddities.[24]

I think it would be a mistake to take 'being essentially a creator' to be a different attribute from 'being a creator'. In saying something is a creator we do not state whether the thing has the attribute by nature or in some other way. In the other case we specify the mode of possession. The mode of possessing an attribute cannot itself be con-

[24] Now all we need to do is explain what the difference is between a quality and a quiddity, without going in a circle by saying that quiddities are essential notes (or their concepts) and qualities are accidental notes. I see no way to do this; and to avoid an extensive and distracting metaphysical speculation, I will take it that whether or not we can perform the task I have just outlined, we are not seriously in difficulty to know the difference between quiddities and qualities with respect to most objects of our experience.

sidered an attribute (unless we want to face an infinite regress), although to possess an attribute F essentially, rather than accidentally, constitutes a difference in the *sort* of being and may even determine some of the attributes. We need not pursue this metaphysical matter here.

Return briefly to the utterance of the pious Euthyphro, "Zeus is omnipotent." Suppose that in his additional claims Euthyphro is found to be taking "Zeus" *primarily designatively*, so that his claim " 'Zeus is omnipotent' is necessary" is equivalent to "It is an essential attribute of Zeus that he be omnipotent." He is not now claiming that 'omnipotence' is part of the signification of "Zeus," although we may as well assume that he has made a separate claim to that effect by using the term "Zeus" *primarily significatively* in another utterance, " 'Zeus is omnipotent' is necessary." Naturally one *could* make both claims by means of a single utterance employing the words " 'Zeus is omnipotent' is necessary," but logically the two claims are distinct; for neither the utterance in which the term "Zeus" occurs *primarily designatively* nor the utterance in which "Zeus" occurs *primarily significatively* entails the other (as was demonstrated above when we showed that they could have different truth-values).

Assuming that Euthyphro has made both claims, and assuming that his second claim has been granted, we must now consider his first claim. First, there is no Zeus; hence, Euthyphro was mistaken in belief when he used "Zeus" in primary reference.[25] Now how does one determine whether or not the claim "omnipotence is an essential attribute of Zeus" is true when there is no Zeus?

Suppose someone says that 'being a pure spirit' is an essential attribute of King DeGaul I of France. Assuming that there are some pure spirits, there is no reason to say that no possible referent of the name "King DeGaul I of France" could have such an attribute essentially. We shall in this case have to grant that the statement "King DeGaul I of France is a pure spirit essentially" is true, but true vacuously, since we have no way of knowing whether any pure spirit is properly so called. Moreover, since there is no referent to be considered, although there are things which might have been referents, we must grant that the claim is necessarily true. As a result, we conclude that in a statement of the form "*A* is essentially F," when the proper

---

[25] As we will assume he has, although it must be noted that a proper name could be used primarily designatively in a modal claim *even if* it is used only to make a purported or a secondary reference.

name "A" occurs primarily designatively, the statement is either necessarily true or necessarily false, but the necessity is determined not solely by the signification of "A" but by the essence or quiddity of the thing which has been referred to by "A" (irrespective of whether that thing is really an existent).[26] Now if someone should say "A is essentially F" when he does not have any *other* quidditative concept (than 'being essentially F') which he applies to what he considers to be the referent of "A," then we can either say his statement is necessarily true because it *provides* a quidditative concept (assuming that F is not a merely qualitative concept, in which case his claim would be inconsistent), or we can say that his claim is indeterminate and that his mode of expressing himself is linguistically improper. This latter judgment seems the more appropriate. For anyone to say "A is essentially F," using "A" primarily designatively,[27] and for him not to possess a quidditative concept of the referent A to which analysis can be applied, is to misuse this form of expression.

(7) There is another relevant situation concerning proper names and logical modalities: that in which a proper name is used as subject term in a simple, *false* statement.

9: *God is female.*

10: *'God is female' is necessarily true (when "God" is used primarily significatively).*

11: *God is essentially female (when "God" is used primarily designatively).*

12: *God is evil.*

13: *'God is evil' is necessarily true ("God" used primarily significatively).*

14: *God is essentially evil ("God" used primarily designatively).*

15: *God is material.*

16: *'God is material' is necessarily true ("God" used primarily significatively).*

17: *God is essentially material ("God" used primarily designatively).*

18: *God is essentially material ("God" used primarily significatively).*

[26] Notice that this does not conflict with the claims in subsections 2 and 3, above, in which decision about modality in terms of the essential attributes of the referent was ruled out. There we were emphasizing the cases where the signification of the name must be considered; here we are concerned with claims *about* the essential properties of things. These are quite different matters.

[27] Such a use tells us that the modality of the statement is not to be determined by analysis of the signification of the proper name A.

Let us deal with the most obvious case first: proposition (18). This could be classed as a linguistic impropriety, since when the term "God" is used primarily significatively, the logical subject is the *signification* of the proper name. Significations do not have essences, though they may, sometimes, *be* essences. Hence, we could dismiss the claim as a misuse of the term "essentially" in a context which determines that "God" occurs primarily significatively. However, this expression (18) may be used as the parenthetical remark indicates, to make a claim *briefly* which is not simple to phrase accurately: that the attribute 'being material' is included in the signification of the term "God" and is included *as* an attribute which is part of the quidditative concept of what is referred to (or is said to be referred to) by the proper name "God." In that case, (18) is a contingent statement which is false. The same somewhat quixotic form of expression, with a different predicate (e.g., 'immaterial') could be used to make a contingently true statement. Whether or not an impropriety is involved in this expression can be determined only if we know the context of the utterance or the relevant habits of the speaker (just as knowledge of how the proper name is primarily used in a particular context is person-dependent).

The next most obvious case is the set (9), (10), and (11). The first, (9), is, of course, false. The second, (10), is contradictory, since the signification of "God" (as the name has signification among orthodox Christians) involves the concept 'pure spirit', which is incompatible with the predicate ascribed. The third, (11), is false. It is not an essential attribute of the entity referred to by "God" that it be female. Is (12) necessarily false? To determine this we must appeal to the appropriate quidditative concept of the referent (which concept may or may not be part of the signification of "God"). There is no case I can think of where the signification of a proper name consists entirely of essential or quidditative notes of the referent, although we could easily construct such a proper name. When I do appeal to the appropriate quidditative concept of God (here presuming that there is such a concept, although our quidditative concept is not complete and cannot be completed purely descriptively), I discover that 'being a female' is not only not an element of it but is furthermore excluded from it. We therefore decide that 'God is essentially female' is necessarily false.

More difficult to treat satisfactorily are statements (12), (13), and (14). Certainly one says (12) is false (for reasons not to be given here). One also says that (13) is necessarily false, since the signification of "God" does not include 'being evil'. In order to determine the truth-value of (15) we must again consult the essential or quidditative concept of God. In this case, we might not expect to find 'good' or 'evil' among the quidditative notes of God, since 'being good' and 'being evil' are not quiddities at all, but moral qualities. However, we may find among the quidditative notes, or the modes of these notes, something which entails that the entity has one or another moral quality. There is, after all, a sense in which quiddity determines quality. Not every quality of a thing is determined by what sort of thing it is; and yet, given any quiddity, some qualities are eliminated in that they suppose a quiddity incompatible with the one given. Whether the concept of what God is actually includes such a note as would be needed to determine that God is not evil will be left for discussion in the sixth chapter. But we can conclude that if a statement of the form of (13) is false because the signification of the subject *excludes* a given attribute signified by the predicate, then the corresponding statement of the form of (14) must be false, and necessarily so.

Last, we consider (15), (16), and (17). Again, by supposition, (15) is false. Statement (16) is necessarily false; (17) is also false, and is necessarily so according to the rule enunciated in the previous paragraph. For the reason why (16) is false is not because the predicate is not included in the signification of the subject term, but because the predicate is explicitly excluded by means of an incompatible attribute. Moreover, following the rule given earlier,[28] we discover that 'being material' is excluded by the quidditative concept of the being referred to. Hence (17) is false and necessarily so, according to both methods for deciding this.

(8) From this discussion we can draw some general conclusions about statements of the form 'God is or has F.'

(a) In determining the existential commitment of a speaker who makes a statement of this form, we must determine what mode of reference (primary, purported or secondary) he employs. This will tell

---

[28] That in order to determine the truth-value of simple statements when "God" is the subject term and is used primarily designatively, and when predicates are said to inhere in the referent essentially, we must consult the appropriate essential or quidditative concept of the referent.

us whether his existential commitment is conditional, unconditional, or not present at all. In only one case, the existential commitment is by way of an entailment holding between a proposition of the form '*n* is or has F' and the proposition '*n* really and actually exists'.

(b) In assigning modalities to statements of this form, we must determine for each case whether the proper name occurs primarily designatively or primarily significatively, since a decision on that point determines where we should *look* for the grounds of the logical modality.

(c) In considering the truth-values of statements of the form 'God is essentially F', where "God" occurs primarily designatively, we must consult a quidditative concept of God (the referent) to make a decision unless we already know that " 'God is or has F' is necessarily true" is false because the signification of the subject term *excludes* that predicate.

(d) In considering the truth-value of statements of the form "Necessarily 'God is or has F' "—where "God" occurs primarily significatively —we must consult the signification of "God" as we have settled it in terms of orthodox Christian teaching, knowing that a decision upon "true" as the value for a statement of this form does not commit us to a value of "true" for a statement of the form 'God is essentially F' where "God" occurs primarily designatively. Many elements of the signification of the term "God" are not attributes that God has essentially. This disparity between what is analytically involved in the signification of a term and what is essential to the referent is even more obvious with respect to the casual associations and meanings attached to the proper names for other beings.

(e) In considering the interaction between the existential commitment of a person who uses "God" in primary reference and the modal operator involved when he says " 'God is omnipotent' is necessarily true," etc., we emphasized the bivalence of proper names and insisted that such a situation constitutes a conjunctive claim because the primary reference requires that "God" be taken designatively, whereas the modal operator requires that "God" be taken significatively and the context suggests that the latter is the *primary* force of the name. This leads us to insist that the logical modality accruing to a statement in virtue of one aspect of the proper name (e.g., its signification) cannot simply be transferred to the statements entailed in virtue of the other aspect of the proper name (e.g., its designative function). Hence, even though 'God is omnipotent' may, as someone uses it, entail both 'It is analytic that God is omnipotent' and 'God exists', the modal operator accruing to the first cannot simply be transferred to the second.

3 ✒ The logical

status of 'God exists'

If you confess, as every reasonable person must,
that every existential proposition is synthetical, how can
it be maintained that the predicate of existence cannot
be denied without contradiction—a property which
is the characteristic of analytical propositions, alone?
                    Immanuel Kant, Critique of Pure Reason

It is not possible for something not-to-exist unless
something positively or privatively incompatible can exist.
                    John Duns Scotus, De Primo Principio,
                                        Chapter 3, Conclusion 5

When we say of this being that it exists, we mean that
its non-existence is impossible.
                    Moses Maimonides, Guide for the Perplexed,
                                        Part I, Chapter 58.

In this chapter, we shall investigate the dispute over the logical
status of 'God exists', with particular attention to the reasons why
that proposition is or might be thought by some philosophers to be

not logically necessary; next, we shall develop some hypotheses which may account for those concepts of "possible" which have caused many philosophers to think 'God exists' to be an absolute necessity; finally, we shall resolve the issue in favor of the latter thesis, adopting the position roughly sketched as follows.

1: It is possible that any given fact should have (or have had) an explanation, either extrinsic (causal) or inherent (self-evident).

2: Suppose God does not exist: ~g.

3: ~g cannot have (and could not have had) an explanation: it cannot be caused and cannot be self-explanatory (since 'God exists', g, is not contradictory).

4: Therefore, ~g cannot be a fact.

5: Then g is true necessarily.

SECTION 1: THE PROBLEM

Despite the conviction of David Hume and many contemporary philosophers[1] that all consistent existential statements are logically contingent and that, no matter what is said to exist or what is said to obtain (as a fact), the opposite state of affairs is always logically possible, a strong current in traditional Judaic-Christian thought considers the existence of God absolutely necessary, something which could not have been otherwise than the way it is.

This current of thought is seldom unambiguous, although some distinguished philosophers—Avicenna, Averroes, Maimonides, Aquinas, Scotus, Occam, Spinoza, Leibniz, and even some of our contemporaries among them—have been *emphatic* enough; usually it is accompanied, even in the best of its expressions, by confusion as to

[1] For example, Alvin Plantinga—introducing the collection *Faith and Philosophy* (Grand Rapids: Eerdmans Publishing Company, 1964), pp. ix and x—describes his own paper (Chapter 4) as follows: "Arguing that the proposition *God exists* is neither analytic nor logically necessary, Plantinga suggests that *God is the necessary being* may be understood as the claim that some proposition referring to God is the final answer in a certain series of questions and answers." He says on page 103: "I suggest that non-contradictory existential statements are all synthetic. It follows, then, that 'God exists' is not analytic." We shall consider his most interesting argument to support this conclusion below. Plantinga's paper attempts to accommodate the tradition I refer to with the proposal summarized above.

just what is meant by the terms "contingent," "necessary," and "self-evident." There is even greater confusion about the relationship of the "absolutely necessary" to the "logically necessary." Yet A. N. Prior rightly ascribes to the Christian tradition a definite commitment to claiming that God's existence is unconditionally necessary[2] (in some sense other than "hypothetical necessity" as a condition for creatures). The confusion of concepts is illustrated by Leibniz's unorthodox account of the nature of truths of fact, an account which entails that a given truth may have two modalities—one in my knowledge, one in God's—and which apparently confuses logical and epistemic modalities. Yet Liebniz exhibits a profound intuition of the necessity in question when he says, "If God is possible, then God exists"—a contention we propose to prove.

A sophisticated but somewhat mysterious reconciliation of our tendency to consider God's existence an absolute necessity, and our experience of being unable to derive a contradiction from the denial of the statement 'God exists', was offered by St. Thomas Aquinas when he said that 'God exists' is *per se nota in se sed non quoad nos:*[3]

In part the abovementioned opinion comes about because of a failure to distinguish between that which is self-evident in an absolute sense and that which is self-evident in relation to us. For assuredly that God exists is, absolutely speaking, self-evident, since what-God-is is His own being.[4]

The usual explanation of this position is that if we had a *comprehension* of the essence of God to associate with the subject term, instead of the confused *apprehension* now available to us, we would see the analyticity of the proposition 'God exists' from our realization of the nature of *what* is said to exist. Now suppose that Aquinas is right; then one of these must be the case:

Either (a) there is some set of characteristics such that if some being has them by nature (i.e., by definition, which is merely the conceptual

---

[2] "Can Religion be Discussed?" *New Essays in Philosophical Theology* (New York: The Macmillan Company, 1955), p. 4.

[3] *Summa Theologica*, I, q. 2, a. 1: "A thing can be self-evident in either of two ways: on the one hand, self-evident in itself though not to us; on the other self-evident in itself and to us." To equate 'self-evident' with 'necessary' is to confuse the logical and epistemic modalities; whether Aquinas did so is not clear.

[4] *Summa Contra Gentiles*, I, Chapter II, tr. A. Pegis, and published as *On the Truth of the Catholic Faith*. Image Books (New York: Doubleday, 1955), p. 81.

expression of a nature, which is prior), then such a being exists: *some set of properties entails existence.*

Or (b) there is some set of characteristics such that if some being has them by nature (in virtue of *what* it is), then *if* such a being exists, the proposition that such a being exists is a logical truth, and the fact that such a being exists is an element of all possible worlds: *some set of predicates determines the modality of the being.*[5]

If either (a) or (b) is true, and if God has the characteristics in question, then His existence is a necessary fact. As Aquinas explicitly said,[6] we cannot have precise enough knowledge of God's attributes to spell out the relationship between these attributes and existence in the manner necessary to exhibit the self-evidence of the proposition 'God exists'. But this would not suggest that it is not necessarily true; for St. Thomas did not think that all propositions expressing necessary facts *(necessitates de re)* are analytic. Therefore I think he held that if you knew God directly you would *see* the necessity of His existence, yet would still not say 'God exists' is analytic (since "exists" is not a predicate), although it would be self-evident.

An objection to Thomas' doctrine must be considered: that he merely appears to be discussing a single proposition, self-evident in itself but not to us; whereas in fact there are at least two propositions involved in his claim, since the concept of the subject *admittedly* differs in the two cases: (a) in which God, or the person brought face to face with God in heaven, knows "God exists," which is self-evident; and (b) in which Thomas Aquinas (in his earthly state) knows "God exists," which is self-evident in itself but not to Thomas. In most phases of theological discussion, it would be appropriate to ignore the fact that the proposition God understands, when He understands the self-evident-to-Him truth that He exists, and the proposition which Thomas understands, when he understands the *not*-self-evident-to-him proposition that God exists, are not the same proposition, since the subject-concepts differ. But at the point where we discuss the

---

[5] The latter proposal seems plausible. For what accounts for the fact that it is a contingent matter that black cats exist unless it be *what* black cats are? Moreover, we will see in Chapter V that it is manifestly possible to construct definitions of such properties!

[6] *ST*, I, q. 2, a. 1: "If, however, there are some to whom the essence of the predicate and subject is unknown, the proposition will be self-evident in itself but not to those who do not know the meaning of the predicate and subject of the proposition. . . ." *Introduction to St. Thomas Aquinas* (New York: Modern Library, 1945), p. 21.

necessity of the proposition Thomas knows, it is very important that it is not exactly the same as the one God knows; from the fact that the proposition God knows is a necessary truth, we cannot infer that the proposition Thomas knows is a necessary truth unless we employ the premise that there is such a proposition which is actually known by God. If it be admitted that there is a difference in the propositions known by God (or the beatified) and those known by Thomas, then we must establish that the proposition Thomas purports to know is true before we can premise that there is any proposition at all which God actually knows. This is, of course, the reason St. Thomas rejected what was later to become the Cartesian form of a priori argument. That there is a logically equivalent but not synonymous proposition, which God knows and which is self-evident to God, will follow if Thomas can establish the proposition which is not self-evident to him.

The angelic doctor's taking an expression like "self-evident"—which is normally both *epistemic* (in that a relation is ascribed to someone's knowledge) and person-variant (in that it is in principle possible that what is self-evident to one person is not to another)—and his employing it in a context (the "self-evident in itself") where both its epistemic overtones and its person-variant nature are ignored, suggests that he did so because he lacked a more appropriate term. We can supply that lack and dispel much of the mystery in his solution with a more fruitful way to interpret Aquinas' position on this matter. This interpretation preserves the assumption that it is one single proposition which is both *per se nota* and *non per se nota quoad nos;* if we put the term "self-accounting" in place of "self-evident," we can work it out as follows: a fact can be self-accounting even though we do not know the explanation of it. Many children know that there are no square circles, but do not grasp the explanation thereof, which is intrinsic to the state of affairs itself. A teacher might tell them that the fact that there are no square circles is self-accounting, and they might come to know *that*, as well as know that there are no square circles; still it might not appear self-accounting to them. They will see it to be self-accounting that there are no square circles only when they understand how the very structure of what would otherwise be the case defeats itself. This is the analogue by way of which I suggest we interpret Aquinas.

Let us read him this way: he says he knows that God's existence is self-accounting *(per se nota)*, not because he *sees* it to be so but because he sees that it *must* be so; he sees the truth of premises which entail this meta-proposition—that is, entail that God exists, that God could not have failed to exist, and that God must understand the necessity of His existence through self-awareness. The philosopher does not see the elements of the fact which render it self-accounting because he does not have an adequate comprehension of God. Hence, we do not see it to be self-explanatory that God exists, and, in fact, we *cannot* see it to be so during our earthly lifetime; but from the things we know, we can infer that the fact is self-accounting.

Such a doctrine is not *logically* odd. We can *refer* to analytic propositions which do not appear analytic to us; for instance, I know there is a proposition which I know to be analytic but do not *see* to be analytic, namely, the last analytic proposition to be formulated in English. Why should we not be able to do the same thing with regard to self-accounting facts? Since being self-accounting is not the same as being analytic (although every analytic proposition "pictures" a self-accounting fact), we shall have to find a supplementary argument which shows that such a non-analytic self-accounting proposition is logically necessary—a project that is carried out in the latter part of Section 2.

I am ready to admit at once that this interpretation does not respect the ordinary meaning of *"per se nota"* as Aquinas used it; what I offer is technically a gloss, not a literal reading. Its merit is that it captures something which St. Thomas understood but which he could not better formulate at a time during which *per se* facts and *per se nota* propositions were not rigorously distinguished; which, even if he did clearly understand this, he could not succinctly incorporate into the tradition, formed by Peter Lombard's authoritative text, of discussion on the question of self-evidence.

No matter how one tries to handle the various interpretations by western philosophers (prior to the twentieth century at least) of the claim that God's existence is a necessary fact, one seems to run across the incompleteness of the conceptual schemes those writers possessed. It might be concluded that since Avicenna, Maimonides, Aquinas, Scotus, Anselm, Spinoza, Leibniz, and Descartes were, each in his own way, confused, the contention that 'God exists' is a necessary proposition ought to be abandoned as one which was never well formulated or understood. But, on the other hand, there was a continuous interest in that claim, formulated through a series of concepts partially grasped by those writers as individuals and inconsistently described by them as a group; perhaps a reconsideration will disclose terms by which their theses can be better formulated.

Before entering definitely upon the attempt to explain and defend the claim that 'God exists' is necessarily true, I shall describe what I consider the more challenging reasons that have caused another large group of philosophers, led by Hume, to reject it.

Suppose I were to invite the classical authors mentioned above to reopen the debates, adding to their number the testy David Hume. To these guests assembled, I observe, "Lucky thing that God exists." They seem astonished, so I add in explanation, "Well, it might have been otherwise, you know." Several would point out that nothing could have brought it about that God should exist or not exist, because His existence is unproducible and unpreventable in principle. To this, I calmly reply: "That makes it all the more lucky He exists; if He didn't things might have gone on that way forever." Before long it would be plain that these philosophers, with the exception of David Hume, do not think God is the sort of being that might *happen* or *happen-not* to exist. In fact, everyone but Hume would undoubtedly accept some form of Spinoza's contention that God is a self-explanatory, a self-accounting entity, the kind of entity for which no explanation need be sought outside its own nature; above all, the kind of entity which does not have inexplicable or even unaccounted existence (the most that Hume would want to say).

The discussion might then turn to how we know that any self-explanatory beings exist, and the old issue of whether the reasoning for such a proposition is a priori or a posteriori, and hence valid or not, would be joined anew.[7] However, leaving this for later, we now attend only to problems connected with various replies to our main question: what is the logical status of 'God exists'?

Suppose I say to Aquinas, Spinoza, Scotus, Maimonides, Leibniz, Descartes, and Anselm:

You gentlemen think 'God exists' is not like 'The earth exists', in that an explanation of how it happened that the earth began to exist and continues to exist cannot be arrived at from an examination of *what* we say exists; there

---

[7] This question is addressed directly in Section 1 of Chapter IV.

is nothing about what the earth is which requires that, or accounts for the fact that, it exists. But this supposes that there is something about the nature of a divine being which requires that it exist and precludes its being either produced or prevented. Several of you have said this nature consists in being the most perfect possible being; others, being the completely independent being; and others still, that being self-accounting (a-*seity*) is *itself* a nature and that to be self-accounting, to have essence identical with existence, *is* the property which accounts for the existence of what is self-explanatory. These assertions all lead one (but not by any apparent logical entailment) to say that the nature of divine beings is such that if one exists at all, it exists necessarily.

Now it is not obvious that any one of the offered characterizations of the divine nature does in fact imply that if such a being existed it would exist necessarily. Why couldn't it exist (logically) contingently? What property can a thing have such that if there *is* anything of that sort, things couldn't have been otherwise at least in that respect? By what *logical* deduction can you show that if a thing is not *metaphysically* contingent (that is, if it cannot be produced or prevented) it follows that its existence is not *logically* contingent but is, rather, logically necessary? You traditional philosophers do not have a precise answer to this, even though you often speak of "independence" and "uncausability" as if they do the trick, and even though the subtle Scotus came very close, indeed, to success. For, you often say, if a divine being is not producible and is unpreventable, then what could account for its non-being?

Undoubtedly, [says Hume,] I agree with this line of reasoning: nothing could account for its non-being. But that does not disturb me; nothing could account for its existence either. Certainly, the fact that something is by definition unpreventable does not entail that it exists, even if it were a possible being. [Here Scotus would try to interrupt with reasoning which we will examine later.] For one thing, it has to be more than unpreventable to exist. An unpreventable what? Suppose it were an unpreventable unicorn. You have to be more than unpreventable to be divine. For another thing, it might just *happen* that such a being does not exist and that there is no explanation for its nonexistence, since, by part of its definition, there *couldn't* be an explanation of its nonexistence. This is just the way it is with God.

Duns Scotus counters:[8]

If we ask why there is no square circle on the table, the correct reply is that there is something about the nature of a square circle which precludes one's

---

[8] I have made Scotus spokesman here because of his very similar concept in *De Primo Principio*, Chapter III, Conclusion 5, quoted at the beginning of this chapter.

being there by positively requiring that it be square whenever it is circular, and vice versa. The square circle is its own sufficient reason for not existing. Its not-existing is necessary. The fact that there are no square circles is self-accounting. So, too, whatever is its own sufficient reason for existence necessarily exists.

Hume replies:[9]

Very well: I grant the principle that if there is any self-explanatory existent, it is in some sense necessary; but this proves nothing until we are shown that there *is* some sort of thing which is self-explanatory rather than unexplained.

The tendency of the Christian community to assert through its philosophers that God's existence is in some sense *absolutely* necessary (and not merely necessary as a condition for the existence of creatures) was brought up short by my bald denial that *no* matter of fact is necessary;[10] for the Christians' "sense" of their doctrine has run far ahead of the logical theory to explain it.

You might be right to claim, on strictly historical grounds, that the so-called a priori argument for the existence of God—which I present in the *Dialogues* and refute by denying the supposition of the argument that there can be necessary facts of existence—is not an adequate representation of the Christian position, since no really close analogue of this can be found in your Christian writers; but still, you must admit that I caught the spirit and tendency underlying many of the scholastic arguments, laying bare at a stroke the backbone of the theory: that some matters of existence are necessary, are parts of all possible worlds. The very acme of absurdity!

Now, [continues David Hume,] I am so sure that 'God exists' is not self-explanatory or self-accounting (for I see that 'being self-explanatory', like 'being self-accounting', is an ontological and not an epistemological relation for you) that I see no contradiction in denying 'God exists', even if I spell out all that I know about God and all that I have been able to elicit from any other philosopher about Him; and you have already made it evident from your example, 'There are no square circles', that you think the denial of whatever is self-accounting must be inconsistent in itself.

Here St. Thomas Aquinas interjects:

But only a comprehension of God in direct acquaintance could reveal to one the self-explanatory character of the divine existence, whereas all that is

---

[9] It is merely a literary device that I attribute to Hume reasons which he did not actually give but which he would surely accept.

[10] See the explicit assertion in *Dialogues Concerning Natural Religion* and in the *Inquiry*.

available to *homo viator* is a confused apprehension of God's essence, derived through description. You may know that Alexander the Great was a
great man; you may even be able to give some plausible reasons for believing
this. But with your fragmentary understanding of the person, you ordinarily
do not *see* that Alexander, Caesar, or Plato was great; you infer it from fragmentary information or learn it from scholars who make the inference. You
would have to know these men or their like by acquaintance. "You don't
know what a great man is unless you have known one" is not nonsensical or
trivial; some things are made intelligible only through experience. So too,
by well-justified analogy, you don't know what divinity really is, what self-
accounting being or *a-seity* is, until you have known God in direct acquaintance. Man conceives God in terms of the world he knows, eliminating implied imperfections from his concepts as far as he can; but he has no knowledge by experience of anything whose existence is self-explanatory. Hence
his concepts of God are taken by analogy from a world in which explanation
is necessary; neither the concepts nor the experiences from which the concepts are formed contain *positive* elements for those aspects of God which
render Him self-existent. Therefore, the fact that the negation of the proposition 'God exists' appears consistent merely shows that Hume, like everyone
else, has an incomplete concept of God.

Hume rejoins:

To say that I do not see the necessity of 'God exists' because I have a human
conception of God may beg the question; to argue in this way we must
employ "God" as a proper name with a description associated with it, since
we are implying that if I *knew* God, I would see the necessity of the proposition. Please spell out the descriptive content of that concept which you have
in mind, and which you say I do not have in my possession.

I think Aquinas and the others would have to reply that we cannot
spell it out (although some contemporaries, like Hartshorne, claim
to do just this), since we do not have it either. They must then say to
Hume that they came to know the necessity of 'God exists', not by
considering the conceptual content of the subject term, but in some
other way.

Hume replies, "Perhaps that way will be good enough for me; please
show me."

The philosophers then repeat the conditions for God's existence:
since He cannot be produced, He must be self-explanatory if He
exists. Some might even point out that they came to know that the

proposition 'God exists' is true by a divine revelation, and came to see that it had to be necessary by speculation upon the fact that, if it is true and is neither caused nor necessary, then its truth is as accidental and random as an event can be; we might just as well not look to such a being as an explanation of the being of all else, since we have explained nothing with the supposition of His existence that we could not have explained without it just as well.

Hume smiles with satisfaction:

I agree that if 'God exists' is true and not necessary, its being true is as accidental and random as an event can be—and as every event really is. And I agree that we might just as well not look to such a being as an explanation of the being of all else, since we have explained nothing with the supposition of His existence that we could not have explained without it just as well.

What species of speculation and what logical peculation could have led you from those things we both admit to the conclusion that 'God exists' must be necessarily true? Ordinarily I would repeat my fruitless request that you "spell out" for my obtuse mind exactly what your reasoning was. But you have failed me often enough, as have your followers in the last three centuries. Therefore, I will save you the trouble of trying to find the logical connections you need by showing you that such connections do not exist and are not possible.

I shall give you *six* arguments:

(1) You assume [says Hume] that everything must have an explanation; that's about the same as the medieval assumption that everything must have a cause because "*ratio*" and "cause" derive from Aristotle's and Plato's broader notion of "explanatory factor." Moreover, it is similar to the grandiose Principle of Sufficient Reason that was so popular on the Continent. No proof of these assumptions has been offered.

If you treat 'Everything has an explanation or sufficient reason' as a universal synthetic truth established by induction, there is logically compatible with your available finite body of evidence a set of exceptions which will falsify the principle. Hence, you cannot establish the *absolute universality* of this unrestricted universal principle by any finite body of evidence; you will never have enough evidence to establish its absolute universality by induction. Hence, it cannot function as a premise for establishing the existence of God.

If, on the other hand, you treat this principle as a *necessary* truth, you will have to hold that 'there is something for whose being there is no explanation whatever' is self-contradictory, since the contradictions of necessary truths are self-contradictory. But in order for this principle to be *established* as necessary, you will have to produce the proof that the negation in question is self-contradictory. No one has succeeded in doing this, and there is no reason to think you will. Experimental attempts with propositions like 'There is no explanation for the existence of the moon' will show that the contradiction is at least elusive, if not absent.

Hence, if you base arguments for the existence of God on the Principle of Sufficient Reason, you will either be basing them upon a synthetic principle of doubtful truth, from which you cannot properly deduce that the conclusion is true, much less that it is necessarily true; or else you will be basing them upon a principle which is said to be necessary, but from whose denial no contradiction has been deduced or is reasonably expected. In either case the arguments will be philosophically worthless. For if we take the principle to be synthetic, and take it to be analytic that God's *non*-existence cannot be explained, then in order to know that the principle is *universally* true, we shall *already* have to know that God exists. Hence an argument for the existence of God based upon this principle will be epistemically circular: we shall have to know that the conclusion is true in order to know that the main premise is true. On the other hand, if we take the principle to be necessary, we shall have to know that its denial is contradictory. We have no grounds for believing this; in fact, my third argument, below, will show that the Christian has even less reason than anyone else for thinking the principle necessarily true. Your followers have been backed up against this wall for centuries. Let me proceed with further arguments.

(2) You assume [argues Hume] that self-explanatory existence is possible. I cannot conceive of such a thing, and challenge you to show me one case of it. But to be brief, I will save your time and show you that such a thing is impossible. For if there is any singular proposition of the form 'a exists' which is logically necessary, then a statement of the form 'Something exists' is entailed and is also necessary, since nothing is entailed by a necessary proposition but a necessary proposition. 'Something exists', if it be necessary, will have a necessarily false denial, because the denials of all necessarily true propositions are necessarily false and are impossible. But I see nothing inconsistent about the proposition 'Nothing exists', nor do I think it impossible that nothing should have existed—even though it is, of course, false that nothing ever existed. I therefore concede your claim that *if* God exists, since God is self-explanatory, God necessarily exists. But since a proposition entailed by 'God exists'—namely, 'Something exists'—is *not* necessary, it follows that 'God exists' is not necessary; therefore, granting your major

premise, by *modus tollens* it follows strictly that the antecedent is false and God does not exist! Put more formally, the argument is as follows:

1. $(\exists x)Gx \rightarrow \square (\exists x)Gx$ (*"Gx" means "x is divine".*)
2. $\square (\exists x)Gx \rightarrow \square [(\exists x)(\exists \Phi)(\Phi x)]$
   (*Proved: rules of EI and EG.*)
3. $\square [(\exists x)(\exists \Phi)(\Phi x)] \rightarrow \sim \lozenge [\sim (\exists x)(\exists \Phi)(\Phi x)]$
4. *But no contradiction is derivable from:*
   $\sim (\exists x)(\exists \Phi)(\Phi x)$. *Therefore:* $\lozenge [\sim (\exists x)(\exists \Phi)(\Phi x)]$
5. *By modus tollens of (4) and (3), we get:*
   $\sim \square [(\exists x)(\exists \Phi)(\Phi x)]$
6. *By modus tollens of (5) and (2), we get:*
   $\sim \square (\exists x)(Gx)$
7. *By modus tollens of (6) and (1), we get:*
   $\sim (\exists x)(Gx)$

Therefore, by assuming the main premise of the theists, premise (1), I can prove that God does not exist. Hence, I have saved you the trouble of proving (1) by showing that if it is true, its antecedent must be false; and, therefore, that were we to prove (1), we should prove that God does not exist.

(3) It is to be noted [Hume continues] that argument (2) is logically independent of whether the assumptions challenged in (1) are true or false.

(4) Furthermore, [Hume adds,] you cannot escape (1) by saying that denying that everything has an explanation leads to absurdity. That would be the same mistake as is made by those scholastics who say that a denial of the principle of non-contradiction necessarily leads to absurdity. For if a man says there is one exception to the principle of non-contradiction, he denies the principle; but as long as he does not pretend to offer us that exception— the proposition which is both true and false—he will not fall into the wilderness of confusion Aristotle anticipated, since his statement that there is such a two-valued proposition has only one truth-value. If a man says that some things lack explanations, he is not involved in absurdity, even if he purports to tell you what things they are. Hence, no obvious and systematic repugnancy follows from the rejection of your basic principles; on the contrary, argument (2) shows that absurdities will *follow* from your basic premises.

(5) Moreover, there are two further difficulties with the principle that everything has an explanation or sufficient reason, which appear to make it a poor starting point for the traditional theists.

First, it cannot be treated as *regulative* (equivalent to "Presume that everything has an explanation"); for then the assertion that God exists will not be independent of all other propositions, but will stand as an hypothesis contingent upon the fact that this regulative principle will never lead us into error. The whole question of the truth of the conclusion would again revert to a question of fact: Are there any exceptions to this rule? If there are, they may be just the things we postulate the existence of God to explain. And even if there are not, the argument is incomplete until that is *shown*, and since one would have to show the conclusion to be true in order to show the premises to be true, arguments with such a premise would be worthless.

Second, the principle "Everything has an explanation" seems to run counter to the theory of creation: the Christian who wants to maintain that God necessarily exists also wants to maintain that this world is necessarily contingent, and further, that the world has its explanation in God. Now if the mere existence of God were said to account for the existence of the world—that is, if God's *existence* were a sufficient condition for the existence of other things—the world would exist necessarily. If, on the other hand, the Christian wishes to say that it is the *choice* of God which accounts for the world, not His mere *being*, then we must ask whether 'God chooses our world' is a necessary proposition. If it be said that it is not, we must seek the explanation of the fact that God chooses our world. If it is replied that the nature of God accounts for this fact (that God's choice is necessitated by His nature), then 'God chooses our world' is a necessary proposition and not, as by hypothesis, contingent; for whatever follows from (as distinct from "follows in accord with") the nature of God—His existence or omnipotence, for example—follows therefrom necessarily. In this case, creation would not be free. If, again, it is said that 'God chooses our world' does not follow from the nature of God, then what explains God's choosing our world? No matter what is named, it will either be a necessary fact or a contingent one. If it is necessary, so is God's choice, and this falsifies the Christian's supposition that the world is contingent. If what is discovered is a contingent fact, then what we have is, not an explanation, but something that itself needs an explanation. Therefore, [concludes Hume,] there is a glaring counter-example to the claim that everything has an explanation, a counter-example that is built right into the Christian conception of the relation of the world to God. Moreover, this position is shared by Spinoza, who has accepted the *only* compatible conception of God: that God does *not* choose freely.

(6) Finally, [Hume says,] I can prove that no existential statement is analytic. I shall restate briefly an argument developed by Alvin Plantinga.[11]

No existential statement is analytic because no existential statement has a contradictory denial, and all analytic statements have contradictory denials. Why say that no existential statements have contradictory denials? In making an existential statement, I assert that there is at least one thing which satisfies

---

11 *Faith and Philosophy*, chap. 4, "Necessary Being," pp. 100–102.

a certain description. This description is logically complex in existential statements like "There are some rational animals," which contain a composition
of logically independent propositions. The *denial* of such a statement, its
contra-existential, is equivalent to a universal statement asserting of each
individual that it is either non-animal or non-rational. In Plantinga's words,
" . . . the truth of any instantiation of such a statement requires only that one
of its disjuncts be true. But if so, the statement in question does not and
cannot entail *two* statements one of which is the denial of the other. Hence
it cannot be contradictory. And of course the point may be put more generally; to deny that there are any *x*'s is to assert that no individual has all the
properties comprising the connotation of *x*. But such an assertion is not
complex in the above sense and cannot, therefore, be contradictory. And if
no contra-existential statement is contradictory, no existential statement is
analytic; accordingly, 'God exists' is not analytic."[12]

Now, [concludes Hume,] what more decisive reasoning do you need? Here
is an out-and-out logical demonstration of the falsity of your "ontologistic"
assumptions.

These six points complete the "Humean" case against the position
taken by Aquinas and others. They are designed to bypass the distinction between comprehending and apprehending God's nature
by attacking the two roots of the Christian position: first, that the
Principle of Sufficient Reason, or something quite like it, is an appropriate premise for theistic arguments; and second, that if God exists,
then it is necessarily the case that God exists. The sixth argument is a
direct attack upon the idea that an existential statement could be
analytic; its relevance to the "necessity" thesis is based upon the
widespread belief that absolutely necessary statements are analytic.
We shall consider these arguments at appropriate places in this
chapter and later ones; and in Chapter VII we shall devote extensive
consideration to the second part of the fifth argument. Here, we shall
reply directly only to the second and sixth arguments.

In replying to the second "Humean" objection, we distinguish between two notions of inconsistency that we often employ in ordinary
language. The one has a syntactical counterpart if it involves an
expression whose syntactical structure is of the form $(p \cdot \sim p)$; the inconsistency may be either "truth-functional" or "quantificational."
These are the paradigms of formal inconsistency—the explicit affirmation and denial of the same thing. However, there are other incon-

sistent statements which do not have such a structure, for example, "Some bachelors are married." The inconsistency here depends upon the *meaning* of the terms involved; we would need a formal semantic system to create an exact formal counterpart, although we usually get along by generating a syntactical counterpart, using definitions like ' "bachelor" means "not married." '

Now the statement 'Something exists', which is entailed by 'God exists', is not like either of these examples. It involves a structure whose formal analogue is $(\exists x)(\exists F)(Fx)$, where we are dealing with an individual variable and a property variable. If, contrary to Hume's supposition, there is an existential statement, involving a definite individual and a definite property, which is necessarily true, then this generalized analogue (or statement-form) will be necessary, provided we believe there is a philosophically acceptable interpretation of quantification over properties. However, the only way to discover the necessity of such a generalized form of statement and the absurdity of its denial will be from the fact that its denial entails the negation of the particular existential which is in fact necessary.[13] Nothing about the semantical structure of the generalized form 'There is something of some sort or another' requires that it be necessary: that depends upon what sorts of things there are. But we must not bypass something which is quite central to this problem, even though it will be more carefully discussed in Chapter VII. This is the fact that the formula $\sim(\exists x)(\exists\Phi)(\Phi x)$ and its correlate $(x)\sim(Fx \vee \sim Fx)$ are *quantificationally* inconsistent. Hence, line 4 of the second "Humean" objection is false, and necessarily false. The quantificational logic we employ is simply incompatible with the hypothesis that nothing exists.

Yet it seems unfair to reject that argument on these grounds alone, for it obviously demands the deduction of a semantical inconsistency as well as a merely syntactical one. But once we understand that *this* is what is required, then we can realize that the consistency of some *uninterpreted* formula is not really the point at issue, and the considerations that follow will have greater force.

No doubt some philosophers will object to this conclusion, saying

---

[13] A statement is contradictory if it entails a conjunction of statements one of which is the negation of the other. (We are bypassing the "problem of synonymy," admitting that for a formally perfect order, your concept of synonymy must be prior to your concept of inconsistency, since we must know that *p* is synonymous with *p* before we can know that '*p* • ~*p*' is inconsistent.)

that we are now committed to holding that the same expression "$(\exists x)(\exists F)(Fx)$" may have *two* modalities, namely contingency and necessity; for in some formal system the expression may *not* have a contradictory denial (although in such language as that of *Principia* it does), while on some interpretation the formula is necessary. Put entirely in terms of interpretations, it will be objected that I am saying that on one interpretation the formula is necessary, and on another contingent. But neither is the case. Rather, if on *any* interpretation the formula is necessary, then the formula, uninterpreted, is entailed by *every* interpretation of it, and the formula is necessary. Thus, the statement 'There is a cat', represented as $(\exists x)(Cx)$, entails $(\exists x)(\exists F)(Fx)$. Since on some true interpretation the latter is necessary, the statement 'There is a cat' entails the necessary truth 'There is something of some sort or another'. In effect, in an interpreted system, a statement form which is necessary on some interpretation (permitted in the system) of its predicates is necessary when uninterpreted (that is, when it is considered as containing only predicate *variables*). This is not the only way to avoid the charge that we are committed to claiming that the same expression can have multiple, and incompatible modalities. But it is one which makes it clear that whether or not it is necessarily the case that something or another exists depends entirely upon what sorts of things are possible.

What right have we to assume that whether or not the generalized statement $(\exists F)(\exists x)(Fx)$ is necessary (given its truth) depends upon what *sorts* of things are possible?[14] What accounts for the fact that 'The earth exists' is a contingent rather than a necessary statement? Three kinds of answer might be given. The contingency may be said to depend upon (1) what sort of thing the earth is; (2) whether or not human convention has developed our natural language in such a way that 'the earth does not exist' is absurd (as it would be to say 'The universe does not exist'); (3) the fact that all existential statements are contingent, that there is no contradiction in denying them (as David Hume would say and as Plantinga claims to have shown).

---

[14] This is paradoxical only in the absence of the relationship between possibility and existence which is developed in Section 2 of this chapter. Notice that the phrase "depends upon what *sorts* of things are possible" is ambiguous between the partial formulations $[(\exists F)(\exists x)(Fx)]$ and $[(\exists x)(\exists F)(Fx)]$. Many philosophers would say that these are the same, since the order of existential quantifiers is interchangeable. But I do not think this is so when the logical types of the predicates are discontinuous (not of "next higher type"). However, we need not settle the matter here.

These three answers are not as different as they might appear. The third is stated in the form of a denial of the hypothesis which needs proving if we are to support the Christian tradition; but if put in the form 'It depends upon whether denying such a statement leads to a contradiction', it amounts to a definition of necessity, and is not so much a reason for as a reiteration of the fact which needs accounting. And if we ask for the grounds of the impossibility of something, we will be told either that it lies in the nature of the thing (e.g., a square circle), or else that it lies in the relationships of meaning in our language. How close these two are as answers depends in part upon what connections there are between the natures of things and the concepts or terms by which we think or speak about them; since I am convinced that such connections do exist and that they are relatively close—close enough to warrant our allowing the structure of our language to guide us as to the structure of things—I think we can treat all three answers (with the third rephrased) as equivalent for our purposes. Hence, we shall have to address the question of what there is about the nature of the earth which makes its existence contingent and about the nature of God which makes His existence necessary, in at least one of these three forms. This will be done in the second part of this chapter.

The sixth "Humean" objection is closely related to the second, in reply to which we stated that whether a particular instantiation of the formula $(\exists x)(\exists F)(Fx)$ is a semantically necessary truth or not depends upon what sorts of things are possible, that is, upon what sort of predicate F is. Now the sixth objection (for which Plantinga should receive credit as having offered the first reasoned defense of Hume's easy assertion that existentials cannot have contradictory denials) insists that the logical structure of the contra-existential precludes its being self-contradictory. This is an ingenious argument.

Its full strength is not obvious because one might think Plantinga's point holds for existentials that are thought to be analytic but not for those that are thought to be non-analytic but logically necessary. However, he uses "analytic" to mean "has a contradictory denial" and therefore, uses "analytic" the way most philosophers (especially Hume) use "necessary." Hence the thrust of his argument is more extensive than might at first appear.

The most important refutations of this argument are given in detail later,[15] when, by demonstrating that their denials are inconsistent with an a priori true principle, E, we show that both 'something exists' and 'God exists' have semantically contradictory denials, and hence produce counter-examples to Plantinga's conclusion.

My second refutation of the argument contends that it begs the question. For consider (a)—'There is something which has some attribute or other; let it be F'—and its contra-existential (b): 'Take anything, it is a non-F'. If F is the disjunction of all possible properties and combinations thereof, then (b) will be equivalent to the assertion that there is nothing at all. Whether this is consistent is just what has to be proved before Plantinga will have shown that no contra-existential can be contradictory. Since 'nothing exists' is quantificationally inconsistent in its form and, in addition, semantically inconsistent with an a priori true proposition (as is shown below in Section 2, Part B), it follows that Plantinga's argument begs the question on just that proposition which falsifies it.

To put this point another way, consider the statement:

1: $(\exists x)(Fx \vee \sim Fx)$

2: $\sim(\exists x)(Fx \vee \sim Fx)$ *is the denial for (1)*

3: $(x)\sim(Fx \vee \sim Fx)$ *which we derive from (2) by the rule of quantifier negation. This is the contra-existential of (1), as Plantinga describes it.*

4: $\sim Fy \cdot Fy$ *UI*

5: Fy *Simp (4)*

6: $(\exists x)(Fx)$ *EG*

7: $(x)\sim Fy$ *Simp (4), and UG*

8: $\sim(\exists x)(Fx)$ *QN*

9: $[\sim(\exists x)(Fx)] \cdot [(\exists x)(Fx)]$ *Conj: (6) and (8)*

Hence, the denial of some existential statements does lead to a contradiction! Therefore, the general principle supposed by Hume is false: some existentials do have self-contradictory contra-existentials. What then *is* the generalization which is true, which Hume tried to enunciate and Plantinga tried to prove?

Third, Plantinga's argument is a *non sequitur*. We will admit his premises concerning the nature of an inconsistency, and concerning

---

[15] Part B, Section 2 of this chapter.

dictory,"[17] is false. Since it has not been shown that an existential statement cannot have a contradictory denial, Plantinga has not succeeded in showing that no existential is analytic. Once we find that some existentials have denials incompatible with an a priori true proposition, we will have discovered just the opposite: that some existentials do have contradictory denials.

A final problem: The foregoing description of "Hume's" position omitted a systematic argument, or meta-argument, which will surely fit the Humean tradition. This has been reserved for a separate place because it must be formulated so generally, and with such a sweeping and simplified view of the task of metaphysics, that I might be accused of sabotage against the tradition I attack because I load its cannon with wet powder. Actually, I have the greatest respect for this argument and do not wish to mitigate its force by having indicated that those philosophers who should cherish it most have let their dislike of talk about doing philosophy deprive them of its service.

There are only three alternative outcomes to a completed metaphysical investigation into the origin of the beings of the universe. (I think we can presume that one does not call an abandoned quest, which has no outcome at all, "completed," and can treat a theory which claims that nothing can be explained as an "uncompleted" or "abandoned" metaphysics.) Either (a) we will discover some fact or being which is self-accounting and which accounts for every other thing, insofar as such an account is possible; or (b) we will discover some beings or facts which account for a large part or all of the other beings and facts, but which themselves stand in need of explanation; or (c) we will discover facts or beings which explain everything else but whose very nature renders them inexplicable. That is, if we call the ultimate explanations feasible to the metaphysician his *explanatory factors* or *explainers*, we can say that metaphysics can result in (a) self-explanatory explainers, (b) unexplained explainers, or (c) inexplicable explainers. An empirical scientist's explanations by means of laws and logical constructs are always of type (b), and will always admit of new and simplified hypotheses which will explain the previously unexplained factors but will confront the next generation with a new set of unexplained explainers.

[17] Ibid., p. 101.

the formation of existentials and their denials; we admit al   tra
ment, "The truth of any instantiation of such a statement re   sta
that one of its disjuncts be true." But Plantinga follows this   ce
if so, the statement in question does not and cannot entail   so
ments one of which is the denial of the other. Hence, it cann   pr
tradictory." This simply does not follow, and I cannot se   ex
says "If so, . . ." For Plantinga assumes[16] that in order to ent.
tradictory conjunction of statements, the original stateme   o
itself be logically complex, a conjunction (via interpretatio   fi
predicates) of *logically independent* singular statements. Th   b
correct. The negation of the original statement need only er   a
denial of an a priori true proposition, and from this denial   c
derive all contradictory conjunctions by strict implication. Hen
original existential need not involve syntactical logical comple

But, the author will reply, a logically simple existential stat
cannot have a denial which entails the denial of an a priori true p
sition. To this I rejoin, first, that this begs the question, since we
no reason as yet to think it true. If a is the existential in question
is a priori true, then it does have a denial which is inconsistent wit
a priori truth. Second, in setting out to show that existential st
ments could not have contradictory denials, it was assumed that, si
the denials do not involve the conjunction of logically independe
statements, they cannot be inconsistent. But this is false, since a stat
ment can be inconsistent without involving logically independer
conjuncts; in fact, a statement can never be rendered inconsistent b
its *logically independent* conjuncts, regardless of their truth-values.
Let F be a simple property and let FF be the predicate 'is F and not-F'.
Then $(\exists x)(FFx)$ has as its interpretation FFa. If we reduce FFa by definition, we get $(Fa \cdot \sim Fa)$. These conjuncts are *not* logically independent;
hence, a contradiction can result without independent conjuncts.
Rather, just the opposite of what Plantinga supposes must be the case:
for a statement to be contradictory it must assert or entail a conjunction of statements which are not only not logically independent,
but are logically opposed. Hence, there can be a simple or logically basic statement—one not involving logically independent
conjuncts—which is contradictory, and therefore Plantinga's claim,
"It is for this reason, of course, that existential statements may be con-

---

[16] Plantinga, p. 101, first two paragraphs.

Some metaphysicians have appealed primarily to solutions of type
(c). For example, Kant's noumena are partial and ultimate explanations of phenomena, but are in principle inexplicable. Other metaphysicians have appealed to theories which involve factors of both
type (a) and type (c). Plato's forms are of type (a), but the receptacle
is of type (c). Still others—for instance, Spinoza—have appealed only
to self-explanatory explainers.

Now it is argued upon these generalizations (which boast no special
refinement) that it is a matter of temperament what kind of ultimate
answer one thinks is possible. The Humean tradition sees no evidence in the history of philosophy that any philosopher has ever
succeeded in producing a general metaphysics which established
the first or the third type of explanation. Hence, it is argued that to
postulate the necessary being of God on the ground that *otherwise*
(that is, if God did not exist) there would be no explanation for the
beings and facts of the universe is merely to turn a reasonable predi-
lection as to what one will seek in metaphysics into a dogmatic principle which presupposes what is to be shown: that there really is a
self-explanatory explainer of all things. This is surely what a significant number of minor philosophers have done.

This final problem can be properly answered only as follows: It
would indeed be a mistake to argue that God must exist because
otherwise there would be no explanation for what is the case; perhaps, after all, there is none. But it is not a mistake to say God must
exist because *otherwise it would not be possible* that there be an
explanation of what is the case. The relation between the possibility
of explanation and the existence of God is a purely logical one; it is
also a purely logical matter to decide whether such an explanation
is possible. Hence, it will be primarily a matter of logical analysis to
decide whether God exists. We shall address these matters below.

SECTION 2: LOGICAL AND REAL POSSIBILITY

A: Historical Hypotheses

When we look at the statements of those philosophers (Aquinas,
Scotus, Spinoza, Leibniz) who have claimed that God exists necessarily, we must bear in mind that they did not always consider a

necessary proposition to be analytic (as is perfectly evident when Aquinas distinguished between a *necessitas de dicto* and a *necessitas de re*); for there must be some necessary truths which we cannot formulate, and there may be some conceptual schemes which are impoverished. The obvious intent of these writers, who antedated Kant's concept of the synthetic a priori proposition (which is non-analytic but necessary), is to make a much stronger claim than that which I take Kant to have been making. We shall investigate the relation of real and logical necessity here, and in the next subsection shall develop derived concepts, adequate for philosophical theology and formulated independently (though in the light of these historical considerations).

All these writers held the Principle of Sufficient Reason in one form or another, although it was chiefly Spinoza, Leibniz, Wolff, the later scholastics, and some of those they influenced (e.g., Schopenhauer), who explicitly formulated it as a basic metaphysical principle. In terms of the principle that there is a sufficient reason for or explanation of everything which is the case, we can both understand the sense in which these philosophers thought God's existence to be necessary, and describe the concept of necessity they possessed in such a way that it becomes fairly evident that the really necessary and logically necessary are co-extensive for them.

On many occasions Duns Scotus asserted that God's existence is necessary. Consider one of his arguments:

It is proved that excluding every cause whether intrinsic or extrinsic of its existence other than the thing itself, it is on account of the thing itself impossible for it not to exist. The proof: *It is not possible for something not to exist unless something either positively or privatively incompatible can exist,*[18] because it must always be that one of two contradictories is true. There can be nothing which is not compossible with the uncausable being; nothing either positively or privatively incompossible can exist, whether it derives from the thing itself or from something else. It cannot derive in the first manner, because then it would derive *ex se* . . . and thus incompossibles would exist simultaneously; and by a like reason neither would exist since you concede by positing that which is incompossible that the uncausable thing would not be at all; and the converse also follows. Nor can it derive in

---

[18] It may clarify this for us to take "positively incompatible" to mean "logically incompatible," and "privatively incompatible" to mean "causally incompatible."

the second way because no caused thing can have a more powerful or more tenacious existence from a cause than an uncausable being has from itself, since the causable depends in being, the uncausable does not. *The possibility of the causable to exist does not entail its existence as it does with the uncausable;* nothing incompatible with that entity can exist from a cause unless it receives from that cause a more tenacious and powerful existence than is the existence of that to which it is incompatible.[19]

The sentiments of this profound, but not transparent, argument are exactly those we shall develop by the extensive discussion in sub-section B.

The statements I have italicized have obvious importance, both historical and logical. For instance, the second sentence italicized in the above quotation is merely one of the innumerable times the theological writings of Duns Scotus assert that the possibility of an uncausable being involves its existence; and this is obviously the origin of Leibniz's similar claim. Aquinas' third argument for the existence of God explicitly begins with the notion of possibility and proceeds to a derived notion of necessity.[20] And even such an early writer as Richard of St. Victor employed arguments for the existence of God based upon the notion of possibility.[21] It is the often-claimed logical relation of possibility to existence which we hope to clarify in our study of 'necessity'.

One discovers that '*p* is possible' functions in various ways for these authors, sometimes meaning '*p* is contingent' and sometimes '*p* is really or metaphysically possible'. Dismissing hypothetical possibility of all sorts (including various senses of "physically possible" which we use in talking about means-end relationships and about certain instrument-employment situations), we find two relevant senses in which the expression "possible" is used by classical philosophers.

1: *"p is possible"* means *"p is logically consistent,"* that is, *the logical terms of the statement p involve no incompatible elements; derivatively, "x is possible" (where x ranges over things of a certain sort) means "the appropriate existential statement or proposition that an x exists, p, is possible,*

[19] Duns Scotus, *De Primo Principio*, Chapter III, conclusion 5: "Incausabile est ex se necesse esse." The translation is mine; but an English text of the entire work is available as *A Treatise on God as First Principle*, tr. Allan B. Wolter, O.F.M. (Chicago: Franciscan Herald Press, 1966).

[20] *ST*, I, q. 2, a. 3, corpus.

[21] Richard of St. Victor, *De Trinitate*, P.L. vol. 196, cols. 891–896.

i.e., logically consistent." It is taken as a fundamental and trivial truth that if *p* is existential and *p* is possible, then it is possible that what *p* asserts to exist does in fact exist.

2: *"x is possible"* means:

a: *x is consistent (that is, it is consistent to say that there is an x, or that x exists), and*

b: *If x exists, there is a sufficient explanation of the fact that x exists to be found either in the nature of x, or in something else in combination with the nature of x, and*

c: *If x does not exist, either x could begin to exist or x could have begun to exist, and*

d: *If x does not exist, but could begin to exist or could have begun to exist, there actually exists or actually did exist something which could explain or could have explained the beginning-to-exist of x, or could have produced something which could be or could have been such an explanation.*[22]

For example, why did Aquinas claim that if there had been a time at which nothing existed, nothing would ever exist, and at no later time would it be possible for something to exist or begin to exist? We speak of something's being-possible-at-*t* only in contexts where we are discussing hypothetical possibility of one sort or another; but the possibility Aquinas has in mind is not hypothetical, it is absolute. This requires that the expression "at no later time" should not qualify the expression "be possible," but the expression "exist." Now why should it make any difference to the possibility of something whether or not something else existed in the past or at the same time? In the first sense of 'possibility', hereafter called 'possibility₁', it could make no difference. But in the second sense, hereafter called 'possibility₂', the claim is obvious: see condition (d). It seems evident that 'possibility₂' is the concept directly employed in Aquinas' reasoning. For, if nothing existed, nothing would be possible₂.

Duns Scotus argued similarly, frequently saying that for anything which does not exist but is possible, something else must exist or must have existed which could have produced it or some producer of it.[23] The meaning of Scotus' claim, like that of Aquinas', is obvious

---

[22] It is to be noted that these conditions are selected to fit scholastic usage, *not* because I shall define the terms "possible₂" or "really possible" in this way.

[23] Obviously, he must have been considering things compatible with what has occurred rather than things *alternative* to what has occurred.

if it is read in terms of 'possible$_2$', but is somewhat obscure if read as 'possible$_1$', unless being possible$_2$ is understood to be a logically necessary condition for being possible$_1$, which we shall show is indeed the case.

Why did the philosophers use "possible" in both senses, instead of selecting a separate word for 'possible$_2$'? Two hypotheses occur to me. The first is that the clear notion of 'the possible' as 'what is consistent' developed *after* the second sense came into use; for the earlier sense may have been that something which is not the case is possible if it is in principle producible, since God exists necessarily and can produce anything conceivable. After it became generally accepted that 'x is *conceivable*' is not the same as 'x is producible by God'—for there might be things that are conceivable to *someone* but are not in fact consistent—the notion of 'consistent *in itself*' or 'possible$_1$' developed. This explanation, which supposes the generation of the first out of the second sense by means of the distinction of 'being conceivable' from 'being *thought* to be conceivable', is quite plausible; for it is frequently the case that a concept like 'being conceivable' is developed and applied for some time, before the necessity of a distinction between 'being conceivable' and 'being thought by S to be conceivable' is apparent. The fact that we can be mistaken about the consistency of a concept is easy to demonstrate, once we have found some good examples (like the search for a largest number). Once this distinction is acknowledged, it no longer follows from 'S thinks x is conceivable' that x is conceivable. Hence, 'x is conceivable' becomes equivalent to 'x is consistent', 'x is possible$_1$'. However, the historical evidence is not decisive, since many uses of 'possible$_1$' can be found, even among very ancient philosophers.

Another explanation of the interchangeability of the two senses of "possible" is that the concepts were not clearly distinguished in the Middle Ages, or even later, because it was thought that anything which is impossible$_2$ is impossible$_1$ and that, given the omnipotence of God, whatever is possible$_1$ is possible$_2$. Hence, whatever is possible in either sense is possible in the other. It is even reasonable that both these historical hypotheses to account for the scholastics' failure to make regular and explicit distinctions between the concepts are true. But from a philosophical point of view the second is more important, since an assumption of this sort most certainly underlies a large number of Aquinas' and Scotus' statements.

Let us investigate the contention that whatever is impossible$_2$ is also impossible$_1$. For this purpose we shall construct an argument on behalf of what may have been the scholastic position in general and of what, as we have said, was certainly Duns Scotus' own position.

The form of the argument is as follows:[24]

1: *Suppose y is impossible$_2$. Is y impossible$_1$?*

2: *If y is impossible$_2$ then either (a), (b), (c), or (d) of the definition given below must be true.*

3: *But if (a), then y is impossible$_1$.*

4: *If (b), then y is impossible$_1$.*

5: *If (c), then y is impossible$_1$.*

6: *If (d), then y is impossible$_1$.*

7: *Therefore, if y is impossible$_2$, it is impossible$_1$.*

The definition: '*y is impossible$_2$*' if and only if:

a: *y is inconsistent; or*

b: *y does not exist, could not have begun to exist, and could not begin to exist; or*

c: *y exists and there is no explanation of the fact which can be found or could have been found in the nature of y or in anything else combined with the nature of y; or*

d: *y does not exist, but could begin to exist or could have begun to exist, and there does not exist and has never existed anything which could be or could have been an explanation of the existence of y.*

The argument proceeds as follows:

If (a) is true, then y is impossible$_1$.

Now, since 'God exists' is possible$_1$, the only things which can fulfill condition (b) are things that are inconsistent, since God would have active power to produce any consistent state of affairs.

(c) cannot be true, since the proposition itself is inconsistent. For if something exists, it must be of one sort or another and must be a thing; there

---

[24] This form of argument and the actual instance of it we give below are in a practical sense superfluous for a scholastic. If God can do anything, then God can bring about whatever is consistent. Hence whatever is possible$_1$ is possible$_2$. But whatever is possible$_2$ is possible$_1$, because 'being possible$_1$' is the first condition of being possible$_2$. Therefore, possible$_1$ and possible$_2$ entail each other (since God's existence and omnipotence are considered necessary truths).

cannot exist a thing which cannot have explanatory factors either in itself or something else.[25]

(d) cannot be true (if y is consistent), since God exists and is capable of producing anything which is consistent, and since whatever could be the case could have had an explanation.

Hence it follows that what is impossible$_2$ is impossible$_1$.

Now we must take note of a certain objection. It might be argued that all the Scotist arguments from the possibility of God to the existence of God are defective, since they employ as equivalent to 'possible$_1$' the second sense, 'possible$_2$', which we have explicated by employing the proposition 'God exists'; for Duns Scotus writes that *nothing consistent is both non-existent and unproducible.* (It would be interesting to prove this or to disprove it, would it not?) But such an objection is at least partially misdirected. The proposition 'God exists' was employed in establishing that condition (d) of the definition of 'impossible$_2$' cannot be fulfilled unless y is also impossible$_1$; but that proposition is not *part of the definition* of either sense of "possible"; nor is the proposition 'Whatever exists has an explanation'. Moreover, the entire argument can be restated so that it assumes only that an omnipotent being is possible$_1$ and that such a being can produce whatever is logically contingent.

To this it might be rejoined that the proposition 'whatever is impossible$_2$ is impossible$_1$' is implicitly employed by Scotus in the proof of the existence of God, and a *fortiori* in the proof of the necessity of the proposition 'God exists'. Hence, such an argument is circular, since the truth of one of the premises is dependent upon the truth of the conclusion. There are two things to be noticed about this. First, this same objection might be made against any argument by a Christian for the necessity and truth of the existence of God from contingent premises, since one of his crucial positions (although it is not a premise) is that the truth of every contingent statement is logically dependent upon the truth of the conclusion, in the sense that the premises could not be true unless the conclusion is, since the argument is valid. In every valid argument, this is the case. Does the objection maintain that every valid argument is circular?

[25] It is because the relationship between 'possibility$_2$' and 'possibility$_1$' is essential to arguments for the existence of God and because the *strong* (a priori) form of the Principle of Reason is employed in the definition of 'possibility$_2$' that the "Humean" doubts of Section important.

If the objection is amended to a claim that the two kinds of possibility would not be equivalent were it not the case that God exists, it could be replied that no equivalence at all would hold if God did not exist, since 'God exists' is necessary. In the proof of a logical truth, the premises of a valid argument are not logically independent of the conclusion, since their negation is entailed by the negation of the conclusion.

Yet it must be admitted that there is a circumstantial defect in Scotus' arguments, one which he apparently did not notice: namely, that in order to come to know (by philosophical examination) the truth of the premise stating the logical equivalence of the two kinds of possibility (and all Scotus' arguments for the existence of God logically presuppose this equivalence), one would have to know that the conclusion 'God exists' is true. Otherwise, one would not possess a satisfactory reason for believing that nothing which is logically consistent (and, thus, possible$_1$) could fulfill condition (d) for being impossible$_2$. Hence, Scotus' arguments *as he presented them*—in a context where the two kinds of possibility were treated as equivalent —are epistemically circular.

It should be emphasized that the relationships between the definitions and the argument are constructions of what I take to be the conceptual connections that Duns Scotus and other scholastics supposed. I am certainly not ignoring the fact that we can argue for the equivalence of 'impossible$_1$' and 'impossible$_2$' without supposing that God (an omnipotent being) actually exists; in fact, this is the improvement I expect to offer over what I take to be Scotus' assumptions. In a word, to prove that nothing can satisfy condition (d) without being impossible$_1$, we need only show that for any logically contingent existential statement, p, there is some other consistent existential statement, q, such that there is a consistent law-like universal r of the form 'if q then p' which, when conjoined to make $(q \cdot r / \therefore \cdot p)$, provides a valid deduction. This will show that p is explicable in terms of $q \cdot r$. As long as we suppose that there are at least two existents, at least one of which is logically contingent, it will be inconsistent to say of any one of them that condition (d) is fulfilled but that the existent in question is still possible.

In view of these considerations, there is nothing in principle wrong with equating the two kinds of possibility. We shall take another ave-

nue to the same terminus, but shall lean heavily upon the considerations mentioned above.

Returning to more central matters, two questions can be asked
about the proof of equivalence between the two sorts of possibility
and what is proved: First, is the equivalence between the statements
'x is impossible$_1$' and 'x is impossible$_2$' a material equivalence, or a
logical equivalence? (Notice that this depends upon whether we take
[b, or c, or d] to be false for any consistent thing because it is impos-
sible$_1$, or because it is impossible$_2$ that the disjunction should be fulfilled.) Second, in the claim that God exists necessarily, which will
have to be introduced to answer the first question, is the corresponding claim "It is impossible that God does not exist" to be read as 'im-
possible$_1$' or 'impossible$_2$'?

Neither of these questions was asked by the eminent medieval
writers; nor, as far as I can determine, were they discussed by those
post-Leibniz writers, both scholastic and non-scholastic, who took so
much interest in the Principle of Sufficient Reason. Two causes for
this neglect are to be found. One is that the reasoning I have outlined
appeared to be in no need of analysis, since the proposition 'God
exists' was thought to be true and absolutely necessary (thus making
the equivalence *logical*); instead, the dispute centered upon the
means of showing that the proposition was true. The other is that the
kind of necessity ascribed to the existence of God was not always
labeled, but when it was, it was called *metaphysical, unconditional*,
or *absolute necessity*—to emphasize its objective or factual character. Furthermore, in those days when logic was widely thought to
be concerned with the laws of thought, and metaphysics with the
structure of reality, there was unqualified confidence in that correspondence between the categories of thought and of reality which
some ordinary-language philosophers presuppose today; but since it
was a confidence about correspondence of *categories*, terms applicable to the one were not often applied to the other. Moreover, no
one was very likely to pursue the question of whether it was merely a
contingent fact that 'x is possible$_1$' and 'x is possible$_2$' were exten-
sionally equivalent; since the obvious answer would seem to be
"No," given that the proposition 'God exists' is necessary. That this
reasoning was epistemically circular went unnoticed; for who would
see that the logical equivalence of the two sorts of possibility must

be premised in order to deduce that it is necessarily true that God exists, and that the necessity of 'God exists' was, in fact, being premised to deduce the equivalence of the two kinds of possibility? After all, this would only mean that premises and conclusion were logically equivalent.

Turning to answers that might have been constructed, if the above questions had been addressed, we find that the reasoning which related the two senses of "possible" is not fully satisfactory.

To the first question, it may be replied that the equivalence between the two statements 'x is possible$_1$' and 'x is possible$_2$' is logical. But this requires that everything entailed by the truth-conditions for 'x is possible$_2$'[26] be logically necessary. Condition (b)—"If x exists, there exists an explanation of this fact either in the nature of x or in some other existent in conjunction with the nature of x"—entails 'if there exists anything y which is not its own explanation, there exists something else z which *is* its explanation'. This proposition, which is a form of the Principle of Sufficient Reason, could be considered necessary and a partial definition of "thing," as was maintained by the proof of the equivalence we examined above, and was adumbrated in the medieval Aristotelian metaphysics, which required that every substance be explicable in terms of its formal and material causes or have distinct efficient and final causes as elements of its explanation. If we do not incorporate this proposition into the definition of "thing," then it stands as an explicit assumption whose truth is not apparent.

More important, entailed by (d) is this: if some thing which does not exist is possible, then something exists (or has existed or will exist) which is capable of producing it or some producer of it. This does not appear to be logically necessary; but surprisingly enough, it is considerably more plausible than the conditions supposed by (b), above.

Two lines of argument are open:

(i) If the statement 'x is possible' is necessary, then the statement 'If x does not exist but is consistent, then something exists, has existed, or will exist which can or could produce x' is necessary, since accord-

---

[26] As given on p. 110, above.

ing to condition (d) of the definition above, the latter follows from the former; but where is the contradiction in its denial?

One could say that there is indeed a contradiction in denying 'If something x does not exist but is consistent, then there exists, has existed, or will exist something which can or could produce x', for 'God exists and can produce whatever is possible' is a necessary truth; denying the former entails the denial of the latter, and therefore leads to a contradiction, because a statement entailing the denial of a necessary truth entails a contradiction. However, this recourse in the justification of the claim that whatever is impossible₂ is impossible₁ renders the following reasoning circular:

that God or an unproducible and unpreventable being must exist, if God is logically possible; for God can be possible₂ only if actually existing, and whatever is possible₁ (logically possible) is possible₂ (really possible); etc.

That is, if we justify the claim that 'possible₂' is equivalent to 'possible₁' by invoking the necessity of 'God exists' as a premise, then we cannot, without universal epistemic circularity, invoke the equivalence of the two sorts of possibility as a premise in the proof of the existence of God. This is just what Duns Scotus does, and what causes his arguments for the existence of God ultimately to beg the question.

Let it be observed that we did not say that 'x is possible' is *analytic;* hence we are not committed to saying that the proposition it entails is analytic. Moreover, although every proposition entailed by an analytic proposition is necessary, not every proposition so entailed need be analytic. Therefore, even if 'x is possible' were analytic, it would not follow from that alone that 'something exists which is or could be an explanation of the existence of x' would also be analytic. It seems then that the sense of "necessary" which is connected with the iterative modality belonging to possibility statements need not be that of analyticity; "$\square \lozenge p$" need not mean "it is analytic that p is possible."

Now whether a contradiction is derivable from our saying that something is impossible which is in fact possible depends upon the language system we employ and the completeness of its conceptual interrelation; theoretically, a contradiction *should* follow, and its failure to do so indicates a serious theoretical defect in the language. Whether such completeness is indeed to be found in our natural language is doubtful. If someone says "Unicorns are impossible₁," how can we show him that he is mistaken without producing one for him to see? Yet his statement is necessarily false and should entail a contradiction. It does not seem to be the case that a contradiction or semantic inconsistency can in practice, or even in principle, be derived from every necessarily false statement; our ability to do that depends upon the structure of the language, and the completeness and simplicity of its transformation rules: it is possible to *assert* some propositions in a language in which we cannot decisively *prove* that they are necessarily false. Hence, failure to derive the contradiction may indicate that we should propose tighter connections among certain concepts or further inference rules. Thus for ordinary language, and for theoretical concept-systems built upon ordinary language, we have no reason to expect the formal theorem that a contradiction can be disclosed in a finite number of steps to be unexceptionally applicable.

If one proposed to avoid these points by suggesting that condition (d)[27] is analytic because the sense of "possible" in the expression "x does not exist but is possible" is 'possible₂', then the reasoning which relates logical and real possibility is still circular; for in the definition of 'possible₂' we would now be employing the definiendum in condition (d), making the definition itself circular. Therefore, we must accept the first account of the reasoning, with the attendant consequence that a sense of "necessary" turns up which we cannot fully explicate in terms of syntactical or semantical inconsistencies derivable from the denials.

It may now be clear why the second question—"How are we to understand the claim 'It is impossible that God should not exist'?"— is important. The hypothesis that its negation is analytic is unlikely, if only because 'exists' is an odd thing to treat as a predicate. Either we can say that God's *not* existing is impossible because the negation 'God exists' is necessary, in that undefined and elusive sense we have just encountered while considering the reasoning used to show the equivalence of the two senses of "possible"; or else we can say

---

[27] In the definition on p. 110.

that it is impossible₂ that God should not exist. If we take the former
course, then we must relate this new kind of necessity to the familiar
logical necessity. This is our constructive project in Part B.

It is easy enough to show that 'God does not exist' is impossible₂,
since it fulfills at least two conditions of that concept, given above.
Let us call the purported fact that God does not exist *p*. If *p* is impossible₂, then either

a: *p is inconsistent; or*

b: *p is false and could not begin to be the case and could not have begun
to be the case; or*

c: *p is the case and there is no explanation of that fact which can be or
could have been found in either the nature of p or that of anything else; or*

d: *p is false but could become or could have become the case, and yet
there does not exist, and has never existed, anything which could be or
could have been a sufficient explanation for p's being the case.*

If *p* should be the case, then (c) would be fulfilled, since God's nature is not inconsistent and therefore cannot explain the nonexistence
of the being which has that nature; and God is by nature uncausable
and unpreventable, so that nothing *else* could explain His nonexistence, for then the negation of that explanation would have become
an extrinsic causally necessary condition for God's existence.

If *p* should be false, condition (b) is fulfilled; for if God exists, nothing could bring it about that God should cease to exist and nothing
could have prevented the existence of God. This reasoning parallels
that for condition (c).

Therefore, *p* fulfills the condition of being impossible₂, and does so
with logical necessity, since the disjunction *p* v ~*p* is a tautology.

It is interesting to consider condition (d) briefly. Suppose we assume
that *p* is false; that *p* might have become the case or could become
the case; and yet that there does not exist, and never has existed, anything which could explain *p's* being the case. This is equivalent to
saying that something might become the case which is such that it is
impossible that either its own nature or anything else which exists
should explain it.²⁸ Now if it could be shown that whatever is logically
contingent could have, or could have had, an explanation, then *in*

---

²⁸ This is just what Scotus says is impossible in the passage we quoted at the outset.

principle a contradiction will follow from saying both that p is false and that p is consistent, because the only statements which are both consistent and false are logically contingent. The result would be an explicit contradiction from the supposition that God does not exist. This is obviously what Duns Scotus, Avicenna, and many others had in mind; it is certainly worth developing, is it not? Moreover, what we have just noticed will serve to define a (new?) kind of necessity and form the basis of arguments we shall use later; p is necessary if postulating its falsity and postulating its consistency are incompatible (that is, will lead to a contradiction). This necessity is reflected in the relation between the object-language denial of a proposition and the metalanguage statement that the object-language proposition is consistent. This is broader than the usual concept of necessity, since it includes both semantic and syntactic necessity, as well as the real or factual necessity which attaches to some propositions whose negations are impossible$_2$.

Now it seems that whatever is impossible$_2$ and is not the case is either inconsistent or else could have (or could have had) an explanation, but that such an explanation, which could have existed, does not exist. But 'God does not exist' could not be explained (except upon the supposition that its negation is inconsistent), since it is logically impossible that something should have prevented the existence of God or should come to prevent it. Therefore, if God does not exist, it must be because 'God exists' is logically impossible. But the latter assumption is false; therefore the former is also false. Moreover, the latter supposition is impossible; therefore the former is also impossible. This is the basic reasoning of Duns Scotus and the outline of what we shall adopt.

From the things which have turned up in our analysis it should be clear that philosophers like Duns Scotus reasonably thought that there really is a connection between 'possible$_2$' and 'possible$_1$', a connection which some writers stated in this form: A state of affairs which violates the Principle of Sufficient Reason is a state of affairs which violates the principle of identity or of non-contradiction. Or, as Scotus put it, "It is not possible for something *not* to exist unless something either positively or privatively incompatible can exist." It should be evident from what we have said so far that belief in the grave consequences of violating the Principle of Sufficient Reason was not reached by the leaps and bounds we find in the reconstructions offered by such neo-scholastic writers as Garrigou-Lagrange (where the invalidity is obvious), but by a subtle process which, although implicit in medieval writings and perhaps not fully satisfactory, was still philosophically reasonable. For it is not invalidity at all which is in point; it is merely the circularity of the reasoning process (which guarantees its validity).

In concluding these comments upon traditional philosophers, we may say that educated conjecture as to what reasoning underlay the medieval treatment of logical possibility (possibility₁) and real possibility (possibility₂) as coextensive and equivalent reveals that there was a plausible case for holding that nothing consistent was really impossible (after all, God could produce it). That this might be said to beg the question of the existence of God and of the logical necessity of God's existence, we admit.

But let it be noted that, strictly, it need only be *consistent* that God, an unproducible, self-accounting being, should exist for it to be *true* that the logically possible and the really possible be equivalent. If it is possible that *p* is possible, then *p* is possible. If it is possible that God should exist and if, God existing, a given state of affairs is really possible, then the given state of affairs *is* possible! Therefore, the circularity which plagued the medievals was actually *incidental* and easily eliminable, with the result that the two kinds of possibility are logically equivalent.

B: Constructive analysis

Now the lessons of these reflections upon history can be applied to the development of a simple and direct concept of real necessity and the construction of an a priori argument for the existence of God; and we can directly attack the questions of whether there is another sense of "necessary," a sense distinct from but not opposed to 'analytic' (as explicated in such terms as "the predicate includes or is included in the subject," etc.), by which we can explain the claim that God necessarily exists, in that He has unconditionable being. The matter is complicated, not only because the concept required may be difficult to define, but also because the distinction between analytic and non-analytic statements is elusive; there is confusion as to what we distinguish *from*. Such skilled logical analysts as White, Quine, and Goodman have shown that the concept 'analytic' is closely related to the very unsatisfactorily explained concept 'synonymous'. Further, the considerations, urged by Putnam and others, that a statement may change its status over time—from analytic to contingent (synthetic) or vice versa—indicate confusion about the notion of "same proposition" or "same statement." Nor can this confusion be satisfactorily resolved by simply stipulating that nothing be counted as the same proposition as something else if the two differ in modality; this would make it inexplicable how people using the same form of words and talking about the same objects (if not facts) should gradually cease to assert one thing about those objects and begin to assert something quite different, which may not be about the "objects" at all in the same direct sense as that of the formerly empirical or synthetic assertion.

This confused state of affairs in logic (involving terms like "analytic," "synthetic," "contingent," "possible," "necessary," "empirical," "a priori," etc.) makes it somewhat difficult to say precisely *what* the sense of "necessity" we are seeking is to be distinguished from. Because we cannot explicate the concepts 'synonymy', 'analyticity', and 'same proposition'—and for that matter, cannot explain what *propositions* are and whether they are ontological constituents of the world—our stipulations will very probably have to be modified when more progress is made.

The original trouble over the logical status of 'God exists' was not caused by perplexities the logicians discovered, but rather by Hume's bold assertions that (1) all truths can be divided into true statements which express relations among ideas, and true statements which express matters of fact; and (2) all necessity belongs to the former class; and (3) the necessity of the former class is characterized by the fact that explicitly contradictory propositions can be derived from the negations of such statements. This was an assertoric denial of the supposition of Aquinas and many scholastics that "God exists" is a *real and absolute necessity*, a truth of *fact* (in a context where real and logical necessity are correlative).

Although we have discovered since Hume's time that the concept 'contradiction' is not as clear as Hume supposed, and that the talk of ·· deriving contradictions runs into the same difficulties as the talk about synonymy which is required for other explanations of necessity, such knowledge does not push our inquiry forward. We are not in pursuit of an attack upon the borderline between what is necessary and what is contingent (or synthetic, or empirical, or whatever you choose to call it); rather, our concern is to move the borderline over to include some matters of fact—some statements asserting existence—*within* the category of "the necessary." Thus, the philosopher of religion did not get his problem from the logician; yet now that we are engaged in the project of moving the borderline between necessity and contingency over into the realm of the existential, we are discommoded by the fact that the logicians have—through their very skill, not through ineptitude—blurred the matter so that, instead of moving the sword of Damocles, we may end up moving a bundle of fuzz.

We will dispense with direct consideration of the details of the dispute concerning analyticity and necessity and admit that there is no universally satisfactory criterion for inconsistency in formal languages, much less in informal ones. Some of the technicalities discovered by logicians apply by analogy to the unformalized and partly formalized natural language we use, and we shall keep in mind what may be learned from their work. But we shall still employ the following concepts which involve the basic concept of 'inconsistent', in the firm conviction that inconsistencies can be recognized when they are properly displayed, and that, moreover, if we delay positive argument until we have clarified that notion, we shall never undertake any of the matters we most desire.

1: Logical Necessity: A statement expresses a logical necessity if it expresses either a syntactical or a semantical necessity. (In terms of logical necessity, we define, as usual, logical possibility.)

2: Syntactical Necessity: A statement expresses a syntactical necessity if it has a formal (grammatical schema) counterpart from whose negation we can deduce a syntactical contradiction of the form $(p \cdot \sim p)$; syntactical contradictions may be of two sorts: truth-functional or quantificational. (This difference becomes very important in Chapter VII.)

3: Semantical Necessity: A statement expresses a semantical necessity if its negation involves semantic inconsistency. The former depends upon logical form, the latter upon conceptual interrelationships.

From these concepts and the a priori principle called Principle E, the Principle of Explicability, we shall develop the concept of 'real necessity' and through it define "real possibility." Then we shall argue that what is *really* impossible is *logically* impossible and that, in particular, the nonexistence of God is impossible. Further refinements upon these concepts appear in Section 3 of Chapter VII.

1: PRESENTATION OF PRINCIPLE E

It is necessarily the case that:

a: For any consistent state of affairs p (which involves the existence or nonexistence of something), it is possible that there should have been an explanation (or accounting) for its having been the case.

And it is necessarily the case that:

b: If q (a state of affairs logically distinct from p) should explain p, then q entails the existence of some thing or another.

Using the following terms:

E = *explains*
pEp = *p explains p (p is self-explanatory)*
qEp = *q explains p*

—we can use a more formal statement of this principle.[29] It is necessarily the case that:

a: $(p)\{\{[p \rightarrow (\exists x)(Fx)] \lor [p \rightarrow \sim(\exists x)(Fx)]\} \rightarrow \Diamond \{[\exists q][qEp] \cdot [\sim(pEp) \rightarrow q \neq p]\}\}.$

b: $\Box(\exists q)(\exists p)\{\{[p \rightarrow (\exists x)(Fx)] \lor [p \rightarrow \sim(\exists x)(Fx)] \cdot [qEp \cdot \sim(pEp)]\} \rightarrow [q \rightarrow (\exists x)(\Phi x)]\}.$

There are only two sorts of consistent states of affairs: the auto-explicable and the hetero-explicable. Principle E asserts that *any* given consistent state of affairs which is not equivalent to, and does not entail, the totality of what is contingent but actual is in principle explicable, even though in actuality it may lack an explanation (either because it is not actually the case, or because it simply has no explanation). Those states of affairs which are hetero-explicable, and which

---

[29] This formalization is not intended as an element of a formal language or as a subterfuge for a formal excellence we do not possess, where all relations and predicates are well defined in terms of stipulated basic concepts. These formalizations are merely *schematizations* or shorthand versions of statements made in English and intended to be read in English; their purpose is merely to assist the intuitive grasp of what we claim, not to suggest that it is a logical theorem in some formal system.

are actually explained by something logically distinct, are explained only by a state of affairs which logically involves (that is, is not possible *without*) an existent. Sometimes hetero-explanation involves the higher-level being's producing the lower (metaphysical causality: creator-creature, dreamer-dream); sometimes cause and effect are on the same level (natural causality: someone's striking a match causes it to burst into flame); sometimes the relation is between agent and action (what Jones did was produced through his own decision to act). Auto-explanation involves, evidently, self-explanation or self-accounting through the intrinsic structure of the state of affairs. While it is possible that an actual event or fact may be hetero-explicable without being hetero-explained, precisely because it has no explanation at all (and I shall contend in Chapter VII that there must be such events in the universe), it cannot happen that something auto-explicable is not in fact auto-explained.[30] We shall use the expressions "self-explanatory" and "self-accounting" to mean "auto-explained"; and it should be clear that what is auto-explicable is also self-explanatory by virtue of its being self-explained.

A state of affairs will be shown to be self-explanatory if its contradictory is shown to be incompatible with Principle E, with the statement that every given consistent state of affairs (with the restrictions provided in the preceding paragraph) is either auto- or hetero-explicable. A moment's consideration will reveal that no state of affairs which involves the existence or nonexistence of something or another, and is expressed by means of statements asserting existence or nonexistence, can be such that both it and its contradictory are incompatible with E (assuming that E is consistent); hence any state of affairs whose contradictory is incompatible with E will have this characteristic: it will not be causable, even in principle. If $\sim p$ is uncausable in principle (as it would have to be for it to be incompatible with E), so also is p. If $\sim p$ is not auto-explicable and is also not hetero-explicable, what would have to obtain? The answer: $\sim p$ must be false in all possible worlds, or inconsistent; inexplicable because impossible. If $\sim p$ is false in all possible worlds, p is true in all possible worlds, and is auto-explicable because it is compatible with E and yet is not hetero-

---

[30] See pages 185–186 of Chapter IV, below.

explicable. Hence *to demonstrate that a state of affairs is self-explana-tory, we demonstrate the incompatibility of its negation with* E.[31]

Are we not saying that any consistent but (in the broad sense speci-fied above) uncausable state of affairs must be actual? Indeed we are; and to deny this is to run into logical conflict with E. The logically con-tingent and the hetero-explicable are co-extensive.

Two Auxiliary Proofs: The following arguments show that a state of affairs, ~p, is self-explanatory if its contradictory, p, is incompatible with E. On the left we use a convenient shorthand; on the right, the statements themselves.

Argument 1

1: Suppose p entails ~E	1: *p is incompatible with E: supposi-tion*
2: ~Sp · ~Hp	2: *p is neither auto- nor hetero-explic-able*
3: Ap entails (Sp V Hp)	3: *If p is explicable, it is either auto- or hetero-explicable*
4: Ap → ~(~Sp · ~Hp)	4: *If p is explicable, it is not neither-auto- nor-hetero-explicable: De Mor-gan*
5: ~Ap	5: *Therefore p is not explicable: modus tollens, 2, 4*
6: ◇p → Ap	6: *But Principle É states that if p is pos-sible, p is explicable*
7: ~◇p	7: *Therefore, p is not possible: modus tollens, 5, 6*
8: □~p	8: *So ~p is necessary: def.*
9: □~p → ~pA~p	9: *Whatever is necessary accounts for itself (this follows from the definition of "self-accounting," to be found on page 135 below)*
10: ~pA~p	10: *Therefore ~p accounts for itself: mo-dus ponens, 8, 9*

Therefore, if p is incompatible with E, *then ~p is self-explanatory.*

None of these statements tells us directly what it means for some-thing to be self-explanatory, although we have a way to decide whether a state of affairs is self-explanatory or is not. Yet we cannot go beyond our earlier statement that a *state of affairs is self-account-*

---

[31] Another way of demonstrating that a state of affairs is self-accounting is given on page 135, below.

Argument 2

1: p is incompatible with E: supposition

2: p is neither auto- nor hetero-explicable

3: If p is explicable, it is either auto- or hetero-explicable

4: If p is explicable, it is not neither-auto-nor-hetero-explicable

5: Therefore p is not explicable: modus tollens, 2, 4

6: But Principle E states that if p is possible, p is explicable

7: Conjoin steps 3 and 6

8: Follow rule of Hypothetical Syllogism, to derive: If p is possible, p is auto- or hetero-explicable (E)

9: Principle E is, by supposition, consistent.

10: If E is consistent, no statement is such that both it and its negation are incompatible with E

11: So any statement you choose will be such that it or its denial is consistent with E

12: So either p or ~p is compatible with E: UI

13: p is not compatible with E: supposition of line 1

14: Therefore, ~p is compatible with E: DS, 12, 13

15: Therefore, ~p is possible (because all that is compatible with what is consistent is itself consistent).

16: So ~p is either auto- or hetero-explicable: MP, 15, 8

17: Every hetero-explicable state of affairs has a hetero-explicable contrary

18: If ~p is hetero-explicable, so is p: UI, 17

19: p is not hetero-explicable: simplification of line 2

20: Therefore, ~p is not hetero-explicable: modus tollens, 17, 18

21: Therefore, ~p is auto-explicable (or self-explaining): disjunctive syllogism, 20, 16

1: p entails $\sim E$

2: $\sim Sp \cdot \sim Hp$

3: $Ap \rightarrow (Sp \lor Hp)$

4: $Ap \rightarrow \sim(\sim Sp \cdot \sim Hp)$

5: $\sim Ap$

6: $\diamond p \rightarrow Ap$

7: $\diamond p \rightarrow Ap \cdot Ap \rightarrow (Sp \lor Hp)$

8: $\diamond p \rightarrow (Sp \lor Hp)$

9: $\diamond E$

10: $\diamond E \rightarrow (q)[\diamond(q \cdot E) \lor \diamond(\sim q \cdot E)]$

11: $(q)[\diamond(q \cdot E) \lor \diamond(\sim q \cdot E)]$

12: $[\diamond(p \cdot E) \lor \diamond(\sim p \cdot E)]$

13: $\sim\diamond(p \cdot E)$

14: $\therefore \diamond(\sim p \cdot E)$

15: $\diamond \sim p$

16: $(S\sim p \lor H\sim p)$

17: $(q)(Hq \rightarrow H\sim q)$

18: $H\sim p \rightarrow Hp$

19: $\sim(Hp)$

20: $\sim(H\sim p)$

21: $\therefore S\sim p$

If E is consistent and if p entails ~E, then ~p is self-explanatory.

ing if the structure of what is the case accounts for its being the case. Further explications will be merely repetitious. We have set forth a procedure for showing that a proposition is self-explanatory; this provides a recursive definition of self-explanation.

A reductionist analysis of 'explain' or 'account for', in which we show the concept to be eliminable in terms of some logically prior class of ideas, is out of the question; it cannot be done. As is obvious in the work of Aristotle and Plato, 'explaining' or 'accounting for' is not a species or subclass of some activity; nor is 'being the explanation of . . .' or 'accounting for . . .' a sub-set or species of some more familiar relation, in terms of which we can fruitfully "reduce" the problematic concept; rather, these concepts express an ultimate and irreducible metaphysical simple. *To-be* and *to-explain* (i.e., "to account for") are primary and uneliminable elements of ontology. The epistemic relation by which one proposition is said to explain or account for another is *not* the same as this real relation, which is what is discovered and expressed when we "give" the explanations or account of things.

2: ARGUMENT THAT PRINCIPLE E IS A PRIORI

If there is any substance to the traditional thought concerning logical modalities, a statement *qua* logically modally qualified is a priori. By "is a priori" I mean "either is inconsistent or has an inconsistent negation." Both parts of E are modally qualified; hence E is a priori.[32]

3: DEFINITION OF "REALLY POSSIBLE" AND "REALLY IMPOSSIBLE"

"Real" or "factual" possibility is defined in terms of the possibility of accounting or explanation. Thus a state of affairs is really possible if and only if it is possible that it should have had an explanation; more generally, *p is really possible if and only if p is consistent with* E. We shall use the following symbols:

$\Box p$ = *Logically necessary that p*

$\Diamond p$ = *Logically possible that p*

---

[32] Some formal logicians have held that it is not true that all iterative or second-level modalities are "necessary." They think that in some cases $\bigcirc(\Diamond p)$: that $\Diamond p$ may be contingent. It may be possible to construct a consistent formal system which embodies the situation, although the absence of a general test for the consistency of such systems makes it difficult to evaluate. But in any case, the formal perplexities which stimulate construction of such calculi have no counterpart that I know of in the less well-structured hybrid of ordinary English which we use to consider the existence of God.

$\bigcirc p$ = *Logically contingent that p*

$\boxed{\text{R}}\, p$ = *Really necessary that p*

$\Diamondblack\, p$ = *Really possible that p*

$\circledR\, p$ = *Really contingent that p*

Thus, we will construct our definitions:

1:    $\Box p \equiv \Box \sim (\sim p)$
2:    $\Diamond p \equiv \sim \Box (\sim p)$
3:    $\bigcirc p \equiv \Diamond p \cdot \Diamond \sim p$
4:    $\Box \sim p \equiv \sim \Diamond p$
5:    $\boxed{\text{R}}\, p \equiv \Box \sim (\sim p \cdot E)$
6:    $\Diamondblack\, p \equiv \Diamond (p \cdot E)$
7:    $\sim \Diamondblack\, p \equiv \Box \sim (p \cdot E)$
8:    $\boxed{\text{R}} \sim p \equiv \Box \sim (p \cdot E)$
9:    $\circledR\, p \equiv \Diamond (p \cdot E) \cdot \Diamond (\sim p \cdot E)$

4: THE LOGICAL EQUIVALENCE OF REAL AND LOGICAL POSSIBILITY

It is obvious that if $\boxed{\text{R}}\, p$ ("*p* is really necessary") is defined in terms of the logical incompatibility of some state of affairs, $\sim p$, with a necessary proposition, E, then $\sim p$ must be necessarily false whenever *p* is really necessary. For $\sim p$ is either consistent or inconsistent. If inconsistent, it is not logically possible and cannot be really possible; if consistent, $\sim p$ will be consistent with every necessary truth, since whatever is logically possible is compatible with everything which is logically necessary. Hence, if *p* is really necessary, $\sim p$ cannot be consistent, or it would be compatible with E. Therefore, since "$\sim p$" can stand for any proposition you choose, we have a fully general proof of the logical equivalence of the two kinds of possibility. This realizes one of the pivotal presuppositions of classical natural theology.

5: THE INCOMPATIBILITY OF PRINCIPLE E AND "NOTHING EXISTS"

1: *Suppose 'Nothing exists' is to be:* $\sim [(\exists x)(\exists F)(Fx)]$

2: *Let* $\sim [(\exists x)(\exists F)(Fx)]$ *equal by definition:* a

3: *Now, if we assume E, as well as a, we can deduce* $(\exists q)(qEa)$ *from E, by substituting a for p in the statement of that principle.*

4: $\sim (aEa)$; *for in* (aEa) a *is either necessary or contingent. But* a *cannot be necessary, since we know* a *is in fact false; hence,* a *is either contingent or impossible. Assume* a *is contingent. As is made evident below (page 185)*

the contingent cannot be auto-explicable. Hence, (aEa) will be inconsistent
if a is contingent.

5: $\{(\exists q)(qEa) \to [q \to (\exists x)(\exists F)(Fx)]\}$ by part (b) of E.

6: $(\exists q)(qEa) \to (\exists x)(\exists F)(Fx)$. From 5.

7: $(k)(l)\{(kEl) \to \Diamond (k \cdot l)\}$. Analytic by df: "k explains l," ∴ it is consistent
that both k and l should be the case whenever one explains or accounts for
the other.

8: ∴ $\Diamond (q \cdot a)$. From 3 and 7.

9: $\Diamond \{[\sim(\exists x)(\exists F)(Fx)] \cdot [(\exists x)(\exists F)(Fx)]\}$. From substitution in 8. This is an
explicit contradiction.

10: Therefore, 'Nothing exists' is incompatible with E.

Does this mean that E *asserts* that something exists? It means that E
entails that something exists. Whether we consider that something is
asserted by E is a moot point not material to our present interests. The
group of objections to the deduction which may be based on the
premise that a is quantificationally inconsistent are treated in Section
3 of Chapter VII.

6: THE APRIORITY OF 'G', 'GOD EXISTS'

Let 'g' stand for 'God exists', and let us mean by 'God exists' that a
divine being—self-accounting, uncausable, and unpreventable in
principle, the ground of the being of all else, omnipotent, eternal,
benevolent, personal, perfect, and (dispositionally) creator of the
world—exists. We here contend that 'God exists' is a priori, and give
the following argument:

1: $\sim$g entails $\sim$E.

2: g entails E.

3: Both E and $\sim$E are a priori propositions, one necessarily true, the other
necessarily false; this follows from their over-all modal operators.

4: Suppose that $\sim$E is true.

5: Then $\sim$g is necessarily true, since it follows from lines 4 and 2 by modus
tollens, and since nothing is entailed by a necessary truth but a necessary
truth.

6: Suppose that E is true.

7: Then g follows from 1 and 6 by modus tollens.

8: Either 4 or 6 is true.

9: *Therefore, either g or ~g is necessarily true.*

10: *Any proposition which is such that either it or its negation is necessarily true is a priori.*

11: *Therefore, g is a priori.*

But how do we prove lines 1 and 2? By proving them separately. We shall prove line 2 now, and line 1 in subsection 7, below.

1: *If God exists, an omnipotent being exists.*

2: *It is possible that an omnipotent being exists, just as it is possible that God exists.*

3: *As "omnipotence" is defined in Chapter V, every contingent state of affairs is within the effective choice of an omnipotent being.*

4: *It follows from the fact that it is possible that there is an omnipotent being which can account, through effective choice, for any contingent state of affairs, that it is possible that any contingent state of affairs should have a hetero-explanation.*

5: *Every necessary state of affairs is self-accounting.*

6: *Therefore, if God exists, it follows that any given state of affairs could have an explanation.*

7: *So g entails E. Therefore, line 1 is true.*

Of course, this proof is technically unnecessary. If E is an a priori true proposition, then it follows strictly from any proposition whatever. Therefore, line 2 is a syntactical triviality. But perhaps the semantic considerations provided above will serve to reinforce one's convictions.

7: THE INCOMPATIBILITY OF '~G' AND 'E'

Taking the same meaning for 'g', we show the incompatibility of 'God does not exist' and Principle E as follows:

1: *Suppose that ~ g is true.*

2: $\Diamond (\exists q)(Eq{\sim}g)$. *From Principle E. (It is possible both that q, and that q explains ~g.)*

3: $(q = {\sim}g) \lor (q \neq {\sim}g)$. *Tautology.*

*4: *Suppose $(q = {\sim}g)$*

5: *Then g is either inconsistent or is incompatible with E, because if (q =*

$\sim g$), then $\Diamond (\sim gE \sim g)$. *[But something which asserts nonexistence ($\sim g$) can be self-explanatory only if the existence in question is inconsistent.]*

6: *But g is neither inconsistent nor incompatible with* E.

7: *Therefore, it is false that* $(q = \sim g)$.

*8: *Suppose* $(q \neq \sim g)$.

9: *Then it is possible that* $\sim g$ *is hetero-explicable:*
$\Diamond [(\exists q)(Eq \sim g) \cdot (q \neq \sim g)]$

10: *But, given what we mean by 'God', as stated above, which required that God's being shall be uncausable and unpreventable, and given the explication of "hetero-explainable" given in subsection 1 above, it follows that*
$\sim \Diamond [(\exists q)(Eq \sim g) \cdot (q \neq \sim g)]$

11: *Conjoin 10 and 9 to derive an explicit contradiction:*
$\Diamond [(\exists q)(Eq \sim g) \cdot (q \neq \sim g)] \cdot \sim \Diamond [(\exists q)(Eq \sim g) \cdot (q \neq \sim g)]$

12: *Therefore, 8 is false; that is,* $\sim (q \neq \sim g)$.

13: *Conjoin 7 and 12:* $\sim (q = \sim g) \cdot \sim (q \neq \sim g)$. *This is a contradiction and a denial of what is necessary: line 3.*

14: *Therefore, either line 1 or line 2 is false.*

15: *But line 2 follows from* E. *Therefore, either line 1 is false or* E *is false.*

16: *This constitutes a demonstration of the incompatibility of* $\sim g$ *and* E.

17: *Now since* E *is a priori true,* $\sim g$ *is a priori false.*

18: *Hence, g is logically true, and is necessary.*[33]

Notice that should E be false, this would not mitigate against the first 16 lines of this argument, or mitigate its force as a proof of line 1 of the previous argument, 6. Hence, our proof of the apriority of 'God exists' is independent of the truth-value assigned to Principle E

[33] It may be objected that the argument just given does not establish what it claims because the term "God" in the premises has the signification we have just outlined, whereas the arguments themselves rest mainly upon the properties "unpreventable" and "uncausable"; thus, the conclusion "God exists" is wider than the premises warrant. This objection is well taken, for it has not been shown that a being which has the rest of the properties cannot fail to be unpreventable and uncausable, and vice versa. However, I think the analysis given in Chapter V goes far enough to suggest that this equivalence will be found to hold in all the necessary cases. Hence, while the objection would be technically correct as it stands, the required logical equivalence can in fact, I believe, be established. As a result, having noted that the conclusion is wider in entailment than the premises explicitly warrant, we can treat this as a matter to be completed after the relationships among the divine attributes have been analyzed. The argument at the very least serves to show that the being which God is, exists; if it does not warrant the identification of its existent with God, that step can be completed elsewhere.

(provided we substitute the semantic proof of line 2 of proof (6) for the syntactical argument mentioned). By explicitly prefixing a second-level modality, "logically necessary," to the conjunction of (a) and (b) which we gave in subsection 1, above, we escape dependence in this argument upon the contested modal theorem concerning iterative modalities and rest only upon the theorem that "necessity" statements have inconsistent contradictories or are themselves contradictory.

Thus, this argument, supported by the definitions and principle given in subsections 1 through 6 above, is central to this book; it is the backbone of my contention that 'God exists' is both a priori and true.

8: DIFFICULTIES AND COUNTER-ARGUMENTS

Those who are displeased with the results of our arguments might attack the assumption that if some proposition explains some other proposition which is not self-explanatory and which has existential import, that explaining proposition entails that something exists. One might say that this is not necessarily so. But if this be argued on the hypothesis that p can be explained by the conjunction $(p \cdot r)$, where r is some other true statement (arbitrarily and irrelevantly selected), I reply that explanation is not the same as entailment, which —although no doubt it has some ontological correlate—is a logical relation; something else is required for the relationship of explanation, even though the explanans may indeed entail what is explained or may, in conjunction with true propositions, be made to entail what is explained.

Let us suppose p: my car will not start on a certain day. Suppose this is accounted for by q, the fact that someone purloined the battery. If it be insisted that q cannot be the explanation of the supposed event, p, unless in conjunction with certain law-like statements or certain statements which eliminate alternative sufficient conditions, q entails p, we will suppose that something of this sort may be so when q explains p, wherever q does not by itself entail p. But we can still sometimes call things explanations which *by themselves* do not entail what is explained; for example: Why did Jones visit New York?— Because he wanted to visit the library. This may be the explanation, yet by itself it does not entail what is explained. Therefore, for q

to be an explanation of *p* does not require that *q* simply entail *p;* moreover, the claim that, wherever *q* does not entail, yet explains, *p,* we can *in fact* find other true propositions which together with *q* entail *p,* is yet to be proved in any significant form. (I distinguish a "significant" form of that claim from an insignificant one because we can always conjoin *p* and *q* as a premise from which to deduce *p,* if *q* explains *p;* thus we would have the triviality that whenever *q* explains *p, q · p* entails *p.*)

In attempts to attack E one may ask all sorts of apparently sensible questions. For instance: If my car would not start because the battery was annihilated, where is the existential commitment of the explanation? We are at least committed to the existence of the battery at some time; otherwise it could not have been annihilated. Perhaps we are also committed to the existence of an annihilator (what would "annihilation" have to mean if we were to count such an event as an *explanation,* anyway?).

We may even be asked to explain the nonexistence of unicorns. But this, as such, is not an appropriate task to set for ourselves in defense of Principle E, which says, not that every fact *has* an explanation, but that it is *consistent* to say about any given fact that it has an explanation, even though it might actually not have one. Thus, we are not required to support E by actually explaining anything. We can dismiss the question as irrelevant, unless, that is, we are confronted with a question about the *possibility* of an explanation of the absence of unicorns; and in that case, we may reply that possibly there are no unicorns because the planet Venus never shows her backside to the earth. For it is *consistent* to say that there is a causal law stating that if the planet Venus were to show her backside to the earth, unicorns would be born. Since this is possible (but intentionally ridiculous), there is *possibly* an explanation of the nonexistence of unicorns.

That what is not but could have been, is not, is accountable only in terms of what is. Why is there no abominable snowman? It would be no explanation for me to reply, "Because there is no parent of an abominable snowman"; for we do not know whether there would have to be a parent for an abominable snowman, or whether its parents are snowmen too. And even if there did have to be parents, we would now have to explain *why* there are no parents of abominable snowmen. We cannot end the search for explanations by continually appealing to the fact that things do not exist or did not happen which would have had to exist or happen in order for abominable snowmen to exist; for we can lump all those things together and ask why they don't exist or happen. Ultimately, if there is to be an explanation of the fact that what is not the case is not the case and also of those facts which are the case but might have been otherwise, we shall have to appeal to the *existence* of something and eventually allege that something is self-explanatory. Moreover, if it is even logically possible that there be such explanations, there must be something self-accounting.

A state of affairs is self-explanatory if an explicit contradiction is entailed by supposing that its contradictory negation is so and has an explanation. A statement of a fact is self-explanatory if and only if it is *really necessarily* the case (e.g., there are no square circles) and if the properties of what is said by it, or presumed by it, to exist or not to exist account for its being *really necessary*.[34] More formally, let us define "self-explanatory" thus:

p is self-explanatory if and only if [~p · (∃q)(qE~p)] entails a contradiction.

To see the force of this definition one should note the following: q is either identical with $\sim p$ or is not. If q *is* identical with $\sim p$ and yet $[\sim p \cdot (\exists q)(qE\sim p)]$ entails a contradiction, then p is necessarily true or $\sim p$ is contingent.[35] If q is neither identical with $\sim p$ nor entailed by $\sim p$, then if the contradiction is derivable, $\sim p$ is not hetero-explicable; from this it follows that $\sim p$ is not logically contingent.

I think a successful attempt to reduce the number of concepts and principles in this section and to recast all the arguments upon identical concepts will have the following result: "self-explanation" can be eliminated through being defined in terms of "hetero-explanation"; Principle E and the definition of "self-explanatory" can be derived from the Principle of Hetero-Explicability: that every logically contingent state of affairs (not equivalent to the totality of all the con-

---

[34] Admittedly the second conjunct of this statement is redundant because it is entailed by the first; but spelling the matter out may make things clearer.

[35] If $[\sim p \cdot (\exists q)(qE\sim p)]$ yields a contradiction on the assumption that $q = \sim p$, it is either because $\sim p$ is self-contradictory or because $\sim p$ is contingent; in the latter case $(\sim pE\sim p)$ will be inconsistent because it violates the truth that contingent states of affairs cannot be self-accounting.

tingent and actual) can be hetero-explained. Basically, the arguments appear to come to this: Neither 'something exists' nor 'God exists' is hetero-explicable. Every undisputed case of a contingent statement is hetero-explicable. Therefore, these two propositions must not be logically contingent. But since they are consistent but not contingent, they must be necessary and hence true.

We have discovered *that* g is self-explanatory, but we have not discovered *what about* g makes it self-explanatory. I am not sure how completely this can be done, since the "unconditionability" of a divine being does not constitute the first-level attribute of its divinity but derives from it. In fact, I am inclined to regard the state of our knowledge as very close to that interpretation of St. Thomas' distinction between propositions *per se nota* and *nota quoad nos* which was offered earlier in terms of 'self-accounting'. We can see *that* g is self-explanatory; we cannot see what about the properties of a divine being bestows its unconditionability. Perhaps we can later employ the Anselmian argument in somewhat the same way Scotus did: not to show that God exists, but to show that given that God exists, His *perfection* is what requires His existence by bestowing unconditionability upon His being. In any case, we can see that certain properties of a divine being preclude absolutely that anything else should be an explanation of the existence of such a being, and also preclude absolutely that the divine being should be unaccounted. It is by means of this and of Principle E that we have reached the conclusions that 'God exists' is necessary and that it is self-explanatory.

The Principle of Explicability, E, is a much weaker proposition than the so-called Principle of Sufficient Reason, which was accepted by Spinoza, Leibniz, and the eighteenth- and nineteenth-century scholastics. They assumed that it is the case that every fact has an explanation (a sufficient reason). E is a *fortiori* much weaker than principles Aquinas and Scotus implicitly employed, for they assumed that *it is necessarily the case* that every fact has an explanation. We have assumed only that *it is possible* that any fact (provided it not be the conjunction of all facts) you choose should have an explanation, and that it is necessary that this explanation involve an existent if the fact is not self-explanatory. This is far weaker, and is a priori true. Whether what we have said entails the older principle is not yet decided, since it might (for all we have shown up to now) be that some fact (e.g., that there is a table in my study) has no explanation, although it *might have had* one. That every fact has an explanation (and that an infinite regress of explanations is impossible) might, as far as we have yet shown, be successfully argued on grounds other than those we have given. It is relevant here only that we notice that such things have been neither established nor presumed. As a matter of fact, however, we shall make a pivotal issue of this fact in Chapter VII, insisting that the Principle of Sufficient Reason must be false.

An attack upon E might take this form: "E is false because there is a true statement incompatible with it, 'God does not exist'; see lines 1 and 2 of your argument 6." This is supposed to put the burden upon us of giving a proof, independent of any so far offered, of the falsity of the statement proposed as a counter-example, or of giving an argument that the negation of E is self-contradictory. It is a formidable objection, especially since the derivation of the contradiction from this denial of E would require us to show, *without employing* E, that ~g is impossible—which is the same as being asked to do our work over again, but without our tools.

But we appeal to the structure of the dialectic and contend that 'God does not exist' is what is contested, and that it ought not to be made a counter-example to our premises unless it is first proved to be true. For, if our arguments are valid, 'God does not exist' is indeed a counter-example, because its contradictory is entailed by our premises. Hence, we will not consider the objection in its present form, but rather in the allied form: "It is possible that God exists and that the nature of God does not account for the being of God"; therefore, E is false, since nothing *else* could account for the being of God.

Now to answer the objection directly we must show that it is possible that the properties of God should determine the truth-value of 'God exists.' But how do we do that? To say in the spirit of St. Thomas that it is the essence of God to exist is merely to repeat the claim which stands in need of proof. To argue to this conclusion by employing E is merely to restate the argument against which the objection was raised in the first place. For if our objector concedes that g is possible but contends that if g were true there could be no explanation of that fact, he has denied E, our main premise.

We answer: it is nonsensical to say g is consistent but that if g were true there could be no explanation of that fact, for g fulfills the conditions of the definition of what is *self-accounting*. The proposition [∼g · (∃q)(qE∼g)] does entail a contradiction (on the supposition that g is consistent). For then, ∼g is either contingent or impossible: if impossible, the conditions of the definition are satisfied; if contingent, then we can derive the statement "There is some state of affairs, not identical with ∼g, which accounts for ∼g." We can then unfold the definitions to derive "There is some state of affairs, not identical with ∼g, which accounts for the fact that an unpreventable being does not exist." If a being is *unpreventable*, it is surely the case that nothing else can account for its non-being! Hence we disclose the needed contradiction. Therefore, g is self-accounting and hence cannot be consistent *and* lack an explanation.

But what of the simple denial of E, in the form: "It is possible that there is a given state of affairs, *p*, which is in principle inexplicable"? It can be replied that *p* would have to be either logically contingent or logically necessary. If logically necessary, then *p* fulfills our definition of 'self-explanatory' because [∼p · (∃q)(qE∼p)] will entail a contradiction just because of the necessary falsity of ∼p. If *p* is logically contingent, both *p* and ∼p will be logically consistent; therefore each will be compatible with any statement which does not entail the other. But since each is contingent, any contingent statement which entails the one will fail to entail the other. For any given contingent statement *p*, there is a contingent statement of the form '*q*, and if *q*, then it is causally necessary that *p*' which does entail *p*. Hence, every contingent state of affairs is hetero-explicable; so, every consistent state of affairs is either auto-explicable or hetero-explicable, and it appears that the supposition of the above denial of E is that there is a consistent state of affairs which is neither necessary nor contingent. This seems absurd.

CONCLUSION

Leibniz and Scotus, it seems, were right: if God is possible, God exists. Moreover, we have defined a sense of real, or factual, necessity in terms of the usual logical modalities and have supplied reasons for believing that the proposition 'God exists' is both really necessary and logically necessary—if it is possible at all.

I have offered an hypothesis to explain how the various senses of "possible" were related for some philosopher-theologians of the past and have developed these concepts to assign a more precise sense to the claim that God necessarily exists: namely, that 'God does not exist' is inconsistent with E and is therefore self-inconsistent. In so doing, we have found a form of a priori argument for the truth, the necessity, and the self-explanatory character of "God exists" which admits of the many permutations which Duns Scotus employed in his extensive proofs of the existence of God.

Although we have left open the question of whether it is consistent that God exists, it is not because this is an open question. Rather, it is because the process of showing that 'God exists' is indeed a consistent claim is the same as the process of philosophically analyzing the essential properties of God. Two of these attributes, omnipotence and goodness, are considered in later chapters; but it is obvious that the analytical task is enormous and, perhaps, endless.

As was said in the preface, the object is not to succeed in establishing what we want in one leap, but to approach this end by gradually refining arguments with analytic care; scientific philosophical theology does not have the urgency of apologetics and need not display a façade of completeness.

4 ✑ Examination of some arguments for the existence of God and formation of some theses concerning such arguments

In the four sections of this chapter, we shall, first, examine the a priori–a posteriori distinction as it was used to ground criticism of certain theistic arguments, and shall disclose the form successful arguments for the existence of God must take. Next, we shall briefly consider the Five Ways of St. Thomas Aquinas, and compare his assumptions with the weaker requirements of the Scotist arguments. In the third section, some "approved arguments," similar in form to those of Chapter III, will be presented. Finally, we shall scrutinize two neoplatonic arguments of Duns Scotus: his "coloration" of Anselm's arguments, and his reasoning based upon the levels of reality or perfection.

SECTION 1: THE A PRIORI–A POSTERIORI DISTINCTION

It has long been customary for philosophers to classify theistic arguments as either a priori or a posteriori. St. Anselm's arguments and all forms of "ontological" argument have been classified together, so that the expression "ontological argument" has become almost synonymous with "a priori argument."[1] Usually the Five Ways of Thomas Aquinas have been called a posteriori arguments, although one occasionally finds certain forms of the Third Way (the argument based upon the contingency of the existents that we experience) treated as a priori; David Hume, for example, in his *Dialogues Concerning Natural Religion*, treats a version of the proof in this manner.

The "design," "moral," and "finality" arguments are classified as a posteriori. Philosophers generally maintain, following David Hume, that (1) there cannot be a valid a priori argument with an existential conclusion; and (2) for a conclusion established by an a posteriori argument, there cannot be a sound a priori argument.

The a priori–a posteriori dichotomy is a source of confusion. If we could find a precise criterion to separate the two boxes we are offered, a criterion which would supply grounds for the claim that one cannot derive existential conclusions from a priori premises, then we might permit the out-of-hand dismissal of certain arguments because they are a priori. But the following paragraphs will show that plausible criteria for the division provide no basis for the two claims given above, and, on the contrary, disclose that these claims are false.

(1) Usually, if one asks for an explanation of the distinction, one is told that an a priori argument contains only premises which are logically true or logically false, whereas an a posteriori argument contains *some* premises which are neither logically true nor logically false, but have their truth-values determined by contingent states of affairs.[2]

Suppose a philosopher who likes Anselm's argument is told that this argument is defective because it is a priori. He will repair it by conjoining to his first premise the following one, which is true but contingent: "Some philosophers object to a priori arguments." Now he no longer has an a priori argument according to the usual explanation, given above; he has preserved both the virtues and the defects of his original argument while changing it from the one class to the

---

[1] These two expressions, "a priori" and "ontological," are not really synonymous. An argument to show that something of a certain sort exists is to be called "ontological" when the existential conclusion is purportedly derived solely from premises concerning *what sort* of thing it is which is claimed, in the conclusion, to exist.

[2] As the subsequent analysis will show, this is the best one can do in formulating the classification; but it is not possible to justify either claim (1) or claim (2) on this or any other plausible ground for the distinction.

other, and has thus proved that none of its defects result from the fact that it is a priori.

No doubt this move would incite disgust in the anti-apriorist, who would charge that the additional premise was not essential to the argument, implying that no *real* change has been made—the argument is still a priori. The discussion would begin again, but this time in the awareness that the distinction *as originally stated* was inadequate, and did not support rejection of Anselm's argument *merely* because it is a priori. It would now be demanded that the a priori argument contain only *essential* premises that are logically true or logically false. On the other hand, the a posteriori arguments must contain at least one contingent truth (or falsehood) as an *essential* premise. This is quite a substantial addition to the definition, as we shall see.

(2) Now what makes a premise essential to an argument? Consider the argument:

(A) 1: *All men are mortal.*

    2: *Socrates is a man.*

    3: *Therefore Socrates is mortal.*

Is "All men are mortal" essential? We could replace it by "All humans are mortal" and alter (2), substituting the predicate "human." Or we could read (1) as "All *humans or men* are mortal." Would we say that *any* alteration in the predicates, even the insertion of synonyms, makes a different argument and constitutes an alteration of essentials? Instead, suppose that to premise (1) we add ". . . and no monkeys are divine," leaving the rest unchanged. Do we have the same argument? If one says "no," then very probably all, and *only*, the premises given are considered essential; hence our amendment to the Anselmian argument as offered above will give us a *different* argument, one which is a posteriori, since it contains an essential contingent premise. This would still show that the defects of the original argument did not derive from its being a priori, because a different sort of argument would now have all the same defects and virtues. If, on the other hand, it is said that we do have the same argument, then the alterations must not have been essential. But now we want to know what alterations *would* be "essential." Suppose we replace every premise in (A), for instance:

(B) 1: *All dogs are mortal.*

2: *Plato was not a dog.*

3: *Therefore Socrates is mortal.*

These changes will, perhaps, be said to be essential and the reason we will be given is that they do not preserve the *validity* of the previous argument. But what then of the following alterations in (B)?

(C) 1: *All cats are felines.*

2: *Socrates was not a cat.*

3: *Therefore Socrates is mortal.*

These changes preserve *invalidity* from (B) to (C). Were the alterations essential? Perhaps invalid arguments have no essential premises? This seems unlikely, but let us suppose it for now. Are the premises that are essential to a valid argument those which we cannot replace without loss of validity? But then, of course, we can replace all the true premises with false ones and preserve the argument's validity. Would not such changes be considered essential alterations? No doubt a change from validity to invalidity would constitute an essential alteration in an argument. But this concept of essential change would be much too weak to support an objection to the move by Anselm's hypothetical defender.

Moreover, if a change to or from validity constitutes an essential change in an argument, then we can never repair an invalid argument; we must transform it into a *different* one. This claim seems unlikely, for in many cases an argument can be rendered valid merely by the introduction of an appropriate modal premise. In fact, *any* argument of the form '*p*, therefore *q*' can be rendered formally valid through the addition of 'Necessarily, if *p* then *q*' to *p*. Thus it appears much more likely that any invalid argument can be rendered valid without an essential change. (Notice that if the modal premise we add is true, it renders the argument valid; if it is false, it also makes the argument valid, because (1) it is itself a priori and an a priori false proposition is contradictory, and (2) an argument with contradictory premises is *eo ipso* valid.)

No adequate notion of 'essential premise' is available; nor is there any precise borderline between a priori and a posteriori arguments which will not allow us to convert an a priori argument into an a posteriori one without a significant alteration. This should tell us without further reasoning that there can be nothing wrong with any argument just *because* it has only a priori premises, regardless of the nature of its conclusion. An argument with a priori premises can be valid no matter what the conclusion may be—for example, an argument with inconsistent a priori premises.

Changes which preserve validity can be "essential"; changes which preserve soundness can be "essential"; changes which preserve invalidity can be "essential"; changes which replace invalidity with validity can be inessential. In fact, we cannot define "essential change" unless we do so in terms of sound arguments only (and this would make the a priori–a posteriori distinction utterly useless as an over-all classification of arguments), or unless we do so in such a general way that no argument can be criticized merely because it is of one or the other group. Moreover, given the contention of Chapter II that Principle E and many principles like it are a priori and *entail* that something exists, one cannot object to a priori arguments (arguments which contain only logically true or logically false premises) on the ground that they cannot have existential conclusions. Such an objection will lead to explicit contradictions: if E is false, it is inconsistent and thus entails its conclusion; if E is true, it is a priori true and, as Chapter III shows, entails its conclusion. Therefore, an existential conclusion follows from a priori premises.

(3) Reinforcing the attack upon the use of the distinction in question here to provide a blanket rejection of a priori arguments for existential conclusions, let us without further quibbling about the looseness of the notion 'essential' employ the following working definition (which will be rejected below):

Definition 1: An argument for conclusion c is a posteriori only if it is not possible to construct a valid argument for c which does not contain an empirical premise.

This does not require that only *valid* arguments are to be classified as a priori or a posteriori. But according to definition (1), there are no a posteriori arguments at all, since every conclusion, whether contingent or not, follows from inconsistent a priori premises. Perhaps we should fix this up, requiring that an argument for conclusion c is a posteriori only if no *valid* argument with *consistent* premises can be constructed for that conclusion unless one of the premises is empirical. But again, if the conclusion is a logical truth, then by this definition it cannot be derived validly by means of an a posteriori argument, since it is possible to construct an argument for a logical truth which contains no empirical premises. Consider, for example, the following argument:

If there are tall men, 2 + 2 = 4.

There are tall men.

Therefore 2 + 2 = 4.

Even though it contains an essential empirical premise, this argument is, by definition (1), not a posteriori. But this is certainly *not* an a priori argument. Therefore we must reject this formulation of the a priori–a posteriori distinction.

Suppose we substitute:

Definition 2: An argument for conclusion c is a posteriori only if the argument is valid, has consistent premises, and contains an empirical premise which is essential to the argument.

Definition 3: An argument is a priori if it has a logical truth for its conclusion, is valid, has consistent premises, and contains no contingent proposition as an essential premise.

The provision of validity was required to rule out our constructing both a priori and a posteriori arguments for every conclusion, whether true, false, consistent, inconsistent, a priori, or empirical (with the result that the notion 'essential' becomes hopelessly confused). But this provision has the disadvantage of making all *invalid* arguments unclassifiable within this formulation of the distinction; the trouble with this is that many philosophers, following the Humean tradition, want to hold that an a priori argument consisting of logically true premises and an existential conclusion must be invalid.[3] They cannot on these definitions call the argument whose validity they reject a priori, and hence we can no longer assign a meaning to the contention that all a priori arguments with existential conclusions must be fallacious; for in definitions (2) and (3), validity is a prerequisite of classifiability.

---

[3] As maintained in claim (1), p. 141.

Perhaps these philosophers will want to reject my working definitions (which were constructed only to call attention to certain important facets of the problem); but what can they offer us as a new foundation for the distinction so that we can assess their claim, the claim to which Hume is committed in Part IX of his *Dialogues Concerning Natural Religion?*

Let it be reiterated that an argument with inconsistent premises and a contingent conclusion is valid. Hence, there *can* be a valid a priori argument with an existential conclusion. For example:

If 2 + 2 = 5, then Socrates exists.

2 + 2 = 5.

Socrates exists.

It will be pointed out that this argument does not qualify as a priori under definition (3) because it does not have consistent premises. But then, it will not qualify under definition (2) either, and for the same reason. Hence, definitions (2) and (3) do not make up a dichotomy subsuming all arguments. The only circumstance under which the argument will qualify is our original classification—which is a universal dichotomy, but is incompatible with the two claims we have been considering. If it were held that an argument does not fit into the classification "a priori–a posteriori" unless it both is valid and has consistent premises, then it could not be held that all a priori arguments with existential conclusions are invalid; that charge would be inconsistent wherever validity has been made a necessary condition of apriority.

But since there can be both valid arguments with only logically true premises and valid arguments with some or all contingent premises for the same (logically true) conclusion we must dismiss the objection of the followers of Hume, namely, that the existence of valid a posteriori arguments for a given conclusion shows that a priori arguments for that conclusion are fallacious.

If we do not make consistency a necessary condition of apriority, the contention that a priori arguments with existential conclusions are invalid becomes contradictory. On the other hand, if we *do* make consistency a prerequisite for apriority, then the division of all arguments into the a priori and the a posteriori is abandoned. Hence, the first Humean claim is not compatible with the assumption that we are dealing with a universal dichotomy.

Therefore, we have shown that if the a priori–a posteriori classification is taken as an absolutely universal dichotomy for all arguments, and if the possession of logically-true or logically-false premises (only) is what renders an argument a priori, then: (a) there can be invalid arguments of both kinds; (b) there can be valid a priori arguments with existential conclusions; and (c) there can be both valid a priori and valid a posteriori arguments for at least some conclusions which are the same. Hence, the two traditional Humean assumptions are inconsistent with the nature of the classification we employ. Further, experiment with definitions (1), (2), and (3) indicated that it would not be easy to provide a plausible basis for the a priori–a posteriori argument distinction which would save the two claims we considered and yet would accord with the way philosophers have used this classification. Therefore, we may conclude that it is ridiculous to criticize an argument just because it is a priori; there is nothing inherently wrong with such arguments. Should a "Humean" object: "Yes there is; you cannot have a *sound* a priori argument with an existential conclusion," I reply that that is just what must be shown. Chapter III, and Section 3 of the present chapter, purport to show the opposite; the Humean's denial merely begs the question at issue. Hence, we can dismiss Hume's objection to the "a priori" argument in Part IX of his *Dialogues;* it merely prejudges the very question for which we need a philosophical answer. Moreover, it ignores the evident fact that an existential statement can have a quantificationally inconsistent negation (as in *Principia Mathematica*). and can be derived from a priori true premises (in this case L-true premises).

(4) We shall now say something about the forms of argument which are appropriate to establishing the existence or nonexistence of God. Leaving aside the dispute over this distinction, let us divide all arguments, valid or invalid, as follows:[4]

A posteriori arguments: all and only those arguments which contain at least one premise which is neither logically true nor logically false.

---

[4] It is not important to me that one may change an argument from a priori to a posteriori or vice versa merely by adding or dropping some trivial truth. No critique of arguments will be offered which rests upon the mere fact that an argument belongs to the one group or to the other.

A priori arguments: all and only those arguments which contain only logically true or logically false premises.

Suppose that 'God exists' is contingent. *In that case there cannot be an establishment of it or its negation.*

For an argument to establish any given conclusion, it is necessary (but by no means sufficient) that the argument both be valid and have consistent premises. Now if the conclusion is *ex hypothesi* logically contingent, then there can be no valid and consistent argument for it which does not contain some premise which is *also* logically contingent; contingent truths are not entailed by logical truths alone.[5] If the conclusion is "God exists," then we shall wonder how the contingent premise has come to be employed and by what right it stands as a premise.

That contingent premise will either be a statement of particular and observed facts or it will be a statement of some general or universal empirical truth (or falsity) or a conjunction of the two.

It is apparently possible to construct a sound argument, containing only cited particular and observed facts, which has "God exists" as a conclusion; but such arguments will not fulfill the requirements of a *scientific establishment* of the conclusion, either (a) because our knowledge of the truth-value of the premises is not epistemically independent of our opinion about the truth-value of the conclusion (such arguments are circular), or (b) because the premises will not have the attributes of accessibility and person-independent verifiability requisite to a good philosophical argument.

An example of (a):

(D) 1: *If Socrates was a Greek, Lincoln liked jokes.*

   2: *Socrates was a Greek.*

   3: *Therefore Lincoln liked jokes.*

If the first premise is interpreted as truth-functional and if you will accept my nonscientific assessment of the conclusion, we may conclude that the argument is sound but circular, because we cannot determine the truth-value of (1) without knowing, or having an opinion about, the truth-value of (3).

---

[5] This should be obvious since the contradictory of the contingent truth is *compatible* with the necessary truths, whereas the contradictory of what is *entailed* by a premise is not. See the definition of "entailment."

An example of (b) is:

(E) 4: *If Moses spoke to God, God exists now.*

    5: *Moses spoke to God.*

    6: *Therefore God exists now.*

Now (4) is a logical truth (provided we take 'God' as a proper name used primarily designatively both times but with the same signification),[6] while (5) cites a particular fact or, at least, what will be admitted by a large group of men, some of whom are philosophers, to be a fact. Let us therefore call this argument sound; there is no point in quibbling over this characteristic here, since even a purely argumentative concession of the point will do. Yet even though the argument is probably not circular, it is not philosophically acceptable: an angel might tell you that (5) is true and you would not first have to have known (6), although your commitment to (6) would be logically involved in your belief in (5); yet if you had not yet examined the signification of "God" you might not know that if such a being exists at all, it always exists. Hence, (5) and (6) could be epistemically independent *for someone*. One could discover the truth of (4) without believing either (5) or (6); in fact, if one knew that (5) and (6) were false, one could know that (4) is true. These points do not decisively show that the argument is not circular for everyone, but they make it *likely* enough for us to assume that it is not circular for everyone and has its fault elsewhere.

The reason why the argument is not satisfactory, even if it is conceded to be sound and not circular, is that the empirical premise (5) is not such that each independent investigator can, at least in principle, verify it for himself. Strictly speaking, premise (5) is not a "truth of observation" at all, since we mean by so designating a premise that what is claimed by that premise is in principle *independently* observable by any rational investigator. How can I find out whether Moses spoke to God? Certainly not by any decision procedure generally applicable in philosophy.

It appears from this that singular propositions are not, in general, appropriate premises in scientific arguments (except insofar as they serve as substitution instances for existentially general truths), since

---

[6] See Chapter II, Section 3 for an explanation of these terms.

they are generally not in principle verifiable by every independent investigator. Thus, "Xanthippe loved a philosopher" is not an appropriate premise for a philosophical demonstration (since what it claims is not a matter observable by any disinterested investigator), unless it stands as an *instance* of an existentially general truth confirmable by true singular propositions that are to be furnished by each observer. There are, however, exceptions, in which singular propositions are publicly assessable through historical research.

It is true that philosophers often use arguments which are identical in outward structure to argument (E). But when they reasonably expect such arguments to have force, they intend to illustrate a kind or form of argument whose particular or singular premises can be replaced by things of our own observation; thus the real premise is existentially general and intended to be confirmed in each appraiser's own experience. This would not apply here since it would be foolish to suppose that every independent investigator can supply appropriate particulars to substantiate the existentially general "Someone spoke to God" for argument (E); who will suppose that all men have had a personal encounter with God or know someone who is known to have had one?

Hence it seems that the premises of every a posteriori argument which is *of scientific standard* will have to contain, not only simple truths of observation, but either a general a priori truth or a general or universal empirical truth. An example of the former:

(F) 7: *Some things are alive* $\qquad\qquad p$

     8: *It is not possible that some things are alive* $\qquad \sim \Diamond (p \cdot \sim q)$
        and God does not exist.

     9: *Therefore God exists.* $\qquad\qquad\qquad\qquad \therefore q$

This is the only form of a posteriori argument which offers hope; and premise (8) has to be demonstrated in terms of conceptual relations or a priori truths alone.[7] For suppose the premises do not contain the a priori claim that the truth of one empirical and particular prem-

---

[7] It will be suggested later in this chapter (a) that in order to make such a demonstration one will have to employ a premise similar to our Principle E; (b) that the premises required to establish (8) are all logical truths; and (c) that since they alone entail q (as our earlier arguments based upon Principle E indicate), this argument serves as what could be called an a posteriori argument for an a priori conclusion.

ise and the falsity of the conclusion are logically incompatible $[\sim \Diamond (p \cdot \sim q)]$, then (given also our rejection of the two earlier forms of argument) there is no way left to connect the observational premise p and conclusion q but that which depends upon a general or universal empirical truth. For a valid a posteriori argument presents its conclusion either as a logical consequence, or else as a causal or material consequence of some empirical truth.

Yet any argument which has as its connecting premise some general truth of observation, like "All events have causes," "All chains of movers are finites," "All living beings act for an end," or even something much more plausible, cannot possess these premises as established universal and unexceptionable truths. Such premises can be shown to be more or less generally true, more or less or even most probable, but not strictly speaking *true*, since we do not possess decisive evidence of their truth—it being granted that they are not a priori true. (Notice that I distinguish what can be *shown* to be true from what can be *known* to be true.) Where there is a potentially infinite body of instances some of which are unexamined, we are warranted in assigning to a conclusion no greater probability than we may assign to the hypothesis. Thus, the conclusion can be said to be only more or less true or even most probably true, but not strictly speaking true. If it is insisted that one can *know* that such propositions are true although one cannot *establish* them, I shall not quibble; for such premises will still not serve as elements in a demonstration or establishment of the conclusion since they themselves are not susceptible to decision by direct observation or the application of analytic methods.

Yet another qualification is needed. We must still consider that such universal hypotheses *can* be known to be true, and that such hypotheses can be decisively falsified. Hence, they are "not susceptible to decision by direct observation or the application of analytic methods" in the sense that they cannot be fully confirmed by observation or deduced from necessary truths. This is obvious; by definition they are contingent, and by supposition they cover unobserved instances. But if we can know that such premises are true, why may we not use them as premises? (Not every premise must be demonstrated.) The answer is that a universally general contingent truth which relates some existential truth to the existence of God will of necessity have the existence of God as one of its substitution instances. Hence, in order to know that such a premise is true, one must know that the conclusion is true. It is hard to conceive that there will be anyone who realizes the import of the premise for whom the argument will not become epistemically circular by requiring of him an experience —independent knowledge of the conclusion—that the argument is designed to obviate. Where the conclusion is a substitution instance of a universally general empirical premise, and where we cannot discover the truth of the premises by any philosophical procedure that does not require us to have decided the truth-value of the conclusion, we shall call the argument evidentially circular. The fact that there is someone for whom it is not *epistemically* circular (because an angel reveals the truth of the premises to him, or the like) will not mitigate against the fact that the premises are not accessible to philosophical determination in isolation from the conclusion. Hence, such an argument is defective. Thus, if the conclusion 'God exists' is contingent, and if we cannot produce a sound example of the third form of argument (F) for that conclusion, then the arguments which best fulfill the requisites of scientific method—that is, the arguments we here describe as of this fourth and last group, (G)—will be able to assign only a probability to the conclusion or its negation.

Whether the philosopher is inclined to religious belief, revolted by the idea, or merely indifferent, he will never be satisfied with such arguments: he wants an unequivocal decision. Only arguments of the form illustrated in group (F), or else arguments which contain *no contingent premises at all*, will do to establish what is desired. Those who contend that 'God exists' is a contingent truth must employ arguments of form (F) or they will surely fail to establish the conclusion; for contingent truths do not follow from a priori premises alone.

On the other hand, if the conclusion is a logical truth, both arguments without contingent premises (a priori arguments) and arguments of form (F) will be acceptable as fulfilling the conditions for establishment (though not *all* such arguments, certainly). In the case of the proposition 'God exists', I do not think the second premise of arguments of form (F) can be properly supported without appeal to such a priori principles as will by themselves entail the conclusion. Hence, the conclusion cannot be contingent. But if I should be in error about this, then only arguments of form (F) will establish the conclusion, or its negation.

Let us digress briefly. Some philosophers think that we will have an established conclusion if our premises are "certain truths." But their position is ambiguous. Perhaps they mean that the premises will be observational truths verifiable by any disinterested investigator. In that case, the premises will not be sufficient, since they need not be absolutely without exception—as was shown in our consideration of group (G). If they mean only that someone knows the premises to be true, then that contention is rejected by our consideration of groups (D) and (E). Not all knowledge comes up to the standards for premises in philosophical demonstration. If it is meant that the premises are a combination of observed truths and logical truths—an argument illustrated by (F)—then they might be right. For, of course, even if the conclusion is a logical truth, such an argument could establish it, even though such arguments may not appear formally the most elegant. If the conclusion were a contingent truth, the argument of form (F) might also succeed.

Many neo-scholastics, like Father Copleston, have used the expressions "certain truth" and "certain knowledge."[8] Is it claimed that such propositions as 'Some things are in motion' are "certain truths" because they are *independently observable* truths, or that such propositions as 'The number of caused causes essentially ordered is finite' are "certain truths" because they are a priori truths? I think the expression "certain truths" is ambiguous, and is used to cover *both* cases. If so, not every argument containing "certain truths" as premises will establish its conclusion, even if we also assume that it is valid; for some would be of forms (D), (E), and (G). It would be much clearer to abolish the expression, or restrict it in such a way that we knew what basis of certainty was presupposed in each case where the expression "certain truth" is used. In any case, we see that valid and consistent arguments involving "certain truths" and having 'God exists' for a conclusion will either be of form (F) or else will contain only *logical* truths as premises if they succeed in establishing the conclusion. Making this clear has been the objective of this digression.

(5) Even if 'God exists' should be established by arguments which contain only necessary truths as premises, it does not follow that all arguments of form (F) are irrelevant and useless. For it will follow that there are valid, consistent arguments with true premises—some of

---

[8] F. C. Copleston and A. J. Ayer: "Logical Positivism," BBC discussion, 1949; printed, McGregor, Geddes, and Robb, *Readings in Religious Philosophy* (Boston: Houghton Mifflin Co., 1962).

them empirical—which entail this conclusion, and to which the contingent premises are essential (in what little sense I can assign to "essential"). Because they are much simpler to grasp than are the more formal ones, such arguments are often useful; there is often a psychological cogency about them which is unavailable in the maze of qualifications and formalizations required for an adequate a priori argument. Hence, the discovery of a purely logical proof of the existence of God will not mitigate the value of other sound arguments: if the conclusion is logically true, it will, after all, *follow* strictly from any premises whatever. Thus the choice of a sub-set of the true premises will merely center upon those which exert the most immediate evidential force to bring the reader to *know* the conclusion. For "scientific" purposes, an argument of type (F) will be just as useful as an a priori argument.

(6) The "Kantian" difficulty: Against the whole project of Chapter III, that of providing a priori theistic arguments, and against the efficacy of arguments of form (F), above, there is a profound objection: that such arguments are misguided in principle. I can easily imagine a man of Kantian inclinations saying:

What is wrong with your arguments is this: you succeed only in showing that our concepts are so related to one another that our conceptual scheme has an ontological commitment. This is the net product of any "ontological" argument.[9] But two possibilities are compatible with that. (a) Our concepts may be inadequate, so that we are conceiving the world quite incorrectly; or (b) there may be alternative conceptual schemes which do not have this ontological commitment but which will serve our other purposes quite well. In a word, your implicit premise is that your conceptual scheme represents the world adequately; how do you show that this is so? As Immanuel Kant wisely observed: "The unconditioned necessity of a judgment does not form the absolute necessity of a thing."

All we have done, it is objected, is to show that our conceptual scheme has an ontological commitment.

What does this objection mean? In Chapter III, I think that I showed an existential proposition, g, to be true by means of premises which are a priori true. If doing this *successfully* is what is meant by "show-

---

[9] This suggests another concept of what an ontological argument is; it may be an argument from premises which express certain of our *conceptual* commitments, to a conclusion that things must be the way we conceive them.

ing that our conceptual scheme has an ontological commitment," then it can be no criticism of our achievements to say we have shown this. But, of course, our critic alleges that we have *failed* to show the existential proposition to be true, an allegation made on the ground that we can be shown to have done *something else*. Actually, that, as such, is not a sound criticism: if doing-something-else is not incompatible with doing what we set out to do, then we may have done both; and if doing-something-else *is* incompatible with fulfilling our own objective, then the proof of that incompatibility ought to be made part of the objection. Now the "Kantian" does not hold that it is *incompatible* with our showing that we have a certain conceptual commitment that we should also have shown that something is the case. Hence, the objection is too strongly stated. It merely contends that we have not shown what we claim to have shown: that the conclusion is true; thus it is, in effect, a disagreement with us about the nature of the logical modalities. We had assumed that if p is true and if we have shown that $\sim \Diamond (p \cdot \sim q)$, then we can and indeed *must* insist that q is true. Now we are told that this is not the case. Why, pray tell, not?

The key elements of a demonstration that our conceptual scheme has an ontological commitment seem to be to show that someone who has concepts x, y, z, etc., which are related logically in certain illustrated ways (to form certain *a priori* propositions) cannot consistently maintain the negation of a certain existential proposition. Hence we suppose that there is someone who has concepts x, y, and z in the stated relations and that he denies the existential proposition. If we can deduce a contradiction from the negation of the existential proposition compounded with various logical truths in which the concepts x, y, z, etc. occur, and if we assume that the set of "logical truths" really is consistent, then we say that we have shown that the conceptual scheme x, y, z, etc., has a commitment to a certain existential proposition. If the set of concepts can be arranged to form a conjunctive a priori proposition p, and if we can show that some existential proposition q is related to p as follows, $\sim \Diamond (p \cdot \sim q)$, then we can say we have shown our conceptual scheme p to have an existential commitment to q.

Notice, in this way of putting it, what we have demonstrated is *not* —as the Kantians would see it—a relationship between our *belief* in *p* and our *belief* in *q*. We have demonstrated a relationship between the *truth* of *p* and the *truth* of *q*, a relationship which holds regardless of what we believe. If the ontological commitment of a certain conceptual scheme (a set of a priori truths) is described as a relationship between our *belief in* the one set of propositions and our consistent *denial of* the existential proposition in question, the Kantian objection will have force. After all, suppose I cannot consistently believe *p* and deny *q*; this does not tell me whether I must *believe* both or *deny* both. To have such a commitment tells us little about the world. Now if we say that my belief in *p* is not within the power of reason and is not based on evidence, but rather that it *precedes* the power of reason and the recognition of evidence—so that *p* does not represent the world but preconditions my representations of the world—then the fact that I cannot consistently deny *q* and maintain *p* only shows me that ~*q* is incompatible with *p*; nothing is shown about the world. Within their own epistemology, then, the Kantians are right in this objection; not every necessity of thought is an ontological necessity.

But *we* explain ontological commitment in terms of the truth of *p* and *q*, not in terms of belief. If *p* is true and it is not possible that ($p \cdot \sim q$), then *q* is true. After all, this is what we mean by "is entailed by." Our arguments are attempts to show that certain a priori truths entail the existence of certain things. Ours is a logical process from an unconditional a priori truth to the unconditional assertion that something must be the case, regardless of our beliefs.

This seems fairly to represent what we claimed to have done, and I believe it to be well worth doing. For as I have explained "showing our conceptual scheme to have a certain ontological commitment," this is about the same as deducing an existential conclusion by indirect proof from a set of a priori true premises. But to the "Kantian" the result is worthless: he says that it is a deduction from the forms through which we think about the world of a proposition about what the world contains. While his latter point is true—we *have* deduced a proposition about what the world contains—the former is misstated. We have not deduced anything from the forms (or categories) through which we think about the world; deductions are possible only from propositions.

Now a priori propositions might indeed be called formal propositions—propositions which express the form of the world and determine the form of our thought. But the forms embodied in a priori propositions are the forms of *all possible worlds*, not only of our actual world; hence, existential propositions that follow from such analytic propositions will also express the form of all possible worlds. There is nothing absurd about a discovery that the form of a possible world is in part *that* the world should have content (be non-empty). It *is* absurd to claim that such deductions will have shown nothing about the world, but merely about how we think about the world. If p conjoined with $\sim \Diamond (p \cdot \sim q)$ does not unconditionally yield q, but only 'I must believe that q', and if 'I must believe that q' is considered by the "Kantian" to be compatible with $\sim q$, then $\sim \Diamond (p \cdot \sim q)$ will yield an explicit contradiction and we may as well give up modal logic at once. This seems to me to be a decisive refutation of the cruder forms of Kantian dismissal of our admittedly a priori reasoning.

A preliminary examination of this "Kantian" objection—an objection we find expressed in the works of many philosophers—indicates that it has no weight apart from the Critical Idealist system of which it is a basic element. Insofar as we can assign sense to it, it consists of two elements: an admission that we have done what we claimed, that is, validly deduced an existential conclusion from a priori premises; and a denial that our task is worth while, basically because the a priori premises "tell us nothing about the world" and hence cannot lead to a conclusion which does. We have rejected that denial, claiming that a priori propositions do indeed tell us about the world—and about all possible worlds into the bargain—and that the conclusion of our argument has the same scope.

Nevertheless, the "Kantian" objection has some aspects which, although they are not easily explained or justified, ought to be at least adumbrated in fairness to the point of view from which the objection originates. The premises of our argument are taken from those a priori commitments or judgments that serve as the form to which all other judgments are, or should be, fitted. Our conclusion is supposed to hold not only of the world as conceived, but also of the world as it is, independently of the consideration of it by any mind at all. But do we *know* that a form of inference which holds for our thoughts about the world-as-conceived will hold at all for the world-apart-from-conception? This epistemic attack that says we have no evidence upon which to ground our acceptance of a form of reasoning to a transcendental conclusion can be directed as well against any type of argument, whether it contains empirical premises or not, containing a transcendental conclusion (i.e., a conclusion about the world as it is, apart from our conception of it). Since the scope of this objection is so broad, we shall not reply to it here, except to note that the objection presupposes that we do wish to speak of things "apart from our conception of them," and that it does make sense to seek "transcendental knowledge"—a theory of perception which has not been found satisfactory by the epistemologists who have examined it.

Sometimes the objection above is stated simply as follows: "The fact that we think of the world in a certain way, particularly a way which makes our thoughts inconsistent if we deny a certain existence, is no evidence that it is that way." This statement of the objection is simple, but it is not really clear. There is no doubt that my thinking that the world is a certain way (that certain things are the case or that certain things exist) is no evidence that the world is that way. But there is considerable doubt as to whether my thinking *of* the world in a certain way (forming my judgments by means of certain interrelated concepts) is not evidence *that* it is that way—that the things which fall under the concepts are subject to some of the relationships of the concepts. In fact, the analytic movement in philosophy seems to be largely dedicated to the thesis that an investigation of our concepts and their interrelation will disclose important truths about the world we conceive through them.

Of course, arguments that employ no premises which are to be established by empirical means do have one inherent disadvantage: the investigation of their suppositions is unending. Thus, when confronted with the arguments of Chapter III, the philosopher is naturally drawn to re-examine the concept of 'explanation', to wonder again about the notions 'causal production' and 'possibility'; he is naturally drawn to ask questions which will continue to stretch out the chain of premises that are needed to get to our conclusion.

From the existentialist point of view, it is a disadvantage that criticism constantly draws our argument toward greater abstraction and away from the commerce of life which requires decision on the conclusion rather than excellence in its establishment. But from the analytic point of view, this is exactly what philosophers seek. Moreover, it is simply false to think this disadvantage applies only to a priori arguments. Any argument containing any premise that cannot be decided by direct observation is susceptible to the same unending analysis. All philosophical arguments are subject to unending analytic reduction. Philosophy is pursued as a science and not as a healing art; naturally it tends to withdraw from the existential predicament, even while accounting for it.

From an analytic point of view, those a priori arguments which have the least psychological force for the man seeking a way of life may be the most excellent establishments of a truth, even though they plunge the investigator into an unending search for a more perfect statement of conceptual interrelationships. The unending analytic reducibility of our concepts and logical forms is not peculiar to an a priori argument and is not, therefore, its characteristic defect.

In conclusion: in this section we have considered two general attacks upon a priori arguments with existential conclusions. Neither of them is consistent with the exhaustive classification employed; nor can the grounds for the exhaustive classification of arguments as a priori or a posteriori be defended in the terms in which they have usually been put, unless we admit that there is to be no critical use of the distinction to reject whole classes of traditional theistic arguments as fallacious. We have gone on to show that if the conclusion 'God exists' is logically contingent, there is only one general form of establishment for it or its negation. It is, however, my opinion that the conclusion is *not* contingent, and that there is another form of argument which is also appropriate to an establishment of it.

SECTION 2: EXAMINATION OF THE FIVE WAYS OF THOMAS AQUINAS

The Five Ways of Aquinas (*Summa Theologica*, I, 2, 3) are, of course, not original with him. Some of the arguments have definite antecedents in the works of Plato, others in the works of Aristotle; all of them are employed by one or another of the medieval predecessors of St. Thomas, although none of those predecessors, as far as I know, listed all five together. An examination of the other works of St. Thomas and those of his contemporaries and successors shows that neither he nor his followers considered these to be the only good arguments for the existence of God; nor did they privilege the formulations of the *Summa Theologica* above other, more complete formulations. Rather, these arguments are representative of the style and logical form which St. Thomas and his followers considered most appropriate. All five arguments are of type (F), described in the preceding section: they first cite some truths confirmable by independent observation, and then they claim, by means of purported a priori truths, that these obvious facts could not obtain unless the conclusion asserted is true.

In the following pages I shall briefly criticize some of the a priori assumptions present in St. Thomas' arguments; then I shall indicate certain weaker assumptions which are entailed by St. Thomas' premises and show how they are employed in a form of argument dear to Duns Scotus, in which the conclusion is derived from a priori premises, with the only function of the original empirical premise being to provide us with an indubitable premise concerning the *possibility* of what we know to be actually the case. It is the general thrust of my comments that whatever is worth while about St. Thomas' arguments can be achieved by means of the Scotist arguments, without Thomas' commitment to premises which may very well be false.

The following statements of the arguments are summaries; but they are carefully chosen to expound the main consequential relationships Aquinas was presenting.

The first way

1: *Some things are in motion and not self-moved.*

2: *What is moved (in motion and not self-moved) must be moved by another (a priori).*

3: *The series of moved movers cannot be infinite (a priori).*

4: *Therefore, there is a first mover which is not moved.*

Premise (1) is intended as a truth of observation independently verifiable by all investigators. Premises (2) and (3) are clearly intended as a priori truths, as the modal terms "must" and "cannot" indicate.

Here we are interested only in premise (2). Why cannot something be in motion, and not be self-moved, and still be not moved by another? Because there would then be no cause, explanation, or sufficient reason for its being in motion. So? It is assumed to be a fact not only that

a: *every case of something's being in motion has an explanation, cause, or reason;*

but also that

b: *it is necessarily so that every such case has an explanation, cause or reason.*

But (a) cannot be demonstrated unless (b) is assumed, since inductive evidence would not establish the absolute universality of (a). Now I do not see why we should accept (b). What is inconsistent about saying that x moved but is not self-moved, and was not moved by anything else?[10] I admit that we could not in the normal course of events come to know that that was true if it were true, but I see no *contradiction* in supposing that it is so;[11] hence, I suspect (b) to be false. Premise (a) becomes, as a result, unacceptable or unassessable independently of the conclusion. We could not claim to know premise (a), admitting that (b) might be false, and still propose to use (a) as premise in a non-circular argument for the existence of God, because once we discard the deduction of (a) from an a priori truth (b), we cannot discover the truth of (a) by a philosophical investigation without presuming to know the truth-value of the conclusion. This would make the argument circular.

Another objection is that (3) is both false—since it is a necessary

---

[10] Some philosophers may object that we have not employed a fair disjunction here: "the universal generalization" or "the logical truth"; for there is another possibility: the "*law-like universal*," the natural law. That every change has a cause might be more than a mere universally general truth, and *less* than a logical necessity. Now we cannot deny that some generalizations have been *shown* to be laws; hence we cannot deny that a generalization like this one might be shown to be a natural law also. While it might have been that some changes would not have causes, it in fact is necessarily so in changes in *this* universe: hence, there is a first mover, etc. In effect, it is claimed that the modal premises in some demonstrations are causal and not logical. But I do not consider this alternative at all likely. Causal laws hold *within* the realm of physical objects. This is no evidence whatever that they hold for anything which is cause of all the changes of physical bodies. In effect, while I agree that physical necessities have been discovered, I deny that any evidence we possess could justify extending such principles to cover an investigation of the causes and moving agencies for the universe as a whole.

[11] It is interesting to note that this supposition, which no experience could establish for us, fulfills the positivist criterion of nonsense and allows the Principle of Sufficient Reason back into philosophy as a meaningful principle. This is one more case in which the positivists have failed to exclude what they intended to exclude.

truth that an infinite series, such as the real numbers between one and two, *can* have both a first and last member—and a priori, and is therefore contradictory. However, I think that, despite his statement to the contrary, St. Thomas merely wanted to claim that there cannot be a series of moved movers which does not begin with an unmoved mover, regardless of whether the series is infinite or finite. When this claim is substituted for (3), we get a much more plausible argument. Yet this premise has not been shown to have a contradictory denial, and since it is a priori it can be established only in that manner; therefore we can still wonder about its consistency and can still feel obliged to investigate it. But, as we have said several times now, incompleteness is not by itself a defect since all deductive establishments are incomplete and not all of them are defective.

Nevertheless, there is a fallacy of logic in Aquinas' reasoning from the claim that every moved thing is in a chain of things with a first mover to the conclusion that there is one first mover of all moved things. There is no set of a priori truths by which to justify this step.[12] Hence, the argument contains an unjustifiable inferential step. We shall return to assumptions (a) and (b) in Section 3.

The second way

1: *Some things stand in an essential ordering of efficient causes.*

2: *Nothing can be an efficient cause of its own being (a priori).*

3: *A series of (essentially ordered) efficient causes of being cannot be infinite (a priori).*

4: *Therefore, there is a first efficient cause.*

Premise (1) is intended as a truth of observation independently verifiable by all investigators; we accept it without further comment here. Premises (2) and (3) are intended as a priori, as the modal term "cannot" indicates. But—since it is assumed that a chain of efficient causes cannot end in a being which is an efficient cause but for whose own

---

[12] This claim is *itself* a priori and should have a contradictory denial. Since the contradiction in the denial is not offered here, it must be realized that we have merely indicated the *locus* of a defect but have not *established* that Thomas' argument has that defect. For with *some peculiar relations*, $(x)(\exists y)(Rxy)$ *does* entail $(\exists y)(x)(Rxy)$. My contention, not proved here, is that 'being moved by' is not such a relation.

being there exists neither a cause nor some natural necessity—the reasoning is not tight unless we add another premise, which can be put in two forms:

c: *For every thing which is an efficient cause there is either another efficient cause or there is some self-explanation for its being.*

d: *It is necessarily the case that for any efficient cause there is either a cause of its being or there is something which renders its being self-explanatory.*

But (c) cannot be demonstrated, established by an argument which "comes up to standard," unless (d) is assumed, since inductive evidence could not establish the absolute universality of (c). Now, why should we accept (d)? Why should we think it inconsistent to say that some chains of efficient causes have a first uncaused cause which cannot possibly be God because this cause is not in principle uncausable but simply exists without any explanation at all? Since we have not been given a derivation of the fact that the negation of (d) leads to a contradiction—since, in fact, it appears very likely that (if 'God exists' is not a logical truth) it does *not* lead to a contradiction— we must either suspect that (d) is false and, furthermore, contradictory, or that (d) is epistemically posterior to the conclusion and, hence, not usable as a premise to establish it.

I do not think (c) and (a), the premises in the earlier arguments, are actually false, though I do think (b) and (d) are. But my reasons for this stem from my conviction that 'God exists' is a logical truth and from the fact that (c) and (a) are *epistemically* posterior, for me, to the establishment of that claim. Before the conclusion of the argument is shown to be true, there is no philosophically acceptable reason for accepting (c) or (a), the premises. As a result we must say that (c), as a premise, is evidentially posterior to the conclusion; this would not be the case if St. Thomas' tacit supposition, (d), were true. But since it is false, one could discover (c) to be true by means of a philosophical investigation only if he knew already whether or not the conclusion is true.

Other objections, not emphasized here, include:

(i) The fallaciousness of inferring from the fact that every efficient cause must belong to a chain which has a first member to the conclusion that all efficient causes belong to chains which have the *same* first member (or a first cause with the same essential attributes). This

164 : Philosophical Theology

could be repaired, but only by our assuming some premise like (d), to which we have already objected.

(ii) The fallaciousness of premise (3), in which it is assumed that an infinite chain cannot have both a first and a last member. Once it is admitted that such a series can have first and last members, the argument requires an extensive set of a priori truths to replace (3). But I think this could be provided in view of the relationship 'essentially ordered cause of'.

Therefore an abiding and irreparable defect of the argument is the fact that (d) and (c) are presupposed, that (d) is false, and that (c) is so strong a claim that it could not (in any philosophically practicable way) be established without our first taking "God exists" as a premise.[13] Hence, once the a priori principle (d) is rejected, premise (c), which is required to complete the reasoning—with appropriate repairs in (3), as indicated in (i) and (ii) above—cannot in principle be established independently of the conclusion and must be declared in the context of this argument to be inaccessible to philosophical substantiation.

The third way

1: Some things are such that both to-be and not-to-be are possible for them.

2: It is impossible for these things always to exist (a priori).

3: If everything can not-be, then at one time there was nothing (a priori).

4: If at one time nothing existed, nothing would now exist (a priori).

5: If at one time nothing existed, it would be impossible for anything to begin to exist (a priori).

6: Therefore, not all things can not-be.

7: Therefore, something exists which cannot not-be and has this attribute of itself.

---

[13] In the broadest sense, a conclusion is epistemically prior to a premise for someone if he would have to know the conclusion to be true in order to know the premise to be true. From this, I have extrapolated the case of evidential posteriority. A premise is evidentially posterior to a true conclusion if we could not by philosophical investigation establish the true premise to be true unless we employed the conclusion as a premise of that establishment. We have a case of that sort here. This is a philosophically serious deficiency where there is actually reason to believe the premises false, as there is with the case of premise (c).

Premise (1) is intended as an independently verifiable truth of observation. We can accept it as such. The presence of the modal term "impossible" tells us that premise (2) is intended as a priori. But I see no contradiction (as St. Thomas admitted in other places when discussing the eternity of the world) in supposing that God *from eternity* created a universe which is *possible*-not-to-be, with that possibility deriving from the mere fact that we suppose God *freely* created it. Hence, (2) must be both false (as a priori) and contradictory, since it has a consistent negation. Suppose we replace (2) with "No such things always exist." This cannot be established by any argument stronger than an induction, and cannot therefore come up to standard for the type of argument we need, since the conjunction of (2), (3), (4), and (5) must give us an a priori truth if we are to have an argument of form (F), as described in the first section of this chapter. However, we can pass over this, because other objections are even more fundamental.

Premise (3) cannot be an a priori truth since it has a consistent denial; in fact, (3) is necessarily false. For even if we assume that every contingent being ceases to exist at some time, it does not follow that there is any time at which *all* have ceased to exist. Why could God not make an infinite number of contingent beings which succeed one another during an infinite time and, perhaps, even during a finite time? Hence, (3) must be false and contradictory.[14]

Nor does (3) follow from (2). 'For every being there is a time at which it does not exist' does not entail 'There is a time such that no being exists'. This is an illegitimate reversal of existential and universal quantifiers: from a statement of the form $(x)(\exists y)(\phi xy)$ we have illegitimately concluded $(\exists y)(x)(\phi xy)$.

Premise (4) seems obviously true. But we must remember that (4) supposes that for it to be possible for something, z, to exist which did not always exist, it *must* be the case that z was produced. This can be put in the following form:

e: It is necessarily the case that whatever begins to exist is produced by something else.

---

[14] It must be remembered that if a proposition in the mode of necessity is false, it is necessarily false or contradictory.

Now (e) is supposed to be a necessary or a priori truth; therefore it should have a contradictory denial. But where is the contradiction in my supposing that a table begins to exist right here in my study and that for it there is no cause, producer, or explanation at all? Certainly given that God exists and is *Creator Omnium* (that nothing can begin to be apart from His effective choice), and that these are necessary or a priori truths, we can derive (e). But how can we do so without those premises? Hence, (e), which is presupposed by the Third Way, cannot be established by an argument which is epistemically independent of the conclusion: you would have to know the conclusion to be true —indeed, to be true a priori—in order to have *found out for yourself* that (e) is true.

To premise (5) the same principle (e) is supposed and the same comments are applicable.

In sum, it can be said that this argument involves two false a priori premises, at least one logical fallacy of illegitimate quantifier-reversal, and one premise, (4), which presupposes a principle which, even if it were true, would be evidentially posterior to the conclusion.

The fourth way

1: Some things are more or less good, true, noble, etc.

2: "More" and "less" are applied to things insofar as they resemble some maximum or standard (a priori).

3: Therefore there is something which is noblest, best, and consequently greatest in being.

4: The maximum of any sort is the cause of all in that class.

5: Therefore, there must be something which is cause of being, goodness, and perfection in all other things.

Premise (1) can be taken as an independently verifiable truth of observation. Premise (2) is a priori in the sense that it is supposed to state the relationship between the concepts 'more' and 'less' and certain of our other concepts. Let us accept (2).

But (3) does not follow from (2). It need not be the case that what is the standard of nobility for someone is also his standard of perfection in being; moreover, it does not follow that *what* is the standard or maximum for someone actually exists, but only that there actually *is* such a standard; i.e., that someone *takes* something he conceives of, as the standard. Hence the argument as given presupposes:

f: *It is necessarily the case that the true standards of nobility, goodness, and other perfection are all the same thing.*

g: *It is necessarily the case that what is taken as standard (or presupposed by what is taken as standard) actually exists.*

Now, (g) is just what was to be proved and hence causes the argument to beg the question. Since (f) is taken as a necessary truth, I would like to see the contradiction in its denial shown in a way which does not beg the question also. It seems that neither (f) nor (g) is true; (f) is false because there is nothing which is uniquely the true standard of perfection to the exclusion of everything else. This will yield the negation of (g).

Premise (4) cannot be intended literally. The biggest liar is not a cause of all the others. Satan does not *cause* the sins of others. On any literal and reasonable interpretation, (4) is false.

Hence this argument must be rejected.

In this unsympathetic treatment of an argument which clearly represents an achievement of the neoplatonic tradition, I have provided no account of the quite different aspect it presents in the context of that tradition's metaphysics. My reason for not doing so is the fact that the general metaphysical background of the argument has already been found wanting in many respects, even by St. Thomas himself. Hence, any consideration we give the argument must be apart from its metaphysical background; it is not surprising that in this context too it is defective.

The fifth way[15]

1: *Some things which lack knowledge act for an end.*

2: *Whatever lacks knowledge cannot act for an end unless it be directed by some being endowed with knowledge and intelligence (a priori).*

3: *Therefore, some intelligent being exists by which all natural things are directed to their end.*

---

[15] The Fifth Way is a paradigm of the argument form (F), discussed in Section 1, subsection 4 of this chapter.

Premise (1) is clearly intended as an independently verifiable observation whose truth is disclosed by our noticing the regular action
of natural objects to obtain the best available result, where "obtaining the best result" involves adjusting action-resources to the state
of the environment so as to maximize the degree to which the agent's
needs are fulfilled. There is a sense in which the actions of non-
knowing things are evidently *purposive*—that is, done *as if* on purpose. What is to be shown is that they are also *purposed*, not indeed
by the object but by a "cosmic archer."

Premise (2) is ambiguous. In one sense it is true: it is impossible that
a non-knowing thing should move toward an end in a *purposed* manner unless it is directed by some being endowed with knowledge and
intelligence. But if this is the sense of (2), the argument will be a *non-
sequitur* unless another premise is added.

h: *It is false that action which is purposive in natural things is not also purposed.*

i: *It is necessarily the case that whenever actions of natural things are purposive, they are also purposed.*

Premise (h) cannot be established universally by induction, and
hence cannot function as the needed premise to provide an argument which establishes its conclusion. But (i), which would serve this
objective, is itself undiscoverable independently of the conclusion's
being considered true a priori. For suppose God did not exist; the
universe might still be *purposive*, act as if on purpose, but it would,
ex hypothesi, not be *purposed*. Now if you tell me the supposition of
God's not existing is logically impossible, I will welcome a convert to
Chapter III (though probably not a convinced one) but will point out
that this only shows that for you (i) is apparently not epistemically independent of the conclusion to be established: you have to regard
the conclusion as necessarily true in order to assure yourself that (i) is
true. It is an unsuccessful argument in which one needs to regard the
conclusion as a logical truth before he can accept the premises as
being themselves "of knowledge standard."[16]

We shall pass over with scant notice certain formal inadequacies of

---

[16] Of course, if one merely needed to know the conclusion was a priori but did not need to know its
truth-value, no circularity would result. But this does not apply here.

the argument. For instance, even if every action in the universe by non-knowing things is purposed by some intelligence, it does not simply follow that all these things are purposed by the same intelligence; to say this is to commit the same reversal of quantifiers we noted in the earlier arguments. Perhaps this defect can be repaired by a proper selection of a priori truths to add as premises; but I am inclined to think that such premises will be found to beg the question. For in order to make the required correction, one must prove it a *necessary* truth that all purposive action by non-thinking things is the result of the direction of some one intelligent being. This will require that one regard 'God exists' as true and as *necessarily* true.

In conclusion to this section: The five arguments of the *Summa* are defective for the various reasons indicated (although some of these defects are remediable). But, most important, each argument involves an assumption which cannot without begging the question be established empirically, but must be established a priori. Yet in each case the *appropriate* a priori premises—that is, (b), (d), (e), (g), and (i) —can reasonably be doubted, although there is evidence that if it is necessarily true that God exists, at least some of these principles could be deductively established from that premise; but this only shows that these propositions are evidentially posterior *for us* to the conclusions St. Thomas attempted to derive.

The defect common to the Five Ways is simply that in order to provide the a priori premises (b), (d), (e), (g), and (i) with the grounds we would need to render a revised version of each argument deductively sound, we would have to employ the conclusion as a premise. Thus we are required to perform, independently of the premises, the very same task—the methodical determination of the truth-value of the conclusion—that the arguments were supposed to perform for us.

SECTION 3: COMPARISON OF THE ASSUMPTIONS OF THE FIVE WAYS
TO DUNS SCOTUS' METHOD OF ARGUMENT

(1) Each of the Five Ways involves a premise which is a priori, and which we have found to be doubtful because of the apparent consistency of its negation, apart from our premising the conclusion in its support. These premises are:

First Way: (b) It is necessarily the case that every being in motion should have for its motion an explanation, cause, or reason.

Second Way: (d) It is necessarily the case that for any efficient cause there is either a cause of its being or there is something which renders its being self-explanatory.

Third Way: (e) It is necessarily the case that whatever begins to exist is produced by something else.

Fourth Way: (g) It is necessarily the case that what is taken as a standard (of perfection), or presupposed by what is taken as a standard, actually exists.

Fifth Way: (i) It is necessarily the case that whenever actions of natural things are purposive, they are also purposed.

(2) Each of these claims entails a weaker principle, which is not assailed by the objection to the stronger, and which when combined with Principle E (see Chapter III) provides an a priori argument for the original conclusion.

Premise (b) entails: It is possible that every being in motion should have for its motion an explanation, cause, or reason.

This is semantically compatible with the existence of some efficient cause which does not have a cause or explanation, but which might have had one.

Premise (e) entails: It is possible that whatever begins to exist is produced by something else.

This is semantically compatible with something's beginning to exist which is not produced, but which might have been.

Premise (d) entails: It is possible that for every efficient cause there is either a cause of its being or there is something which renders its being self-explanatory.

Premise (g) entails: It is possible that what is taken as a standard of perfection, or is presupposed by what is taken as a standard, actually exists.

Premise (i) entails: It is possible that whenever actions of natural things are purposive, they are also purposed.

Each of these principles seems quite plausible.

Duns Scotus was convinced that decisive arguments for the existence of a divine being could be constructed from several of the above principles.[17] For example, the first, in conjunction with the obvious a priori truth that not every series of movers, causes, purposers, and producers *must* be infinite, will entail that a first mover, cause, producer, and designer is possible. One then argues, in effect, that such a being could not be possible unless it exists. This is similar to the two forms of argument given in the next section, which I consider to be basically sound. However, it must be emphasized that the key steps in showing that such a being as a First Cause, First Mover, Unconditioned Being, or Designer must exist if it is possible, absolutely must employ some general and a priori claim (Principle E) of the form 'For every being which is possible, it must either be the case that it is self-existent or self-explanatory or that it is *consistent* to say something else produces or accounts for it or might have done so'. Then it is argued that it is not consistent to say that a First Cause, First Mover, Designer, etc., can *consistently* be said to be produced or accounted for. Hence, it is concluded that such beings exist.[18]

---

[17] See both *De Primo Principio* and *Lectura In Librum Primum Sententiarum*, (Vol. XVI, J. D. Scoti *Opera Omni*, Civitas Vaticana, 1960). Important passages on the proof of the existence of God can be found in Duns Scotus, *Philosophical Writings*, ed. A. Wolter, O.F.M., "The Library of Liberal Arts," No. 194 (New York: The Bobbs-Merrill Company, Inc., 1962).

[18] An argument following Scotus' plan would look something like this:

1: *It is possible that whatever begins to exist is produced by something else.*
2: *Some things begin to exist.*
3: *It is not necessary that there be an infinite chain of causes of beginning-to-exist which does not have a first member.*
4: *Therefore it is possible that there is a first unproducible producer of those things which begin to exist.*
5: *It is either (a) consistent to say something produces a first unproducible producer or (b) it is true the being of such a thing is self-explanatory.*
6: *It is not consistent to say that something produces a first unproduced producer.*
7: *Therefore the being of such a thing is self-explanatory.*
8: *Whatever is such that its being is self-explanatory exists.*
9: *Therefore an unproducible first producer exists.*

Subtle refinements are lacking in this sketch and, as the argument stands, we have not a proof but rather a rough outline, just as a charcoal sketch is not itself an oil portrait, but is a useful guide to the design. In particular, this "lining" of the proof directs attention to lines 5 and 6, whose presupposition of Principle E is what is so crucial. Consider what St. Thomas says in the *Compendium*, chapter 6: "The same line of reasoning clearly shows that God necessarily exists. For everything that has the possibility of being and of not being, is mutable. But God is absolutely immutable, as has been demonstrated. Therefore it is impossible for God to be and not to be. But anything that exists in such a way that it is impossible for it not to exist, is necessarily Being itself, *ipsum esse*. Necessary existence, and impossibility of non-existence, mean one and the same thing. Therefore God must necessarily exist." Compendium of Theology, tr. Cyril Vollert, S.D., S.T.D. (St. Louis: Herder Book Company, 1949), p. 11.

The principle which we supposed as the required additional premise is basically the same as Principle E, which was involved in our more rigorous examination of the claim that *real* or *metaphysical* possibility is the same as logical possibility.[19] Hence, if our main arguments are sound it will be only a matter of routine care to construct a great number of sound arguments, taking the premises above, or quite similar ones, and adding Principle E.[20] In effect, Duns Scotus has discovered a recipe for large-scale production of theistic arguments based upon the reduction of real or metaphysical possibility to logical possibility that I indicated in Chapter III.[21]

Now a brief *ad hominem* circumstantial argument for the Thomists: if the a priori principles (b), (d), (e), (g), and (i) are not true, there is no possibility of rehabilitating the set of St. Thomas' arguments as deductively valid establishments, since each of these arguments requires one of these principles if it is to be "of demonstrative standard."

But since we have already found the truth of the conclusion to be a logically necessary condition for the truth of these premises, and to be evidentially prior to them as well, the conclusion must be logically true, if the premises are true, because the *only* logically necessary conditions upon a logical truth are other logical truths.[22] Thus, I think that the Thomists who might question whether Aquinas really held 'God exists' to be a logically true statement must either accept my contention that that conclusion is a logical truth which can be estab-

---

[19] See Chapter III.

[20] In the manner indicated in the previous paragraph and note 18.

[21] The formula Duns Scotus developed was basically this: to use the traditional "motion," "cause," and "design" reasoning to establish not the actuality but the possibility that there is a being which is divine, and then to argue from Principle E that it is not possible that there should be such a being unless there actually is such a being. The formula is utterly simple, and its applications are manifold: we can devise endless forms of Principle E which will say, in effect, that a divine being is not possible if it does not exist because divinity involves self-accounting being, a-*seity*, and to say that a being is by nature self-accounting but that it does not exist is to talk nonsense or to assert an explicit contradiction. How do we decide the truth-value of such propositions as "It is necessarily the case that all self-accounting beings actually exist" or "It is impossible that there should be a *merely possible* self-accounting being"? This was explained in the final pages of Chapter III, where the implications of the definition of "self-accounting" were traced, and where we considered the relationship of the definition to the Principle of Hetero-Explicability: that every contingent state of affairs is hetero-explicable.

[22] This is equivalent to an additional proof that St. Thomas' philosophical system was *committed*, regardless of what statement he actually made, to the doctrine that 'God exists' is a necessary truth. It should be obvious that the truth of the conclusion 'God exists' is a logically necessary condition for the truth of several of the assumptions of the Five Ways. Now what is logically necessary for an a priori truth is *itself* a priori true, since nothing is entailed by an a priori truth but an a priori truth.

lished by arguments employing only a priori premises and such obvious truths as "Some things are caused, moved, designed, etc." or else must entirely abandon their own arguments! There is no point in expounding this *argumentum ad hominem* in detail, since it is merely circumstantial and is designed to suggest the systematic commitment of St. Thomas' philosophy to the main contention of this book: that 'God exists' is an a priori truth. This argument certainly is not intended to suggest that the Five Ways can be suitably repaired for their task.

SECTION 4: SOME ACCEPTABLE ARGUMENTS

Here I shall briefly state two arguments which, I believe, adequately establish the existence of a being which is properly called "God" (although they do not establish that the being *is* properly called "God," or that there is only one such being). These arguments are simpler in form, less precisely qualified, but generally adequate specific forms of the Modal Argument of Chapter III. Moreover, the second argument has quite definite antecedents in the works of Duns Scotus, and by reason of its distinguished classical authorship deserves to be included among the basic attempts by Christian thinkers to establish the existence of God.

Both arguments presuppose the principle that for any particular *contingent* state of affairs, it is possible that there should be or should have been an explanation of its being the case; this principle is a specific form of what in Chapter III was stated (in terms of "consistent" states of affairs) as Principle E; we may as well give this specific principle a name, and call it the Principle of Hetero-Explicability, or Principle H. Its special distinction is that from it, combined with the definition of "self-explanatory," we can actually deduce Principle E. Moreover, in addition to the intuitive obviousness of Principle H we will discover, while considering the following arguments, that it is well supported by general considerations accepted in other areas of philosophy, particularly in the philosophy of science.

A: The argument from "self-explanation"

The two forms of this argument are "modernized"; but like every philosophical classic, it is replete with antecedents in the writings of many, many predecessors—in this case, Duns Scotus,[23] Leibniz, and Spinoza.

FIRST FORM

1: It is possible that whatever is not the case should have either a self-explanation in terms of the inherent absurdity of its having been the case, or a hetero-explanation in terms of causes, agents, or producers whose actions prevent its being the case or whose own failure to act or to obtain is causally sufficient for its not being the case.

2: 'God does not exist' cannot be the case, because:

a: There is no absurdity or contradiction in 'God does exist', and hence 'God does not exist' is not self-explanatory.

b: "God" cannot denote anything unless that thing be both uncaused and unprevented by any other thing and, furthermore, be both uncausable and unpreventable by any entity whatever. Therefore, "God" cannot denote anything which is such that 'God does not exist' is hetero-explicable.

3: Then 'God exists' must be the case.

Part (1) is somewhat ambiguous, but we can supplement it by an interpretation. Let us suppose that 'God exists', or *g, is not the case.* Now part (1) says that it is possible that either:

a: ~g should be self-explanatory (in view of the inherent absurdity of g).

or

b: ~g should be hetero-explicable (in view of the possible prevention of g by something else).

The remainder of the argument is:

1: g is not inherently absurd, and hence ~g is not self-explanatory.

2: g is not preventable, since God is uncausable and unpreventable.

3: Hence, the supposition that 'God exists' is not the case is false.

4: Therefore, 'God exists' must be true.

---

[23] In *Reportata Parisiensia,* I, d. 2, q. 2, n. 6, Scotus says: "Si potest esse et non ab alio, igitur necessarium est": "If it can exist but cannot exist *ab alio* (as accounted for by something else), it is, therefore, a necessary being" (my translation). This is central. Since no one will deny that a divine being is precisely the sort of thing which cannot exist *ab alio,* the greatest importance must be assigned Scotus' claim that a being which cannot exist *ab alio* exists necessarily. If this can be shown to be true, the whole question of the existence of God is decided affirmatively. If it can be shown to be false, then an adequate establishment of the existence of God can be shown to be impossible.

The only objection to this argument which seems to demand immediate treatment is the objection to the use of the proper name "God." But here "God" functions primarily significatively, and insofar as it is incidentally designative it can be disregarded, since we can substitute an indefinite description without loss of validity. And "God is unpreventable" is merely shorthand for "the proposition 'something prevented its being the case that a divine being exists' is absurd and contradictory."

SECOND FORM

1: It is logically possible that there exists a self-explanatory being.

2: It is either the case that:

(a) There actually exists such a being; or

(b) There does not exist such a being and there exists, did exist, will exist, or could have existed some other being which could have produced a self-explanatory being; or

(c) There exists, did exist, will exist or could have existed some being which could produce a self-explanatory being (in the present or future); or

(d) Such a being, though not existing, could have begun to exist without an explanation's being possible for its beginning to exist; or

(e) Such a being could have begun to exist without an explanation for its beginning to exist, although such an explanation is possible.

3: Assume that (a) is false.

4: Then b ∨ c ∨ d ∨ e.

5: Not-b: for a being which could have been produced cannot be self-explanatory. (See the definition in Chapter III)

6: Not-c: for a being which could be produced cannot be self-explanatory.

7: Not-d: for nothing can begin to exist which is such that it is logically impossible for its beginning-to-exist to have an explanation even though it does not. (From the Principle of Hetero-Explicability)

8: Not-e: for it is not possible that the beginning-to-exist of a self-explanatory being should have an explanation. (Since the beginning-to-exist is inherently impossible)

9: Therefore, supposition (3) must be false, since (b), (c), (d), and (e) are all impossible.

10: Since (3) is false, there exists a self-explanatory being.

Despite the apparent difference, this is the same as the first argument; hence it is treated as a second form of it.

We shall not examine objections to these versions of the Modal Argument[24] here, because I think the most important points have already been raised in Chapter III. Instead, let us look at still another argument.

B: The Scotist argument[25]

1: That there is at least one Uncausable Producer is logically possible.

2: Whatever is logically possible is either actual or potential.

3: Whatever is potential is causable.

4: No Uncausable Producer is causable.

5: Hence, no Uncausable Producer is potential.

6: Therefore, at least one Uncausable Producer is actual, that is, exists.

STIPULATION OF SOME DEFINITIONS

a: a is the cause of b if there is some self-consistent causal universal of the form $(x)(\varphi x NPC\phi x)$, where "NPC" means "non-paradoxically causally implies," according to which a statement of the form 'a exists' or 'a occurs' causally implies a statement of the form 'b exists' (with or without the specification of further conditions or further characteristics of a and b).[26]

b: a is an uncausable producer if a has properties such that there is some thing or event, b, such that "a is the producer of b" could be true, and there is no consistent set of causal universals according to which the statement "there is a z which is sufficient cause of a" is logically consistent.

---

[24] This name has been given by Charles Hartshorne to a similar argument in his *Logic of Perfection* (Open Court, pages 49–52). I came upon his work after already having given this name to the arguments central to these Chapters III and IV; the similarity in structure between these arguments and his reworking of the Anselmian argument appears great enough to justify our using the same name for both sorts of argument.

[25] In preparing this "Scotist" argument I have not taken any particular argument of Duns Scotus as a whole, but have rather synthesized the spirit of his "touching-up" of Anselm (*Opus Oxoniense*, I, d. 2, q. 2, n. 32 and 43; *Reportata Parisiensia*, I. a, d. 2, q. 2, n. 73), "first cause" argument (*De Primo Principio*, Chapter III), and parts of the argument for the existence of an infinite being (*Opus Oxoniense*, I, d. 2, q. 2, n. 25). A somewhat more elaborate form of my argument appeared in *Theoria*, XXVIII (1962), 2: "Does 'x is possible' ever yield 'x exists'?"

[26] The expression "non-paradoxically causally implies" is herein employed in the sense explained by Arthur W. Burks in his paper "Dispositional Statements," *Philosophy of Science*, Vol. XXIII, no. 3 (July, 1955), pp. 175–193. If p, the first existential statement, causally implies r, a second existential, then there is some causal universal, q, such that $(p \cdot q)$ logically entails r.

c: *a is actual if a is an element of this possible world; that is, if "a actually exists" is ever true.*

d: *b is potential if "b exists" is logically possible but is not actual.*[27]

e: *b is causable if it is not logically impossible that there should be some set of consistent causal universals according to which there could be some entity, y, which is a causally sufficient condition for b—in short, if it is logically possible that b should have a cause.*

f: *a produces b, either if a is the cause of b (on definition [a] above); or if a has a disposition to free agency, the supposed exercise of which "accounts" for the existence or occurrence of b. No producer is both agent and cause with respect to the same thing, b; moreover, whenever a is agent of b, it is false that there is anything else, c, which is sufficient cause of b.*[28]

PROOFS FOR THE PREMISES

Premise 1: At least one Uncausable Producer is logically possible.

1: *Some things are actually produced.*

2: *Some producer is logically possible (entailed by [1]).*

3: *This producer is either*

    a: *An element of a series of producers, each of which is causable; or*

    b: *An element of a series of producers at least one of which is uncausable.*

4: *(3a) is not analytic.*

5: *Therefore, (3b) is not self-contradictory.*

6: *Hence, at least one Uncausable Producer is logically possible (premise 1).*

Suppositions of the proof:

a: *That the disjunction contained in statement (3) is complete.*

b: *That it is a priori true that if one element of a complete disjunction is not analytic, the other is not self-contradictory; this rule is used to infer (5) from (4).*

[27] We more often use "actual" and "potential" in other ways; these definitions are unusual in that what is actual is never potential, and vice versa. These definitions are stipulated in order to simplify our considerations; no presumption of accord with traditional usage (or usage elsewhere in this book) is supposed. Note that whatever is potential *might* have existed or obtained, had things been other than as they are.

[28] It would be possible to make 'agency' a subclass of 'causing' in a wider sense than I have employed in definition (a). But it might then be argued that the import of the proof for premise (1) is not clear. This usage is stipulated in order to avoid the appearance of equivocation, but it is not intended to carry beyond this argument and, hence, should not be thought to conflict with the explicit provision to the contrary in Chapters III, V, and VI.

Both these suppositions are true.

Premise 2: Whatever is logically possible is either actual or potential.

This premise is a priori true; it is a complete disjunction equivalent to the statement that every thing which is logically consistent is such that either it exists at some time or it never exists, although it might have existed.

Premise 3: Whatever is potential is causable.

1: Whatever is potential is contingent. If something does not exist but might have existed had things been otherwise than as they are, the statement asserting its existence is contingent; for if the existential statement were contradictory, the entity would not be logically possible, and logical possibility is, according to definition (e), necessary for potentiality. If the existential statement in question were necessary, it would be true; but potentiality supposes (as the concept is employed in this particular argument) the falsity of the appropriate existential statement. Hence, whatever is potential is said to exist, if it is said to exist at all, by our employing a contingent existential statement (which is false).

2: There is no contingent existential statement which is not such that it can be consistently causally implied by some other contingent existential statement, according to some causal universal of the form (x)(φx NPC φx). This is another statement of the Principle of Hetero-Explicability, which is central to all the arguments and is a logical truth.

3: Whatever can be described by a contingent existential statement is causable, according to statement (2) and definition (e). But whatever is potential can be so described. Therefore, whatever is potential is causable.

But is statement (2), that every contingent existential statement can be causally implied by some other contingent existential statement, true? Here we come upon some of the grounds for what I earlier called the "intuitive" obviousness of Principle H.

This is equivalent to the claim that for any property, G, which can be possessed by anything whose existence is contingent, there is some property, F, which neither entails nor is entailed by G, such that (x)(Fx NPC Gx) is consistent and such that (x)(~Fx · Gx) is also consistent (although, of course, these are not co-consistent). Hence in some possible world (∃x)(Gx) is causally implied by (∃x)(Fx). This claim seems obvious enough.

It may be wondered why no exception to this rule might be supposed. Assume that there is some statement, *p*, of the form (∃x)(Fx), where F is a property which cannot consistently be said to be non-paradoxically causally implied by any property G. The truth of *p* is thus causally independent of the truth-values of all other existential statements; to posit that *p* is true can never lead to an inconsistency with any true existential statement conjoined with any set of causal laws; there are no conditions under which *p* would be hypothetically impossible. Hence *p* is compatible with all other states of affairs (except, of course, its own negation). Is it not true of every necessary statement that it is neutral to the truth-values of all contingent statements, and consistent with all other states of affairs except its own negation? And is it not true that a contradiction is consistent with no state of affairs, whereas what is *contingent* is compatible with some states of affairs but *not* with others? Thus it follows that *p* is not contingent.

Further, let us suppose that *p* is false, but logically possible; it could have been true had things been otherwise. But what would have had to be different? What difference in the things which are actual would have had to occur? None; for the supposition that *p* would *become* true if things were not the way they are is either utterly trivial or self-inconsistent. *P* could not become true; if it were possible for it to do so, it would have done so already, since by hypothesis nothing prevents or could prevent this becoming. Thus it seems that the supposition that *p* is false is inconsistent with the claim that *p* is possible: this is a general feature of all logically necessary existential statements. This is what we suggested, at the end of the first part of Chapter III, as the "encompassing" sense of "necessary."

Someone may argue that this theorem is not universally true, that there is at least one contingent existential statement which is not causally conditionable, that is, 'God exists'. The appropriate reply is a denial of the example's supposition: that 'God exists' is contingent; next, consistency forces one to deny the wider supposition that all existential statements are contingent. And this move merely highlights the very point at issue. It is of very great importance to the would-be theist employing this argument that the existential *p* should not be considered contingent; it is of equal importance to the would-remain atheist or agnostic that *p* should not be considered logically necessary. If one accepts the argument of Chapter III, that *g* is an a priori proposition, this main element of dispute is automatically decided, and Leibniz is instanter shown to have been right. If the theorem in question is true of all contingent existentials, the theist's argument stands. And there seems to be ample weight on the theist's side here, since a contingent statement is one whose truth-value could be different under different causal conditions. Yet, given a statement which cannot possibly be causally conditioned by other contingent statements, it is difficult to see how its truth-value could be different under different conditions; for no other statement or change of statements makes a difference in the truth-value of p; there can be no difference of truth conditions when nothing whatever can make such a difference.

Premise 4: No Uncausable Producer is causable (analytic).

Premise 5: Therefore, No Uncausable Producer is potential (follows from [3] and [4] by *modus tollens*).

Conclusion, 6: At least one Uncausable Producer is actual, i.e., exists. This follows from (5) and (2) by disjunctive syllogism.

Thus, the premises stand justified, and the conclusion is established. It is to be emphasized that what is crucial to this argument is whether or not 'God exists' is either a priori true or a priori false. Hence, the independent proof of apriority given in Chapter III, Section 2, is of immense importance.

An Historical Comment

Leibniz is often said to have inferred the existence of God from the possibility of God.[29] Yet it should be emphasized that he merely claimed to do this, and did not invent the argument which underlies that claim.

---

[29] "If there is a reality in essences or possibilities or indeed in eternal truth, this reality must be founded in something existing and actual, and consequently in the existence of the necessary being, in whom essence involves existence or with whom it is sufficient to be possible in order to be actual. Hence, God alone (or the necessary being) has this prerogative, that He must exist if He is possible." Leibniz, *Monadology*, pars. 44 and 45, in *Leibniz Selections*, ed. Philip P. Wiener (New York: Scribner, 1951), p. 541. See also the *Discourse on Metaphysics*, sec. XXIII (p. 324 of Scribner edition).

There seems to be little reason to doubt that the general form of this argument originated with John Duns Scotus.[30] Crucial elements of the arguments from possibility were extant much earlier in the Christian tradition than the time of Scotus, but they had not been forged into one claim. Richard of St. Victor (ca. 1150), for example, argued for the existence of God as the ground of the possibility of all other things and as an entity whose possibility was necessarily independent of anything else.[31] He almost paraphrases Aristotle[32] when he says, "Those things which are eternal are such that it is entirely impossible that they should not exist. . . ."[33] It would not be correct to suppose that Richard's argument has any refinement or subtlety comparable to that of Scotus' proofs, which were presented in the framework of his developed metaphysics; although Richard anticipated Scotus, Scotus went far beyond any of his predecessors, even Avicenna.

It was not by a happy accident or even on the grounds of persuasiveness that Scotus elected to produce his theological arguments in terms of possibility. He had decided that all metaphysical explanations, to count as explanations, had to take note of the conditions of the real *possibility* of what is actual; thus there is good reason to see Duns Scotus as a direct ancestor of Kant's desire to account not only for phenomena but also for the conditions of the possibility of phenomena. Scotus asked not only how it was that things were the way they were, but how it was *possible* for them to be so.[34] In such employment of the term "possible," Scotus is clearly relying upon a notion of metaphysical or real possibility. In Section 1 of Chapter III,

---

[30] None of the historians who have discussed Scotus' proofs for the existence of God (all of which are based upon the notion of possibility) has mentioned any other source of this argument form, other than the weak adumbration of it by Richard, which I note below. See E. Gilson, *Jean Duns Scot;* E. Bettoni, *L'Ascensa a Dio in Duns Scoto* (Milano, 1943); Pluzanski, *Saggio sulla filosoia di D. Scoto* (Firenze, 1892); also the works of F. S. Belmond, Allessandro Bertoni, Glorieux, Heiser, Longpré, and Alan B. Wolter, O.F.M. However, there is some reason to think that Avicenna and other medieval Arabic philosophers used arguments which, at the very least, would have suggested this form to the perceptive theologian.

[31] Richard of Saint Victor, *De Trinitate*, P.L., Vol. 196, cols. 891–896.

[32] Aristotle, *Physics* III, 4, 203b29: "In the case of eternal things, what can be must be."

[33] Richard of Saint Victor, *De Trinitate*, P.L., Vol. 196, col. 894, D.

[34] Duns Scotus: "I prefer to submit conclusions and premises about the possible, for if those about the actual are conceded, those about the possible are conceded, but not conversely; those about the actual are contingent, though manifest enough; those about the possible are necessary." *De Primo Principio*, Chapter III, p. 41. Compare Fr. Wolter's translation of *A Treatise on God as First Principle*, cited above, p. 42.

we discussed the relationships between this notion and that of logical possibility; it was suggested that by employing Principle E as an a priori premise and by defining "g is really necessary" as "~g is incompatible with E" and "g is really possible" as "g is consistent with E," etc., we can show that whatever is really possible is logically possible, and vice versa, with the result that what is really necessary is also logically necessary.

SECTION 5: TWO INTERESTING ARGUMENTS

A: A "coloration" of Anselm's argument

1: *Definition:* The *Summum Cogitabile* is the most perfect being whose existence is consistently conceivable.

2: It is possible that a *Summum Cogitabile* exists intentionally, is actual object of thought rather than potential object of thought; for it is actually an intentional object for the person who grasps the definition.

3: It is possible that the *Summum Cogitabile* really exists.
   a: What is consistently conceivable is possible (such that the proposition that it exists involves no contradiction).
   b: The *Summum Cogitabile* is conceivable. This follows from the definition of the expression "*Summum Cogitabile*" as something both consistently conceivable, and unequaled and unsurpassed in perfection by anything else which can be consistently conceived.

4: Whatever is possible either actually exists at some time, or else does not exist but might have existed.

5: The *Summum Cogitabile* must account for its own existence or non-existence (since this is clearly more perfect than to have existence accounted for by something else, or by nothing at all).

6: The *Summum Cogitabile* cannot be such that it does not really exist but might have really existed, for no non-existing thing which might have existed can be self-explanatory.

7: Therefore, by disjunctive syllogism from (4) and (6), the *Summum Cogitabile* must really exist.

SOME COMMENTS

Definition (1) is similar to the following definition: The *Summum Difficile:* the most difficult person anyone could ever imagine. Now, suppose someone says to me: "Does the *Summum Difficile* exist?";

and suppose I do not know but will try to find out. First I must know whether the expression "the most difficult person anyone could ever imagine" is *consistent*. For it may be that difficult persons are like the possible worlds discussed in a later chapter of this book: your selecting one as prime example brings it about that there is a better instance which you have not chosen, in the same way that saying "God can think of any possible world" is not at all the same as saying "God can think of *all* possible worlds." It may be that there is not and cannot be something which is the one and only person imagined by someone, *than whom no* other person whom anyone could imagine could be more difficult to get along with. It is not at all easy to decide this point; but let us answer that we have decided that there is no "most difficult person anyone could ever imagine" just *because* my imagining a person who is difficult to degree *n* makes it possible for me to imagine a person who is difficult to degree *n* + 1, and makes sense to me out of my saying "just a little *more* difficult than the last." Thus I am able to imagine of a new Difficult Person. Hence, we can answer the question, "Does the *Summum Difficile* exist?" with the reply "No, and necessarily no." Therefore an expression of the form "the most ———— anyone can consistently conceive of" does not guarantee that there is such a thing, even intentionally or conceptually; so that premise (3b) is probably false.

One might think that something really exists which it is in fact not possible for us to think of, despite the fact that we have a *name* (or sometimes a definite description) for it; and we can talk and think about what would be the case if there were such a thing. For example: let "N" mean by definition "whatever is consistently conceivable, is a number, and is unequaled by any other number and unsurpassed by any other number." Someone might say, "There is something I am thinking of, namely, N." It would not follow that N exists (even intentionally), or even that the person had consistently conceived of N. For it is not possible that N exists; it is impossible that something exists which fulfills the conditions for being *properly* called by the name "N."

This example shows us that the subtle Scotus blundered when he thought to gain by adding the qualification "consistently conceivable" to the definition of the *Summum Cogitabile* in conjunction with other implied and stated attributes (for instance, that the thing *properly* called "the *Summum Cogitabile*" must be unsurpassed in perfection by anything else which is consistently conceivable). For if it should be the case that nothing (actual or possible) is properly called "the *Summum Cogitabile*" because each thing can be surpassed in perfection by something else which is consistently conceivable, then the fact that the definition specifies that this is the one and only consistent exception leads to a contradiction. Therefore, if the attributes assigned are not inconsistent, there is no need to specify that they are not; if they are inconsistent, an additional inconsistency follows from the specification that they are not.[35] Hence, nothing is gained by such addition, and there is nothing to be said for Scotus' "coloration" of Anselm's argument.[36]

It is interesting that Duns Scotus might be quick to point out one difficulty with my criticism of his "improvement" of Anselm's argument. This difficulty follows from the line of criticism that I have pursued that something, x, which is *by definition consistent* can be inconsistent.[37] Thus N, as we defined the term above, is an attribute such that $\lozenge (\exists x)(Nx)$ will entail that it is possible that something exists about which it is consistent to say that it exists *and* that it has the attribute of being largest among all numbers. But we can deduce an explicit contradiction from this; therefore we must conclude that it is not possible for anything to exist which has that attribute; i.e., of being the largest number and a possible existent. It would seem, then, that we have admitted that something may be both possible and impossible at the same time.

However, this would be incorrect. We can treat the definition of N as the definition of a second-level property '$N\phi x$.' And 'N' is the second-level property of being such that $[\lozenge (\exists x)(\phi x)]$ and

---

[35] The same problem arises for those apparent counter-examples to Principle E which are like the following: (a) an unproducible and unpreventable man; (b) an unproducible and unpreventable man which is not actual but which is possible. Despite the fact that the *description* in (b) specifies the possibility of there being such a thing, such a being is *impossible*, and the addition of 'possible' as a predicate is of no force in mitigating the contradictions involved in the two attributes. (b) is very much like 'a triangular circle which is possible.'

[36] *Opus Oxoniense*, I, 2, 2, n. 137–139: "Deus est quo cognito sine contradictione maius cogitari non potest sine contradictione. Et quod addendum sit 'sine contradictione' patet. . . ." See also *De Primo Principio*, Chapter 4: "Summum cogitabile non est tantum in intellectu cogitante; quia tunc posset esse, quia cogitabile et non potest esse, quia ratione ejus repugunt esse ab alio . . ." (p. 123 in Fr. Wolter's text, cited above).

[37] I do not think it follows that *everything* which is by definition consistent can be inconsistent; for suppose I say "x" shall be the name of any and every thing which is human and which is such that 'x exists' is consistent." Certainly nothing properly named (according to the definition of "x") can be inconsistent.

[$\sim \Diamond (\exists x)(\phi x)$] could both be true. That is, a modal operator is explicitly incorporated into the definition of a second-level property N; and the contrary modal operator is incorporated into the definition of the first-level property ϕ, which is a prerequisite for the occurrence of N. The fact that modal operators occur on two levels at the same time violates the type-relationship among concepts and causes the modal operators of all higher-than-first-level properties to be *canceled out*, since the weakest modality of the statement $(\exists x)(\phi x)$ determines the maximum modality of all statements involving higher-level properties of any x such that (ϕx) is true of it.

Thus, if $\Box \sim (\exists x)(Fx)$, then it cannot be the case that $\Diamond [(\exists r)(\exists x)(rF \cdot Fx)]$. This matter is, of course, beset with formal complications. But in the absence of a well-developed formal modal logic, it seems that this matter must be decided upon its intuitive obviousness (but almost always with at least some reservations), and hence, we must conclude that to introduce this supposed improvement (which has been highly praised by various commentators as a great advance by Duns Scotus) makes no advance and merely begs the question of whether the entity which is purportedly conceived really *is* conceived.

Proposition (b)—that what does not exist, but might have existed, cannot account for its own existence—seems evident enough. For whatever accounts for its own existence must do so by nature, and thus whatever is accounted (in the absence of all presupposed external causal conditions) must happen independently of any merely possible state of affairs. Thus, the nature of man accounts for man's rationality and hence for the rationality of any man that exists, even though some other thing may be required to *produce* and *sustain* a rational animal; any man, whether existing or not, is rational. Therefore, *if anything accounts for its own existence, it must not be a possible state of affairs that such a thing should not exist.*

But there is no way to determine the truth of premise (2) without settling the question of whether the expression 'the most perfect being that a man can think of' is consistent. For, if such a thing is consistent, then it can be thought of; if it is not consistent, then it can only be *thought* to be thought of. Thus, the main point of the argument can be put very directly as follows:

1: *It is possible that there really exists something which is properly called "the* Summum Cogitabile," *which is the most perfect being which any man can think of.*

2: What is possible either actually exists at some time or never actually exists but might have existed.

3: Nothing which is properly called "the Summum Cogitabile" *can be such that it does not really exist but might have really existed, since (a) it is a necessary condition for being the most perfect being that the thing should have self-explanatory existence if it exists and (b) it is impossible that something which does not exist should have had or should come to have self-explanatory existence.*

4: Therefore (by disjunctive syllogism of [2] and [3]) there must be something actually existing which is properly called "the Summum Cogitabile."

Now premise (1) is either a priori false or a priori true. If we assume that it is true, the key to the whole argument is premise (3). I think almost anyone would agree that if it is possible that something should account for its own existence, then a thing which *does* account for its own existence is a more perfect being than anything which *does* not. Thus (3a) is an a priori truth. So also with (3b). If something which is supposed to have self-explanatory existence does not exist, then either it is possible, or it is not, that the nonexistence of such a being is self-explanatory. It is impossible that both the existence and the nonexistence of one and the same thing should be self-explanatory, since in the latter case an inconsistency in the definitive (essential) characteristics is a logically necessary condition, while in the former, consistency is a logically necessary condition; and nothing can have both a consistent and an inconsistent set of essential characteristics. If the nonexistence of such a being is not self-explanatory, it cannot be *hetero-explicable* either, since the *absence* of that causal relation would be a necessary condition of its existence; thus it could not have self-explanatory existence. Hence, if something is such that when it exists, its existence is self-explanatory, then if it is possible that that thing exists, it is the case that it exists.

It might be argued that perhaps something which does *not* exist would have self-explanatory existence if it existed, but that there is no explanation for the nonexistence of this thing. Now either it is possible that there should be such an explanation, or it is not. It is our basic and a priori premise that it is possible for any particular contingent state of affairs that it should have an explanation (the Principle of Hetero-Explicability). Employing this premise, we can assume that it is the case either that the nonexistence in question is impossible, or that it is possible that it should have a hetero-explanation (since we can employ the previous argument to say that both the existence and the nonexistence of the same thing *cannot* be self-explanatory). Now since we have also just shown that the nonexistence of a self-existent being cannot be hetero-explained, we can conclude that the non-existence in question cannot have a hetero-explanation. Therefore, the nonexistence in question must be impossible, and the hypothet-ical objection we are considering must be inconsistent.

But we have employed Principle H, a sub-form of Principle E, as a decisive premise of the above argument. Thus, the argument is only a more extensive statement of the arguments given in Chapter III and in Section 3 of this chapter, and gains nothing from the addition of the concept '*Summum Cogitabile*'.

This argument has no special virtues. It is very similar to Argument I: it employs the same proposition, similar to Principle E, which all the arguments employ; moreover, it has the defect of employing what at first looks like the very profitable concept '*Summum Cogitabile*' as 'the most perfect being whose existence is consistently conceivable', but upon inspection this is found to be merely a name whose signifi-cation is no improvement over Anselm's concept.

My main purpose in presenting the argument is to state my dis-agreement with the historians' usual assessment of Scotus' "Colora-tion" of Anselm and to show in a practical way both how the intro-duction of the modality "consistently conceivable" as a property of things gained nothing, and that the apparent strength of the argument rests upon its containing the hard core of reasoning from possibility to existence by means of a Principle of Explicability which, according to my hypotheses, is distinctive of Scotus' thought and does not de-rive from those aspects which are "Anselmian."

B: The reality-levels argument

The work of Duns Scotus suggests another line of reasoning which, although it is basically neoplatonic in outlook, is deserving of consid-eration.

1: Suppose that all possible things are divided into levels of reality, accord-ing to some rule such that (a) no member of a lower level of reality could in any way account for the fact that some higher level of reality has any actually existing members; and (b) no lower level of reality could itself have mem-bers unless some higher level of reality has members.

2: Suppose it is evident that the level of natural beings is not the highest possible level of reality, and yet that this level has existent members.

3: It will follow from (1a) plus Principle E (and from the truth that whatever is possible either exists at some time or might have existed) that the highest level must have a member or members, and by virtue of their being of the highest level of reality the member or members of this level must be self-explanatory or self-accounting.

4: It will follow from (1b) and (2) that the highest level must have members.

5: If we use "Absolutely Perfect Being" as the common name of any and all members of the highest level, it will follow both that some absolutely perfect being exists, and that all absolutely perfect beings exist.

COMMENTS UPON THIS ARGUMENT

First one needs a definition of the expression "a is of a lower level of reality than *b*." There are many ways of forming such definitions, and the selection of one over another cannot, as far as I can see, be made apart from those important considerations which would be supplied by a general metaphysical system; a definition is to be offered below, repeated in Chapter VI, and extensively examined in the Appendix to Chapter VI. Hence, there is a sense in which all the arguments pre-viously discussed (with the exception, perhaps, of the Five Ways of Aquinas) are system-invariant with respect to metaphysical systems, although they lean heavily upon the logical devices we possess for handling the matter of modalities and upon our intuitive notion of explanation (this aspect might be greatly improved by the develop-ment of a precise and broadly applicable concept of 'explanation' for the sciences). But the argument just stated makes all of the assump-tions of the earlier arguments; it is, in addition, dependent upon the concept of 'reality level', a concept which is not employed by the earlier arguments and which is not system-invariant. Duns Scotus dis-tinguished levels of reality in terms of the *perfection* of the things of the various levels, so that the world (as is generally found in the neo-platonist–Augustinian tradition) is divided into levels of perfection. It was taken by him to be analytic that *the more perfect thing cannot have its existence explained (exclusively) by the less perfect*. Hence, he argued, suppose that the universe is divided into two levels, *A* and *B*, where *A* is a level of things that are more perfect than the things of *B*, and that these two levels are all that are possible; then if some member of *A*, called *a*, exists, its existence cannot be accounted for by some member, *b*, of *B*. Now, he argued, suppose *b* exists (some member of a lower level than *A*); it would not be true that it is possible that some member, *b*, of *B* exists unless there existed some member, *a*, of *A*. For no member of *B* can account for its own existence, since only the most perfect beings are self-accounting. Hence, the members of *B* are possible only if something exists which could bring it about that level *B* has members; and that something cannot be of the same or of a lower level than *B*, since the less perfect cannot produce the more perfect. Hence, there must be some member of *A* which actually exists. Now, let *B* be the name of any level of being which is not the level of the most perfect beings which are possible. It follows that in each case there is a member of some higher level than *B*. From this it follows that the highest possible level has actual (existing) members; and, since the highest possible level is the level of self-existent beings, such a self-existent being must exist.

It would not be an adequate objection to this argument to say that the number of levels of reality may be infinite. For the fact that the number of possible levels might be infinite is compatible both with the assumption that there is a lowest level and with the assumption that there is a highest possible level, just as there is an infinite series of real numbers between zero and one, yet a termination of the series in both directions. Moreover, by postulating the existence of members of a level of reality which is not the highest possible level and then concluding that the highest level should have members, the argument does not commit itself to *all* intervening levels. Rather, given the definitions and the axiom that for any thing that exists it is possible that there is something which accounts for its existence, the argument merely claims that since something which is not of the highest level actually exists, it follows that something which is of the highest level actually exists. Whether or not the intervening links have members and whether or not such intermediates are finite or infinite in number is not determined by the structure of the argument.

Hence, the argument does not commit one to saying that the universe is a plenum with respect to levels of perfection or with respect to things of any level short of the highest.

Naturally the main focus of attention with respect to the form of the argument we have given, as we have derived it from Scotus' formulation in terms of perfection, must be upon the specification of the 'difference in reality-level' relationships and upon whether or not it is possible that there is a highest level. For the sake of better exposition, let us employ the definition of this relationship which will function importantly in Chapter VI—even though it is not an entirely satisfactory definition, for reasons which are given in the Speculative Appendix to that chapter.

Definition: b is of a lower level of reality than a if and only if b belongs by essence to a class of things, B, such that no member of that class could exist unless:

1: some member of the class of things, A, to which a belongs by essence, actually exists;

2: some member of class A actually produces the existing members of class B;

3: some member of class A maintains a conserving relationship to that member of B throughout its existence; and

4: no member of class B has any property whatever that is not bestowed upon it by some member of class A or some member of some class of things to which the members of class A stand in relations (1), (2), and (3).

We know that there are some things related to others in this way, as is indicated in Chapter VI. The question is: are natural things, human persons and physical objects, for example, related as the members of B to something else?

The first step in answering that question is to determine whether it is *possible* that there is something of a higher level than human beings. If it is possible that there is something higher than a human being, then it will follow analytically that human beings are not of the highest level of reality. Since it cannot be true, according to the argument, that anything on any level is actual or that it is even possible that something not of the highest level should exist unless something of the highest level possible be also actual, it would follow that there actually is a higher-level being upon which human beings depend, and that this being is of the highest level.

That it is possible that there is something upon which all natural objects are dependent as upon a being of a higher level of reality seems evident—as evident, at least, as the traditional claim that it is possible that a creator exists. So the conclusion may appear to follow.

But the difficulty with the argument is that it maintains that there is a contradiction in supposing it to be the case that a lower-level creature exists or could exist if no higher level being (granted that its existence be possible) actually exists. This is argued because of the *definition* of 'being of lower reality level than. . . .' which we have employed. Consider the following reasoning:

1: It is possible that human beings, b, stand to something else, a, as the members of B to those of A (in the definition above).

2: There exist human beings.

3: It is impossible that b should stand to a as metaphysically dependent and that it should be true that b exist and false that some a exists.

4: Therefore it is true that something else, a, a member of class A, exists.

This appears to be coercive reasoning; and yet there is something puzzling about the way the modal operators in (1) and (3) function. For there is no doubt that (3) is analytic; it is no more than a part of the definition of the relation between the members of B and A, and (putting it very roughly) it merely states: $\Box \sim (b \cdot \sim a)$. This is a perfectly intelligible claim; for "*b*" and "*a*" might designate, respectively, ideas and minds.

Yet one might want to say that the truth of (1) is dependent upon whether or not *a* really exists, since we know that *b* does really exist. Hence, it might be further claimed that (1) is not properly formulated, since by the presence of its modal operator it purports to be a priori, when in fact its truth depends upon a contingent fact, whether or not *a* actually exists (though, of course, if *a* is of the highest level, its existence will not be contingent). But this proposal reflects an understandable misconstruction of premise (1): this premise does *not* presuppose or entail (2); it merely asserts that there is no contradiction in the claim "it is a necessary truth that no human beings exist unless a higher level being upon which they depend also exists." But therein lies the rub.

It has been widely thought for many centuries (although sometimes quite reasonably disputed of late) that the modality of all necessary truths is itself *necessity*, although *possibility* is compatible as a weaker iterative modality. Thus it has long been thought that $\Box p$ entails $\Box\Box p$ and $\Diamond \Box p$. But now we have a case where someone might want to say we cannot know whether $\Diamond \Box p$ is the case *unless* we know that $\Box p$ is the case, since if it is the case that $\sim\Box p$, then it follows that $\Box[\sim \Diamond (\Box p)]$. This seems to be quite correct. The Reality-Levels Argument will not work unless we show that it is *necessarily* the case that human beings do not exist unless a higher-level being exists; and since the argument is supposed to *decide* that question by showing that such a higher-level being exists, it follows that the argument begs the question. Hence, this argument is of no value despite its outwardly solid appearance.

In Duns Scotus' form of the argument, he took it as evident that a human being is not the most perfect possible being and, as we said, employed the auxiliary premise that the less perfect cannot be caused or accounted for by something less perfect than itself, and by virtue of its not being the most perfect possible, it cannot account for itself. But this form of argument supposes that whatever exists is *actually accounted for* by something; whereas it might be the case that the less-than-best-possible-thing is accounted for by nothing.

The addition of Principle E would not help directly, since it would only show that it is possible that there is something which accounts for this lower-level being. But, of course, we might reinstate the argument as follows:

a: *For anything, b, which is not on the highest level of reality, it is possible that there is something of higher level which accounts for its existence.*

b: *Therefore, it is possible that the highest level of reality has members which are actual.*

c: *Since the existence of the members of the highest level cannot be explained by anything which is not of the same nature as the members of the highest level, these entities must have self-explanatory existence.*

d: *The members of the highest possible level of reality cannot have self-explanatory existence unless they exist. Therefore, they exist.*

We have in effect re-presented the arguments of Chapter III and of Chapter IV, Section 3, under confusing neoplatonic metaphysical trappings. Hence, Duns Scotus' insight here achieves nothing which has not already been achieved in simpler form elsewhere, although this expression of the argument may appeal to the neoplatonist more than the earlier forms.

The trouble with the earlier versions of the Reality-Level Argument resulted from the fact that we employed an *iterative* modal operator, "possibly," which implicitly contained another operator, "necessarily," within its scope, when in fact we did not know whether the proposition in question (that human beings are causally dependent upon some higher being) actually bore *that* modal operator; and since it was a logically necessary condition for the whole proposition's bearing the iterative modality "possibly" that the proposition about humans should bear the modality "necessarily," proposition (1)[38] will be contradictory if it should merely be a contingent truth that human beings depend upon some higher being.

In order to rescue the argument from the difficulty that we have developed, one would have to do one of two things. One could write a reinstatement such as I offered above, which really converts this into our other pattern of argument. Or else one would have to show that it is impossible for any human being to exist unless something else existed upon which human beings are metaphysically dependent. But this is what the argument is supposed to settle for us, and therefore we must conclude that it is unsatisfactory.

Yet the result of all these reasonings about the unsatisfactory arguments is not nugatory, as it might appear; rather, it is *premonitory*. For it will be remembered that we said that the claim "It is possible that there is something upon which all natural objects are dependent as upon a being of higher level of reality" seems at least as evident as is the traditional claim "It is possible that a creator exists." The warning from all this is that there may be something peculiar about the notion "creator" which is not apparent in our frequent uses of that term in contexts concerning *production* rather than metaphysical dependence. For the relation of creator and creature as it has been traditionally described contains not only the implication that the

[38] See p. 191.

creature is produced by the creator but also the implication that the creature could not have existed *unless* it was produced by a being as perfect as the creator. The premonitory information we have gleaned is this: it is one thing to prove that natural objects were produced by something higher; it is quite another to show that they could not have existed if they had not been so produced. Certainly the second claim would not follow simply from the first.

5 ✒ The analysis
of 'S is omnipotent'

*Some agents can do some things which an omnipotent
being cannot do.*

This chapter is concerned with the project of providing an analysis
of the meaning of the general expression 'S is omnipotent' by means
of a set of logically distinct truth-conditions (the set of logically distinct things which must be the case if 'S is omnipotent' is true). The
term "S" in the expression is purely indexical, a non-connotative
"referring" term.

The discussion is in three sections. First, there is an historical consideration of some medieval antecedents of the contemporary tendency to speak of God's power in terms of what He can do; for instance, we say "God is almighty because He can do whatever is possible." This discussion concludes that on contextual grounds St.
Thomas Aquinas must be said to have *transcended* the usual pattern
of medieval discussion, a pattern which has been carried over to our
time and with which his insight has been confused.

Next, there is a fairly extensive critical attempt to show that the
analysis of 'S is omnipotent' by means of truth-conditions expressed
in the form 'S can do everything, x, such that. . . .' will surely fail.

Finally, in the constructive section of the chapter, we shall propose an analysis of the expression 'S is omnipotent' and make brief applications of it to several problems, contemporary and traditional.

SECTION 1: HISTORICAL CONSIDERATIONS

Our text will be: *Some agents can do some things which an omnipotent being cannot do.*

(1) This may be bewildering. But the idea of the text is not new. Magister Peter Lombard (d. 1173) says:

> But we ask: how can He be said to have power over all things when we can do some things which He cannot do?[1]

And illustrations are offered:

> For he cannot walk, speak, etc., things which are entirely alien to the nature of divinity, since an incorporeal and simple substance can have absolutely no need for the instruments of such things.[2]

These passages are representative of the common belief of scholars in the eleventh and twelfth centuries that God cannot do everything every agent can do and that this fact must be reconciled with the theological doctrine that God is almighty. Moreover, even the method of reconciliation adopted by the later tradition is already grasped; Peter Lombard says:

> But there are other things which God can in no way at all produce: sins, for instance; nor can He lie; nor can He sin. . . . But it does not derogate or detract from His omnipotence if God is said to be unable to sin because this would not be a power but an infirmity.[3]

This passage, without any doubt, establishes the problem of what we mean by 'omnipotence' within the context of what God can do; and it suggests the answer which we find in Bonaventure and to some

---

[1] "Sed quaeritur quomodo omnia posse dicatur (Deum) cum nos quaedam possimus quae ipse non potest" (*Sent.* I, d. 42, ch. 2).

[2] "Non potest enim ambulare, loqui et huiusmodi, quae a natura divinitatis penitus sunt aliena, cum horum instrumenta nullatenus habere queat incorporea et simplex substantia" (*Ibid.*).

[3] "Sed sunt quaedam quae Deus nullatenus facere potest, ut peccata: non enim potest mentire; non potest peccare. . . . Sed ideo, non omnipotentia Dei in aliquo detrahatur vel derogatur, si peccare non posse dicitur, quia non esset hoc potentia sed infirmitas" (*Ibid.*).

extent in St. Thomas, that the things which other agents can do but which God cannot are things whose doing proceeds, not from a power alone, but from an infirmity or defect in a power.

(2) Consider *Bonaventure* (1221–1274). Like his contemporaries teaching theology in the Universities, he was required to lecture on the *Libros Sententiarum* of Peter Lombard, and hence lectured on this particular passage. His commentary takes up four questions, one of which is of great significance:

Granted that His power extends to something different from Himself, it is asked whether it extends to everything which is possible should some other agent be acting.[4]

This is a very cautious translation, made cautious in the light of points to be raised later. Ordinarily it would be translated:

Granted that His power extends to something beyond Himself, it is asked whether He can do everything which can be done should someone else be acting.

The Latin admits of both translations; only because of the subsequent context, which clearly concerns "doing," are we justified in employing the second and more determinate rendering—yet there is no doubt that that is the correct one in this particular instance.

Responding to the question posed, Bonaventure, like Lombard, quotes Aristotle,[5] saying that some things require impotence: *"ut posse mori,"* and *"posse corrumpi,"* etc. Then, in the *corpus* of his response to the question, Bonaventure distinguishes transitive action (which results in distinct effects) from immanent action (which has effects internal to the agent) and from subjective potency (the passivity and receptivity that Aristotle had in mind). Bonaventure decides that God cannot simply be said to have power to do everything that any other agent can do; rather, He has the power to do only the things which do not imply imperfection, although with respect to each thing which implies imperfection of a true power, God can act eminently. I will not stop to explain this last point, which occurs in Bonaventure along with a series of interesting distinctions, because I do not want

[4] "Dato quod possit (aliquid aliud a se) quaeritur utrum possit omnia quod alio agente est possibile" (Bonaventure, *In Sent.* I, d. 42, 2. c).

[5] *V Met.*, text 17, IV, ch. 2.

to obscure the main point: that Bonaventure, through the suggestion of Lombard and Lombard's citations of Augustine and Aristotle, follows the pattern set by his predecessors, attempting to reconcile the claim that God is omnipotent with the premised fact that God cannot do everything every other agent can do. As a result, he is forced to accept the reconciliation suggested by Peter, that some actions require a perfect agent while others exclude such an agent. Omnipotence is a characteristic only of an agent which is perfect and without infirmity.

(3) *Anselm* (1033–1109). Stepping backward in time, because we wonder where these ideas arose, we find that, as is often the case in medieval philosophy, the real trouble began with St. Anselm. However, if only to distribute the blame equitably, we must mention Boethius, in whom we find the following:

"No one can doubt that God is almighty," Philosophy began.
"Certainly not, unless he is mad," I answered.
"But nothing is impossible for one who is almighty."
"Nothing."
"Then can God do evil?"
"No, of course not."
"Then evil is nothing, since God, who can do all things, cannot do evil."⁶

From a man who wrote a logic text, the blithe mixture of formal and informal fallacies is refreshing. The effect of the passage, when one ignores the fallacies, is that what God cannot do is either impossible for anyone to do or impossible for Him. But the passage leads to disaster, for the reasoning entails that *no one* can do evil; moreover, the only possible explanation of why something is impossible for God which is not so for another, would be in terms of the imperfection required for its execution.

Still, the real culprit is St. Anselm, whose very terms and examples became the parameters of later discussion.

But how can you be omnipotent if you have not power over all things? But if you cannot be corrupted, nor lie, nor make the true be false, nor make what has been done to have been left undone, and other things alike: how do you have power over all? Yet, to have power over these is not power but

⁶ *The Consolation of Philosophy*, Book III, prose 12. Tr. Richard Green, "Library of Liberal Arts," No. 86 (New York: The Bobbs-Merrill Co., Inc., 1962), p. 72.

impotence? . . . Therefore, O Lord God, you are the more truly omnipotent because you have power over nothing through impotence and nothing has power against thee.[7]

So it began with Anselm (although it was probably presaged in Augustine), and has continued till now. God's power is seen in terms of what God can do; what He cannot do but others can is seen as the result of their debility, infirmity, and *impotentia*. Our text, therefore, is precedented and appropriate; moreover, it will become useful.

(4) And now I turn to St. Thomas Aquinas, whose classic formulae have overshadowed succeeding debates.[8]

1: Constat ergo quod Deus ideo dicitur omnipotens quia potest omnia quae sunt possibilia secundum se (*De Pot.* 1, 7, c).

2: Relinquitur ergo quod Dei potentia ad ea se extendat quae sunt possibilia secundum se (*De Pot.* 1, 7, c).

3: Relinquitur igitur quod Deus dicatur omnipotens quia potest omnia possibilia absolute (*ST* I, 25, 3, c).

I have given these three formulae in Latin. Only the last is usually translated into English, though the first two have correlate passages in *Contra Gentiles* which have been translated. The third is usually rendered: "It remains therefore that God is called omnipotent because He can do all things which are possible absolutely." And judging from the way the expression "potest omnia" has been handled in various translations of *Contra Gentiles*, the first formula would get the same treatment: "God is omnipotent because he can *do* whatever is intrinsically possible." And only the second formula would receive a less determinate reading: "The power of God extends to everything which is intrinsically possible."

Translations like these have caused the few British and American philosophers who consider the matter[8] to conceive of God's power in terms of *what God can do* and to work within the limits of the medieval discussion, assuming that some actions require an imper-

---

[7] "Sed et omnipotens quomodo es, si non omnia potes? Aut si non potes corrumpi, nec mentire, nec facere verum esse falsum: ut, quod factum est non esse factum, et plura similiter: quomodo potes omnia? Aut, haec posse non est potentia sed impotentia? . . . Ergo, Domine Deus, inde verius es omnipotens quia potes nihil per impotentiam et nihil potest contra te" (*Proslogion*, ch. 7).

[8] See, for example, *Mind* and *Philosophical Review*.

fect agent and that this explains why God cannot do everything any-thing can do.

But that shift from a less determinate translation of *potest*—"has power over," or "has within his power" (where the verb *potest* is not functioning as a modal auxiliary verb)—to a more determinate "can do" or "has power to do" is of great importance. Most trans-lators would see the latter only as more facile and felicitous English. But in this case the Latin text of St. Thomas trips the translators nicely; for the shift to a more determinate reading causes the passage which is consistent in Latin to become logically inconsistent in English, and moreover, loses sight of a basic philosophical intuition. We shall explain this. As Aquinas defines the notion 'absolutely possible',

A thing is said to be possible or impossible absolutely with respect merely to the terms. It is absolutely possible because the predicate is not repugnant to the subject, as that Socrates should sit; and absolutely impossible when the predicate is repugnant to the subject, as, for instance, that a man is a donkey.[9]

As translators render the passage, that Socrates should sit is abso-lutely possible and God can do anything which is absolutely possible. *But* God cannot do "Socrates sits"; nor can God sit (except in the metaphorical sense of sitting in judgment), since a divine substance has no body. Hence there is a state of affairs, "Socrates sits," which by Aquinas' explicit statement is absolutely possible; yet God cannot *do* it, even though the general definition says that God is omnipotent because He can do whatever is absolutely possible.

It might appear that Aquinas has given a counter-example to his own general definitions. Yet the original text contains no inconsis-tency—on this point, at least. The phrase *Socratem sedere* is put in the infinitive mode when Socrates' sitting is said to be absolutely possible, to indicate a *state of affairs* expressed by a statement of cer-tain logical form (where its subject and predicate are compatible). Thus Aquinas implies by his very grammar that the divine power ex-tends to *states of affairs* and is not to be spoken of as "doings."

The English rendition of "*Deus potest omnia quae possibilia sunt*

---

[9] Dicitur autem aliquid possibile vel impossibile absolute ex habitudine terminorum; possibile quidem, quia predicatum non repugnat subjecto, ut Socratem sedere; impossibile vero absolute, quia predi-catum repugnat subjecto, ut hominem esse asinum. (*ST*, I, 25, 3c. The translation in the text is mine.)

secundum se" should be "God *has within his power* anything which is intrinsically possible." Thus God has within his power that Socrates should sit.

(5) The translators are not to be blamed unreservedly, for three reasons. First, these forms of Latin expression often occur in other contexts where the best translation of *potest omnia* is "can do everything." Second, the whole tradition from Boethius, Peter Lombard, Bonaventure, and Anselm thinks of God's power in terms of what God can do. Finally, St. Thomas, in his own discussions, lapses into the old forms of thought when he treats allied problems and objections. He asks whether God can do evil, can undo what is done and do what is not done, and can make the past not to have happened. (Of course, these questions were imposed upon him by the tradition that was to be expounded.) Moreover, in answering an objection he even uses the expression "Deus potest aliqua agere . . .";[10] and, when he asks whether God can do certain things, he uses the active and transitive verb *agere*. So we can partly excuse the translators, even though they make the key passages inconsistent. What is missed is that St. Thomas, using the old formula in a new way in his definition, transcends the limits of the previous tradition and escapes its terminological poverty; yet he is forced to return to the older terminology, in order to answer traditional subsidiary questions imposed by his authoritative text (Peter Lombard).

(6) Why do I make so much of this slight difference in reading? Is the strictly formal consistency of a passage so important that we must face a whole barrage of Latin? I want to read three occurrences of one expression, *potest omnia*, a bit differently in each of three statements, admitting that it occurs in another meaning in thousands of places in this and other writers on the same topic. Why do this to save formal consistency when we could merely claim the passage is consistent in what is intended? The answer is that an important *philosophical* point would be missed and actually has been lost in all those writers who understand God's powers in terms of what He can do. If a person wants to find out what it means to say "God is omnipotent" and has to set up an analysis in terms of "God is able to do everything, *x*, such that . . . *x*," he will surely fail. He will either have

---

10 *ST*, I, 25, 3 ad 2.

to invoke the notion 'perfect agent' and face the hopeless task of giving a quidditative explanation of 'perfection', a concept which was always taken to signify a mode of being, an existential non-quidditative mode, or he will meet circularity and vacuity.

Let us turn now to why analyses of the form 'S is omnipotent if and only if S is able to do everything x such that φx' will fail.

SECTION 2: THE FAILURE OF ANALYSIS IN TERMS OF 'DOING'

Imagine that a philosopher wants to know what it means to say that something is omnipotent—not just God but anything at all: for now let us use "S," a purely indexical, non-connotative constant whose referent is not yet determined, but whose referent would be, when determined, unique. The philosopher wants to know the truth conditions for 'S is omnipotent' and, being caught by the tradition, he wants them in the form: 'S is omnipotent if and only if S has active power to do everything x such that φx.'

What are the attributes we can substitute for the blank "φ" to determine the things S has active power to do?

(1) We can at once eliminate the following: 'S has active power to do every x such that x is intrinsically consistent'. (This is the most common way St. Thomas' formulae are explained.)For both 'Socrates sits' and 'Jezebel fornicates with the heathen' are intrinsically consistent. But S cannot do both unless S is identical with both Socrates and Jezebel; and even if S achieved that, it could not achieve identity with every agent. The analysis fails.

It may be wondered why we should bother to consider any other analyses in terms of 'doing', since we have just shown that all such analyses will be too narrow. Our counter-examples to the first analysis are based upon the fact that although the things that fall within the *range* of S's doings are the largest set possible, still an infinity of things which we think must fall within the power of an omnipotent being have been left out simply because S cannot *do* them without becoming identical with a multiplicity of agents—which is surely impossible.

This argument is devastating to the hope of analyzing 'omnipotence' entirely in terms of what some agent can do; yet many philosophers, like the medievals quoted in Section 1, have thought that, with refinements, such analyses or definitions would be possible. So it is instructive to consider a few further proposals, examination of which discloses that there is no convenient restriction upon what an omnipotent being can do which will both place everything we wish within its power, and exclude what we do not approve, and at the same time provide the concept with any measure of clarification.

Moreover, objections to formulae (4) through (7), below, will apply just as well should we substitute 'bring it about that *x*' for 'do *x*', so that these objections apply not only to the 'doing' formulae but also to the most obvious substitutions for them. Hence the objections to be developed will guide us away from obvious pitfalls when we try to replace 'doing' with some more appropriate concept.

(2) '*S* has active power to do everything, *x*, such that *S* can do *x*'. This, as Aquinas said, is defining God's power in terms of God's power: it is circular.

(3) '*S* has active power to do everything, *x*, such that an omnipotent being can do *x*'. This is likewise circular, although it is true enough. The number of possible analyses based on patterns (2) and (3) appears to be infinite—which only shows that there are more chances to miss the point than hit the mark.

(4) Now we come to more significant ideas. '*S* has active power to do everything, *x*, such that "something, *z*, does *x*" is consistent'. To be able to do everything which any being can do, or can consistently *be said* to do, requires an omnipotent being. This would truly be omnipotence if it were logically possible that any being should do so much. Since it is consistent to say 'Socrates strangles his mother', *S* would have to have active power to do the same not only to his own mother (unless *S* is Socrates) but to Socrates' mother. Many people would accept this analysis, but the tradition is against it, since the omnipotent being is thought within that tradition to be *incapable* of such things. As Anselm says, "How can you be omnipotent when there are things you cannot do?" and Peter Lombard adds: ". . . and others can do them?"

As is clear from the passages quoted, the philosophers have thought that whereas there are some acts whose performance requires an imperfection in knowledge, there are others that could *not* be performed by a being whose knowledge is imperfect. Some acts, therefore, require a perfect agent while others exclude a perfect agent, and so we cannot analyze '*S* is omnipotent' as "*S* has active power to do anything, *x*, such that 'something does *x*' is consistent," because *S* would have to be both perfect by nature and imperfect by nature.

Some of the arguments by which the medieval philosophers tried to show that certain actions require an imperfect agent are clearly unsound—for example, St. Thomas' argument that God cannot do evil (he treats "doing evil" and "sinning" as alike in this passage):

> To sin is to fall short of a perfect action. Hence, to be able to sin is to be able to fall short of a perfect action, which is repugnant to omnipotence. So it is that God cannot sin, because of His omnipotence. . . .[11]

We are given no reason why being able to fall short of a perfect action should be considered repugnant to omnipotence, since it is also supposed that God is able *not* to fall short of a perfect action, and in fact, will not. From the fact that I am *able* not to throw the ball as well as I can, it does not follow that I am limited in ability to throw the ball; "as well as I can" may be "perfectly." I think Aquinas assumes that if God were able to do evil, God would not be able to act perfectly: and that is based upon the idea that being able to sin follows from a defect in a power (but certainly not a defect in the power of producing transitive effects, i.e., in omnipotence). As a matter of fact, he argues this point at length when he proposes that the ability to sin follows from limited knowledge or weakness of will. But it is to be emphasized that even if those arguments be correct, it would not follow that sinning is impossible for a divine being because of its *omnipotence*, but rather that sinning is impossible for an omnipotent being because of its perfection or divinity. Hence St. Thomas was mistaken.

Let us return to our formula (4); as it stands, it is technically absurd. Jezebel can fornicate with the heathen at t₁. This is something that one agent other than *S* can do. But *S* cannot do *numerically* the same thing unless *S* is identical with Jezebel, which, *ex supposito*, is false. Therefore, taken strictly, the formula is inconsistent. Because of the strength of the former objection that *S* could not do everything that

[11] *ST*, I, 25, 3 ad 2.

something can do because S would have to be both perfect and imperfect at once, we shall not consider restricting x to things *specifically* the same as those something else can do, since that objection
would still apply.

Moreover, our intuitive feeling for what omnipotence should be
tells us that somehow or another the particular act 'Jezebel's fornicat-
ing with the heathen at t₁' *should* fall within the power of an omnipotent being. Thus this form of analysis is totally misconstrued, because it requires us to exclude (in the interests of consistency) precisely those particular acts of other agents which should fall within
the power of an omnipotent being.

(5) Another analysis:

S is omnipotent if and only if S has active power to do anything, x, such that
'S does x' is consistent.

Informally put: S is omnipotent if and only if S has active power to
do anything that S can consistently be *said* to do.

The only point in our discussing this analysis is its retroactive indication of a mistake in St. Thomas Aquinas' statement "God has power
over everything which is absolutely possible."[12] Now to avoid difficulties of translation one might premise that the consistency of 'God
does x', where x is 'causes or prevents a' and where "a" designates
some particular state of affairs (such as "Socrates marries Xanthippe"),
is entirely determined by the consistency of a. St. Thomas explicitly
says that a state of affairs is absolutely possible if the predicate is not
repugnant to the subject; that is, that the absolutely possible is the
consistent. But surely, when he says that the power of God extends
to the absolutely possible, he means to a *sub-class* of the consistent,
namely the *contingent*. The formula "Deus potest omnia possibilia
absolute" could not place every consistent state of affairs within the
power of God, because some states of affairs are necessary conditions of God's existence, and because God's existence itself is not
within the power of God, although it is consistent. Moreover, it is
consistent that bachelors are unmarried and that plane triangles have
three angles; and we know that Aquinas would not want to join

---

[12] "Deus potest omnia possibilia absolute" (*ST*, I, 25, 3, c).

Descartes,[13] who says in his "Reply to the Sixth Set of Objections" to his *Meditations:*

And it is because He willed that the three angles of a triangle be necessarily equal to 180 degrees that this is true and cannot be otherwise. . . . Thus that supreme indifference in God is the supreme proof of His omnipotence.[14]

Therefore, *possibilia* must be *contingent* states of affairs and not merely consistent ones. So to amend St. Thomas' passages and to repair the formula we are presently considering, we must replace 'consistent' with 'contingent', whereby we mean that a proposition is contingent if and only if both the proposition and its negation are consistent.

Unfortunately the more important difficulties cannot be amended away. First, since "*S*" is a purely referential or indexical term, it could refer to a substance which has no active powers whatever—a substance unable to produce a single effect upon any other being. Such a thing would fulfill the conditions of the definition and would therefore be omnipotent. On the other hand, another substance designated by "*S*" could fulfill the requirement of having active power to do everything which it is *contingent* to *say* it does, by being able to act, but performing its every act through necessity. This being also will be omnipotent, since it has active power to perform every act which it is contingently true to *say* it does, namely, none. In both

[13] The doctrine that whether or not a state of affairs is possible is within the power of God is called "metaphysical voluntarism" and has been attributed to Descartes on the basis of the passage quoted here. But we should, perhaps, have the same kindness for Descartes as we have for Aquinas, to whom we will not attribute the position despite his having phrased his doctrine in a way which commits him to the view. Perhaps there has never been a philosopher who really *was* a metaphysical voluntarist; perhaps it was just looseness of thought which made Descartes appear so confused.

For metaphysical voluntarism could not be true. Suppose that God exists; then it is both true and possible that God exists. Whether or not it is possible that God exists cannot be within the will of God, since for God to will that it should not have been possible for God to have existed would require that God should actually have existed and that it should therefore be both possible and impossible for God to have existed.

Put another way: Suppose that whatever God chooses to be the case will be the case. Suppose that God chooses that 'God exists' be necessarily false; then 'God exists' will be both necessarily false and true. Hence, *metaphysical voluntarism* is inconsistent. It can neither be the case that whether or not p is consistent lies within the will of God; nor can it be true that whether or not p is the case lies within the will of God for every consistent p, since that would entail the former position because having within one's control the truth-value of a necessary truth is equivalent to having control over the consistency of a state of affairs. Neither is possible for God.

[14] René Descartes, *Selections,* ed. Ralph M. Eaton, pp. 264–265.

cases the bi-conditional is true because the antecedents (and hence the consequents) are necessarily false. And, as St. Thomas knew,[15] a conditional with a necessarily false antecedent is true.

Further clarification of these two exceptions to our amended definition may be helpful.

An entity with no active powers whatever—call it "Jones" (letting the name connote what sort of a thing it is)—an entity which is by nature incapable of doing anything, would fulfill the conditions. It would be omnipotent because all antecedents of the form 'Jones does x' would be inconsistent, with the result that the bi-conditional (given in the suggested analysis) would be true because of the necessary falsehood of both its antecedent and its consequent.

The other difficulty is encountered in, for example, a Spinozistic or Leibnizian world. For Spinoza nothing other than what is the case is possible: only the things that I actually do are things that are possible to me, and only they are things which it is consistent to say I do. Hence, if Spinoza were right about the way of the world, I would, by the definition at hand, be omnipotent. So too would every agent. (This would hold, too, if we replaced 'consistent' with 'contingent', because I would have active power to do whatever is contingent for me; namely, nothing).

The same would be true in a Leibnizian world, in which every true statement about a finite monad is, from God's point of view, analytic; hence there would, from God's point of view, be no contingent statement of the form 'Jones does x' which would be true of Jones. In that case, Jones (finite monad), would be omnipotent by default: anything which can do anything which it is contingent to say it does, and for which there is nothing which it *is* contingent to say it does, is omnipotent according to the fifth analysis.

Those who do not fear the "fallacy of facile amendment" might think that there is nothing crucial about the cases I have constructed. They will eliminate the first case by stipulating that there are *some* things which S can do; to get rid of the second, they will specify that

---

[15] "Now it is true that the philosopher says that God can deliberately do that which is evil (Aristotle, *Topics* IV, 5, 126a34). But this must be understood either on a condition the antecedent of which is impossible— . . . as, for instance, if we were to say 'God can do an evil thing, if he chooses to.' For there is no reason why a conditional proposition cannot be true, even though both the antecedent and the consequent be impossible" (*ST*, I, 25, 3, ad 2).

S can do some things *contingently.* Yet from our intuitive ideas about an omnipotent being, we know the set of things which can be done contingently will have to be infinite in size. Shall we specify that as well? How shall we do so? We can consider the following two definitions as attempts to show just how the set of contingent effects will be described, and we will see that the "fallacy of facile amendment" has kept many philosophers from the diligent pursuit of the outcomes of such amendments, a re-examination which would soon disclose that the original analysis was misbegotten.

If we merely specified, in order to avoid the difficulties mentioned above, that *S* should be able to do an infinity of contingent things, we would soon have to decide whether *R*, which can also do an infinite number of things but can do nothing *S* can do, would be omnipotent (for instance, a computer capable of an infinite number of output states). This would require that we talk about the actions compatible with *S*'s being an agent of a certain sort. We actually find this type of discussion in some scholastic writers, who say God can do whatever is relatively and unconditionally possible for a divine being, whereas Socrates cannot do everything which is relatively and unconditionally possible for a *man* to do. The next two analyses illustrate this approach.

(6) Perfection: "*S* is omnipotent" if and only if "*S* has active power to do anything, *x*, such that 'A perfect being does *x*' is logically contingent."

This formulation excludes from the power of *S* all those states of affairs which are necessarily the case. I think that, despite its technical dissimilarity with St. Thomas' formulation, this condition is logically required. We must not speak of doing what is necessary in the sense of "logically necessary"; for we can do that only in doing what is *not* logically necessary.

But why should we make the contingency of 'A perfect being does *x*' an element of our analysis? If no perfect being should exist, and if there should exist a limited and imperfect being, *L*, which can do anything any limited being can contingently be said to do, would not *L* be omnipotent? In order to satisfy ourselves that this state of affairs could not obtain—that we could not have a limited being which can do anything (a numerically distinct token of that type) any other limited being can be said to do—we should have to understand much more fully the relationship between 'perfection in being' and 'action'; we would also have to establish by new arguments the scholastic principles that some actions require an imperfect agent, and that some actions *exclude* an imperfect agent. The scholastics supported the former principle fairly well by appeals to experience; but they did not adequately address the latter (although the matter is treated in the context of showing that finite beings cannot create), and they certainly did not *establish* that some actions *require* a perfect agent.

Even if we could show that '*S* has active power to do everything, *x*, such that "A perfect being does *x*" is contingent' is a complete truth-condition for '*S* is omnipotent', we would still be uncertain what a perfect being is. If we could hope for nothing better, we could enter upon the fruitless task of explaining, to an age of philosophy entirely unreceptive to the idea, what a perfect being is. But in any case, the task is hopeless: perfection was never considered a quiddity or essence but an existential mode not admitting of a conceptualized definition. In sum, this analysis is uninformative and unilluminating: it may be abandoned for greener pastures nearby.

(7) Finally, the last analysis, and the most general.

S is omnipotent if and only if S has active power to do everything, x, such that 'A being of S-S does x' is contingent.

(i) I am using "S-S" to indicate—without signifying or connoting, but rather by referring—the essence, nature, type, or *sort* of *S*. In effect, *S* is omnipotent if *S* has active power to do whatever a thing of that *sort* can *contingently be said* to do. The advantage of indicating without signifying the nature, essence, or sort to which *S* belongs is that one avoids having to provide a quidditative definition of God. But unfortunately, there are also ineluctable disadvantages.

(ii) The analysis does not avoid the difficulties that arose against analysis (5) above: that a being, *S*, of a sort where no statement of the form 'A being of S-S does *x*' will be contingent, will be omnipotent by fulfilling the conditions vacuously. There will be two classes of these beings at least: (a) those that are capable of no action at all, and (b) those that are capable of no *contingent* action, although they are capable of necessary action.

(iii) Furthermore, the analysis admits the possibility of at least two omnipotent beings of different sorts—beings such that each has power over everything which anything of its sort may be *said* to do, but neither has the power to do or prevent anything which something of the other sort can be said to do or prevent. This tells us that there is something wrong with this conception, not because some being can do what an omnipotent being cannot do, but because some *omnipotent* being can do what another omnipotent being cannot.

Therefore, it all comes down to our specifying what sort of a being an omnipotent being is; but that is just what we started out to discover.

Let me summarize the argument of this section. The main premises are:

1: *If S is omnipotent, S does not have the power to do everything that it is logically possible for some being to do. (We take that premise from tradition.)*

2: *Therefore, if S is omnipotent, S must have active power to do everything which it is possible and contingent for a certain sort of being to do.*

But we cannot specify the *sort* without circularity ("a divine being") or vagueness ("a perfect being"). Failure to specify the sort by providing only a referring term, as in (7), permits defeating counterexamples and leaves an infinity of things outside God's power, as the objection to the first analysis showed. Therefore, we must stop thinking of God's power in terms of what God can do, and find another way to specify its extent. We do so in the following section, with the result that many side problems discussed by Lombard, Bonaventure, and Aquinas become trivial—while one or two others take on added importance.

SECTION 3: THE ANALYSIS IN TERMS OF CHOICE

The best analysis is often the simplest. Aquinas says: "Deus potest omnia possibilia absolute." We shall take our answer from his, generalizing by means of the term *S*, and taking *"possibilia"* as "contingent states of affairs."

S is omnipotent if and only if for every logically contingent state of affairs,
p, whether p or ~p is the case is logically equivalent to the effective choice,
by S, that p or that ~p (respectively).

Symbolized, where "$_xW_y$" means "x effectively chooses that y be the case":

$$(p)[(\Diamond p \cdot \Diamond \sim p) \rightarrow (p \mathrel{\underline{\underline{\Leftarrow}}} {_sW_p})]$$

This is a very strong definition. It does not say that whether or not *p* is the case is *within* the power of *S*'s choice, but rather that whether or not *p* is the case is *logically equivalent to* a choice by *S* that it be so. Several questions need to be taken note of here.

(1) Why do we use "logical equivalence" rather than "material equivalence" for the relationship between *p* and $_sW_p$? Because the traditional conception of God's power is not only that whatever He chooses is *in fact* the case and vice versa, but also that whatever He *might* have chosen *must* have been the case.

(2) Then why not use the "fishhook" or "arrow" to suggest that *p* entails $_sW_p$ or vice versa? Because the entailment must go both ways: not only must whatever God might have willed have been the case; but also, nothing could have been the case had God not willed it. Hence, we require a logical equivalence. Admittedly this is a little stronger than the articulated tradition, but it is not, I think, stronger than the implicit tradition.

(3) Why not a "horseshoe" or "material implication" sign for the main connective? Because we do not want to assert merely that it is a fact that any contingent statement must stand in a logical equivalence with God's effective choice, but rather that it *could not have been otherwise*. Then why not use the "logical equivalence" connective which occurs within the second element? I think that perhaps it would be stronger than is needed to capture the traditional conception of God's power; yet if we allow that $(p)[({_sW_p}) \rightarrow \Diamond \sim ({_sW_p})]$, and also that $(p)[\sim ({_sW_p}) \mathrel{\underline{\underline{\Leftarrow}}} ({_sW}{\sim}{_p})]$ are parts of our conception of 'W' or 'chooses effectively that', then I think there is no logical difference between using the "arrow" pointing to the right and the "double arrow" or "logical equivalence" connective between the two main parts of our

definition. (It is, of course, assumed that "*p*" stands only for contingent states of affairs.)

Some philosophers, doubting the consistency of the definition, will give the following example:

p: Jones freely chooses to murder Smith.

~*p: It is false that Jones freely chooses to murder Smith.*

It will be granted that *S* could by merely so willing prevent Jones from freely murdering Smith. But that *S*'s choice can be entirely sufficient for *p* to be the case is said to be inconsistent, because what is a free act of Jones cannot have sufficient conditions in the act of any other thing. (Materially sufficient conditions in the acts of another are possible, of course; but not logically or causally sufficient ones.)

This problem is an old one; Augustine saw it as a conflict between providence and free will, and between grace and free will. Later medieval philosophers considered other versions in terms of conflict between divine governance and free will, and between predestination by grace and free will. Yet it may be simply put that the effect of God's choice with respect to Jones is not to make Jones murder *against* his will, but to make Jones murder *at* will.

The details of this controversy are not important here, since the antinomy in question is usually dealt with in other contexts. Yet one very common error must be indicated. It does not follow from the fact that '$_sW_p$ entails *p*' is a necessary truth that *p* is not a contingent state of affairs. There is absolutely no justification for transferring the modal operator from the conditional to the consequent of the conditional. (The same rule applies to $_sK_p$, where "K" means "knows that.") This is just a case of mistakenly inferring from $\Box[_sW_p \supset p]$ by way of $_sW_p$ to $\Box p$. It is a mistake Aquinas pointed out in *De Veritate*, centuries ago.

Despite the fact that the modal operators do not transfer, there is still something mysterious: corresponding to the logical equivalence between the divine choice and certain states of affairs, there must be an ontological dependence of the state of affairs which is *not* identical with the divine choice. After all, one of our central and anti-Kantian premises has been that there is an ontological correlate to the logical relations of possibility and necessity, and that this correlate is found in the metaphysical relation of 'accounting-for'. Where

God's choice is logically sufficient for the occurrence of some non-identical state of affairs, then the relations of creation, conservation and causation must obtain.[16] Every orthodox Christian theologian for twenty centuries has conceived the relation of the divine will to human events in this way. Examine the more general, non-theological provisions of the classical metaphysical systems—those of Plato, Aristotle, Aquinas, Scotus, Berkeley, Kant, etc. Each system has two kinds of causality, one "metaphysical," the other "natural." In any case, it is this problem that becomes more serious because of my definition. Other traditional puzzles, as will be seen below, evaporate.

Necessarily existent beings

The definition I have given may be considered defective in that it requires that the proposition $\sim g$, where it means "S never existed," be necessarily false. For if $\sim g$ were contingent and true, then according to the definition, it would entail $_sW\sim_g$. But 'S exists' must be true in order for $_sW\sim_g$ to be true, and $_sW\sim_g$ entails $\sim g$; thus in order for 'S never existed' to be true, 'S exists' must be true. This is an explicit contradiction, from which it follows that $\sim g$ is *not* contingent. Hence, only a being, S, which is such that 'S exists' is necessarily true can fulfill the conditions of the definition.[17] All omnipotent beings (if there are any) exist necessarily; and all that are possible actually exist. If the definition is consistent, at least one such being is possible.

Since I think there is at least one such being, I find no difficulty in the condition upon referents of "S" which is entailed by the definition. Those who do not like the fact that "existence" is derivable will have to treat 'S exists' as contingent and restrict the states of affairs falling within the decision of S to a *sub-class* of contingent states of affairs. This will make it very difficult to specify the range of things which fall within the choice of such a being. As Chapters III and IV should have indicated, I consider that it is a mistake to treat 'God exists' as a contingent statement. Hence, far from finding it a difficulty

---

[16] How we are to reconcile the apparent conflict between the determining causality of God and the freedom of the created agent is not to be explained here; it is discussed in Chapter VI, where we consider the problem of evil.

[17] This is the insight which underlies Spinoza's botched argument for the existence of God from God's omnipotence, in Part I, Proposition XI, of the *Ethics*.

that no being whose existence is contingent can be a referent for "*S*," I regard this fact as a great advantage of the definition.

Omniscience

The same result can be achieved through a similar definition of "omniscience":

S is omniscient if and only if for every logically consistent state of affairs, p, whether p or ~p is the case is logically equivalent to $_sK_p$ and $_sK$~$_p$ respectively.

$(p)[\lozenge p \rightarrow (p \equiv _sK_p) \cdot (\sim_sK_p \equiv _sK\sim p)]$

(1) This may seem too weak, because *S* would have to know necessary truths; but we have already made the slight alterations necessary for that.

(2) Suppose *p* is "*S* never existed." Then, if *p* is consistent, it is not possible that *p* be true if $_sK_p$ is false. But since, in any case in which $_sK_p$ is true, *S* must exist, and therefore $_sK_p$ must be false, it follows that supposing *p* to be consistent leads to an explicit contradiction. Therefore, ~*p* is necessarily true. Hence, any and all beings that are omniscient exist necessarily. But it is possible that an omniscient being should exist necessarily; therefore, at least one omniscient being exists and exists necessarily.

What is the significance of this? Ignoring technical defects in the formulation of the two definitions (although it is exciting to think that we may be able to derive the one property from the other), something important has occurred: we have realized Anselm's dream. We have shown that from a definition which says nothing whatever about the existence of any entity, but which expresses a conceptual relation for whose consistency there is at least a millenium of support, we can validly and ineluctably deduce the existence of any and all things which could fulfill its requirements. Both definitions are consistent; therefore there can be a substitution instance of each. But if each can have a substitution instance, then in each case something exists which satisfies the conditions of the definition, and the statement that such things exist is necessarily true.

We shall not stop here to consider the many objections which can be presented; but it is worth noting that one of the most fundamental will take the form of a denial that any attribute of any thing can be such as to involve in its nature a logical relation (such as logical equivalence in the truth values of certain statements, etc.). As I have sketched this objection, it is not, of course, well stated. But enough is indicated to show that it will probably never get off the ground for two reasons, one circumstantial and the other logical.

First, all the "higher-level properties"[18]—"uncausable," "unpreventable," "eternal," "omnipotent," "omniscient," etc.—by means of which we describe God, can be analyzed only in terms of the logical relations among certain states of affairs. Hence, the sort of objection we are discussing would require that we consider the whole tradition of western theology, insofar as it theoretically explicates the religious conception of God, to be nonsensical and entirely misguided. This is implausible enough.

What makes it entirely unlikely is that those "projectable" physical properties which we find it practically necessary to ascribe to natural objects cannot be defined without our invoking logical relations among states of affairs and, in addition, the notion of natural or causal necessity. Hence the implausibility of the line of objection is increased by the fact that, were it correct, we could not account for a large segment of our analytical practice in the philosophy of science. It appears, then, that apart from technical defects in the definitions, we shall have to accept the consequences and admit that the existence of some things can indeed be a logical consequence of what sort of thing they are.

A plurality of omnipotent beings

The analysis of 'S is omnipotent' given in this section does not exclude the possibility that "S" may refer indifferently to two beings, S_1 and S_2, both of which fulfill the conditions of the analysis—provided that both exist necessarily, and that $(p)[(\Diamond p \cdot \Diamond \sim p \cdot p) \rightarrow (s_1 W_p \triangleq s_2 W_p)]$. Which of the two beings would be said to account for what is the case? It would be a matter of indifference, since if $(s_1 W_p)$ is contingent, then $(s_2 W_{s_1 w_p})$ is also contingent, etc., and wherever $(s_2 W_{s_1 w_p})$ is true, then, both p and $(s_1 W_{s_2} W_{s_1 w_p})$ will be true, ad infinitum. These iterated formulae become vacuous. As a result, we can say that nothing about the definition excludes the possibility of an infinite number of necessarily existing beings each of which is omnipotent, provided their natures be constituted in such a way that there is a logical equivalence among their decisions; that is, that it be logically impossible that one such being should decide that something should be the case where another decides that its negation should.

Some philosophers think that uniqueness is a presupposition of omnipotence. I do not think that the sort of plurality which is compatible with the definition offered can be considered of the same sort as that excluded by ordinary religious discourse. Moreover, the requisite uniqueness of God will be a consequence of other conceptual relations among the divine attributes, and need not be demanded at this point.

Consider two of the conundrums debated recently in the journals.

(1) It is asked: Can God make a being He cannot control? Suppose we put this problem in a form appropriate to our definition. It is suggested that God choose that there exist a being, K, which God cannot control. What does that entail? It entails that there should exist a being, K, which may cause the occurrence of a state of affairs, q; and that this occurrence cannot be logically determined by the will of God. Now according to our definition of "omnipotence," the only circumstance under which a state of affairs, q, is *not* determinable by the will of God is if $\Box q$ or else $\Box \sim q$. It is inconsistent that something should cause q when $\sim q$ is necessarily the case; it is also inconsistent that God should choose that K exist, where K causes q and q is necessarily the case. The existence of K falls within the power of God only if it is contingent, as the definition provides. It is inconsistent that a being whose existence is contingent should be cause of q where q is necessarily true. Therefore, it is impossible that K should exist and be able to cause a state of affairs which does not fall within the determining will of God; consequently, it is inconsistent to say that God makes a being He cannot control.

(2) The same sort of confusion is involved in an older question: Can God make a stone He cannot lift? First—since 'God lifts a stone' cannot be true—we shall delete the metaphor and substitute the following: Can God bring it about that there is a stone, x, which is such that 'x moves' is not a state of affairs God can bring about? Only if 'x moves' is either inconsistent or necessarily true could it not be a state of

affairs God could bring about: But if *x* is a stone, as is supposed by the very form of the problem, then '*x* moves' cannot be simply inconsistent. Nor can it be logically necessary: the stone could exist alone in the physical universe. Therefore, it is inconsistent that '*x* moves' should not be a state of affairs which God can bring about, since the state is contingent and all contingent affairs fall within God's choice. No limitation upon a power whose exercise is conditioned by consistency can be disclosed by a task which is inconsistent in nature.

(3) There is a very old problem which arises from Occam's enthusiastic dictum: "God can do immediately whatever He can do by secondary causality." This principle, developed in the context of discussions concerning the nature of miracles and of supernatural interferences in nature, was widely believed in the fourteenth century, despite the fact that it is a model of confusion. Like most of the conundrums, it is expressed in terms of what God can do, and it contains all the confusion entailed by this mode of expression. Taken seriously in the form it was first given, the principle is false for events which are the same numerically, specifically, or generically. For those particular events which are worked by secondary causes, their numerical identity logically involves the agent which produces them; thus it is absurd to say that God can produce numerically the same event as *my writing this page* without the mediation of the secondary cause.

Nor is the truth of the principle assured by our understanding it to claim that God could have produced an event not numerically but *specifically* the same in the absence of the particular secondary cause. God cannot bring about the playing of a certain piano concerto without any secondary causes: even though He could dispense with a particular pianist, he would still need an *instrument*, since being performed upon an instrument is a necessary condition of being a performance of the particular work.[19] Hence, there are occasions when God cannot, without secondary causes, produce an event which is specifically the same as one produced through secondary causes.

Finally, suppose we describe an event *generically* as "a human composer's writing a new sonata." It makes sense to call this a generic description, since a species of that event would be "a human com-

---

[19] There are endless borderline cases; would God's producing radio waves which deliver me what sounds just like a performance of a certain work, with no instrument or instrumentalist involved, be a case of producing a performance of the work?

poser's writing a twelve-tone sonata between 1960 and 1965"; and particularly, it might be Hanson's writing his thirteenth sonata. God cannot produce tokens of that type without secondary causes.

Thus, in most plausible interpretations, Occam's principle seems false. Yet there is a form in which it is true:

> For any consistent state of affairs, p, which is brought about through the causal sufficiency of an event, q, such that p does not entail q nor does q entail p, it is within the power of God to effect p while effecting ~q, all causal laws remaining the same.

This revised Occamist principle is a trivial consequence of the definition of omnipotence. Its only application, so far as I can see, would be to one of two projects: that of defining a miracle, or—the project for which the Occamist principle was applied—that of showing that God can produce all the subjective grounds for a *justified* perceptual claim in the absence of the physical object or event.

Whatever real problems arise in the analysis of 'S is omnipotent' are problems in preserving the consistency of such a notion, while taking account of the believer's conception of the power of God. Yet not all the alleged inconsistencies are significant in that they require qualifications in or additions to the truth-conditions for 'S is omnipotent'. For instance, Paul Ziff has argued that the discoveries of physical science provide evidence that God, an omnipotent being, does not exist, since God cannot make a stone fly to the sun in a second. Explaining why, he says that physicists have discovered that *no one* can make a stone fly to the sun in one second. Therefore, he concludes, there is evidence that no such being exists.[20]

The confusion here is twofold. First, if Ziff thinks that such an event is really impossible, why does he demand that an omnipotent being be able to do it, when he already has conceded that an omnipotent being can do only what is possible? If scientists have discovered that no one can do it, they must have discovered that an omnipotent being cannot do it; no evidence, then, for the nonexistence of an omnipotent being has been found. If, on the other hand, the author does not think this task is impossible, why does he doubt that God

[20] Paul Ziff's article in *Religious Experience and Truth*, ed. Sidney Hook (New York: New York University Press, 1962).

can do it and credit the scientists with having shown that no one can do it? My guess is that Ziff has confused the physically or hypothetically impossible with the logically impossible, and has somehow taken proof of the one to be evidence for the other.

Pushing such argument further, some thinkers have said that we know that the finite speed of light imposes a limit on all physical events such that none can occur faster; hence God's moving the stone to the sun in one second is impossible. This gets us nowhere. If conforming to the laws of nature is taken as a logically necessary condition for something's being a physical event, then asking God to produce a physical event at a greater speed than those laws allow is asking Him to do what is inconsistent; His not doing so is no weakness of a power which extends only to the possible. If the limiting speed of light is taken as a universal empirical truth, asking God to move the stone in one second is asking Him to falsify the hypothesis that the law is an absolutely universal truth—something He can do readily, and even may have done. If the law is merely a generalization, it is no wonder that there should be exceptions, and there is no point in a philosopher's discussing them. Hence the presentation of such objections can at best involve a confusion of kinds of possibility and cannot constitute any sort of argument against God's omnipotence or any evidence that an omnipotent being does not exist.

There is a general moral to this. Since saying that a being is omnipotent is not saying unconditionally that it can do any particular thing, the discovery that someone's doing certain things is impossible cannot constitute evidence that an omnipotent being does not exist. Hence, it is pointless to argue that an omnipotent being does not exist by beginning from premises about the impossibility of specific sorts of activity; the argument will be a *non sequitur.*

Before concluding, we need a diagnosis of what is wrong with speaking of God's power in terms of what God can do. The defect is that of equivocation. With respect to the production of any real effect, I can do nothing successful without entering into what Aquinas called a *real* relation with my effect, a kind of equal-and-opposite-reaction situation. This is exactly what Aquinas claimed was not present between God and the creature.

Historians sometimes give the impression that there is something mysterious and peculiar about Aquinas' saying:

It is necessarily the case that the relation by which the creature is related to the creator should be real; but in God it is merely an intentional relation. . . . And Peter Lombard expressly said this in *Sent.* I, dist. 30.[21]

There is no peculiarity or mystery about this. First, St. Thomas thinks that certain features which characterize the finite relations between causes and effects are absent in the case of creation, conservation, governance, or providence. Secondly, he thinks that an infinite regress will result from our requiring that a real relation obtain between God and His creatures.

In both *De Potentia* and *Contra Gentiles*, Aquinas emphasizes that creation, conservation, and so forth are not forms of change. The requisites for change are (a) a subject in potency which is altered; (b) a process which is *real*, prior (logically) to the reality of the effect produced; and (c) a real *terminus a quo* or initial state of the subject changed, from which the change proceeds to a final or result-state (*terminus ad quem*) through the intermediary process. None of these conditions obtains for the divine acts of creation, conservation, and governance. For a cause to enter into a real relation, that cause must undergo a change: this is not the case with God. Both in *De Potentia* and in *Contra Gentiles*, Aquinas points out the disastrous results of considering God to be in real relation with His creatures. I call attention to these passages, which presage the arguments of Bradley and McTaggart against the reality of relations:

[If these relations, creation, conservation, etc., were realities outside God,] we should have to consider yet other relations of God to those that are realities since God is the first of beings and the highest of Goods. And if these also were realities, we should be compelled to find third relations; and so on endlessly. The relations in which God stands to other things are therefore, not realities existing outside Him.[22]

---

[21] Opportet quod relatio quae creatura ad creatorem refertur sit realis; sed in Deo est relatio secundum rationem tantum. Et hoc expresse dicit Magister in *Sent.* I, dist. 30" (*Questiones Disputatae de Potentia Dei*, 3, 3, c).

[22] *Summa Contra Gentiles*, Book II, ch. 13, n. 2; translated by James F. Anderson as *On the Truth of the Catholic Faith* (Book II: "Creation"). "Image Books" (New York: Doubleday & Company, 1956), II, 45.

It is not necessary to regress infinitely because the relation of creation is not related to God by some other relation which is real but is related to God through itself. As Avicenna says in his *Metaphysics* (Chapter X), no relation is related by another relation. . . .[23]

Let us apply these ideas to the case at hand. Whenever I do anything which produces what might be counted as a distinct effect, I must undergo some change and must act upon a subject which also undergoes change. God's conservation produces no changes in things or in God; nor does God's governance or providence; nor, indeed, does creation. The actions of God are simply not in the mode of change. When I do something, change is so intricately involved with it that entirely the wrong connotations are carried when we speak of God's power as a power of *doing*. All my doings, but none of God's acts as Creator, involve change; the exercise of divine power is purely intentional.

[23] *De Potentia*, 3, 3, ad 2.

6 ✐ "God is good"

and the problem of evil

Some philosophers have thought the dogmatic commitments of Christians to be incompatible with the evident truth that there are moral and physical evils—pain, ugliness, and anguish.[1] Others have supposed that the evil in the world is evidence which, even if not conclusive, provides a high probability that certain Christian beliefs about God are false (in particular, either the belief that God is morally perfect or the belief that God is all-powerful).[2] The "problem" for Christians has traditionally been to reconcile their claims to the premises of these contentions.

Both points of view appear to me to be in error. I think we can show that Christian belief is logically consistent with the evils in the world, insofar as it is possible to establish the consistency of any set of propositions as formulated in ordinary English. Moreover, I think we can show that in order to argue that the evils of the world provide significant evidence against the moral perfection or the power of God, it is

[1] H. J. McCloskey, "God and Evil," *The Philosophical Quarterly* (April, 1960), p. 97.

[2] See Hume, *Dialogues Concerning Natural Religion.*

necessary to beg the question, by assuming as a premise the very thing for which one is attempting to provide evidence. We shall attempt to establish these points.

But there is another sense in which the problem of evil has not been resolved and, perhaps, cannot be. David Hume asked "Whence is evil?" That is, assuming that God is both good and powerful, *why* is there evil in the world? Many of the twelve standard hypotheses which we shall criticize in Section 3 have been put forward to reconcile the goodness of God with the evil in the world, but all depend entirely for success as reconciliations upon whether they are in *fact* answers to Hume's question. We shall reject these hypotheses because we do not and cannot know that they are true.

There is still another sense in which the problem of evil cannot be settled. Many human beings meet with or hear about some tragic event to which they cannot but respond, "All right; I'll give God the benefit of the doubt with respect to everything else: but *why* did He command or allow *this*?" (That is, "Explanations which cover the rest do not cover *this*.") Sometimes we are concerned with the manner of death or illness of one close to us, or with some hideous crime upon the innocent and helpless; sometimes, with the wanton destruction and suffering wrought by an evil or misshapen human soul; in all such involvements we face particular sets of events that are relatively small in the course of history. The fact that we might have espoused some general answer to "Why does God permit evil in the world?" will not help us, for we are now asking an even more difficult question: "Why did God permit *this* evil in the world?" It is logically possible that any general purpose which allows *some* evil in the world (as a logically replaceable means to some end) could have been achieved without any particular, *given* evil (taken in isolation from the rest of events).[3] Therefore, for each particular one of these upheavals of the human spirit where we confront the cruelty and irrationality of nature or of man, a special and quite personal explanation is necessary. Even if

---

[3] This is trivially true, but not a trivial truth. A careful distinction of general purposes from particular purposes is needed here. For if God's purpose is that $(p \cdot q)$ should occur (where q is an evil), then this purpose entails that *some* evil occur, q, but cannot be achieved apart from *this* particular evil. Hence, strictly speaking, it is not possible that every purpose which permits some evil should be achievable without some particular evil. But a *general purpose* for which evils are a logically replaceable means is by definition not one which logically involves any *particular* (given) evil (though it may require *some* particular evils); hence, the claimed possibility should be obvious.

there is a general purpose which requires or allows some evils, and even if we were to discover what that general purpose is, we would still be unable to explain the occurrence of a given, particular evil, since by the very concepts we employ, *this* particular evil is not a logically necessary condition for the realization of the general purpose. Hence, a new explanation is required in addition to the general one we *ex hypothesi* possess.

And if, on the other hand, we were finally to discover that God's purpose was to produce the particular state of affairs *p* · *q* (where *p* designates the conjunction of all other particular facts and *q* the particular evil event which puzzles us), we would simply ask: "Why would God choose (*p* · *q*) rather than (*p* · ~*q*)? Thus the whole question of explaining whence the evil event, *q*, would be opened again. There is *nothing for us to know* which can provide a philosophical answer to the personal and existential question "Why did God allow *this* evil?"[4]

SECTION 2: SOME SENSES AND USES OF "GOD IS GOOD"

A person saying "God is good" in a discussion of religion might mean that God is a worthy object of our desire and our knowledge (that God is *our* good);[5] he might be attributing to God a firm adherence to the right (determined, perhaps, independently of the will of God); or

---

[4] In much of the "existentialist" philosophy of our time, the attempt to assign meaning to human effort in a world replete with evil and with frustration of man's deepest desires has played a fundamental part. Even the Christian religion may be seen as an answer to the same sort of puzzle: Every human being has a desire for unlimited life, complete knowledge, and uninterrupted possession of some object worthy of possession to the exclusion of all else; every evidence in all of human experience of the natural world seems to indicate that these desires will in the end be frustrated, and even though we might in death not know this, the *anticipation*, while *living*, of this outcome jades all human pleasure and makes very rare the man who can be said to have been "happy" (in any profound sense) throughout his natural life. It is an obvious fact that every man wants to be divine in power, in immortality, and in happiness. Christianity proposes just this: the opportunity, as St. John says, to be sons of God and to be made divine by participation in the divinity of Christ. The "meaning" or "point" to earthly life is provided by the *anticipation* and *expectation* of the end to be achieved in life: St. Thomas Aquinas says "Faith is the foretaste of the knowledge by which we are to be rendered happy in the life to come" (*Compendium of Theology*). (My translation; cf. p. 5 of the Vollert translation cited above.)

[5] Of course, it might be argued that if God is *not* morally good, then God is not the worthy object of our desires and knowledge; thus, if argument against the moral perfection of God were to succeed, it might show the falsity of the belief that God is a worthy object of man's will and reason.

he might be attributing to God the benevolent desire to produce the happiness of His rational creatures, insofar as doing so would accord with their states of will. He might be saying these things to inform us, to commend God, or to exonerate Him (perhaps even to ridicule us!). There is no doubt that if one examined other uses of the expression "God is good" by nominal Christians one would find other meanings too, some fairly orthodox and others bizarre. These statements are made for various purposes, and have various *uses* beyond their employment as vehicles of information. Two of these uses concern us: the commendatory and the exculpatory.

The commendatory and the exculpatory *uses*[6] are related. A man horrified at the extermination of six million Jews might insist "God is good," intending to exonerate God. His primary intention in saying "God is good" is to dismiss blame, to assert the moral purity of God and to disclaim His moral reprehensibility for what is evil in the situation. Sometimes there is a belligerent tone to such utterances, a tone which indicates another dimension of meaning: that God *will* right the balance, that justice will be done and the injured avenged. Thus the *exculpatory* assertion "God is good" is sometimes based upon one's confidence in the hidden purposes or supreme wisdom of God, and sometimes upon the additional confidence that God will set things right again, redressing grievances and punishing the evildoers.

The same man might, upon winning the Irish Sweepstakes, say "God is good," praising God and indirectly attributing *responsibility* to Him for the good event. Note the differences between the two uses: (a) in the one case, one means to assert God's moral purity in contexts where moral censure might otherwise seem appropriate; whereas (b) in the other, one means to assert God's *active* benevolence in a deed which resembles a personal kindness. It is the difference between denying God's moral responsibility for a characteristic of the event (its being evil), and attributing moral (and benevolent) responsibility for a characteristic of the event (its being desirable for us). It is precisely these different usages which have confused philosophers and have caused them to wonder what would ever be taken to falsify

---

[6] We deal here with *uses* of a phrase, uses which can be found for the expression in several of its *meanings:* The *benevolence* ("to all," "to me," "to some") meanings and the *moral* meanings admit of these as well as other uses. The variety of *uses* profoundly affects the matter of verification and falsification.

the claim "God is good," since the practice of believers is to attribute everything good to the authorship and direct benevolence of God (the commendatory utterance) and to attribute everything evil to the depravity of man and the influence of devils (the exculpatory utterance). If "God is good" is taken to be the *same* statement in both cases, then it would naturally appear to be used unfalsifiably and non-empirically. (Both uses appear to require that "God" be used primarily designatively and only incidentally significatively.)

In various contexts, moreover, the expression "God is good" is used synonymously with "God is benevolent"; but the latter expression is a model of ambiguity and even in technical contexts has never been particularly clear. There is considerable difference between saying "God is benevolent" (that is, "God wills the happiness of each rational creature, subject of course to the free decision of the creature") and saying "God is morally good" (that is, "God always freely does what is morally perfect and avoids what is morally prohibited"). For it might appear possible that a being could be sometimes benevolent but not morally perfect. The fact that there is evil in the world is sometimes thought to mitigate against the benevolence of God, and sometimes also against His moral perfection, by those who hold that it is wrong and a defect in God for Him to have brought about the dire misery in the world which He could have avoided without cost or moral defect. The "problem of evil" can therefore be conceived as the problem of theoretically reconciling the *benevolence* of God with the misery of His creatures, or as that of reconciling the moral perfection of God with the apparently gratuitous production of evil things. But more mature consideration shows that consideration of God's benevolence can be made secondary, and derived from an examination of more general concepts.

Consider the ambiguity of the claim that God is benevolent. Benevolent to whom? *To me*, let us say; we could as well say "to everyone," or "to His friends." But let us content ourselves with "God is benevolent to me"; God not only *wishes* me well, He wills me well; He *does* something for me.

The necessity of two uses of the claim "God is good," the exculpating and the commendatory, carries over to contexts where "good" means "benevolent." When things turn out the way I like them, I commend God's action by saying that He is benevolent, that He has bent the course of the world to my taste; when they turn out the way I do not like them, I exonerate God's actions by affirming that my happiness is being wrought in the fire, not that my hopes are being consumed. The fact that there is an exonerating usage of the "benevolence" meaning of "God is good" shows that at least some believers think particular states of affairs, however miserable they may appear, serve God as a means to their ultimate happiness. Orthodox Christian believers, in fact, teach that the right state of mind—the trust in God to bring them to happiness in union with Him—will dignify any state of suffering; that suffering is a means to happiness because it allows the person to enter the state of mind which Christ freely chose in the redeeming act of His death: complete union with the will of God, complete acceptance of the choice of God.[7]

The person who says "God is good," meaning "God wills my happiness" (i.e., provides all the means to happiness short of my own free decisions), does not usually mean that in each event of that person's life God brings about what in particular that person desires at that moment. He means only that happiness is made available in the form of tranquility of soul, the happiness of faith and confident expectation for homo viator, and that that happiness is promised through possession of divine life for homo victor. When God is said to be benevolent in this way, the use of the phrase is often commendatory, as in prayers and meditations, and the use of the term "God" is primarily designative.

The preceding comments have indicated that there is a wide divergence among the meanings in which Christians use the expression "God is good," and that, among the uses to which the statements expressed are put, some are primarily commendatory (as in prayers and meditations) and some are exculpatory (as in arguments and apologies). Variations of the "problem of evil" can be played upon this breadth of meaning, for example: How can God be benevolent to all men when so many suffer unequally? How can God be benevolent to me when I must constantly seek happiness? Why does anything

---

[7] However, the spiritual writers try to teach detachment and trust in God which is so complete that no matter what happens the Christian wills what happens and would not wish anything else than what God has chosen to happen to him, regardless of the latitude of choice that might be imagined for him; thus a person's desires become consequent upon the actual.

occur from which God must be exonerated? But the fundamental arguments and counter-arguments have their paradigms in a discussion of the *moral* goodness of God. *Mutatis mutandis*, our comments may be applied to the other senses of "God is good," senses whose existence and importance we have both acknowledged and indicated.

As we examine uses of the expression "God is good" to express claims that God never does what is morally reprehensible and is, moreover, in all His acts worthy of praise and admiration, we ask two questions: (1) Is the statement analytic? (2) Is God *essentially* good?

I think there is no doubt whatever that the statement 'God is good'— where "God" functions primarily significatively but incidentally designatively—is analytic. Further, to allow even the possibility of moral defect in God is repugnant to the Christian way of thinking of Him; the Christian would not think 'God is morally defective' merely false; he would think it ridiculous, and would very probably say that you do not understand "who God is" if you say this about Him.

It does not follow from our admitting that 'God is good' is analytic that we think God is *essentially* good—that moral goodness is an essential attribute of God (in the primarily designative sense of the term "God"). Rather, as Section 3 of Chapter II indicated, the fact that 'A is good' is analytic (for one who understands the statement as it occurs in the discourse of religious teachers and thinkers) does not entail that the being referred to by the name "A" has goodness as an essential property (i.e., by nature). As I stated above, it is a very important feature of analytic statements expressed by sentences with proper names to indicate the subject that some of the elements of the name's signification may be found in the referent only contingently; moreover, they are sometimes *absent* in the referent, with the result that consistent thought requires an alteration in the name's signification. It may seem absurd to the Christian for someone to think God is not good (because for this Christian 'being good' is part of what is signified by "God"), but this is not the same thing as saying that the attribute belongs to God essentially (that is, as a *constituent* characteristic). Therefore, it is quite appropriate for a person to believe that 'God is good' is analytic, and yet to investigate arguments for and against the claim that God has His goodness by nature—or that He has that quality at all.

Even in the context of moral goodness, the statement "God is good" is ambiguous. When I say, "Jones is good," I usually mean that some act or set of acts or disposition to act (of Jones) is in accord with the standard of moral rightness. But I make this claim in the context of thinking it possible for Jones to have acted, or have had a disposition to act, in a way which does *not* accord with the standards of rightness.

Yet is it possible that *God* should not act in accord with the standards of moral perfection? If so, then God is not essentially good—although, of course, 'God is good' remains analytic. If it is *not* possible, then something about the nature of God (apart from any moral or aesthetic attribute) precludes evil acts, and God is essentially good.[8] In that case, we shall have to decide whether God can possess moral goodness, as we conceive it when we speak of other intelligent beings; we shall also have to decide whether the kind of praise and admiration which it is appropriate to render to God is the same as that which it is appropriate to render to other intelligent beings whose acts also conform to the standards of rightness.

St. Thomas Aquinas[9] argued that God is essentially good. On some occasions he had in mind what we have called "ontological goodness," saying that God is an end to Himself and the end of all other things and, further, that He is that-by-participation-in-which all other things (insofar as they have being) are rendered worthy objects of desire. On other occasions, St. Thomas taught that God is essentially good in the sense that God's actions *cannot fail* to accord with the standards of moral righteousness. We shall consider his position briefly.

Discussing whether God can will evil, Aquinas said:

> The will never aims at evil without some error existing in the reason, at least with respect to a particular object of choice.[10]

This is the assumption behind the argument that God cannot perform an evil act. It is reasoned as follows: A being that does what is evil acts against its nature; God cannot act against His nature; therefore, God cannot perform an evil act. A finite being is able to act

---

[8] It would also seem that a "naturalistic" analysis of 'being a good being' would be possible.

[9] *Summa Contra Gentiles*, Book I, chs. 28, 37, 38, 39.

[10] *SCG*, Book I, ch. 95, n. 3. In *On the Truth of the Catholic Faith*, tr. Vernon J. Bourke. "Image Books" (New York: Doubleday & Company, 1956). The other quotations from *SCG* here have also been taken from this translation, unless otherwise noted.

against its nature because it is ignorant, or weak, or both. God is neither weak nor ignorant.

The keystone is the contention that no being can perform an evil act unless it be in some respect ignorant or weak. This must be reconciled, on the one hand, with the fact that no one is morally responsible for an evil act unless he knows (either attentatively or habitually or *in causa*) that his act is evil; and on the other, with the fact that sometimes people doing evil acts appear to lack no knowledge whatever which is relevant to the character or forseeable effects of those acts. It is not easy to deduce from '*X* broke his promise, freely made, to *Y*' that *X* is weak or ignorant in some respect. I cannot use only premises Thomas provides to deduce a contradiction from the following conjunction: '*X* broke his promise to *Y* and *X* is omniscient and omnipotent'; what is there about complete knowledge and complete power which precludes promise-breaking? Nor can I deduce a contradiction (by means of premises provided by St. Thomas) from the following conjunction: '*X* frustrated the natural desire of *Y* (an intelligent being) for immortality and *X* is omnipotent and omniscient'.

It would appear that the actions of a morally perfect being should be such that no one who fully grasps the circumstances can reasonably disapprove of them. If we postulate that God has annihilated an intelligent creature possessed of a natural desire for immortality, and at the same time assume that God is by nature good, it would appear that one of the following is a consequence: either (a) no one who fully grasps the circumstances can reasonably disapprove of the act supposed, or else (b) that the act supposed is impossible (that is, it is inconsistent to say God does such a thing). Whether or not the supposition of an annihilation is consistent depends upon whether or not that act is morally good; and whether or not someone can reasonably disapprove of the act also depends, in part, upon whether or not the act is good. If a being had to be ignorant or weak to perform the act, we could of course eliminate it as inconsistent for God, but we could not infer from that that it is an evil act; many morally worthy acts— for example, the generation of children—presuppose ignorance and weakness on the part of the agent. Hence, we can settle the matter of whether God can perform this act only by deciding whether it is a good act or not. If we accept Aquinas' main premise that the performance of an evil act is possible only to a being which lacks knowledge, we may ask whether God would have to lack some knowledge in order to annihilate an intelligent creature with a natural desire for immortality. I think He would not; it follows, by *modus tollens*, that this is a morally worthy act, an act which, given our initial premise—that it is not reasonable to disapprove a good act—no one can reasonably disapprove. And yet I think one could reasonably disapprove God's annihilating such a creature; St. Thomas certainly thought so, making this a premise of his arguments for personal immortality. If this is so, then it will follow, again by *modus tollens*, that it is not a necessary condition for x's performing an evil act that x should lack knowledge or be weak in some respect; hence, St. Thomas' necessary condition appears not to be necessary at all, and his argument for the essential goodness of God collapses.

Although I am not satisfied that we have thereby provided a conclusive refutation of St. Thomas' main premise, I think we have cast enough doubt upon it to justify our saying that he has not shown that evil acts are impossible to God.

St. Thomas' reasoning and the difficulties it raises suggest that a more satisfactory premise may be this: *No being can knowingly perform an evil act unless it has some defect in power or knowledge with respect to the means to its own satisfaction.* This may indeed be the way St. Thomas' claim should be interpreted, but deciding that is not important here. The assumption underlying this premise is that the performance of those activities which are in accord with natural inclination (the appetite to fulfill the agent's natural function) and are motivated thereby cannot be morally defective, except circumstantially; hence, the performance of acts which secure one's happiness cannot be morally unworthy. In effect, we presume that the world is so made up that one cannot secure happiness by doing what is wrong.[11] We also presume that no intelligent being can act (transitively) except in pursuit of its happiness, or to bring about the existence of or fulfill the natural inclinations of other beings.[12] When

---

[11] This is, admittedly, a simplification of the basic moral situation. But we must begin with some premises which can be examined later if their consequences look promising.

[12] The concepts 'natural inclination' and 'happiness' are not analyzed here, nor is the principle that one cannot secure happiness by doing what is wrong; for this is a hypothetical deduction we are concerned with. We merely want to find a set of apparently plausible premises from which 'God is essentially good' can be derived.

one intelligent being acts against the happiness of another, it must *not* have attained its own happiness.

It will follow that no being can perform an evil act without having a defect of knowledge or power with respect to the attainment of its happiness; for if no being can act at all unless it be in pursuit of the happiness it does not yet possess (or to fulfill the natural inclinations of other beings, should it possess its own happiness), and if an evil act is one which more or less decisively precludes one's happiness (thus frustrating a natural inclination), no being could choose such an act unless it lacked either power or knowledge with respect to the attainment of its own happiness. If happiness were within one's power and knowledge, one *could not* choose anything else. A being that lacked the power to attain happiness by merely willing it might find itself in circumstances where no course of action (all of whose elements and effects can be foreseen) within its power would achieve happiness; at that point either in ignorance or in weakness, it might select actions which are not compatible with its objective. Man is in just this position during most of his life. He cannot name, act for act, a chain of particular acts which actually lies open before him, within his power, and which he *knows* will confer his happiness. This is because he lacks *power* to bring about those chains of action which he knows would lead to his happiness if they *were* within his power; he has neither the knowledge nor the power entirely to control his future. Even though a being is biased to seek its happiness, it may choose a course of action which it knows will not lead to that goal if it lacks power in such a way that no envisionable unbroken course of particular acts in its power at that time can efficaciously achieve its happiness; evil and good acts may *appear* alike desirable in their immediate consequences when both kinds of choice fail to attain happiness for the agent, and no efficacious choice lies open.

That the evil act is incompatible with happiness is, of course, crucial; but only in the sense that one and the same act cannot both achieve or preserve happiness and be evil. A particular evil act is not absolutely and unconditionally incompatible with happiness attained through other acts; rather, it is incompatible only if it causes the final or attained state of virtue or vice. If conscious wrongdoing is merely a temporary choice of one who, on the whole, acts in accord with his happiness, then the evil acts will not frustrate the happiness of the agent and will, in effect, not be unconditionally evils for him. This suggests that from the point of view of a given agent, whether a particular act is unconditionally evil or not depends entirely upon how it fits into the chain of activities by which the agent pursues happiness; thus vice—that is, habitual evil which perdures—may for some people have a more deleterious effect than maliciousness (conscious intent to do harm), which is sporadic. It is habitual maliciousness which characterizes the unqualifiedly bad man and unconditionally damns him.

That no evil act is by itself capable of frustrating the search for happiness makes it possible for a person to perform such an act, even knowing that if that choice should be the attained state of the will or should form a habit leading to a similar attained state of the will, happiness will be lost. No one intends to make his habit of will evil; one merely intends to do acts, which are evil, to attain some desired object.

A being which attains its own happiness by nature cannot perform an evil act in the pursuit of its own happiness; it does not pursue its happiness, or perform any act with a really distinct effect (any transitive act), in order to attain happiness. Hence, God can act transitively only to bring about the existence of and to fulfill the natural inclinations of other beings.[13] No action of this sort can be incompatible with God's happiness; rather, it proceeds from God's happiness, as from a motive (not a cause). Hence, God cannot perform an evil act; consequently, He is essentially morally good. Therefore, I think it a plausible hypothesis that God is essentially good.

In the light of this concept of 'evil act' we can settle the test cases of whether God can break his promises or annihilate an intelligent being, cases used for criticism of St. Thomas Aquinas' argument in Summa Contra Gentiles. If the acts are evil, God cannot do them; if they are not, He can. A being which is by nature happy can act transitively only to bring about the existence or fulfill the natural inclinations of other beings; thus the annihilation of a creature naturally inclined to immortality would be contradictory to the possible courses of action open to God, all of which must fulfill the natural inclinations of things.

---

[13] This follows from the preceding statement and from Principle I, above.

The matter of breaking promises is not quite so evident, but seems clear enough. It is certainly a natural inclination of a rational creature to expect God to fulfill His promises, since He could gain nothing by failing to do so. Moreover, none of the "excusing" conditions which apply to the failure of others could ever apply to an action of God; and it is a natural inclination of man to trust the word of the being which is believed to be unable or at least unwilling to do evil acts. Hence, were God to break His promise, He would frustrate any rational creature's natural inclination to trust. Thus God cannot break his promises.[14]

We have concluded that God cannot do evil acts and that statements of the form 'God breaks His promises to Y' or 'God annihilates Y, who has a natural and intellectual inclination to immortal life' are contradictory, just as St. Thomas supposed. We reached this conclusion by way of these premises: (a) No being can pursue any end unless it pursues it as a means to its own happiness or unless, possessing its own happiness, it pursues that end as means to the fulfillment of the natural inclinations of some other being.[15] (b) No being can perform an evil act unless that being is defective in either power or knowledge with respect to its own happiness. This defect is a necessary condition for any agent's performing an evil act, since no act that secures the happiness of an intelligent agent can be evil. God is by essence an intelligent being (hence possessed of an intellectual appetite) which cannot be ordered to any end outside Himself; thus, He must be happy by nature and necessarily. It follows from this and from the a priori truths (a) and (b) that God cannot perform an evil act and must in all his actions accord with moral perfection. Nevertheless, we can treat these conclusions only as reasonable hypotheses because no concerted analysis has been devoted to certain key concepts, such as 'natural inclination' and 'happiness'.

Yet it may be that God's actions accord with the moral law, and that nonetheless God is not morally good; a stone is not morally good even though its actions are in accord with the moral law. The obvious

---

[14] This conclusion does not accord well with the doctrine that God can perform the descriptive contrary, though not the moral contrary, of whatever He does. But resolving that would take us too far afield.

[15] This is an a priori claim which, in effect, specifies part of what we mean by "the act of an intelligent being."

reply is that a stone is not a free agent in any of its actions, whereas God is a free agent in all actions *ad extra;* and the obvious rejoinder to that reply is that although God is in one sense free in transitive actions, He is not *morally* free. God could have done the opposite of what He did. If 'creating our world' is the same as *a* then God could have done ~*a*. But if *a* stands for 'doing a good act', God could not have done ~*a*, where this means 'doing an act which is *not* good'. Now some may say that God does not perform a moral act at all, since He could not have performed the moral contrary of His act. Yet we do not make this a condition for a morally worthy human act; we merely require that the agent should have been able to perform something descriptively and not "normatively" incompatible with what he chose to do. In fact, as a man becomes a "moral saint," his inclinations to do the moral opposite of his actual courses diminish. We may suppose that in some extremely disciplined life a man reaches the state of escaping all temptation to morally unworthy acts and attains such habits of virtue that the opportunity to be morally neglectful would have no influence upon him. In that case, we might say the moral saint could not have performed the *moral* contrary of his actual course; but this would not make his action non-moral.

Therefore, we say that God acts *from* His essence in choosing only among morally worthy courses of action. Yet we do not deny that God is a moral agent: His actions *ad extra* are free (in that He could do an act of the complement class), and they proceed entirely from internal causes. If someone wants to make 'being able to perform an act of negative moral value' a necessary condition of 'performing a morally good act', then he will deny that God is morally good (i.e., performs morally good acts). But he will not, in that case, be denying anything I wish to affirm, although the paradoxical character of his utterance would be confusing in religious contexts.

Although we have emphasized that 'God is morally good' is analytic for the Christian and have insisted (in the light of Section 3 of Chapter II) that from ' "God is morally good" is analytic' it does not follow that there are or are not independent grounds—grounds originally suggested by St. Thomas Aquinas—for concluding that God is essentially good. I do not think we should consider the preceding pages as an attempt to *establish* the essential goodness of God, since most of the premises were merely presumed in order to assist the exposition of the kind of reasoning which leads to the conclusion that God is essentially good. We have merely decided upon one of two alternative frameworks in which to consider the claim that there is good reason to think that God is not morally perfect. We have decided to hold both that 'God is good' is analytic and that 'God is essentially good' is true, but we have not pretended to deduce the latter from the former. Finally, we have decided that since 'God is good' is analytic and the second hypothesis is probable, we shall have to find a way to explain away the apparent conflict between these and the empirical evidence we have, based upon the evil we observe in the world.

SECTION 3: EXAMINATION OF THE TRADITIONAL "RECONCILIATIONS" OF 'GOD IS GOOD' AND 'THERE IS EVIL IN THE WORLD'

These "reconciliations" fall into two main groups: Claims that God *could not* avoid the evils we observe; and claims that God *need not* have avoided those evils.

A: *Concerning arguments that God could not have avoided evil*

The key premises in the usual arguments that God could not have avoided the evils in the universe are of three sorts:

1: *that the laws of nature and the nature of free beings could not be of the sorts they are without the occurrence of some evils.*

2: *that some moral goods are impossible without some moral evils: the concept of pleasure is meaningless apart from the concept of pain, in such a way that there would be no sensible pleasure in a universe without pain.*

3: *that a perfect world is not possible without that kind of variety which would allow some physical evils.*

The three premises are not equally well connected to the same conclusion (that God could not have avoided the physical and moral evils which obtain). The third, for instance, deals wholly with physical evils (pain and ugliness), and the first, while permitting us to argue that the occurrence of some natural evil (physical and moral) is *conditionally* necessary, leaves open the whole matter of the avoidability of this world in preference for a more perfect one.

The first of these arguments is one of the more plausible traditional "reconciliations" of the goodness of God and the reality of evil. It does indeed seem that the avoidance by all creatures of some physical evils would require alteration in the laws of nature, and that the very fact that man is a free being, partially ignorant and partially weak in his resolutions, makes it likely that some men will make choices that are incompatible with what is right. But we need not expatiate upon the argument's virtues, which could be increased by other considerations, since the key premise embodies two basic defects.

First, even granting that the evils are unavoidable given the structure of nature, the fact that God could have avoided a universe *with this structure* shows that these evils could have been avoided—that they are only hypothetically necessary, upon the condition that God freely chose to make a world of this sort. But since that condition is present, it follows that avoiding these evils *absolutely* was in God's power. Hence, although it is the case that there are some ends which it is not logically possible to achieve without some evil (e.g., that a murder be committed or that medicines should actually heal someone or that prayers for deliverance from pain should be heard), since none of these ends need have been selected by God, it follows that all such evils were avoidable by God. This argument would then have to be joined to the third, or to some other which makes the ends that are to be achieved in a creation of this sort (a) unattainable by any better means and (b) *worthy* in themselves. But since, as we shall show below, whatever end was to be attained in this creation could have been attained in some other in which these evils are not present, it follows that these evils were avoidable. In fact, it is evident that for any end that God wishes to achieve, which will of course be worthy in itself, no particular creation is logically necessary (unless that end or purpose be defined in a way to make it logically trivial to say so, like 'creating a man who sins and then repents').

Suppose that someone says, "But the purpose God had was to produce events $x, y, z, \ldots n$ [where this constitutes some complete itemization of the actual]; hence evil was unavoidable because y, z, w are evils and thus the occurrence of certain evils is logically necessary for the good universe, which is good over-all. We can ask simply: Why did God choose to make world $x, y, z, \ldots n$? Either God had a purpose or He did not. If He did, that purpose cannot be described as 'purposing to produce events $x, y, z, \ldots n$' and hence could (logically) have been achieved without events y, z, w, the evils. If God did not have a purpose in producing events $x, y, z, \ldots n$, it still remains true that any purpose God had could (logically) have been achieved without events $x, y, z, \ldots n$, since in this case these events are not logically necessary to any purpose at all. Hence it follows that there is no purpose God had in creating this world, $x, y, z, \ldots n$, which He could not have achieved without the world or its evils.

Nor is there any reason to think that, the nature of free agents being as it is, God could not have created only persons who would act rightly throughout their lives. There is nothing about a free person which *requires* that he do evil; only that which *permits* him to do evil. Hence, it is logically possible that all existing persons should have been wholly good.

The second argument has some merit also though it too is insufficient for its object. Many counter-examples could at once be given to the assertion that pleasure is impossible without pain, or moral virtue impossible without vice. Yet this is not the most sympathetic way to interpret that claim. There is no doubt that many people have had pleasures (e.g., of wealth, virtue, and health) without having suffered the corresponding pain. But the same faculties by which a man can experience pleasure or exercise virtue are those by which he can suffer pain or display vice. For, as Berkeley remarked, a certain excess of heat or cold or any other sensation causes pain; in general, excess or defect of what is pleasurable constitutes the painful, just as habitual excess or defect in what is reasonable constitutes the vicious. The same powers by which we can suffer want are at hand for the enjoyment of plenty. Now, the argument suggests that it is not possible for God to construct a universe in which such powers of sensibility and moral choice are present—in which sense gives pleasure and intellect gives virtue—but neither does in fact lead to pain or vice. I do not see why this is impossible. Consider intellectual virtue: there is no reason why a man could not know exactly what he needs to avoid evil in a natural way, even though he does not know everything. Still, the case of pain is different: would the *word* "pleasure" even have meaning under such conditions?

It seems that "pleasure" might not have *our* meaning for a person living in such a world. In such a universe as we postulate, a man might very probably use the term "pleasure" only for those states of delight which are *more* than normal. Yet, notwithstanding the fact that people in such a world might have the same vocabulary as we possess and might lack some of our concepts, theirs would be a world of what we call pleasure. I see no reason why such a world could not exist.

Some pleasures (such as the pleasure of feeling one's toothache stop after the novocaine is injected) are not possible apart from pain and some moral virtues (visiting the sick and burying the dead, and fortitude in withstanding the unjust) are not possible in a world without evil. But no serious argument can be based upon the premise that the goods so achieved outweigh the prerequisite evils, such that a similar balance could not have been attained in some other way. We simply do not know, nor have we the means to discover, enough about the structure of the world to confirm the first part; and we already know enough a priori to disconfirm the latter.

St. Thomas Aquinas[16] has argued in terms of "balance," without, I think, noticing that full support for the conclusion that the balance of good over evil is favorable and not otherwise attainable requires the *assumption* that God exists and is good—the very proposition for which evidence is to be supplied.

The third way of arguing that God could not have avoided the evils in the world is also found in Aquinas:[17] that *a perfect world is not possible without this sort of variety.* This is a typically neoplatonic notion, which occurs again in the work of Leibniz. But there is no reason to think this universe is uniquely perfect. Aquinas himself said in *De Veritate* that God could have created another world, as perfect as this one, or more so; and there is decisive reason to think that no creation could be absolutely perfect in any sense in which all are not (see Chapter VII on the only possible world). If one says that this statement means only that this world is perfect for the end God had in mind, then either this is a tautology or some other world would be equally perfect. If the notion of that end includes "this world," the claim is trivial; if not, the fact that this world attains the particular end excellently does not preclude its being true that some other world with less or no evil would also have attained it excellently. Hence, it is false that the evils were unavoidable because this world is a perfect world and God chose to make a perfect world.

Moreover, variety of perfection does not require either moral or physical evil. Infinite variety is possible within the scope of the plea-surable, the good, and the beautiful; consider the being of God, for example, which is infinitely imitable.

An argument countering the case against the goodness of God by showing that, even though He freely created, God could not have avoided the evil that occurs, must premise at least: (1) that the object God chose for his creation is worthy in itself, although not necessary for God's happiness; (2) that there is no better way to achieve it without the occurrence of some evil; (3) that although other equally worthy ends could have been achieved through a creation without evil, the value of achieving the end is not diminished by the fact that the means must be deficient in some respect in order to be excellent as *means* to that end. Although we have seen that there are some ends which cannot be achieved without the occurrence of some evil, the introduction of the first premise—that God has freely chosen both the world and any object (end) for which this sort of world is a logically necessary condition—vitiates the whole argument, since it establishes as a fact the negation of (2): that God *could have avoided* the evils which obtain. A *fortiori*, if there was *no* purpose to be served by the creation of this world, there is no reason at all to think God could not have avoided the evils which obtain.

B: Concerning arguments that God need not have avoided evil

We can now turn to the arguments designed to show that God need not have avoided evil. These are of two sorts: (a) arguments which concern the permissibility of the creation of the world as it is, and (b) those which suggest that God *ought* to have made things the way they are.

To show that such a creation is *permissible*, various premises have been employed: We shall consider three:

1: The greater good on the whole results from this sort of world.

2: The evils in the world are intended as a warning to man to repent his sins.

3: The evils result from defects in secondary causes which do not imply a defect in the remote cause.

(1) As David Hume apparently admitted in his *Dialogues Concerning Natural Religion*, no one can rightly accuse the Christian of believ-

ing in inconsistent things; the goodness, omnipotence, and perfection of God are not incompatible with the evil in the world because
premises like (1), (2), and (3) are all consistent, and because there are
forms of these premises which, if true, would reconcile the descriptions of God with His supposed actions. In fact, Hume seems to
think—for dialectical purposes at least—that if you knew, as the
Christian claims to know at the *outset*, that God is morally good, you
would have no difficulty in principle, only in practice, in accounting
for the evil in the world. On this point Hume may be over-optimistic,
unless he merely means that there is *some* logically consistent hypothesis which, conjoined with the premise of God's goodness, will
entail that there is evil in the world.

One can, I think, use premises such as these to discredit charges of
inconsistency;[18] but to *resolve* the problem of evil, to say whence the
evil, one must show that such indeed *is* the state of the world, that
evil *is* a means to an actual end that is greater in good and not otherwise obtainable; that the consistent hypothesis is also true. None of
the principles cited, (1), (2), or (3), can function in this way, because
none of these has been or can be established.

(2) The first theory, which is often presented as the "tapestry
theory," suggests that all the moral and physical evils of the world are
resolved into some greater good not obtainable through a better
world. Man cannot know from his finite sampling of the world just
what this greater good is and why it could not have been achieved
without evil; that is why the world is compared to a tapestry of which
man sees only the tangled threads in back, not the beautiful pattern
they create on the right side. Such an argument is found in the works
of Aquinas,[19] Augustine, and Leibniz, as well as in the writings of
many lesser thinkers. It is not to be treated as a version of the earlier
ones that we have rejected, for it is highly improbable that there is any
pattern of good which could not (except in a logically trivial sense)
have been attained with less evil. But from the incredible pain and
moral deformity found in our world, how could there result a
greater good than could have resulted from a harmonious kingdom
of free intellects devoted to God and loving Him, as is depicted in the

---

[18] See the more detailed discussion in Section 4.

[19] *SCG*, III, 71, n. 7.

doctrine of Heaven? That is, Heaven was logically possible for a creation of men without earthly life; supposedly it was intended as the alternative to what is now the case. How can earthly travail bring about any addition to this good? It is answered by some that thereby both the justice and the mercy of God are displayed. Yet this is unavailing: to a beatified intellectual universe both the justice and the mercy of God would be fully evident even though there would be no need to punish or forgive any sinner.

Unmodified, therefore, the "tapestry" hypothesis is simply too vague to have force. It seems a priori false on every sensible interpretation. A *modified* "greater good" theory can be dismissed as not established, although we must grant that it is *consistent* (if we do not speak of a good greater than that achievable by *any* other world) and that it can function as part of a proof of the consistency of the Christian's faith, as is explained in Section 4.

(3) The claim that God is justified in producing this world, replete with suffering and moral evil, because these evils serve to warn creatures that they should repent is plainly false. Most of the evils in the world occur under conditions where they not only do not, but *could not*, serve that function. When a man alone on a mountain is lost in an avalanche and never recovered, this might be taken by his friends, if he has any, as a warning that they could meet a like sudden deliverance to judgment. But the mutilating of children whose parents are morally good, the natural deformities of disease, the hideous crimes which take victims at random—these hardly function as warnings to repent, but rather as warning to repair the course of nature by the application of intellect and law. If one replies that the evils exist because man *ought* to take them as warnings to repent, it can be answered, first, that often the evil prosper and the good decline so that such warnings are ambiguous (we might be being warned to forget "honor" and grasp our neighbors' goods); and second, that the whole point that remains to be demonstrated is that man *ought* to take the evils he knows of to be warnings, since there are more reasonable interpretations of their purpose.

(4) The main thrust of all Aquinas' reasoning, and all the reasoning of the Fathers and other great theologians too, is that *the evils both physical and moral result from defects in secondary causes and do*

not imply any defect in the remote cause; therefore, a morally perfect being need not have avoided a world in which such evils are present. St. Thomas states the whole point at issue:[20]

It is possible for a defect to appear in an effect because of a defect in a secondary cause without there being a defect in the primary agent.

(i) Is this possible? To account for a defect in the effect, Aquinas postulates a defect in the secondary cause. Since the secondary cause is itself an effect of the primary cause, one might well have to account for the defect in the secondary cause by postulating a defect in the primary. This is just what the arguments *against* the combined goodness and omnipotence of God purport to do: to account for the defects in creation by postulating defects in the creator.

For example, if a man is said to be able to sin because he is ignorant, then does not some defect in God result from His creation of ignorant beings? Either He could not or He would not create beings with enough knowledge to avoid sin. Ruling out the claim that He *could* not, is it a defect that He *would* not? Aquinas thinks God's unwillingness to do so need not imply a defect, although he teaches: "Bonum ab integra causa; malum ex aliquo defecto." He holds that a defective effect can result from an integral (non-defective) efficient cause.[21] If that is so, he need not postulate that defective effects have defective secondary causes either, since those causes might be integral. Why is it that sometimes the inference from a defective effect to a defect in its cause is legitimate, and at other times not?

(ii) The principle quoted touches at the heart of the problem of evil, as well as that of determinism.[22] For it is evident that from some, but not from all, defective effects we can infer to defects in the agent. And in the showing of why this is so, and why the relationship of God to the world is a case where such inferences would be illegitimate, lies a crucial piece of the whole puzzle.

---

[20] *Ibid.*, n. 2. (My translation.)

[21] Is this a place where the principle of sufficient reason breaks down? Need there be no explanation of the origin of the defect if the agent be perfect? It is false that ignorance is a limitation but not a defect in an intelligent creature. Ignorance of any useful truth for which adequate evidence is naturally available in the environment is a defect in the endowments of an intelligent being.

[22] We shall develop the connection later.

The last group of traditional arguments purports to show that God *need* not have avoided the evils because He *ought* not to have avoided them. The key premises are:

The physical evils are punishments for the moral evils which God ought not to have prevented.

The physical evils are the natural consequences of moral evil which ought not to have been prevented.

These two premises rest upon a third:

The prevention of evils (especially moral) would involve God's interfering with the natural behavior of things.[23]

We can dismiss the punishment theory very quickly, combining the other parts of that premise into a discussion of the second one. It is most improbable that the events of the world fall upon man and beast as a result of any sin that the *sufferers* committed; first, because animals cannot sin, and secondly, because among men, evils are distributed alike to both the good and the evil, often falling far more heavily upon the former. Such a plan of punishment would be harder to justify than the evils for which it is supposed to account.

The same result occurs when it is said that these punishments befall man not because of his sin but because of Adam's sin. It could hardly make sense to say that because Adam sinned, lions step upon thorns and men suffer cancer in *punishment*. That God took away from these creatures some priviliged protection which was *additional* to animal perfection or to man's nature (as Aquinas thought) would make sense; sin would thus bring loss of privileges to which Adam had no natural right. This loss of protection might be deemed a punishment, but not the evils.

The second claim—that God ought not to have avoided the physical evils in the universe (because they are a natural consequence of the moral evils which, in turn, He ought not to have obviated because it would have required His interference with the natural ordering of things)—is also unsound. There is no reason to think that God could not have obviated all moral evil by His supernatural grace, as He is

[23] *SCG*, III, 71, n. 4 and n. 5.

thought to have done with some of His saints and with the Virgin Mary. The whole Christian tradition asserts that grace *builds upon* nature, and that it does not *work against* nature. Hence, God could have avoided all moral evil through grace without interfering with the natural behavior of things.

Yet it would be a mistake to push this point of view much further. One might be tempted to think that God ought to have avoided all moral evils by the dispensation of grace; but this answer would run counter to the Christian tradition that grace is free and not due to any man. All that the doctrine of grace need contribute to this argument is the counter-example to the claim that God could not prevent all moral evil without interference with the natures of things.

This dispute over the origin of physical evil suggests the following speculative hypothesis: God gave the first men power over nature, by some combination of telekinesis and telepathy, in such a way that they could avoid not only moral evil, but also all physical evil; and He so constructed the laws of nature that with wise interference by Adam's children the glory and the order of nature would ever increase—the very opposite of the otherwise naturally increasing state of entrophy. But sin brought about a loss of these preternatural powers of knowledge and alteration-at-will in distant physical objects; so it is that the universe is running down all the time and disease, disaster, and annihilation become ever more probable as time passes. Physical evil, then, would be explained as a natural consequence of the laws of nature, as these laws operate without the significant interference of intellectual beings who increase the balance and beauty of nature, and in terms of whose interference the kingdom of laws was originally designed. Depriving man of the powers of interference is God's punishment for humanity as such; but the evils result from entirely sufficient natural causes. This somewhat theological hypothesis would have great force did it not simply raise the question asked above: why did God not avoid such a universe as this? If one replies, "Because not avoiding such a universe implies no defect in virtue or in power," I point out that this is just what remains to be shown.

There have been many variations upon these themes, all leading to the same problem: whether it is possible that there could be a world which it would be evil for God to create.[24] The answer seems to be that it is not; God can create any possible world, and He cannot do evil. But can God create a world in which, as time passes, more beings suffer pain and more sins are committed until no finite being loves God and all are in physical torture and surrounded by ugliness? To say "No, for then God would not be good" begs the question. The attributes of such a world are consistent; God can create such a world; since God cannot do evil, the making of such a world would not require God to do evil. So, no matter what sort of world God creates, such creation has nothing to do with His moral goodness. To support this position some reason must be given as to why the character of the world (apart from God's supernatural relationships to it) is irrelevant to the moral character of God. It is just such a reason that we shall develop in Section 5.

SECTION 4: CONCERNING THE CHARGE OF INCONSISTENCY

Sometimes the Christian's beliefs have been said to be inconsistent because he holds both that God is good and omnipotent and that there is evil in the world. But this charge has never been proved.

It may be that those who have urged this objection did not mean that these two beliefs *could not* simultaneously be true, but rather that they *are not* simultaneously true; that is, the charge may be intended as a claim that some of the Christian's beliefs are false. Yet I do not think the Christian could expect much enlightenment from anyone who carelessly calls beliefs "inconsistent" which he merely thinks do not all have the *same* truth value.

If there is a way to give successful proof of the consistency of the Christian's beliefs, the "inconsistency" objection could be definitively disposed of. Such a proof has been proposed by Alvin Plantinga,[25] but as it was presented by him it employed a premise which I

[24] There is an interesting ambiguity here: (a) "It is possible that world A exists and it is evil for God to create A." And (b) "It is possible that some world would be evil for God to create." The latter would be true if creating some world would require that God do evil: a world where God would not keep His promises (if this were consistent). The former would be true even if God is essentially good, provided it was not absolutely necessary that He create the actual world in order for it to have being. The ambiguities in all this seem endless and are not relevant here.

[25] "The Free Will Defense," in *Philosophy in America*, ed. M. Black (Ithaca: Cornell University Press, 1965), pp. 204–220.

consider to be ambiguous: "God cannot *cause* a person freely to do what is right." There is certainly a sense in which this is true. But there is also a perfectly orthodox way of interpreting it so that this premise becomes false: the very important sense in which God's choice is said to be sufficient and necessary cause of whatever finite and contingent events occur in the universe (see Section 5, below). On this interpretation, the definition of "possible person" given by Plantinga is unacceptable: it presupposes that at least some persons have attributes which God does not determine that they have (in the sense that God's choice is logically sufficient and necessary). As a result, I cannot accept the proof of consistency as he has presented it, although it seems that his argument can be reformulated to take account of what I have held concerning the divine causality. A sketch of his proof will do to provide a touchstone for some comments.

The general form of the proof of consistency of two propositions, p and q, may be as follows: conjoin p and q to make $(p \cdot q)$ and provide a proof that the first conjunct, p, does not entail the negation of q. That is, prove that it is false that $(p \rightarrow \sim q)$.

Now to do this, according to Plantinga's plan, we find another proposition, K, which fulfills these conditions:

a: K *is obviously consistent, or can be shown to be consistent.*

b: *Construct* $\Diamond (p \cdot K)$ *(assuming that* $\Diamond p$ *is granted).*

c: *Prove* $[(p \cdot K) \rightarrow q]$.

In effect, p and q are shown to be consistent by our (1) assuming that p is consistent and (2) finding consistent premises, K, such that the conjunction of p and K entails q. Since it is assumed that p is consistent and since K is supposedly admitted to be consistent, it cannot be supposed that both q and $\sim q$ follow from p and K.[26] Hence, if we properly deduce q from $(p \cdot K)$, then, assuming that $\Diamond (p \cdot K)$, we will know that it is false that $\sim q$ follows from p. As a result we will know that $(p \cdot q)$ is consistent.

[26] Some logicians say that it does not follow from $\Diamond p$ and $\Diamond k$ that $\Diamond (p \cdot k)$. Doubts as to the legitimacy of this inference were expressed by Pseudo-Scotus early in the fourteenth century. That the construction described in (b) can legitimately be inferred from our admitting (a) and granting $\Diamond p$ is a major logical assumption of Plantinga's method; but it is one that I myself am quite ready to accept, although we know very well that we cannot allow the general rule that *any* two consistent logical units will yield a consistent conjunction, or even that any two *contingent* logical units will yield a contingent or even a consistent conjuction. Just what general rule of inference justifies the step to $\Diamond (p \cdot k)$ we shall not inquire here.

Now if *p* is 'God exists, is omnipotent, perfect, etc.', and if *q* is 'God creates a world in which there is both physical and moral evil to the degree that it is present in our world', then we must show that *p does not* entail ~*q*—that God did not create a world in which there is both physical and moral evil to the degree that it is present in our world. To do this we must select K.[27]

Several candidates, suggested by the "reconciliations" we rejected earlier, offer themselves:

K₁: *God chose some morally worthy end which cannot be achieved apart from the balance of physical and moral goods and evils which we find in our world.*

K₂: *God chose such a balance of goods and evils as we see in our world because a greater good on the whole could be achieved by such a balance than could be achieved without the evils.*

K₃: *God chose such a balance of goods and evils as a warning to man of the wrath to come in judgment.*

K₄: *God chose such a balance of goods and evils as the natural consequence of an evil action by which men lost the knowledge and power to control nature and avoid the evils in a way fitting human nature.*

If we add K₁, K₂, K₃, or K₄ to *p*, we can (with some appropriate qualifications and additions) deduce *q*.

Some philosophers may doubt the consistency of these principles. We shall not present the lengthy analysis required to show that *these* principles are consistent; instead, let us informally remark, with respect to K₁, that no one can give any reason to show that, in a world where goods and evils are distributed as they are in ours, it is *not possible* that the goods should greatly outbalance the evils. As the Liturgy says: "O felix culpa quam meruit tamquam salvatorem." The matter of balance is closely tied to the ends achieved. If it is possible that the goods outweigh the evils, it is also possible that God should have chosen this world with a worthy motive. Hence, there seems to be no reason to think that K₁ is inconsistent, regardless of what its truth-value may be. I am inclined to consider K₄ as obviously consistent, and even quite plausibly true.

---

[27] We shall not trace out the Plantinga argument with the particular examples he employs, since his paper is readily available.

Another principle—call it Ks—which will provide the necessary proof of consistency is this:

Ks: *An essentially good deity is not reprehensible for the physical or moral evil in any world he creates and it is not possible that any world should exist which God does not bring about. (It is assumed to be necessary that some world obtains even if it be the world of God existing alone.)*[28]

The whole project of giving a proof of the consistency of *p* and *q* depends upon our selecting certain propositions (K$_1$ through Ks, for example) which are themselves consistent, form a consistent conjunction with *p*, and, when conjoined with *p*, will entail *q*.

But no matter what premise K$_n$ we pick, we can be asked for a new proof of the consistency of K$_n$ or that of the conjunction ($p \cdot K_n$). This, of course, can always be supplied (if the original K$_n$ or the conjunction is consistent) by means of new premises, which will in turn be challenged. If the consistency of principles K$_1$ through Ks were universally obvious, then I doubt that reasonable philosophers would have been as troubled by the consistency of *p* and *q* as they have professed themselves to be. Whether we will reach premises which are *obviously* consistent in a reasonable number of steps has yet to be shown. Certainly K$_2$ seems less evidently consistent than K$_4$; and K$_3$ seems far less obviously consistent than K$_2$.

Hence, although sound proofs of the consistency of *p* and *q* can be provided (and, indeed, Plantinga has neatly provided the plan for an ample supply), and although these proofs may *establish* that the Christian's beliefs are consistent; they will also involve the questioner in an endless chain of proofs of the consistency of various other propositions. For the man who thinks he *knows* that God is not morally good, any set of premises which appears to prove the consistency of the "theistic set" will probably appear to him to be of doubtful consistency. Therefore we must buttress the rebuttal of "inconsistency" with reasoning to show such a person that he *cannot* be in a position to know that God is not good.

We shall do this by way of a quasi-Humean proof that there cannot

---

[28] Again, it is possible for someone to dispute the consistency of Ks. But upon what grounds? As will be seen in the next section, there have been few reasons given as to *why* a good and all-powerful God should not have created a world like ours, and the best reasons we can supply for this claim are such that no one should ever claim to have *established* them by acceptable philosophical procedures.

be acceptable grounds for the disbelief in the moral perfection of God, as this disbelief is expressed by philosophers on the basis of the evil in our world. Our reasoning will not show that God is morally perfect; but it *will* show that no one can discover from an examination of creation or of our conceptual orientation that God is not good.

SECTION 5: A FRESH EXAMINATION OF THE CASE
AGAINST THE GOODNESS OF GOD

(1) Let us consider the following passage from St. Thomas:

Every agent produces its action by acting through the divine power and consequently God is the cause both of all effects and of all actions, and since it was also shown that evil and defects occur in things ruled by divine providence as a result of the establishment of secondary causes in which there can be deficiency, it is evident that bad actions according as they are defective are not from God but from defective proximate causes; but in so far as they possess something of action and entity they must be from God.[29]

(2) We must premise, in accord with traditional Christian thought, that:

a: *Every agent produces its actions by acting through the divine power and that God is cause of all effects and actions.*

b: *Evil results from a defective cause.*

c: *Not every defective cause results from a defective cause (of itself), although if it is defective it results from a cause.*

Aquinas implicitly supposes at least two *levels* of causality. God is said to be the *sufficient* cause of whatever is done by His creatures; but in some other sense, the creature-cause is also said to be the sufficient cause of what is done. This is not to be taken as alternative sufficiency, but as simultaneous but imparate sufficiency.

As we said earlier, the basic questions were raised by Aquinas, in his thirteen arguments[30] to reconcile Divine Providence with evil;

---

[29] *SCG*, III, 71, n. 13. In *On the Truth of the Catholic Faith*, tr. Vernon J. Bourke "Image Books" (New York: Doubleday & Company, 1956).

[30] *SCG*, III, Chapter 71.

in the passage quoted above, he has stated some fundamental elements of the answer, but has not made explicit just what is illegitimate about the project of holding God morally responsible for the defects in the world. This is what we will undertake now.

(3) The arguments we examined in Section 3 (with the exception of the third, that God need not have avoided the evils of our world because the defects of secondary causes cannot be traced to a defect in the ultimate cause), acknowledged a *prima facie* case against the goodness or existence of God by implicitly conceding that there are two sorts of evil in the world and by pleading "necessity" or "permissability" for God's activity. One might think that the *prima facie* case against the goodness or existence of God is strengthened by St. Thomas' unequivocal claim that God is the cause of all effects and actions; yet the opposite turns out to be the case. It is just *because* God is sufficient cause of all effects among creatures that the *prima facie* case is destroyed.[31]

Concerning God's goodness and the evil in the world, many reconciliations or exonerations have been offered, in order to defend or excuse His creating our world. The main defect in these defenses and excuses is that we do not know whether their premises are true.[32]

(4) What we shall pursue now is an investigation of the case which these reconciliations and defenses were supposed to answer: That q, 'God is good', is found to be false on the basis of p, 'There is moral and physical evil in the world which God could have avoided'. It is obvious that some additional principle, r, will have to be introduced to connect p and $\sim q$. It will be our dual contention (a) that the proposition r, which is usually presupposed (but very seldom even crudely stated), is false and is based upon a mistaken analogy; and (b) that

---

[31] What is involved in a *prima facie* case? According to custom, "A litigating party is said to have a *prima facie* case when the evidence in his favor is sufficiently strong for his opponent to be called upon to answer it"—*Black's Law Dictionary*, p. 1353 (4th ed., St. Paul: West Publishing Co., 1951). Also, "A *prima facie* case is one in which the evidence in favor of a proposition is sufficient to support a finding in its favor if all the evidence to the contrary is disregarded" (*Ibid.*). For an investigator S, there is a *prima facie* case against proposition q based upon p if, in the light of what S knows, p entails $\sim q$, or p conjoined with some probably true proposition, r, or some necessary proposition, r', entails $\sim q$. If in honest defense of q one must concede the truth of p, the necessity or truth of r and the validity of the entailment, then one must concede the case. But if the propositions involve questions of responsibility, freedom, one's purpose, or one's intentions, then exonerations and excuses may be alleged. One concedes the *prima facie* case but denies its final force; he pleads excuses or defenses (e.g., necessity).

[32] These "reconciliations" were criticized in Section 3.

there is no proposition, r, which can be philosophically established and can be added to supply the required connection. Therefore, there is no problem of evil, as it has traditionally been conceived—namely, as a problem of reconciliation between p and q; for there is no ground for thinking p and q to be incompatible, or even for thinking that they have different truth-values.

(5) For the sake of this discussion, we do not need any more precise analysis of 'evil' than the following: moral evil is real in the universe if and only if some intellectual being knowingly does anything which he ought not to have done, and does it in the absence of conditions defeating his voluntariety of action. There has been much of such evil, and no one can properly employ the premise that God is sufficient cause of all effects to conclude that a condition defeating voluntariety has always been present.[33]

Physical evil: There has been physical evil in the universe if and only if some beings have suffered, or have been ugly to behold; and if these events are caused by non-rational beings or by the actions of rational beings not acting *qua* rational (though they may result from rational beings acting rationally).

This is not a perfectly clear definition: one might wonder whether a man who desires knowledge, or a bridegroom who desires to consummate his marriage, is suffering. Further qualifications of the concept of physical evil are also required. We want to be able to distinguish between a beast's pain, which causes him to withdraw from a fire, and the suffering caused by his stepping on a nail; one is an evil "with a purpose," whereas the other seems pointless. But for the present we shall not differentiate these formally; it is evident that all such kinds of suffering have occurred in our world, and the number of occurrences or the relative misery constituted by such suffering is not material to the argument we expound.

Employing Aquinas' principle that God is sufficient producer of all finite events, we know that in some sense He is the cause both of the

---

[33] We shall not examine why this is so here, although it is worth noting that one cannot demonstrate that the *non sequitur* is as I suggest by giving cases where besides the free agent's volition to do x there is also present a condition which would have forced his doing x (e.g., appearing in court); for, although this *looks* like a sufficient demonstration at first glance, it fails: the analogy is not accurate. God's sufficiency for my action is not sufficiency *alternatively* to my will's sufficiency, as is the sufficiency of the officers of the court to drag me to appear in court; rather, God's sufficiency is integrated with my own sufficiency in a peculiar way which must be explained in its proper place.

sufferings and of the immoral acts of men. Yet we cannot think that He should cause these events in such a way that the acts of men would cease to be immoral, and the events would cease to be sufferings. God must be cause of my sinful actions in such a way that I still do what I ought not to do with full knowledge, forethought, and responsibility; for our investigation supposes that moral and physical evil is real. Any interpretation of God's relation to the world which conflicts with that supposition is obviously false and contrary to those prevailing Christian doctrines to which the analysis is primarily relevant.

(6) These presuppositions suggest that the question of whether God is to be blamed for the evils in the world is closely connected with the question of whether God's predetermining and foreknowing the events of the world precludes the freedom of creatures and undermines the logical contingency of propositions about what is future to a given creature. That is, seeking to blame God for the evils in the world involves the same sort of mistake as saying that, because all has been set forth by God from eternity in His divine plan and is carried out under the sufficiency of His will, human choice is unavailing, prayer useless, and the future outside of our power to determine.

Aquinas says:[34]

> It is also apparent that the same effect is not attributed to a natural cause and to the divine power in such a way that it is partly done by God and partly by the natural agent; rather it is wholly done by both, according to a different mode, just as the same effect is wholly attributed to the instrument and also wholly to the principal agent.

Our solution involves a proposition such as that of Aquinas: that for the same event two chains of causal sufficiency and necessity are simultaneously present, and simultaneously required. This is possible only if, as was emphasized in Chapter V, there are logically diverse kinds of dependence and causality.

The general religious doctrine of Christianity involves a skeletal ontology which places God and creatures on different levels of reality.

This doctrine is traditionally interpreted as follows:

[34] SCG, III, 70, n. 8.

a: Since God is almighty, nothing is possible which God cannot create.

b: Nothing finite could have been actual had God not willed it to be.

c: God's creative and conserving power extends, by His explicit attention and willing, to every act and every positive aspect of every act of every being in the universe.

d: Some actions by creatures are morally evil.

e: God's willing that the events other than His own being should occur is both sufficient and necessary for their occurrence.

f: There is also real natural sufficiency upon the part of created agents, and there are natural causes for their effects (the concourse of nature being postulated).

(7) Difference of Reality Levels: What does one mean in saying that two entities are of different levels of reality? One means, quite obviously, that one of the entities is of a lower level of reality than the other; so we shall define that relation.

b is of a lower level of reality than a, if and only if b belongs by essence to a class of things B such that no member of that class could exist unless: (1) some member (or members) a of the class A exists; (2) produces the existing members b of class B; (3) maintains a conserving relation to those members (b) throughout their existence; and (4) no member of class B has any property whatever that is not bestowed upon it by a or by some member of A or some member of some class of things to which the members of A stand in relations (1), (2), and (3).

As this definition stands, it does not preclude an infinite set of levels of reality; nor, as we examine some cases of reality-level dependence, will we find any reason to think there could not be such an infinity. We shall give the name *metaphysical dependence* to the relation a thing of lower level of reality has to the particular thing of higher level which produced it, conserved it, and determined its properties. Thus, metaphysical dependence will be the relation which obtains between particular effects, *b*, and their causes, *a*, which are of different levels of reality.

This is not a relation of simple or "natural" causal dependence, even in the more ancient sense of "cause," for several reasons; most obviously, because particular effects can often perdure when all members of the class to which their causes belonged have ceased to exist.

(There is no reason why automobiles might not continue to exist after all living beings have been poisoned by their fumes.)

Neither is it a relation of simple logical dependence; even though there can be no children without parents, it is possible that particular children might exist without any parent continuing in being or exerting any conserving force upon them.

The relationship requires three sorts of dependence:

(a) The one-way logical dependence of the classes, such that the lower cannot have actual members if the other does not. Thus some mind might exist even though no imaginary being exists; but there cannot exist an imaginary being unless some mind exists which imagines. We often name such relations by contrast-dependent expressions, like "dream–dreamer"; in that case, neither the class of dreams nor the class of dreamers can have members unless the other class has members. But, of course, things-of-the-sort-which-dream, that is, minds, can exist even though no dreams occur. Hence, while there is a logical dependence between the class of dreams and the class of dreamers, between the things which can dream and the dreams there is no such logical dependence, although there is between the dreams and the things which can dream them. The same relationship holds between jumps and the things which can jump. If we define "dreamer" and "jumper" in terms of powers rather than acts (as we define "pointer" when we call a dog a pointer who has never pointed and is as yet a pup) the contrast-dependency is found to hold only in the one direction.

(b) Dependence in beginning-to-exist upon one of the relata but never mutual dependence in beginning-to-exist (although a common dependence upon a still higher-level being is possible).

(c) Dependence in continuance-in-being; that is, there can be no time at which b exists (where the time is calculated by relationships among things of the same sort as b) when it is not also true that a exists or some member of the class A to which a essentially belongs exists.

Imaginary beings stand in just such a relation to the minds which conjure them. It is impossible that an imaginary being should exist if no mind ever existed; it is impossible that an imaginary being should be produced by anything other than a mind upon which it depends.

Hence, it follows that imaginary beings are of a lower level of reality than the minds which imagine them, and that each imagined being is metaphysically dependent upon the particular mind which imagines it.[35]

It is to be emphasized that the contrast-dependency found among pairs of concepts does not reflect the relationship of difference-in-level-of-reality or metaphysical dependence among things, since it is not sufficient for such a relationship. Thus, "creator–creature" and "thought–thinker" are cases of both relationships; but "parent–offspring" is not, and we see that two concepts can be contrast-dependent without the entities which fall under them being of different levels of reality. Hence, contrast-dependence of the relational concepts is not a sufficient condition for metaphysical dependence of the things so related.

An interesting example having to do with differences in levels of reality is the relationship between persons and nations. If there were no persons at all, there could be no nations. Yet this is not sufficient for a reality-difference; the persons that produce the nation need not, as individuals, co-exist with the nation (although at all times there must be some persons to conserve the nation). The chief reason that one might hesitate to call this a case of reality-difference is that the conserving cause seems to be disjunctive over groups of persons rather than over specified individuals. As a result, we shall leave the matter open as to what specifications we shall have to add to the definition of "difference-in-reality-level" in order to decide whether this is a case of that difference.

We shall meet several other borderline examples which beg for an "analogous" application of our concept in the next pages, and will provide some speculations in the appendix to this chapter which show that we have not yet achieved a satisfactory view of metaphysical causation. Moreover, the example of this dependence that will be most important in our analysis is that of fictional characters' dependence upon their authors. The first part of the appendix will clarify

---

[35] This, of course, raises the question of whether two minds can imagine the same imaginary being. If one says this can occur, it would look as if the same thing is metaphysically dependent upon two entities at once. It seems that one should say these imaginary beings are not the same, but that the respect in which they differ, that of depending upon different minds, is most often not relevant to any purpose two people could have in imagining things otherwise the same.

and settle (at least arbitrarily and provisionally) the objection as to how that relationship fits our definition.

(8) The Limitation of Inferences: To justify some steps in the forthcoming argument, it is necessary to introduce an obvious rule which sets limits upon what inferences are legitimate with respect to things that are known or assumed to be of different levels of reality.

If a and b are of different levels of reality such that a is of a higher level than b, no inference from the fact that b has a property, F, to the conclusion that a has the property F is warranted unless it is logically impossible that Fb if it is false that Fa or unless there are inductive grounds that if Fb then Fa when the induction is based upon independently known instances of pairs of things related by that difference in level of reality.

In the former case, Fa follows logically from Fb; in the latter it follows only probablistically. We shall subsequently claim that this rule is violated by the arguments against God's goodness based upon the evil in the world, and those against God's providence and predestination based upon the observed freedom of creatures.

Let us suppose that a student, asked to give reasons why Othello might be said not to have murdered Desdemona, replies not by denying the existence of premeditation or by invoking the fact that passion mitigates responsibility, but by saying, "He couldn't have murdered her—Shakespeare made him do it." Suppose also that in an essay on the qualities of the man Shakespeare the same student says that he was wicked because he frustrated the eager assassin in Macbeth, tortured the hesitant Prince in Hamlet, and, in other plays, exults in bloodshed, tears and tragedy so that evil triumphs, virtue is scorned and the innocent are star-crossed. The student errs in both cases—most evidently in the former, but equally so, although not so obviously, in the latter. The mistake of the latter case is obscured because of the fad some psychologists and critics have followed of trying (sometimes successfully) to read the personality of the author out of his works.

Consider the claim that the fact that the author determined the activities of the character implies that the character did not act freely. To know that this claim is true, one would have to have found it to be false that any thing which acts freely is metaphysically dependent upon something else (since, by definition of *that* relation, it is of a lower level of reality than something else and received *all* its properties from something else). If that were so, it would be impossible to create a character which is free since all characters are dependent in this way. But we know this is false; from that we know the falsity of the premise that nothing which is metaphysically dependent is free.

Since this is so, an argument that God's predestination of human action is incompatible with human freedom is unsound because it includes a conditional premise which we know to be false: "If *x* acts freely, *x* is not metaphysically dependent upon something else."[36] Moreover, it is to be noted that no good argument can be constructed to replace the one we have rejected. For if it does not follow from the mere fact that *a* is a sufficient condition for everything which happens that *b* (which depends entirely upon a) cannot be free, then it cannot be argued without additional established or known premises that in some particular case this is so. This is the more obvious because we cannot think of any case where it follows from the mere fact that *b* is metaphysically dependent upon *a* that *b* cannot act freely. What premise could be added, and would it be an acknowledged truth?

(9) But, knowing that one cannot use the unrestricted and false premise that metaphysically dependent entities cannot be free, what would happen if we tried to introduce the more restricted premise, "*A being entirely determined by a higher-level being which is divine cannot be free*"? But what special knowledge of divinity would we have to possess to know that this is so? The premise seems to deny to a divine being a power which every literary creator has; moreover, it would beg the question of whether a divine being can really create and predestine free beings.

Attempting to avoid this circularity, one might select the premise that *real* beings all of whose actions are determined by a metaphysically superior cause cannot act freely. But this, too, begs the question: it is generally conceded that the only possible case (granting the consistency of the proposition 'God exists') of the metaphysical causation of the attributes of real beings is the case of God's causality. Moreover, the premise we are considering involves a modal term, and

---

[36] The facile amendment which would restrict this claim to beings of different levels of reality is treated in subsection 21; the facile amendment restricting the claims to real, as opposed to legendary or fictional, beings is treated afterwards in the same place.

entails that it is *inconsistent* to say that God metaphysically determines the actions of free beings. This again begs the question; it is just what has often been contended by the opponents of "predestination," but it has never been supported by a deduction of the claimed inconsistency.

(10) It has been shown that it is not logically necessary that for *b* to be free, *a* (a member of the higher-level class *A*) must not have predetermined *b* by choices which are *logically sufficient* for what *b* does; therefore it cannot legitimately be inferred simply from the freedom of men that God has not predetermined all events and all finite choices. Moreover, since no inductive evidence that God has not done so can be found or manufactured, it cannot be concluded that the freedom of man lends any noteworthy probability to that claim. Therefore, we know no true and a priori proposition which, when conjoined to "God predetermined causally and sufficiently all events in the created universe," will yield "Man is not a sufficient and free cause of any of his acts": there is no basis for the charge that divine governance or causality is incompatible with human freedom.[37]

(11) Now let us turn to a more difficult matter. From the observed states of good or ill in some lower being that is metaphysically dependent upon a higher-level being, is it legitimate to infer the moral character of that higher-level being? In particular, we shall consider those objections to the moral perfection of God which are based upon the physical and moral evils we observe in the world.

We shall divide the first stage of the argument into two parts, one concerned with those evils whose causes in nature are non-rational and the other concerned with evils whose causes are rational *qua* rational.

(12) Physical Evil: The following four paragraphs seem to make what a theist must call true claims—claims which appear to demand reconciliation.

(a) If it is true that *x* suffered deformity or pain, generally there is something, *y* (usually but not always distinct from *x*), which is the sufficient cause of *x*'s suffering that deformity or pain. Furthermore,

---

[37] The premises for this conclusion are of great strategic importance, not only in the discussion of evil which follows, but in the possibility they hold out for a reconciliation between the Thomists and the Calvinists on the question of the character of divine foreknowledge and the determination of future events.

given the general concourse of nature, y is of the same level of reality as x and is a natural cause (a cause operating under general laws of nature) of x's suffering or deformity.

(b) If it is true that x suffered deformity or pain for which y is a sufficient natural cause, it is also true that God, unaided by anything, brought it about that this should be the case (in particular, by establishing the laws of nature by which the occurrence of y causes x's suffering). God's decision that it be so is a sufficient and necessary cause of its being the case.

(c) y and God need not be identical. The natural cause of an event is not usually something upon which x, the participant in the event, is metaphysically dependent, but is, rather, something which is related to x by causal laws. Thus the natural cause of the king's death is Macbeth's stabbing him, although Shakespeare's decision that it be so (given his supply of symbols, etc.) is a sufficient condition for Macbeth to kill the king. But Macbeth's action, the natural cause of the king's death, cannot be identified with Shakespeare's willing that the king fall at Macbeth's hand. For two different kinds of causality are involved, kinds which parallel the two kinds found in Berkeley's metaphysics: that which obtains among ideas, such that nothing can be the cause of an idea but another idea; and that which relates minds and ideas, such that the ideas exist only in the perceiving mind. The former, *natural causality*, relates items of the same level or category (e.g., ideas, physical objects, events in space-time, embodied minds, etc.);[38] the latter, *metaphysical dependence* or *ontological posteriority*, relates elements within the basic categories of reality or basic levels of being.

[38] I shall do no more than mention that the mystery of the Incarnation, which figures so strongly in Christian theologies, seems to involve a situation in which the natural cause of some events (e.g., Jesus Christ, cause of His audible words at the Last Supper) is in some special way identical with the higher-level cause: God. This will no doubt give considerable difficulty to one who wishes to reconcile it with a general doctrine that metaphysically diverse entities *cannot* interact as equals. The same question arises when we discuss salvation; for there can be no other sense assigned to "being made sons of God," which is promised to the elect by St. John, than that the elect will be raised to direct knowledge of God without intermediary sensations, and will by grace be raised to a *supernatural* state of being.

Cognizant of these theological problems, I have stated this third principle in the form which says that the natural cause and the metaphysical cause of a given event *need* not be identical, rather than that which says that they *cannot* be. This is all that is needed philosophically, since it is a supposition of the "problem of evil" that there are physical evils which have sufficient natural causes—natural causes which are not identical with God and which are related to their effects by laws for which God is the metaphysical cause.

(d) If y is a sufficient cause of x's being in a certain state of pain or deformity, nothing else can be, although other things might *have been* the sufficient cause. This is the very common claim, mentioned earlier, that there can be only one sufficient cause for a natural event. Of course it will be somewhat arbitrary how we distinguish the sufficient cause of any physical event from the surrounding and presumed necessary conditions. Shall we call the knife (which is at best the instrument) the cause of the king's death and presume the swinging arm of Macbeth? This depends upon one's purposes and needs; the cloak of *"ceteris paribus"* covers myriad alternate distinctions between the necessary conditions and the attendant circumstances. ("Bad money drives out good money, *all other things being equal.*") Different causes can be sufficient simultaneously (depending upon the points of view and upon what question is asked). From the coroner's point of view, the fact that the knife struck the main heart valve may be the sufficient cause of the king's death, whereas from that of the criminal prosecutor the sufficient cause of the king's death is the action of Macbeth under the incitement of his wife and with a demonstrated motive.

But the claim that God and the human agent are both sufficient causes of the same event is not a claim from two different points of view. Rather, a natural explanation of an event includes a statement of its natural cause and of the law under which it operated; a metaphysical explanation of an event involves a statement of its metaphysical causes. Neither God in His world nor Shakespeare in his play is an agent with regard to any event like my falling off a cliff or Mercutio's being stabbed (unless it is a miracle).

The possibility of different points of view in the previous examples springs from the complexity of the set of necessary conditions for natural causality between events. Thus a coroner may not care whether it was Macbeth, Jack the Ripper, or the electric fan that threw the knife; he may have some reason for determining only whether death resulted from a knife wound. There is no parallel in the case of metaphysical dependencies. I am not an instrument of God in my actions: God does not pick a man's pocket when I do or help a blind man across the street when I do; for in order for b to be the instrument of a, the effect c must be attributable without qualification as an action to a, and as an effect to b. Thus, creatures are not instruments of the Creator, despite St. Thomas' infelicitous comparison in *Summa Contra Gentiles*.[39] But since they, and all their actions, are effects of the Creator, it is appropriate to attribute to the Creator whatever happens, but *as an effect;* it is appropriate for the blind man to thank God for having provided help across the street, since whatever help is had is a positive provision of God, although "helping across the street" is not in this case an action of God.

Without further elaboration, we can conclude that there can be only one sufficient cause of a given event from a given point of view; and, where a difference of points of view is not relevant, there can be only one sufficient cause of any event, unless the difference is in the kind of sufficiency in question.

(13) One might be inclined to conclude that one of the preceding four claims must be false: the first postulates a natural sufficient cause for every physical evil; the second postulates a metaphysical sufficient cause for every event in nature; the third states that the natural and metaphysical sufficient causes of an event need not and in some cases cannot be the same; and the fourth states that there can be at most one sufficient cause of an event from a given point of view.[40]

(14) If God wills that Jones stab Smith and God's will is effective or sufficient (as it is), then Jones stabs Smith. This is an essential part of the Christian doctrine that whatever God wills to be the case, *is* the case *ipso facto,* and that nothing contingent can be the case that God has not willed to be so. (It should be obvious that 'God wills that

---

[39] III, 70, n. 8.

[40] But what this shows is that the expression 'x is the sufficient cause of y' is equivocal. This was evident in our two earlier references to the existence of two *kinds* of causality in systems like those of Berkeley, Plato, Aristotle, Aquinas, etc. Every large-scale metaphysical system has had one sort of dependence which holds among elements that are fundamentally or categorically different, and another sort which holds among things of the same basic kind or category. Since all metaphysical systems have some class of things which are ontologically prior to things of other classes, and since there is a dependence between particular things of the prior class and things of the posterior class, there is an exact parallel of the relations of higher-level-of-reality and metaphysical dependence which have been defined here. The briefest consideration will disclose that the relationship of God to the world, by which He produces or causes the world, is not like the relationship between created things, where one produces or causes another thing or event. For one thing, there are presupposed conditions which are hidden in some phrase like "*ceteris paribus*"; the acid causes the litmus paper to turn from blue to red, *all other things being equal;* this is because adding entities or events can prevent the effectiveness of natural causes (like adding a plastic cover to the litmus paper). There can be no such conditions upon God's power, for God can bring about any contingent state of affairs; His causality is *unpreventable.* Hence, the kinds of sufficiency are different, and are not exclusive.

Jones stab Smith' does not entail 'God approves of Jones' conduct in his act of stabbing Smith'.)

(15) For every cause of physical evil which is of the same type as the thing which suffers the evil, there is a higher-level sufficient cause which brought it about *that* the lower level thing or event was cause of the suffering. This is a consequence of the doctrines of creation and of governance. The higher-level thing, God, could have avoided the occurrence, which is a physical evil, by alterations in what exists or in the causal laws governing what exists—by adding a causal law, for example, that whenever a man strikes at another with a knife, it turns into a lily. (Notice that such a "law" would actually have to be incredibly complex.)

But to *blame* the higher-level cause, or to argue that there is a moral defect in that cause, is either to employ as a warrant for such an inference a proposition which is false and which, even if it were true, would not be a necessary truth (such as is needed to provide the force of the deduction); or to employ a proposition which is equivalent to what needs to be proved. This latter point is explained in subsection 21, below; here, we want to establish the falsity of the principles involved in the first and general course of argument.

Suppose we have the following premise:

God, Who is of higher level than His creatures, could have precluded all the sufferings in His creatures, without performing an act of lower moral value than He has performed.

How do we get from this statement to the conclusion that God ought to have done so? By means of a second premise:

R_1: *Any being that could avoid or preclude the sufferings of others without performing an act of lower moral value than it would otherwise perform ought to do so.*

This looks plausible until we see that it commits us to

R_2: *Any being that could (without performing, etc.) preclude the sufferings of other beings on a lower level of reality, or in beings which are metaphysically dependent upon it, ought to do so.*

The more specific form R_2 is necessary because it has been amply illustrated that, from the very notion of sufficiency and the Christian doctrine that God's choice is sufficient and necessary for what happens, God cannot be on the same level as His creatures. By the same arguments with regard to sufficiency, Shakespeare cannot be on the same level as his characters. But we know it is false that Shakespeare ought to have prevented the wounding of Paris just because he could have performed an equally worthy act which did not involve the suffering of any creature of his. Furthermore, we know that a person who deliberately imagines a suffering lion, to whose thorn-pricked foot a little mouse ministers, is committing no moral crime. The imaginary lion is not on the same level of reality as the imaginer; so also with the literary creation and its author. Hence the general principle R_2 is false. The obvious next step, the restriction of R_2 to metaphysical causes with *real* effects, is treated in subsection 21, below, and constitutes an example of the fallacy of facile amendment.

(16) Premise R_2 might reasonably be thought to ascribe an *objective* moral defect to God for His failure to prevent all physical evil; and indeed, it is reasonable to say that if A can prevent the suffering of B without cost or moral fault, he ought to do so and is morally imperfect if he refuses. For now we have introduced the qualification "without cost," which was not present when we considered R_2 above. In beings of the same level, all this is true. But the qualifications "without cost" and "without performing an act of lower moral value than it would otherwise perform" make no headway against a situation which involves metaphysical dependence, and in which nothing the divine agent could do would cost Him anything.

It is not necessarily true that if a being of higher level is the cause of the existence and attributes of lower-level beings which suffer, and if that higher-level being could morally and without cost have avoided this creation, that it is morally defective. It is at least *possible* (if one does not wish to admit my examples of Shakespeare and his characters as cases in fact) that this suffering of creatures should occur without moral defect or imperfection in the higher being. Therefore, the inference from the physical sufferings and evils in the world to the moral imperfections of God is invalid, since it does not conform to the rule of limited inference cited earlier; the possibility mentioned is just what we must have grounds for rejecting in order to produce a valid deductive argument against the goodness of God. As in the case of foreknowledge and determinism, whatever inductive evidence there is from the analogy with literature supports the claim that premise R$_2$ is false. Therefore the inference from the physical suffering observed in the world to the moral imperfection of God is entirely unwarranted, both on purely logical grounds and on inductive ones.

(17) Moral Evil: If Jones sins in murdering Smith, then Jones must have been the sufficient cause of the murder; otherwise he would not have been responsible and could not have sinned. But if Jones sins in murdering Smith, it is also true that God *willed* that Jones sin in murdering Smith; and God's will is sufficient for this to be the case.

Is every sufficient cause of morally evil action morally responsible for that evil? Obviously not; for if Jones sins in murdering Smith, why should we say God sins in bringing it about that Jones sins in murdering Smith? By a principle, some may reply, that whenever *A* causes *B* to sin in doing *x*, *A* sins also. But this is an obvious equivocation of the term "cause." Ordinarily, if *A causes B* to do *x*, this exonerates *B* from the charge of having sinned. This means that *God can be morally responsible for the moral evils of his creatures only on the condition that they are not guilty.* This is logically equivalent to saying that God is morally defective for creating a world with moral evil in it only if He did not do so.

But God did create a world in which there is moral evil. Hence it follows that God is not to be blamed for the evil in the world as long as we maintain the principle that if there is a sufficient cause in something other than *B* for *B*'s performing an evil action, then *B* is not responsible.

But when the beings are of different levels of reality, that principle cannot apply, for the term "cause" becomes equivocal. This now requires that a new principle be employed:

R$_3$: *When a being of higher level is sufficient cause for the free evil action of a being of a lower level, the higher being is morally defective and ought not to have done so.*

But this principle is demonstrably false, for the same reasons as were given above. Therefore, the inference from the moral defects of creatures to a moral defect in God is unwarranted.

(18) If one wishes to argue that since there are morally evil beings in the world who will be damned for their sins, God must be imperfect because He could have created only blessed men, there will have to be some principle to connect the argument's antecedent with its

consequent. Since the most likely principle, R_3, is in general false, there is no logical warrant for the inference; all inductive evidence, moreover, seems to imply the falsity of that premise. Hence, the inference is not even *probably* valid, much less logically certain.

(19) Attempting to reinstate the argument by treating God and creatures as being of the same level of reality will not help; for then God's sufficiency for what is done will destroy the freedom and responsibility of the agent, making it absurd to blame God for the evil I freely do (since I would now do none). In this case it would become a necessary condition of God's being blameable for the morally evil act that I perform, that I should not have done it freely; that is, God's being responsible and reprehensible for the free acts of creatures has as a necessary condition that the creatures should have performed no such acts. This is a sufficient and definitive proof of the absurdity of denying man freedom of action because of God's pervasive causality, and of blaming God for man's morally evil acts.[41] Moreover, such an assimilation of God and His creatures neglects certain basic notions of the dependence of creature upon creator, and consequently is inconsistent with Christian doctrine.

If it were argued that no relationship other than that between God and His creatures fulfills the conditions for metaphysical dependence (and thereby difference in level of being or reality), and that in particular literary creators and their creations do not parallel this relationship, it would (were the argument sound) show no more than that the principle upon which the argument to God's moral defect was based has not been proved false. However, since the negation of that principle is consistent, there is still no sufficient warrant for the nontheist's inference.

(20) In order to warrant the inference in the *prima facie* case, either the necessity or the truth of R_1, R_2, or R_3 must be established, or at least be accessible to human knowledge. Even if my proofs of falsity be rejected, one still needs to show that the principles are true, or else that they are necessarily true.

Proofs of the truth of these principles will beg the question if they do not involve a proof of their necessity. And proofs of their necessity

---

[41] An act can be morally evil for S only if S performs the act. When one creature murders another, it is he that performs the act, not God. Hence, despite God's sufficient causality, the acts of creatures are not attributable to God as to an agent.

will surely fail; for consider that there is no contradiction in the following:

1: A is of a higher level of reality than B.

2: B does evil freely.

3: A's choice is a sufficient condition for B's doing evil freely.

4: B is responsible for the evil B does freely and is morally imperfect.

5: A is responsible for its being true that B does what B does and A is not morally imperfect.

A contradiction can be derived if we add a few definitions and:

6: Whenever a being of lower level of reality sins or suffers, the being upon which it is metaphysically dependent is imperfect.

Since no contradiction follows from 1–5 without 6, and since the negation of 6 does not entail a contradiction (which is the least proved by the examples of the author-character relation), any contradiction which follows from the conjunction of 1–6 must follow because of the addition of a false proposition to a true one or vice versa.

Since 1–4 are granted as data of the problem, either 5 or 6 must be false. But 6 is, as the examples showed, not *necessary*; there is no reason to assume that it is *true*, since that constitutes begging the question against 5. Hence, the inference to the moral imperfection of God violates the principle of limited inference.

Suppose one wished to argue that since there are morally evil beings in the world who will be damned for their sins, God must be imperfect, for He might have created only blessed men. Some general principle is required to connect the antecedent to the consequent; that principle will be another version of R: "A being which makes entities that will be damned for their sins is morally imperfect." This principle is even less plausible than the others. Why should a man not be damned for his sins? Why shouldn't Macbeth have been damned for his murders? Why shouldn't a perfect being create those who are *justly* damned?

Since it is the case that no matter what world God creates, He could have created a more perfect one (see Chapter VII), it is always the case that what is actual is defective in comparison to something God might have produced had He chosen another. Yet since this would always be the case, it cannot function as a reason in God's selecting one world over another because it cannot help to single out one world or provide a reason for its creation. Therefore, the mere fact that God chose a world less perfect than he might have chosen is not a reason for blaming God unless one wishes to contend that it is an imperfection in God to create at all. On what grounds could *that* be argued?

Moreover, for these reasons, one cannot properly claim that the connecting rule between "God should have made a better world than the one He made" and "God ought to be blamed for having made the world He made" is: "A creating being which does not do the best it can do is imperfect." For no matter what God does in creating, there is something better which He might have done; prior to God's act there is no best world. To say that there could have been a better world than x is to say that there is some consistent state of affairs, y, which when compared with God's perfections is a better imitation of God than x. Since this holds for any possible world, the result of applying Principle R_4 is that of any two worlds, God ought to choose the better; it will follow that if God adheres to this principle with respect to any x and y, He will simultaneously violate it with respect to some other possible choice, z. Hence creation of any world would become an imperfection. This should be sufficient evidence that Principle R_4 is false, and that God has no obligation to choose any world merely because it is better than another. From all this it follows that since there is no "worst world," there is no defect in God no matter what world He creates, however miserable the creatures may be.

(21) The main counter-argument, which brings the whole matter to its basic elements, must be answered. But first, a word of caution is necessary. The preceding pages have contained so much talk about the relations of mental beings to the minds that conceive them, and the relations of fictional or imaginary beings to their authors, that it might be concluded that I am drawing an analogy between these relationships and that of God to the world, or that I am arguing by analogy. This is not at all true. Rather, what I am showing is that there are only two sorts of principles about the moral relationships between higher-level beings and their metaphysical effects which could validly connect the proposition 'God is good, Creator, omnipotent,

etc.' and the proposition 'There are evil and suffering in the world'. The first sort is a general proposition of the forms R_1, R_2, or R_3 (given above); each is clearly false because the author-character and dreamer-dream cases are counter-examples which fulfill the conditions of the dependence relation. The other kind of principle, which concerns only metaphysical causes with real beings as effects (the proposition R' discussed below) will be rejected because it begs the question. Thus, the point of the discussion of metaphysical causality is to clarify a fundamental element of God's relation to the world so that it will be evident that these two sets of principles (R_1, R_2, or R') are of the only sorts that will make valid the usual inference against the goodness of God; ignoring the reality-level difference causes equivocation. We have rejected R_1 and R_2 as plainly false. Let us see what happens to R'. If, as I contend, it begs the question, then the argument against the goodness of God, though valid where R' connects the main premise to the conclusion, is not and cannot be made successful; and this is what we want to show.

(a) It might be said that Principle R_2 may be true when restricted to actual or real beings.[42] Now *why* there should be this restriction, I do not see (beyond its apparent value as an *ad hoc* escape from the argument), since all the cases I have given fit the definition of metaphysical dependence. But I will grant the restriction. Thus we get this principle:

P: *Any being which could, without cost or moral defect, preclude or avoid the evil acts and sufferings of other real beings and fails to do so is morally imperfect.*

(b) But this principle, which is confirmed by our moral experience or at least by our moral *ideals*, does not entail R', the principle that is needed.

R': *Any real being which could, without cost or moral defect, avoid or preclude the evil acts and suffering of real beings which are metaphysically dependent upon it and fails to do so is morally imperfect.*

For to say R' follows from P is to equivocate upon the term "cause" which is involved in "preclude" and "avoid." There are at least *two kinds* of precluding or avoiding. Our evidence for P is based upon

---

[42] This option was left open in subsection 15.

experiences which involve natural causality. How can we, without further reason, swing to a principle involving metaphysical causality, especially when cases (now conceded for the argument) were given in which the stronger rule, R₂, did not hold—that is, in which the dependent beings were not restricted to real beings?

(c) That God could have avoided the evils in the world without moral defect and without cost must be granted by theist and non-theist alike. The theist must hold that there is no end which God in any way needs for His happiness, pleasure, or moral perfection which can be provided *only* by creation: God did not *need* to create; hence, no cost, if no creation at all. The theist must also grant that God failed to avoid or preclude these evils.

(d) The non-theist needs R' to make his *prima facie* case. For if R' is false, the fact that God created a world with evils He could have avoided entails nothing which would supply any reason for our believing that God is morally imperfect. If it cannot be established that R' is true, there is no *prima facie* case to be answered.

(e) The establishment of R' as a premise cannot succeed. It begs the question; and it cannot be shown to be true.

(f) R' begs the question.

1: There is only one possible substitution instance for the first occurrence of "real being" in R', since God alone can create other beings which are real.

2: Hence, R' is equivalent to a: If God fails to avoid the evil acts and sufferings of real beings metaphysically dependent upon Him when He could do so without cost or moral defect, God is morally imperfect.

3: Now both theist and non-theist must grant this antecedent: that God could have avoided all evil and suffering of real beings, without cost.
The non-theist wants to grant this to urge his opponent into the consequent; the theist, because he holds that no creation is necessary for God's beatitude. Hence, no creature could be avoided only at a cost to God.

4: The theist thus sees the whole matter as an issue of denying the inference a, which he takes the non-theist to be bent upon establishing.

5: But the non-theist's principle R', used to establish this inference a, is nothing but a restatement of a. Hence to insist that R' is the premise the prima facie case employs is merely to beg the whole question of whether God is morally perfect or not, unless the non-theist will go on to show that R' is true.

(g) But R' cannot be shown to be true; it cannot be established by philosophical analysis. Two avenues are open: to show that R' is necessary (and therefore true); or to show that R' follows from premises we know to be true, or else to show that some experience confirms it. I cannot imagine a proof of the necessity of R', since it is possible that although God could have eliminated the evils without cost there might be some balance of good and evil which would justify those evils, just as several other of the twelve "reconciliations" of divine goodness and evil in the world are possible (i.e., consistent).[43] Nor can there be a proof of the truth of R' from things we know to be true. R' does not follow from P and other truths about the relationships of natural agents (that is, agents of the same level of reality). For any proposition K from which R' follows, it will be quite evident that K is no more surely a matter of knowledge than R'; and R' is now in doubt, because our knowledge of metaphysical dependence is limited indeed and easily surveyed.[44]

There cannot, moreover, be a proof of the truth of R' from experience; for if it is not a revealed truth, what experience other than that of a divine revelation would tell us it is true? And if it were said to be revealed, it would, in combination with the observed evil in the world, convict God of moral defect; in that case we would have good reason to doubt the truth of the "revelation," since God's veracity would go the way of God's morality.

Suppose it were said that R' needs no proof, that we all know it to be true. That assumption would be false; I do not know that R' is true —I think, in fact, that it is false.

It cannot be shown that there is or could be any reason to accept R' either from logic or from experience or from whatever else we know;

---

[43] See Section 3 of this chapter; see also Alvin Plantinga, "The Free Will Defense," pp. 204–220, *Philosophy in America*.

[44] One should remind oneself that there is no advantage to be gained from denying that God and creatures are of different levels of reality, for it will still be true that each of the conditions given as part of the definition of "reality-level difference" will hold of God's relation to the world; quite adequate evidence for the sufficiency of God's choice to effect contingent states of affairs is provided in Christian teaching. It is this sufficiency which provides our solution by requiring that the type of influence God exerts must be quite different from that with which we are acquainted in ordinary life. Hence, denying the reality-level difference between God and His creatures will only embroil one in serious problems of internal orthodoxy and will not get rid of the "sufficiency" relation which is the basis of our answer to the "reconciliation" problem.

hence it is indeed unjustifiable for a philosopher to employ R' as a premise to attack the goodness of God, since doing so begs the question.

As a result, there is not and cannot be a *prima facie* case against either the moral perfection of God or the all-pervasive determining will of God.

(22) Does this mean that the moral character of God cannot be established through knowledge gained from the structure of the world, as Hume contended? It does. Yet we do not deny that, in observing the world, one finds many things to rejoice in and admire God for. If the question to be answered is: "Has God acted in a morally perfect way in His acts?" I think we might be able to discover that this is so. But we cannot establish from a single act (that of creating the world) that God has the dispositional attribute of moral excellence. Therefore, while a person might conceivably come to see and discover the inherent truth of 'God is good' (where "God" is used primarily designatively) from his contemplation of the excellence of the natural world, there is no deductive argument by which we can proceed with logical exactitude from what we know about the excellence of the world to establish the conclusion that God is morally excellent or that He is essentially good. (Remember that in the *analytic* statement 'God is good', "God" is primarily significative; in the *empirical* statements 'God is good' and 'God is essentially good', "God" occurs primarily designatively.)

SPECULATIVE APPENDIX

The following considerations are presented as a *speculative appendix* because, although they are important and relevant to what is considered in the foregoing chapter, they are too tentative and fragmentary to be treated with assurance. Their concern is with the question of how we handle borderline cases of the reality-level definition.

Let us suppose that an author creates a character today, writing a play in which that character figures. If human life were subsequently destroyed and, a millenium afterwards, were to appear again on the earth, would we, discovering the manuscript, say that in the interval the character had ceased to exist? The same question might, of course, be raised about the briefer periods of time in which no one reads, performs, sees, or thinks about the play. It does not seem correct to say the character ceased to exist; yet this makes it appear that although the activity of some mind is necessary for the beginning-to-exist of the character, this condition does not hold for its continuance in being. Hence, the condition in our definition that there be a conserving cause of the same level as the originating cause, or at a higher level, does not seem to be fulfilled. This may show merely that fictional beings are not at all the same as imaginary beings.

For a fictional being to exist, it is necessary that an imaginary being should have existed in the mind of the author. (We shall pass over objections concerning the literary creations of automata.) There need not always be an imagining being corresponding to the fictional one. Being a fictional, legendary, mythical, or other literary creation involves more than status in the imagination of the author; it also involves enshrinement in language or other symbolic forms (e.g., choreography). These symbolic forms are partial causes of the fictional entity and serve as its conserving cause, for if all such embodiments were destroyed and the character did not exist as imagined by any mind, the character would surely be destroyed. Thus, if the character existed in a play, the destruction of the play would mean the destruction of the character. (There is an exception to this in the possibility that a play is lost although the character is remembered and continues to be described in terms of fragments, snatches, or conjectures about the lost play; this is just the borderline of a different horizon.) To say that a character is thus *symbolically* embodied does not imply that anyone has ever interpreted, or ever will interpret, the symbols to reveal what they symbolize. These symbols, *as* symbols, are themselves of a lower type than the minds for which they are symbols. For there could be no such thing if there were no minds; upon the destruction of all minds there will be no symbols, although there may be things which once functioned as symbols and which could again do so. It seems that in our case of the thousand years when there are no minds, there are only *potential* and *former* symbols. There is something which they once symbolized, and might again if properly understood; but in the meantime, it must be said that there is no such character as the inscriptions might embody when they again function as symbols. This is something of an oversimplification of the matter, but we shall be content with it; for it is not important whether or not the character is destroyed in the meantime, once the complexity of the way in which the fictional being is dependent upon beings of other levels has been made clear. It is dependent both for its possibility and for its continuance in being; yet its dependence is not necessarily (and in the case of fictional beings necessarily *not*) upon the same thing for both production and continuance in being. It is not necessary that the beings of higher level upon which a given being depends should be all of the same level of reality. The mind is of higher level than the symbols; but the characters in the play depend upon both.[45]

Why, according to our definition, is not a forest on a lower level of reality than the trees which constitute it? A platoon on a lower level than the soldiers who make it up? A handmade suit, than the tailor who cut and sewed it? A machine-made suit metaphysically dependent upon the machines that made it?

Some of these are cases of "accidental wholes," as distinguished from organic units or essential wholes. I know no way accurately to clarify this difference. There are (1) natural substances or first-level units (e.g., a tree); and there are (2) natural aggregates, or second-level units, which have as parts the natural substances (e.g., a forest); there are also natural units constituted of (3) the natural materials (lumps of coal, drops of water, etc.), partitioned by natural or rational agencies. There are third-level units, natural materials arranged to constitute things: a desk is an *accidental* unit created by the arrangement of a *natural material* (e.g., wood or metal) within its natural dispositions. This is somewhat different from the forest, which is a natural aggregate of natural individuals (first-level units). For with respect to a given amount of material many accidental unities are possible, whereas with respect to a given set of natural individuals

---

[45] These conjectures raise another difficulty because they imply that what is symbolized is of lower level than the symbols. Since facts are often thought to be what are symbolized—for example when I write to a friend that it snowed here in November—it might be thought that the facts are thereby made of lower level than the symbols. But this seems to be patently false; thus something is wrong with this distinction of reality levels, or with this characterization of symbols. The latter seems to be the case, although it is not easy to state exactly what is the proper way of describing the matter. Symbols do not symbolize facts, but rather statements of what is purported to be a fact. The medievals would say that judgments (actual or potential) are symbolized—or at least what we intend that others take to be our judgments and expressions of attitude.

the resulting aggregate is determined, within the natural dispositions of the *materials* involved.

There is no doubt that the term "thing" applies primarily to natural individuals or first-level units and secondarily to those accidental units constructed from natural materials, for our treatment of the latter as individual things is always a consequence of our experience of first-level things. In a much more extended sense we occasionally speak of the accidental aggregates of natural individuals as *things.* Would we call a pride of lions a *thing* or a *group?* Would we call a forest a *thing* or a *group?* I think we would usually, but not always, employ a term like "group," or "arrangement," or "collection"; for the *unity* is one such that we could readily imagine that every tree be replaced and yet that it remain the same forest. Despite this, we do call every group, collection, set, etc., "something" and, hence, do in some cases call it a thing. Of course, there is more to the matter than this, for the accidental unities produced from natural materials are more than aggregates; they have a structure which is *imposed* upon the material, not derived entirely from it, although that structure is dependent upon the natural attributes and dispositions of the material. This is not the case with the aggregates, where there need be no cause of the aggregate unity in addition to the causes of the individual units.

Whatever be the structure of the aggregate unity, it is not imposed upon the natural individuals; rather, it is derived entirely from the summation of the attributes of the individuals. A forest is a set of things of a certain sort; a pride is a set of things of a certain sort; so also with a brace, a pack. But what of a village, a town, a university, an institution? These can be called "things"; they can be said to "exist" in a more basic sense than that in which we say that forests, prides, braces, and packs, exist (for the latter sense is usually closely allied to a contrast with purely imaginary or fictional entities of those sorts). The village, town, university and institution seem to be constituted of a combination of places, times, natural individuals, natural materials, and accidental unities, all of which can change within broad limits. For example, you cannot have a university without teachers and students, buildings, etc.; but you can change all of these over time without loss of identity. You cannot have a village or town without people, structures, and conventional relationships among the people, all of which evolve and change entirely. How such things as these are related to the natural individuals, the accidental unities, and the natural aggregates which are their constituents, is not clear. Hence, it is extremely difficult to answer the question of whether such things are metaphysically dependent upon the natural individuals.

But I think we can say this much. Nothing made of a natural material can be said to be metaphysically dependent upon that material, for the simple reason that the material cannot be a sufficient cause of the individual or the things which are made up of it: this would require either that the form not be imposed upon the material, or that the form and the material always exist conjoined. Both are impossible. It is also impossible that a natural individual or an accidental unity should be metaphysically dependent upon its inherent form or structure, since, by our definition, the form cannot exist apart from the individuals which have that form. Hence, whatever the *constituents* may be, they cannot be of a higher level of reality; they are probably (if a reality-level comparison were possible) of a lower level of reality, since it seems impossible that any material should exist without some determinate form, even if it be a powder, rock, etc. So also with forms such as "powder": there cannot be a powder which is not some *kind* of powder, some material in powdered form; the same is true of "crystal," "liquid," etc. Perhaps it will be necessary, in order to gain clarity in these matters, to distinguish the *states* of matter from the *forms* of matter and to discover distinctions in other ways—to re-institute, in effect, Aristotle's metaphysical and categorical analyses.[46]

The very incompleteness of the logical network among the various units about which we think is the basis of the doubt I expressed earlier[47] that borderline cases of this reality-level distinction can be satisfactorily decided. On the one hand, the ontology supposed by the Christian doctrine of God's relationship to the world is merely skeletal; on the other, our philosophical ontologies (even were we to take Aristotle and Aquinas wholesale) are fundamentally incomplete in their analysis of just those matters which are on the border-

[46] In the last few years many philosophical analyses of "mass nouns," "abstract particulars," etc., have appeared, forming an extensive body of material to serve as a base for such an enterprise.

[47] End of subsection 7, above.

line of the reality-level distinction. Hence, we cannot determine whether there is some crucial condition that is absent from our analysis of the reality-level distinction, or whether this appears to be so only because we do not know what to say about the peculiar things given in the examples; our explicit concept system is simply not intricate and well-developed enough to provide obvious answers.

It seems that we use the term "thing" not only for primary substances, accidental units, aggregates, and so forth, but also for *events*, realities which involve in their conception the passage of time in the form of changes in the states of other things. It is perfectly correct English to say: "A funny *thing* happened to me today; I found out that eating people is wrong."

Is the whole set of events on a lower level of reality than the things involved in the events? Most of the classical metaphysical views seem to indicate this, by their acceptance of the *omne agens agit sibi simile* principle, which required a *seccnd* kind of producing power, whereby the *things* could produce *events*, and agents could produce actions. This is quite different from the causal sufficiency of an event to bring about another, and that of one primary thing to bring about another.

Perhaps we have several different sets of basic categories partially represented in our thought at once. That is, it is possible that a description of the world in terms of things and attributes is not *prior* to a description in terms of events, but is rather supposed to be *alternative* to it—as two descriptions of a gas, one chemical and the other statistical, might be alternative for a scientist.

Is a fist of a lower level of reality than a hand? It appears to be: a fist can be produced only by a hand, can exist only as long as the hand keeps a certain position, and has all of its properties determined by the hand. This may indeed be so. Let us assume that it is, since we can then appreciate a serious and related problem: does the series of differing levels of reality form a single ladder, or a pyramid? Is everything either higher, lower, or of the same level as everything else? Suppose both *a* and *b* are of a lower level of reality than *c;* nothing whatever follows about whether *a* is lower than *b* or whether they are identical in level of reality. Suppose we find out that *a* and *b* are of a lower level than *c* and that *a* is of a lower level than *b;* then should we discover something, *d,* which is of a lower level than *b,* we will not thereby know its relationship to a. Although the relationship 'be of lower reality level than . . .' is known to be transitive, that information is not sufficient to tell us whether or not there is a universal system of reality-levels into which all things are integrated. However, the Christian religion claims not only that God is of higher level than men, but also that God is of higher level than *any finite* thing, attribute, event, or relationship. Hence, the Christian faith is committed to a reality-level difference in which all things other than God are of lower level; but this does not resolve our question about the logical relations of the "event," "fact," and "substance" descriptions of the world. This appendix must conclude that we know too little about metaphysics to answer with much confidence the questions we can frame about the concept of metaphysical dependence. Let us hope that what we do not know is not antithetical to what we now believe.

7 ✒ Possibility

and sufficiency

This chapter should tie together several of the earlier chapters and resolve some questions yet unsettled; in particular, we must reply to the "Humean" criticism presented in the first section of Chapter III: that the Christian, least of all men, can hold that the Principle of Sufficient Reason is true. And, in settling that matter, we shall commit ourselves to interpreting Principle E (which functions centrally in Chapters III and IV) in a way which, despite its wholly technical appearance, has vast importance. In the process of settling these questions about the Principle of Sufficient Reason and the nature of God's reason for creation on the supposition (not to be debated, substantiated, or explicated here) that God really did create the world freely, we shall appeal to certain things that we have already supported in the discussions of the power and the goodness of God (Chapters V and VI). Further, we shall propose solutions to several other matters which have long been contested: for instance, whether there can be a best of all possible worlds, or a worst of all possible worlds; whether the actual world is the only possible world; how God might be imagined to have chosen among an infinity of possible worlds; and how these matters affect the Principle of Sufficient Reason and Principle E.

We shall begin by contrasting three classical positions on whether God created the only or the best possible world. After appraising these positions, we argue that God may very well have had reasons for creating our world rather than some alternative, and that the nature of God may very well have imposed some reasons for creating something or another, rather than not creating at all. But God's having had *those* additional reasons for creating our world (rather than reasons which would have led to a different outcome) is not explained; there *is* no explanation or accounting to be found for that fact. This will bring us to the heart of the Sufficient Reason dispute.

SECTION 1: DID GOD CREATE THE ONLY POSSIBLE WORLD?

(1) It would seem that the absolutely perfect Creator produced the only possible world. Three philosophical positions discussed below, despite their obvious disparities, seem to entail that: (1) 'God is the absolutely perfect creator of the world' implies (with certain auxiliary premises) 'This is the only possible world'; and (2) 'God created the world by an act of free will' entails (with certain auxiliary premises) 'This is not the only possible world'. Two of the positions, those of Aquinas and Leibniz,[1] appear to be committed (contrary to their author's intentions) to both antecedents and to the resulting inconsistency; the third position, that of Spinoza, seems committed to the truth of the antecedent of (1) and to the falsity of the antecedent of (2). I shall briefly establish these points first; then I shall directly consider the problem of free creation.

One would think that we cannot say both that this is the only possible world, *and* that God created it by an act of free will. If this is the only possible world, it is logically impossible that God could have decided otherwise than as He did (assuming that God decided that it be this way); for God could not have created an impossible world. Yet 'its being logically possible that one should have done other than as one did' is thus taken as a logically necessary condition of 'having done freely what one did'! Spinoza, Leibniz, and Aquinas accepted

---

[1] So, too, Plato's cosmology of the *Timaeus*, despite its avowedly mythological character, depicts the Creator as seeking the best possible arrangement of things, moved by the Love of Good; and apparently this was the origin of the Augustinian doctrine that this world is the perfect work of a perfect artist.

such a condition; further, they agreed that 'God could not have done otherwise than as He did' entails 'What God did not do is logically impossible', since the only limitations upon God's powers are limits of logical possibility.

(2) Spinoza, as is well known, held both (1) and (2) explicitly, and concluded that God does not act from free will. In the *Ethics*, he says, "Although it be granted that will appertains to the essence of God, it nevertheless follows from His perfection that things could not have been by Him created other than they are or in a different order."[2]

Spinoza's arguments for the incompatibility of free will and absolute perfection[3] are not cogent; his point might be dismissed were it not for other considerations which arise when we turn to Leibniz and Aquinas.

(3) Leibniz held (1) that God creates all things other than Himself, freely, and (2) that this is the best of all possible worlds. But he also held (3) that God is determined, not by coercion but by reason, to choose the best.[4] "In regard to will in general . . . choice follows the greatest inclination. . . . When God chooses, it is by reason of the best." And, in refuting Spinoza, Leibniz says, "God has been inclined towards those individuals by a determining reason, but He has not been necessitated." "God exists necessarily, but He produces things freely . . ."[5]

In spite of his expressed difference from Spinoza, Leibniz said of our world in the *Theodicy* that we know "*the best plan for the universe, which God could not fail to choose, made it so:* We judge from the event itself; since God has made it, it was not possible to do better."[6] Answering the objection that *Whatever cannot fail to do the best is*

---

[2] Note II, Prop 33. See also Prop. 32: "Will cannot be called a free cause, but only a necessary cause." And Corollary I: "Hence it follows, first, that God does not act according to the freedom of the will." In Prop. 29: "Nothing in the universe is contingent, but all things are conditioned to exist and operate in a particular manner by the necessity of the Divine Nature." All quotations from Spinoza are taken from *The Chief Works of Benedict de Spinoza*, tr. R. H. M. Elwes (New York: Dover Publications, Inc., 1951).

[3] See Note to Prop. 33.

[4] *Leibniz Selections*, p. 435.

[5] *Ibid.*, pp. 486 and 489. "The world is a voluntary effect of God, but on account of inclining or prevailing reasons. And even if the world should be supposed perpetual, nevertheless, God either could not have created it or could have created it otherwise, but He was not to do so. Spinoza thinks (*EP* 49) that 'God produces the world by that necessity by which He knows Himself.' But it must be replied that things are possible in many ways. . . ."

[6] *Ibid.*, pp. 519–520.

not free, he replies that if doing the best is action by inclination based upon reasons and without constraint or displeasure, then this is the highest form of free action.[7]

Nevertheless he could not avoid Spinoza's position. For he describes God as the Absolutely Perfect Being, and says that an absolutely perfect being must act for the best,[8] since to act for anything less, or to decide for reasons less than the best *not* to act, would render such a being imperfect. Moreover, by granting the assumption of the objection that God cannot fail to choose the best, he generates the position that this is the only possible world, as follows.

a: *God is an absolutely perfect being.*

b: *God exists.*

c: *The perfect being does what is best.*

d: *Everything which differs from what God does is, in some way, less than the best. This is true and necessary, since God could not choose between two things which are equally "best," and therefore could not have acted at all unless the proposition were true.*

e: *Since whatever differs from what is best, qua best, must be in some way imperfect, God cannot do anything other than what He does, given (c).*

If God cannot do anything other than what He did, then all alternatives are logically impossible; for it is a logically necessary condition, for anything other than God to exist, that God be able to produce it or have it produced. Thus Leibniz is committed to the first of our propositions, namely, "If God is absolutely perfect, this is the only possible world." But by his own insistence he is also committed to the second: "if God creates freely, this is *not* the only possible world"; since he maintains both antecedents, he contradicts himself. Like Aquinas and Spinoza, Leibniz holds that it is a logically necessary condition for the truth of any proposition of the form 'x exists', where x is not identical with God, that God could have willed that x exist,

[7] Anticipating a difficulty we might raise, he says: "Nevertheless, although His will is always infallible and always tends toward the best, the evil or the lesser good which he rejects does not cease to be possible *in itself;* otherwise the necessity of the good would be geometrical or metaphysical and altogether absolute. . . ." (520–521). This, of course, trips Leibniz up; for nothing is possible *in itself* if it is not such that God can produce it (if it be different from God). One could escape this difficulty by saying 'God is perfect and acts perfectly' is contingently true; but Leibniz would not accept this proposal.

[8] Pages 521 and 522.

since it is absolutely impossible for anything to exist which God has not willed to exist. Hence, for anything y which is not an element of the best, it is impossible that 'y exists' be true, since, for Leibniz, it is impossible that God should will that y exist. Therefore, for Leibniz, the actual world is the only possible world.

(4) The same inconsistency arises for Aquinas, who teaches that (a) God is an absolutely perfect being; (b) God created the world freely; (c) this is not the only possible world. The inconsistency arises, just as it did for Leibniz, because Aquinas interprets the statement 'God is absolutely perfect' in a way that is incompatible with the statement 'God's decision might have been different from what it was'.

An objection was put to Aquinas as follows:

God wills things other than Himself in as much as He wills his own goodness. God wills his own goodness necessarily. Therefore He wills things other than Himself necessarily.

To this Aquinas replies:[9] (a) It is true that God wills His own goodness necessarily; (b) it is true that God wills other things as ordered to His goodness, i.e., as embodiments of His goodness and perfection; but (c) when one wills an end one must will a particular means only if it is logically impossible to achieve the end without that means (in cases where the one that wills has complete knowledge).

Hence, since the goodness of God is perfect and can exist without other things in as much as no perfection can accrue to Him from things, it follows that for Him to will things other than Himself is not absolutely necessary.[10]

That God does not *necessarily* will some of the things that He wills does not result from a defect in the divine will, but from a limitation belonging to the nature of the thing willed, namely, that the perfect goodness of God can exist without it.[11]

In this way Aquinas tries to show that God *could not* have created *except* by an act of free will, since the only things God necessarily

---

[9] *Introduction to St. Thomas Aquinas*, ed. Anton Pegis (New York: The Modern Library, 1948). All quotations from *Summa Theologica* which occur in this chapter are taken from this work, which is in turn an abridgment of *The Basic Writings of St. Thomas Aquinas* (New York: Random House, 1945). I, 19, 3, corpus and ad 2.

[10] I, 19, 3, c.

[11] I, 19, 3, ad 4.

wills pertain to His nature, and no finite thing is a necessary condition for the attainment of the object of will imposed by the nature of God. This is also his way of arguing that 'God creates necessarily' is incompatible with 'God is perfect'.[12]

Yet to the question, "When God, who freely decides to create, makes His decision, by what reasons is His will moved?" Aquinas replies:

It pertains, therefore, to the nature of the will to communicate as far as possible to others the good possessed; and especially does this pertain to the divine will from which all perfection is derived in some kind of likeness. Hence, if natural things, in so far as they are perfect, communicate their good to others, much more does it pertain to the divine will to communicate by likeness its own good to others as much as possible.[13]

Hence, although God wills things other than Himself only for the sake of the end, which is His goodness, it does not follow that anything else moves His will except His goodness.[14]

[The divine will] wills nothing except by reason of its goodness.[15]

If, by the nature of His will, God communicates His goodness (even freely) to other things as far as is possible, then what is created is the only world that could have been created: the world which contains the best possible expression of the divine goodness. Were God to create a different world, He would act in a manner contrary to the nature of His will.[16]

---

[12] Aquinas and Spinoza are diametrically opposed. The former says that absolute perfection and necessary creation of finite things are incompatible; the latter, that free creation and perfection are incompatible.

[13] I, 19, 2, c.

[14] I, 19, 2, ad 2.

[15] I, 19, 2, ad 3.

[16] Commenting on this argument at the APA Detroit Meeting, May 5, 1962, Professor Thomas Langan suggested that there is another interpretation of the expression "as far as possible" in this context, an interpretation which will keep Aquinas' treatment consistent. He proposes that to say God communicated His likeness as far as possible to x, something God created, merely means that x, inasmuch as it has being, is a likeness of God, and that God could not have made it more like Him, given that x is the sort of being it is. I think this interpretation is defensible, although it seems to make the statement "God communicates His likeness as far as possible" a trivial thing to assert, since no one would ever have doubted its truth. Moreover, interpreting Aquinas this way exposes the fact that his theory can offer no reason whatever for God's creating the world He did create.

Thomas Aquinas concurs with Leibniz and Spinoza in premises which entail that anything is impossible absolutely if it is such that it is impossible that God should will its existence. All worlds other than the actual one fulfill that condition, given what has just been presented; therefore the actual world is the only possible world. From this it follows that God does not create freely, since He cannot do the impossible, and all alternatives to *this* creation are impossible. Therefore, the free will of God and the perfection of God are incompatible, and Aquinas, like Leibniz, is inconsistent.[17]

Taking as premises some propositions held in common by the three writers, let us consider the factors which generate this puzzle. All three hold: (1) "God exists" is true, and God is an element of all possible worlds; (2) God is absolutely perfect; (3) if God acted freely He might have done otherwise than He did, since any end toward which creation was freely ordered could have been attained with another creation or none at all; (4) He could not have done otherwise than He did for the *same* reasons as those which determined Him to do what He did, since His reasons would be based upon merits perceived in the particular case: (5) whether God acts from free will or not, He must still act from internal inclination based entirely upon reasons; (6) there is some object, namely God's goodness or perfection, to which God inclines by nature, the divine will being the inclination toward that object.

Aquinas and Leibniz maintain that the creation which God selected is one of a set of alternatives ordered to that end; these are not alternative ways of *producing* that end, however, but alternative sets of things which might be produced and perfected by being directed to it.[18] In other words, the divine goodness or perfection is not an effect of creation but a *reason* or motive for it, or that which gives creating its point;[19] in *that* sense, creation is ordered to God's goodness as to an end. The goodness or perfection of God is that-on-account-of-which God acted and in *that* sense serves as end.

---

[17] Unless we take Professor Langan's interpretation, given in the note above; in that case, Aquinas is merely incomplete.

[18] Aquinas offers this qualification in *De Veritate*, 23, 4, c.

[19] My wishing all men well might be the reason I do a kindness to another, but is not an effect of it, although my doing the kindness is "ordered to my benevolence as to a Final Cause."

In fact, Aquinas says:

1: The divine goodness serves His will as the reason for His willing all things, just as His essence is the reason for His knowing all things.[20]

2: If natural things in so far as they are perfect communicate their good to others, much more does it pertain to the divine will to communicate by likeness its own good to others, as much as is possible.[21]

These last propositions, which I have called (1) and (2), are central to the paradox. The second seems to be plainly false, as well as incompatible with the possibility of alternatives to what God has done. It seems manifest that no matter how perfect the likeness to God in anything He has created, He could always create something else which is more like Him. Hence the apparent[22] paradox that it is not possible for God to communicate His likeness *as far as possible*. In fact, Aquinas virtually says this:

No matter how much more nobly any pure creature is related to God, it is still possible for some other creature to be related to God and to represent the divine goodness in a manner equally noble.[23]

Given this, (2) would be fulfilled only if God created *simultaneously* everything He could have created alternatively. It is obvious that He did not,[24] and could not do so. Let us dismiss (2) as false both for creatures and for God, unless we accept the interpretation of note 16; then it is false for creatures but not for God, although Aquinas thought it to be universally true.

Proposition (1) is a more serious matter. Aquinas clearly intends the expression "all things" to mean all things which exist. But why should not the divine goodness be equally a reason for creating all things which are compossible? One would wonder why, if God did not create the most perfect set of compossibles, He failed to do so; for

[20] *DV*, 23, 4. In *Truth*, translated from the Leonine text by Robert W. Schmidt, S.J. (Chicago: Regnery, 1954).

[21] *ST*, I, 19, 2c. *op. cit.*, p. 194.

[22] Apparent; for notice that "It is not possible" qualifies a proposition, while in "communicate His likeness as far as possible," "possible" ranges distributively over states of affairs which *collectively* are not *compossible*.

[23] *DV*, 23, 4.

[24] This is obvious because not everything which (considered in isolation) God could create is compossible. God must have some additional reason by which to select among sets of things.

He had *reason* for doing so—the only reason He could have for doing anything at all.[25] It is partly because of this that Leibniz took the position he did, a position as inherently contradictory as that of maintaining the possibility of a largest number. For it is self-evident that if God is infinitely perfect, there is no finite embodiment of divine perfection which is the most perfect possible.[26]

Leibniz is, therefore, necessarily wrong in his reason for thinking that God *had* to follow the "principle of greatest variety and minimum hypothesis" in making his choice, since neither that principle nor any other will select "the best possible world."

Nevertheless, all three authors seem to think a free Creator would employ as a reason *some* standard, p, in selecting a world to create. Now either what is actual is the only set of things fulfilling p (the rule of selection employed), or else some other set also fulfills p. If the former is true, and if it is also the case that a perfect being must follow p, then the actual is all that is possible. If the actual is not all that satisfies p, the Creator needs a new standard, p', in order to select among the worlds satisfying p. If p' is also such that a perfect Creator must adhere to it, the world which satisfies both p and p' is the only possible world. In a word, in order for the actual world to be both created by a perfect God and be only one of a number of possible worlds, it must *not* be the case that there is some standard of perfection, p or p', which it is necessary that a perfect Creator follow and which, when followed, selects the particular world made actual.

But if we assume that the Creator chooses among possible worlds by employing some reason, r, which it is *not* necessary that a perfect Creator employ in creating, then how does He decide upon r as His reason? Presumably He does this by employing principles for selecting reasons; but by what principle could He select r over r'? Either He has some reason, q, for His selection or He does not. If He does, either He has q by the fact that He is perfect, or He does not. If He

---

[25] "God creates by reason of His goodness" may be read in Aquinas either as I have read it, "with His goodness as the reason or motive," or it may be read "because He is Good." In the latter case, His goodness is not asserted to be *His* reason, but *our* reason for what He did (or explanation of why He did it). This second reading will not avoid the problem I raise later, although it will absolve Aquinas from my charges that he assigned an *insufficient* reason for God's doing what He did (since it would equally have been a reason for God's doing anything else you choose); on that reading, Aquinas assigned no reason whatever.

[26] As Aquinas undoubtedly saw; see *DV*, 23, a. 4.

does not, He must have a reason for q, and so on. If He has q by nature, He could not fail to have r and hence may be said to have r by nature, with the result that the actual world is the only possible world. If He does not have q by nature and has no reason for q or has no reason for some reason for q by nature, then He would fail to act, since at some point He would lack a reason for choosing.[27]

For authors like Aquinas and Leibniz, who implicitly suppose it impossible that God should create without a reason—or with a reason for which there is no reason—this dilemma is insoluble; for these writers' inconsistencies followed from the tacit assumption that God's determining reason is imposed by His nature in such a way that He could not be the sort of being He is if He did not follow that reason. Among other things, they failed to distinguish between the question concerning God's choice whether or not to create at all, and the logically posterior questions concerning God's choice of a *particular* world among an infinity of possibilities.

The failure to make these distinctions put Aquinas and Leibniz into a logical box: Assuming that it is not possible (except in a logically trivial sense) that God should have a reason for every reason He has, and ruling out creation from no reason, we conclude that God must have some reason because of what He is. This reason must be sufficient to move Him to what He does, rather than to something else. Therefore, it cannot move Him among alternatives which stand equally with respect to that reason, since He could not then decide without new reasons, ultimately founded in His nature. Hence, He could have created only the world He has, and the other worlds become impossible.

Considerations such as these show that the concepts of *free action* which we apply to God, like those employed by Aquinas and Leibniz, emphasize two different conditions: (a) that the activity proceed internally from the agent on account of its reasons and in the absence

---

[27] This consequence is avoidable, as we shall see below, if we postulate that God has by nature (i.e., in His goodness) a reason for creating rather than not creating; then he will lack a reason, at some point, for the particular choice He makes, but He will, by nature, have a reason for choosing some created world or another. In this way, I think we can arbitrate between the intellectualism of St. Thomas and the voluntarism of Duns Scotus, taking over the essentials of both: (a) the divine nature provides the reason for creating rather than not creating (the intellectualism aspect); (b) the divine will provides, ultimately without reason, the particularity of what is chosen, as something among an infinity of alternatives (the voluntarism aspect).

of sufficient external causes or conditions; and (b) that it should be compatible with the nature of the agent that it should perform actions other than those it actually performs.

It is seemingly plausible that God could be free in the first sense but not in the second, since the fulfillment of (a) does not have the fulfillment of (b) as a logically necessary condition. Spinoza described the situation in which (a) is satisfied and (b) is not, as a case of acting according to one's will, but not freely. His proposal that God acts thus fails, simply because we know that things other than what is actual are possible, and we will allow no argument to convince us of the contrary. We would more readily reject the proposition that God exists, or that God is absolutely perfect, or that every possible world contains God as an element, than we would the obvious consistency of some false propositions.

Nevertheless, Aquinas and Leibniz have succeeded no better with what looks like the only alternative to Spinoza's view.

The nub of the whole problem seems to be this: When God created the world, He did so either from the *necessity* of His nature (in the way in which Aristotle thought man willed his own happiness, Aquinas thought God willed His own perfection, and Spinoza thought He willed the world); or else from *external* causes which moved Him to create; or finally, from reasons which moved Him to create. We reject the first alternative because of our insuperable belief that things other than the actual are logically possible; we reject the second, also, as inconsistent with the notion of God as the perfect (and therefore independent) creator.

The last alternative admits of three interpretations: (a) God may have derived His reasons from the necessity of His nature, in such a manner that, being what He is, He could not have had any reason other than the reason He did have; (b) God may have derived His reasons from external causes; (c) God may have freely chosen His reasons.

(a) If God derived His reasons from the necessity of His nature, He could not have had reasons different from those He had. If those reasons were sufficient to move Him to what He did and to no alternative, then alternative courses of creation are impossible. But this is false; therefore the supposition that the reasons for creation were entirely derived from the nature of God is also false.

(b) That external causes should have supplied God with reasons (in the manner in which some of our reasons are imposed upon us by our environment) is absurd, and incompatible with the nature of God.

(c) Therefore, God must have chosen His reasons. But this choice is either based upon reasons or it is not. If it is not, then God can be said to have had, at bottom, no reason for what He did; there is no sufficient reason for the fact that what was done is what it is, rather than something else. To imagine the selection of this world to be entirely arbitrary because God chose His reasons arbitrarily seems incompatible with our concept of God as the fully intellectual being. But if God's reasons for creating were chosen on the basis of other reasons—reasons for His reasons for creating—then we must inquire into the origin of those reasons. Either (a) God has a reason for each reason He has, and has each reason because of a choice based upon some other reason which He also chose to have, or (b) He has some reason from His nature. The infinite series of reasons based upon prior choices is as much in need of a sufficient reason as any series of things. Why did God employ the series r, rather than some other series? If it be said that, of all alternatives, r alone is compatible with God's nature, then the first alternative (a) is reduced to the second (b) and what happens is all that is possible. If r is not the only set compatible with God's nature, then there must have been a reason for His following this rather than the others. This reopens the whole mystery. Thus the only alternative to Spinoza seems to be a theory that God's decision is based upon an infinite series of reasons plus an infinite series of reasons for the selection of the series of reasons selected.

SECTION 2: REASONS, EXPLANATIONS, AND "SUFFICIENT REASONS"

Our critical excursion into the history of philosophy suggests that there are glaring inconsistencies in the way God's relation to the world has been conceived by western philosophers, whether they be at the heartland of Christian orthodoxy with Aquinas, on the enthusiastic periphery with Leibniz, or beyond the fringe with Spinoza.

There must be some very basic confusions throughout the entire western tradition. I will venture (even though space and my other purposes will not let me prove it) that confusion over the notions of "free choice" and "free will" is basic to the problem; but so, too, are confusion and outright error on the matters which are more germane to our over-all purposes.

So, in this section we shall not canvass the whole epistemological wasteland surrounding the concepts "reason," "explanation," and "sufficient reason"; rather, we shall concentrate on a few points which are connected with these concepts and are directly related to positions taken elsewhere in this book (particularly in Chapters III and IV, and in Section 1 of this chapter).

Everything I have said in the previous section confirms "David Hume's First Objection," as it was sketched in the first section of Chapter III. There, he was imagined to object that the Christian, *least of all men*, can maintain the Principle of Sufficient Reason as it was understood by the "modern scholastics."[28]

The main thrust of our reasoning so far has been to support Hume's objection. We considered two alternatives, on the premise that God created the world and did so freely—not only in the sense of acting from an internal cause without external conditions which are sufficient, but also in the sense of acting under circumstances where a contrary act was equally possible.

(a) First we considered the situation where God would have had no reasons at all for choosing one universe over an infinite number of alternatives. In such a case (where God chooses freely but without a reason) there is no sufficient explanation for or reason why God chose this world rather than another. Therefore, on the first supposition, the Principle of Sufficient Reason would surely conflict with the prem-

---

[28] Two surveys give a fair picture of the extent to which the principle was actually employed: John Edwin Gurr, S.J., *The Principle of Sufficient Reason in Some Scholastic Systems, 1750–1900* (Milwaukee: Marquette University Press, 1959); and Wilbur Urban, *The History of the Principle of Sufficient Reason: Its Metaphysical and Logical Formulations*, "Princeton Contributions to Philosophy," I, 3 (April 1900). As these fascinating surveys of a now-dead debate disclose, some of the very points we shall discuss were examined in the Leibniz-Clarke disputes and in the later scholastic-scientist disputes, such as that between Premontval and the Wolffians (see Gurr, p. 99), or that between Nicholas Beguelin and Cardinal Gerdil; see "Reflexions sur un memoir de Monsieur Beguelin concernant le principe de la raison suffisante de la possibilité du système du hazard," *Opere Edite E Inedite del Cardinale Giacinto Sigismondo Gerdil* (Florence: G. Celli, 1844–1851), Vol. I.

ised free creation of God, and if the first supposition and the doctrine of free creation are both true, the Principle of Sufficient Reason must be false.[29]

(b) But what of the second supposition: that God created freely, and did so on the basis of reasons that He had? As we said earlier, there are three circumstances under which this could be imagined: God's having His reasons by nature; His having them from some external cause (as do men); or His having them through His own choice. We showed that the first two situations turn out to be incompatible with the claim that God created freely, and with the assumption that this is not the only possible world. This convinces us that if God created on the basis of reasons, then He must have selected His reasons by free choice. So, if we explain the existence of our world by appealing to the creation of God, we must appeal to his *reasons* for creating this world to explain the fact that God created *this one* rather than some other.

But we can, in turn, ask for the explanation of God's having had the reasons He had. For they were not imposed, as they are in the case of man, by the knowledge of His environment, or imposed through His ignorance or weakness; rather, God's knowledge of contingent things and states of affairs is dependent upon His will, because the *existence* of the contingent things and states of affairs known is dependent upon God's choice. The only sort of explanation there could be for God's having had the reasons He had is to be found in a further appeal to the divine choice.

But because God's reasons are chosen, the divine choice itself must precede their selection. Hence, however we extend the chain of choices based upon reasons by which God selects reasons for His further choices, that chain always begins with a choice. In a word, even if the chain be infinite (and of what value would such a proliferation be?) it is ordered in a certain way, whereby every set of reasons is posterior to some choice, just as in the set of natural numbers

---

[29] We shall support this claim in the detailed argument which follows. A comparable debate occurred in the Middle Ages: Avicenna rejected the doctrine of free creation with similar considerations. As Giles of Rome (*Errors of the Philosophers*, VI, 4) put Avicenna's argument: "If something contingent proceeded immediately from God through His nature, He would be changed in nature; if through His intentions, His intentions would be changed; and if through His will, His will would be changed." Translated by H. Shapiro, in *Medieval Philosophy* (New York: Modern Library, 1964), p. 396.

every even number is posterior to some odd number. Hence *the divine reasons are ultimately founded upon divine choices*, and not vice versa. In this respect we are defending one of the major contentions of Duns Scotus' metaphysics which postulates that the divine choice is ontologically ultimate as the explanation for the existence of the world. (From this Scotist position developed the radical voluntarism of some later medieval scholastics.) But on this point an important distinction needs to be made, in order to distinguish the voluntarism of Scotus from the intellectualism of St. Thomas. If we make this distinction properly, some compromise can be worked out between the two theories.

In particular, with respect to the reasons for creation, those reasons which account for the selection of *this world* rather than some alternative world must be distinguished from those which account for God's having created a world involving some being other than Himself rather than being content with a world involving nothing other than Himself. The latter case is what we call the choice between *contradictories:* whether there should be or should not be anything other than God. The former is the choice between *contraries:* whether among those things other than God which are possible, the actual should be of *this* sort rather than *that* sort.

Now the reconciliation between Aquinas and Scotus can be sketched in the following way. We can argue, using the principle "The good is diffusive of itself," that God has *by nature* a reason for His choice between the contradictories; that is, the goodness of the divine nature inherently provides a reason for creating. But that reason, which is provided by the divine nature for the creation of *something*, cannot determine God to create (cannot be sufficient for God to create): it provides only a reason for creating some thing or another, but does not provide a reason for creating some *particular* thing rather than another. And the creation itself must be of some thing rather than another. In order for the outcome of an activity to be determined, it is necessary that the *particular* outcome of that activity be determined in accord with the nature of the thing that is said to determine it. The divine nature provides a reason for creating rather than not creating but will not provide a reason for creating some particular thing (such as the world we actually have) rather than some alternative; therefore, the reason for creating which is to be found in the divine nature cannot necessitate the creation. Put simply, it is not sufficient, though it is necessary. Hence we can say the basic reason for creating rather than not creating is to be found in God's knowledge of His own nature; yet we can at the same time maintain the voluntarism of Duns Scotus—that ultimately the character of the creation which is actualized is determined entirely by the divine choice, which is prior to every chain of reasons for one possible world over another.

Thus—on the supposition that God created freely, but that this creation was based upon reasons He had for selecting among the possible alternatives—it will still follow that the Principle of Sufficient Reason is not satisfied. And therefore, on the supposition that God created freely, whether or not doing so involved reasons, the Principle of Sufficient Reason is not satisfied. This is just what the imaginary voice of David Hume contended in Chapter III, and is exactly the view adopted by Avicenna (in his commentary on book nine of Aristotle's *Metaphysics*), who rejected, on a priori grounds, the doctrine of free creation. The Christian, least of all men, can insist upon a strict interpretation of the Principle of Sufficient Reason. He, least of all, can insist that is a priori true: for if it is, the doctrine of the free creation of God becomes a manifest impossibility. Because this point —the insufficiency of sufficient reason—is so important, we shall argue for it in considerable detail below.

The truth of the matter is this: those things that the Principle of Sufficient Reason was introduced to explain can in fact be explained by appeal to much weaker principles. One of these is Principle E, which we have employed in this book. Another is the weaker but still general Principle of Hetero-Explicability; i.e., for any contingent but actual state of affairs (not equivalent to the conjunction of *all* contingent but actual states of affairs), it is logically consistent that there should have been a cause or explanation of its actuality. That is, the most basic metaphysical questions, such as whether God exists, can be handled just as well with Principle E as with the traditional, universally general apodictic statement that every existent, event, fact, and thing has a sufficient reason for being. For when the crucial steps of the argument are reached, it is always asked whether the universally general Principle of Sufficient Reason is said to be true because it is a priori, or because it is inductively confirmed. When the latter position is adopted, it is pointed out that a principle that is universally confirmed by a finite body of evidence may in fact have a finite body of exceptions and that one of these exceptions may be the unobserved case whose existence or occurrence is in question in the argument at hand. Thus the principle is said to be insufficient for its purposes. When, on the other hand, the Principle of Sufficient Reason is said to be a priori true (for what else can one do after seeing the defects of merely claiming that it is a universally general truth?), the following argument is urged: If it is logically possible that God should create freely, then it is logically possible that some event, being, or fact (namely, the initial divine choice) should lack sufficient explanation since the free creation of God and the absolute universality of the Principle of Sufficient Reason are incompatible. Naturally, the Christian will agree that it is possible that God created freely. Therefore, he seems forced to admit that the Principle of Sufficient Reason is a priori false; for that assertion of necessity which is incompatible with a true assertion of possibility (that free creation is possible) is necessarily false. In order to give fuller support to this contention, I offer the forthcoming arguments, which, although they approach the matter in a manner apparently oblique,[30] are noticeably similar in structure to the arguments used in the first section, concerning the multiplicity of possible worlds.

THE INSUFFICIENCY OF THE PRINCIPLE OF SUFFICIENT REASON

(1) A number of great philosophers, Avicenna, Maimonides, and Duns Scotus among them, were convinced that God is a being of such a nature that He exists necessarily; that is, of such a nature that things could not have been otherwise than that He exists. Moreover, Maimonides, Duns Scotus, and their countless followers were convinced that God created the world and did so freely, that the things of the world exist contingently (both logically and causally), and that in God is to be found the sufficient explanation of the being of all things.[31]

---

[30] This obliqueness is accounted for by what I take to be the intrinsic interest and initial plausibility of a particular argument for what I call the Principle of Duns Scotus, an argument which deserves the detailed consideration we provide for it.

[31] They did not presume to say what this explanation was; rather, just how God's choices functioned to this effect was commonly considered a mystery.

I shall here try to show in detail both that the Principle of Sufficient Reason is false and that it is logically incompatible with the conception of God I have ascribed to these philosophers—a conception of God which I take to be "orthodox" and central to the concerns of this book.

There is a general principle used by Duns Scotus, called the Law of the Disjunctive Transcendentals,[32] which entails the statement: if anything exists such that its existence is logically contingent, then there exists something whose existence is not logically contingent. I shall call this latter statement the Principle of Duns Scotus (PS) (although it must be noted that the same principle is found in the work of Avicenna and is, for both these philosophers, a fundamental metaphysical law).

In considering what might have led Avicenna and Scotus to accept this principle, one may discover an argument like (2), discussed below, whose key premise is fundamental to our concern with the Principle of Sufficient Reason. That argument (which has its own interest) suggests that PS is correct; yet further consideration discloses first of all that the argument is unsound and reveals two things which should be disconcerting: (a) that the Principle of Sufficient Reason, interpreted in the broad sense which would allow us to say that in God is to be found the sufficient reason for the actuality of all contingent states of affairs, is incompatible with the doctrine that God is a free cause of all other things; and (b) that the Principle of Sufficient Reason is necessarily false. At the very least, we discover that systems of metaphysics which set out to show that there is a sufficient explanation for the being of the world (where "world" designates the conjunction of *all* contingent but actual states of affairs) are embarked upon a search which fails—not because it confronts a mystery, but because there cannot be such a thing as the sufficient reason (or accounting) of the world, even though we consider "accounting," "rea-

---

[32] Duns Scotus: "In the disjunctive attributes, however, where the entire disjunction cannot be demonstrated from 'being', nevertheless, as a universal rule by positing the less perfect extreme of some being we can conclude that the more perfect extreme is realized in some other being. Thus it follows that if some being is finite, then some being is infinite. *And if some being is contingent, then some being is necessary.* For such cases it is not possible for the more imperfect extreme of the disjunction to be existentially predicated of 'being,' particularly taken, unless the more perfect extreme be existentially verified of some other being upon which it depends" (*Philosophical Writings*, p. 9).

son," and "explanation" to designate a metaphysical rather than an epistemic relation.

In the sense that we have assigned to "world," Spinoza would say, "There is and can be no world." But let us accept Duns Scotus on this: "The proposition 'Some existing thing is contingent' seems to be a primary truth and is not demonstrable by an a priori demonstration." I think, *pace* Spinoza, we can agree; there exists at least one thing such that it is logically possible that it should not have existed.

There is, then, a set of contingent but actual states of affairs, a world. It will follow (by PS) that there is at least one thing such that it is *not* logically possible that it should not have existed. The inference is valid, but is PS true? An argument can be constructed to show that it is; and from this we shall derive our consequences.[33]

(2) Argument in behalf of PS:

1: There is an infinite set of logically contingent propositions which contains a proper sub-set: the contingent propositions which are true. Among these, there is a sub-set which constitutes an inventory of what there is. Now let 'w' be the logically complex proposition constituted by the conjunction of every true contingent proposition which is not equivalent to 'w'. Then let w designate what is expressed by 'w', namely, the entire actual but contingent state of affairs which constitutes (along with any existential necessities there may be) the actual universe.

2: For any actual but contingent state of affairs, p, it is logically possible that there should be or should have been some state of affairs which accounts for the fact that p is the case.

3: But w is a contingent state of affairs.

4: Therefore it follows (from 2 and 3) that it is possible that there is some state of affairs, q, which accounts for w.

5: No contingent state of affairs can account for its own being-the-case. This is evident because if p accounts for p's being the case, then ~p cannot be the case and, thus, p is not contingent. Further, the complex contingent state of affairs w cannot have a constituent element which accounts for its own being the case and which, in turn, accounts for p, of which it is a constituent part, because by (1) the sole constituents of w are contingent states

---

[33] One should note that even though we find the argument unsound and reject the Principle of Sufficient Reason, we shall not have shown that PS is false; we shall merely have failed to show that it is true.

of affairs, whereas by (5) it is evident that what is self-accounting is not contingent.

6: Therefore, it is possible that there is some state of affairs, q, which is not a constituent element of w and which accounts for w.

7: But if q can be actual and cannot be contingent, then q must be necessary. For only the necessary can be actual and cannot be contingent. Whatever is necessary is actual.

8: Therefore there is actually some state of affairs which is necessary and which accounts for w's being the state of the contingent but actual universe.

9: But no state of affairs q can account for any other modally distinct state of affairs w, unless q involves an existent which accounts for w through causality or agency.

10: The constituents of a necessary state of affairs must all be necessary; therefore, the existential constituent q is necessary.

11: Therefore, something exists such that it is necessarily true that it exists.

12: Hence, PS is true: if there is some contingent state of affairs, there is some existent whose actuality is not contingent.

(3) The consequences of this argument are these: (a) if it is sound (or can be made sound by repair), then it follows that God does not account for the world; and (b) if it is not sound, the false premises, when negated to provide truths, yield the same result: that in God there cannot be a sufficient reason for the world.[34] Does this show that there is no being such that it exists necessarily, is free and omnipotent, and is the sufficient explanation for the world of contingent things? That is, does it follow that God, as He is widely (but perhaps incorrectly) conceived, does not exist? It seems that it does; for whatever follows from both p and $\sim p$ is necessarily true, and the conclusion mentioned follows both from the supposition that the argument is sound and from the supposition that it is not.

A: On the assumption that the argument is sound

It has long been thought (see, for example, Maimonides and Scotus) that a free and omnipotent being which exists necessarily can account

---

[34] It is to be repeated that "world" is a technical term, defined as is 'w' in (1) of the argument for PS. 2.

for the being of the world. But let us suppose that there is something, *a*, which exists necessarily and which accounts for the being of the world. Let *q* be the state of affairs constituted by the existence of that being, *a*; let *w*, as defined above, be the world; and let $_qE_w$ designate the state of affairs where *q* accounts for (explains) *w*.

Now it is evident that $_qE_w$ cannot be so *because q* logically involves *w*, as would be the case if the proposition '*q*' entailed the proposition '*w*' (although that is sometimes what renders one state of affairs the explanation of another, namely, the first logically *involves* the second). The contingent cannot be logically involved in the necessary; if *p* is contingent, so is ~*p*. But if p followed from a necessary truth necessarily, then ~*p* would be incompatible with that necessary truth. But every contingent state of affairs is compatible with every necessary one. Thus, ~*p* would have to be both contingent (and hence, possible) and impossible (because incompatible with what is necessary); so the supposition that the contingent is logically involved in the necessary leads to explicit contradiction. Therefore, *a*, the necessary existent, cannot account for *w* by nature because we cannot consistently suppose that '*q*' entails '*w*' and that the former is necessary while the latter is contingent.

But if *q* does not account for *w* because of the nature of *a* (the being whose existence constitutes *q*), then it must do so either through causality (which will require a causal law as connecting link) or through agency, which involves choice.

It is of no avail to suppose that the accounting relation is causal: the causal law cannot be a logically necessary truth, because the resulting *w* could not be contingent if it followed necessarily from the conjunction of logical truths (and it is premised that *q* is a logical truth). And if the causal law is contingent, it would be a constituent part of *w*—of what is contingent and actual—and would require an additional *accounting relation* connecting it with *q*; this relation could not be supplied through another causal law, for that would then require a third, etc., with the result that we meet a vicious regress. To reiterate: Imagine that it is the actual but contingent state of the world that if a necessary being exists, it follows causally that everything else which is actual, exists. What accounts for the fact that *this* is the state of the world?

Hence, if it is true that $_qE_w$, that the existence of the necessary being accounts for the actuality of the world, then it must be thus through some choice. So let us define a predicate "$_xC_y$," "x chooses effectively that y be the case." If the necessary being, a, accounts through a choice for the being of the world, then $_aC_w$ (a chooses that w should be the actual state of things) will be a fact. This state of affairs, $_aC_w$, is either logically necessary or logically contingent. It cannot be logically necessary, if we take the existence of a to be necessary and that of w to be contingent, since a contradiction would result. Moreover, it would be incorrect to say that the "choice" in question was free; when a choice "that-p" is free, it is necessary that the choice "that-not-p" should also be consistent; but if the choice "that-p" is logically necessary, the contrary choice is impossible. Hence, "$_aC_w$" must be logically contingent. But if so, what accounts for the fact that *this* ($_aC_w$) is the way of the world? If 'God chose our world' is logically contingent, then what accounts for the fact (which is part of our world) that God did so? Whatever you propose must be thought either to be a state of affairs which is part of our world but not part of all possible worlds, or a part of our world *and* part of all possible worlds. If what accounts for the choice of our world is part of all possible worlds, then ours is the only possible world—a consequence incompatible with our premise that w is contingent but actual. But if what accounts for the choice of our world is *part* of our world and not of all possible worlds, then what accounts for the fact that *it* is part of our actual world? Some other choice? We reach an infinite regress.

A similar regress can be generated if we imagine that God chose our world, acting upon reasons. Either He chose these reasons, or else He had them of necessity, through His nature. If He had them of necessity, the choice was not free; if He chose them, then He must have chosen His reasons because of other reasons; and the regress is again encountered, whatever His reasons. The whole set of states of affairs indicated by statements of the form 'God has reasons *l–n*' is contingent because it is entirely constituted by the contingent states of affairs designated by statements of the form 'God has *that* reason'. Hence the whole set of states of affairs constituted by God's having a certain reason for choosing the world and having a certain reason for having that first reason, etc., will, if it is actual, be part of w, the state of affairs requiring an explanation.

In other words, it is quite correct for us to admit that if a certain statement of the form 'God chose w for reason r' had been true (as it could, logically, have been), there would have been an explanation of the actuality of w (what is now the case); yet we can still say that there would not, thereby, have been an explanation or account of what *would* have been the case because w would not have *been* the conjunction of all actual, contingent states of affairs. For 'God chose w for reason r' would itself have become part of what required an accounting, with the result that while a given set (however large) of contingent states of affairs could be accounted for through some other contingent states of affairs, the *whole* set of contingent but actual states of affairs cannot be accounted for while it *is* the whole set of the contingent and actual. This should be evident now, since the only way the necessary (not being an element of the contingent world) could account for w would be through logical involvement, a relation excluded by the supposition that the contingent world is logically contingent. Hence, if argument (2) is sound, and if its conclusion that there necessarily exists something which *could* have accounted for w is true, it still follows that this necessary being does not in fact account for w. From this it follows both that the Principle of Sufficient Reason is false (insofar as it requires a sufficient explanation for whatever exists or obtains) and that there does not exist a free and omnipotent necessary being in whom there is a sufficient reason for the being of the world, although there may be an explanation in its choice for everything else which is contingent.

Generalizing the argument, let "N" be the conjunction of all necessary truths (and let us suppose that this includes those statements which require that something exist whose existence is logically necessary). And let "W" be the conjunction of all true contingent statements. There can be nothing true to connect "N" and "W," since whatever it is will be describable in some statement "R." If "R" is true, it will be either necessary or contingent. If necessary, it will already be contained in "N"; if contingent, it will already be contained in "W." Hence, there can be no connection between the contingent and the necessary such that the contingent but actual is accounted for by the necessary; and therefore, there cannot be a free and divine omnipotent being which is a sufficient accounting for everything which is contingent and actual, though it may nature of what exists contingently cannot account for its own existence, for it would have to account for the absence of all possible privations and negations thereof, and would thereby render the existence necessary.

C: If God does not exist, that He does not is true either necessarily or contingently.

   1: If necessarily, the PSR is false because there cannot be a sufficient reason for the actuality of what is contingent but actual, since there is no necessary being in which this reason may be found.

   2: If contingently, the PSR is false because there cannot be a sufficient reason for the non-existence of God, since God is unpreventable by nature.

Either B or C is the case; therefore, either B1, B2, C1, or C2 is true. But each entails the falsity of PSR. Therefore, PSR is necessarily false, since it is false under all circumstances. (This can be said without requiring us to admit that all four situations described are possible, or even that more than one is.) Therefore, the "Humean" objection of Chapter III is perfectly correct.

SECTION 3: FURTHER CONSIDERATION OF THE PRINCIPLE OF EXPLICABILITY

How will the considerations which we employ to reject the Principle of Sufficient Reason affect the status and interpretation of Principle E, which we used as a premise in Chapters III and IV, and similar principles such as "Every contingent state of affairs is hetero-explicable"?[36] We encounter three problems for our basic principles:

---

[36] This latter principle can be made central to a simplified form of the argument of Chapters II and IV, as follows:

1: Every logically contingent state of affairs is hetero-explicable.
2: The state of affairs "God does not exist" is not hetero-explicable, for:
   a: God is such that whether or not God exists, nothing can cause or prevent the state of affairs "God exists."
   b: Whatever is uncausable and unpreventable is not hetero-explicable.
   c: Therefore, "God does not exist" is not hetero-explicable.
3: So "God does not exist" is not logically contingent.
4: Therefore, "God does not exist" is either necessary or impossible.
5: But it is possible that God exists.
6: Therefore, it is necessary. (DS, lines 4 and 5).
7: Therefore, it is true that God exists.

(a) The apparent necessity that there be some state of affairs which is unexplained, while at the same time the same state of affairs is supposed to be explicable in principle. This suggests, first, that the principles are false, and secondly, that the modal operators in our principles are ambiguous—perhaps in such a way that upon their being clarified the principles will be obviously false.

(b) In light of the objections to the Principle of Sufficient Reason, the concept 'explanation' becomes vacuous, so that it does not make sense to talk of events which are hetero-explicable but unexplained. What if the unbroken and complete chain of explanations which is presupposed by the Principle of Sufficient Reason is essential to the concept of an explanation?

(c) Since intuitive considerations which were supposed to be the grounds for acceptance of the Principle of Sufficient Reason (as an a priori truth) were found to be inadequate and to be in conflict with well-established truths, why should we accept Principle E on similar grounds? Even if Principle E survives the clarification of its ambiguities and the challenge to its content, it has still not been established as true and may be inappropriate as a premise. Even granting the claim we made earlier, that Principle E can be derived from the definition of "self-explanatory" given in Chapter III and the Principle of Hetero-Explicability, this merely transfers our suspicion to the latter principle, despite the assurances we were given in Chapter IV.

PRINCIPLE E: EITHER FALSE OR FATALLY AMBIGUOUS?

There must be actual and hetero-explicable states of affairs which are not, in fact, explained! But for any given state of affairs you choose, it need not have been the case that it was actual, hetero-explicable, and unexplained. Is this a case of an existentially general formula which is L-true but is such that *no* substitution instance is true? If both should be provable, is the modal logic or our concept system omega-inconsistent?

One might say that the objection to be found in Chapter III (about the reasons God had for creating the world) conclusively establishes the falsity of Principle E, as well as that of the Principle of Sufficient Reason. For if God had no reason for choosing this world over any other, then there is a fact, "God chose this world," which lacks sufficient explanation and if explained would have left something else without sufficient explanation. Hence, Principle E *must* be false, in that there is an actual and contingent state of affairs which is not hetero-explicable.

But we reply that the argument merely proposes that there is at least one unexplained actual and contingent fact—at least one fact such that in terms of what else is a fact, there cannot be any explanation for it; this is merely *hypothetical* impossibility. The argument fails to show that there could not (logically) have been an explanation for that fact (that, for example, God could not have had a *reason* for creating our world). But it does suggest that if *a* is a fact which is not explained, but which would have been explained by *b* (if *b* had been a fact), then in the case that *b* explained *a*, either *b* or some fact which explained *b* would itself have lacked an explanation. (The "possibility" that the chain of "explainers" is infinite has not been considered; let us put it aside, noting that this hypothesis must eventually be discussed.)

The argument displays the falsity of the claim that for every fact there is a fact, perhaps identical with it, which explains its being the actual state of the universe; all possible worlds include some contingent state of affairs which is unaccounted for (that is, not *sufficiently* accounted for). But it leaves entirely open whether there could have been an explanation for each fact taken by itself, even though the totality will always contain one fact which is unexplained, but which could have been explained.

Yet the argument can be strengthened as follows. Either we are willing to say that one contingent state of affairs can be the sufficient explanation of another, or we are not. If we are, then there still cannot be a sufficient explanation of the contingent world, since the sufficient explanation of any contingent state of affairs must be a logically distinct state of affairs (even this is not at all clear as a principle, because wherever $(p \cdot q)$ explains r by q's being a law-like universal connecting p and r, the conjunction is *not* logically distinct, in the sense of having its truth-value independent of that of r). But there can be no logically distinct contingent state of affairs which will provide a sufficient explanation for the entire actual world. (The ambiguity of this generalization is fundamental to the present inquiry.) We have already shown that a logically necessary state of affairs cannot be a sufficient explanation for the entire contingent world. Therefore, it appears that there can be no sufficient explanation of the entire state of the world, which we call w. This seems to require that there be one actual contingent state of affairs, call it w (namely, the entire set of actual and contingent states of affairs), for which no sufficient explanation is possible. If this reasoning is correct, then Principle E is false.

The state of affairs, w, is to be taken as *what-is-designated by* a definite description, "w": "The one and only actual state of affairs constituted by every state of affairs expressed by a true contingent statement." Now what shall we make of the argument above?

We can piece together a reply gradually. Insofar as w is accountable, the term "w" would not designate all that *would be* actual, were w accounted for. But since anything which would account for w would have to be actual (if it did account for w), and since the accounting (though not necessarily that which does the accounting) could not fail to be logically contingent, it follows that it only *appears* to be so that there is always some actual state of affairs, w, which could not have been accounted for. For it now turns out that this belief would involve an equivocation between the *term* "w," taken as a definite description, and w, taken as *that which is designated by* the definite description. Consider this further.

Take w, the actual and the contingent (taken as a whole) and designated by "w," a definite description: "The one and only state of affairs constituted by every state of affairs expressed by a true contingent statement." Is there anything to account for w? No, as the earlier arguments made clear: w is unexplained, unaccounted for.

Could w have been accounted for? Is w (what is designated by "w") in principle explicable? First, let us distinguish the way w is *named* from *what it is*. For in one sense it is impossible that something, q, should be actual and contingent and account for w; whatever sufficiently accounts for something contingent cannot be a constitutive element of it. Hence, q would have to lie outside w. But, of course, that is impossible: whatever is actual and lies outside the entire set of the contingent and the actual would have to be necessary, or else impossible; and, *ex hypothesi*, q is contingent. Hence it appears that, in one sense, w is not only unexplained, but inexplicable.

However, there is no set of contingent states of affairs, w, such that by virtue of what it is—by nature, from the "list" of its content—it is the entirety of what is actual. This follows from the fact that w is contingent; for if it followed from what w is, that w is the entirety of what is actual, then w would not be logically contingent. Hence, that w

(the conjunction of what happens to be actual) is what is actually designated by "w" is itself contingent. The definite description "w" applies necessarily and by definition to the *entirety* of the contingent and the actual; but that what is contingent and actual is identical with w is itself logically contingent. It is logically possible that w_1 may have been the actual state of affairs, and that it would have been distinct from w (what is in fact actual) merely by the addition of some state of affairs, q, which is a sufficient explanation for the occurrence of all the elements of w_1 which are *not* entailed by q—namely, those things which constitute w.

Therefore, from the fact that every world designated by "w" must contain (or in itself *be*) a contingent but actual state of affairs which lacks a sufficient explanation, it does not follow that there must in any case *be* an actual state of affairs which is inexplicable in principle. Not at all; such an actual and *unaccounted* state of affairs is still *accountable:* it might have had an explanation. It is necessary that there be an unaccounted state of affairs, for example, the "original" divine choice, which is, of course, not entirely unaccounted for, but is still not accounted for *entirely;* but it does not follow from this necessity that there must be a state of affairs which is inexplicable or unaccountable—one that *could not* have had an explanation had things been otherwise than they are.

We must reply to the suggestion that there is omega-inconsistency between our general principle "It is necessarily true that some state of affairs be actual and unaccounted for" and the claim that there is no substitution instance of that formula which is true, because for every case (e.g., 'the cat is on the mat') it is false that it must, if actual, be unaccounted for. This concept of inconsistency apparently originated with Godel and really applies strictly only to formal systems, though an analogous defect can certainly crop up in ordinary language. As Wilder defines it:[37]

A formal system is ω-inconsistent if it contains a formula $\varphi(x)$ such that both $[(\exists x)(\varphi x)]$ and $[\sim\varphi(0), \sim\varphi(1), \sim\varphi(2) \cdot \cdot \cdot]$ are provable in the system.

The analogy here is that 'There is some unaccounted state of affairs' is necessarily true, and

It is false of (a) that it is unaccountable.

It is false of (b) that it is unaccountable.

It is false of (ω) that it is unaccountable.

Inspection shows the analogy does not hold. If the general formula spoke of an "unaccount*able*" state of affairs, we would have had the sort of inconsistency in question. But it does not; thus it is obvious that it could be true that *some* state of affairs must be unaccounted, while it is false that any particular one is unaccountable.

We could conclude, therefore, that those special considerations which show that the Principle of Sufficient Reason must be false *because* there must be, under all possible conditions, some (but no particular) actual state of affairs which is unaccounted for, provide no grounds for our thinking that Principle E and its correlate, the Principle of Hetero-Explicability, are false or even doubtful.

But, it will be rejoined, this defense of Principles E and H rests upon a variety of confusions. First, we take no account of the manifest ambiguity of E, and similar principles; the inadequacy of our defense will disclose itself when those ambiguities are resolved. Second, the falsity—or at least undecidability—of the principles will be revealed when we resolve the ambiguities involved in the modal and universal quantifiers. And, moreover, when we get those ambiguities straightened out, we will find that we have so far violated our intuitions as to what "explanation" consists in, that (a) the sense of the principle (which is derived from its relation to our abandoned sufficient reason principle) is destroyed; and (b) the intuitive justification we supposed for the principle has become irrelevant because of the ever-increasing distance between the sense of "possible" and "explanation" found in Principles E and H, respectively, and the senses of those words in our ordinary language. These latter points are eventually given consideration below; but for now we must concentrate upon the alleged ambiguity concerning the universal and modal quantifiers.

THE AMBIGUITY FOR THE MODALITIES IN PRINCIPLE E

It is objected that to symbolize the Principles of Explicability and of Hetero-Explicability in terms of the standard symbols, " ◊ " and "□," is to give the impression of greater precision in the concepts than is actually to be found there. Notions of the 'logically consistent' are all related to and based upon the concept 'logically impossible', or 'logically inconsistent'. This is evident from the explanations in Chap-

excludes the very existence required for hetero-explicability. More-over, the logical steps of the argument may follow rules which pre-suppose the inconsistency of the hypothesis, but nothing deleterious to the argument results from that: the hypothesis is introduced con-ditionally, and the rules of the system, far from precluding our intro-ducing inconsistent premises, permit us to introduce any conditional premise we please; after all, our conclusion is merely that if the null universe hypothesis and E are both consistent, then contradictory propositions are true. (We then reject the antecedent of the condi-tional by rejecting the consequent.)

Despite some reasonable hesitation, this may be granted, because it serves to disclose the next stage of the objection: namely, that to say that the inconsistency is established on semantical grounds (both in the case of the null universe and in that concerning the nonexistence of God) does not avoid the difficulties having to do with quantifica-tional and truth-functional inconsistency. Principle E involves modal operators, for instance, "possibly" and "consistently." In what sense is "possibly," symbolized by " $\Diamond$," used? In what sense are we saying that for any given *consistent* state of affairs it is consistent (i.e., possi-ble) to say that there is an explanation of that state of affairs? Are we saying that it is "truth-functionally consistent," "quantificationally consistent," or consistent in some other sense? If, for the moment, we treat "truth-functionally consistent" as a predicate, A, which is applicable to propositions, and if we treat "being quantificationally consistent" as a second predicate, B, which is applicable in the same way, we find that there are four schematic interpretations of the formula:[39]

$(p)(Ap \supset Bp)$

$(p)(Ap \supset Ap)$

$(p)(Bp \supset Ap)$

$(p)(Bp \supset Bp)$

Moreover, the whole expression is to be preceded by a modal op-erator, "It is necessarily the case that"; this operator has at least three

---

[39] These simple conditionals are, of course, only crudely schematic for Principle E, since it is obvious that the second half of E does not directly apply the operator to the original propositions but to the statement that some proposition explains or accounts for it. But greater precision is not needed here.

interpretations: (a) "it is truth-functionally necessary that"; (b) "it is quantificationally necessary that"; and (c) "it is semantically necessary that." Thus we have three interpretations of each of the four formulae above. If we introduce *another* predicate, C, for "semantically consistent," substituting it for A or B in the original four propositions, and if we begin to combine the three sets of the two internal operators with the three sets of over-all operators, we can get what I estimate to be 24 different statements of Principle E. And this multidimensional ambiguity does not yet take into account the various combinations of disjunctive predicates which could be made up of the original operators—such as "truth-functionally consistent *or* quantificationally consistent"—or the combinations which would result from *conjunctions* of operators: "truth-functionally *and* quantificationally *and* semantically consistent." What originally looked like a rather simple claim turns out to be highly ambiguous!

Actually, in terms of the definitions given in part A, Section 2 of Chapter III, most of the ambiguities are eliminated: the logically necessary is defined as that which expresses a truth-functionally or quantificationally syntactical necessity, or a semantical one. Thus:

1: "$\Box p$" means that ~p is either truth-functionally, quantificationally, or semantically inconsistent.

2: "$\Diamond p$" means that p is neither truth-functionally, quantificationally, nor semantically inconsistent.

Now the real difficulty with these concepts is disclosed: Does it follow from saying that ~p is logically inconsistent, that p is logically consistent? Is it not conceivable that there should be some proposition which is such that its negation is inconsistent in one way while its affirmation is inconsistent in another?

This does not seem conceivable. If it should be, then despite what may be alleged to be ambiguous about E, there will be the more serious defect that the relations among the operators cannot be as we have presumed. While we are not committed to saying that whatever is inconsistent in one way is inconsistent in every other, we *are* committed to saying that whatever is inconsistent in one way will have its contradictory negation consistent in that way and in the other, provided the contradictory negation is well formed. The null universe, call it *n* in this case, is not a counter-example. *n* is quantificationally inconsistent, but its contradictory negation is consistent in all relevant ways. Can we then design a quantificationally or truth-functionally inconsistent formula whose contradictory will not be consistent in all three ways? I have not succeeded in doing so, but I acknowledge that a major revision of the concepts involved in Principle E would be demanded by such an example.

Now that we have explicated the relationships among the concepts, and need no longer wonder which of the bewildering multitude of propositions is asserted, we can say that Principle E is not ambiguous. Of course, there is no shortage of vagueness in the notion of the "semantically inconsistent," since it is often very difficult to decide for ordinary language whether an expression is consistent. But we need not attempt to improve that situation now.

In the light of this clarification of how the modal operators are to be read in E and in similar principles, we can return to the objection that even a semantic derivation of our conclusions from E is not permissible. If a proposition's being logically consistent entails that it is not quantificationally inconsistent, then Principle E (as well as the Principle of Hetero-Explicability) begs the question against the null universe hypothesis: because 'n' is quantificationally inconsistent, '$\Diamond n$' is false, and we cannot take it as a supposition.

However, put simply, E states that for any given proposition p, if p is consistent, then p is in principle explicable. There is nothing wrong with our taking n as a substitution instance of the variable p. For E is supposed to be "necessary," and therefore, the "if–then" connective is that of strict implication. Now, by our substituting n for p we get "If n is consistent, then n in principle is explicable." This proposition is known to be true (and necessarily true), simply by virtue of our prior knowledge of the quantificational inconsistency of the antecedent. For any conditional (of strict implication) with a necessarily false antecedent is necessarily true.

The fact that we employ our knowledge of the quantificational inconsistency of n in order to guarantee that the conditional, above, is true does not cause our argument to beg the question when we later conclude that n is inconsistent. For we arrive at that conclusion by way of the negation of the consequent, followed by application of the rule modus tollens. And we arrive at the negation of the consequent entirely through semantical consideration based upon what would have to be the case if n were in principle explicable. Therefore, there is no defect in the argument just because both n and the contradictory of E are quantificationally inconsistent. Indeed, its strength is increased: this provides us with knowledge of the truth of the crucial conditional premise, mentioned above, upon whose consequent our key semantical operations are to be performed.

Therefore, I think we can admit that Principle E was in need of the explication it acquires from our making explicit the complex concept 'possible' or 'consistent' which is employed in it. But at the same time we need not admit that any defect accrues to the argument because of the multivalent concept 'inconsistent' which underlies it. Nor need we admit that it is more difficult to decide whether E is true, now that we have explicitly dismissed the host of alternative interpretations, than it was before. Principle E (expanded) states that it is either truth-functionally, quantificationally, or semantically inconsistent to deny that for any given existential state of affairs, p (which is neither truth-functionally, quantificationally, nor semantically inconsistent), it is neither truth-functionally, quantificationally, nor semantically inconsistent to say that there is some state of affairs which accounts for whether or not p is the case. It is evident that E is rendered true just because its negation is quantificationally inconsistent (since its negation will entail ' $\lozenge n$'); but we have not rested on so slight a support and have, additionally, urged semantical considerations to support our belief that E is a priori true.

As we said before, the reasoning process against n was not based upon syntactical forms but rather upon semantical relations. The whole thrust of that reasoning is that hetero-explanation is a relation between states of affairs where the explanation involves an existent, and that the hypothesis in question precludes the possibility of hetero-explanation while at the same time (through its manifest falsity) precluding auto-explicability. Hence, E and n are not compatible. Is this not obvious?

Therefore the objection that reasons that the ambiguities of E will disclose its falsity appears to be unfounded.

CONSEQUENCES OF THE ABANDONMENT OF THE PRINCIPLE OF SUFFICIENT REASON FOR PRINCIPLE E

Philosophical inquiry into the explanations for the general features of the universe began on the assumption that all actual states of affairs are either self-accounting or else hetero-explicable and hetero-explained. Thus, Aristotle is quite explicit that the ultimate explanatory factors of the universe must be finite in number but more than one, and that they will stand in need of no explanation, being necessary unconditionally. It is also obvious that we evolved E (and similar principles) in contrast to the Principle of Sufficient Reason, which had been found wanting.

Since it has turned out that the Principle of Sufficient Reason is self-contradictory—not because of its syntactical form but because of the conceptual interrelationships it presupposes—it may be wondered whether all sense that was to be assigned to the principles derived from it has also been destroyed. Related to this is the question of whether all grounds for accepting such derived principles have been cut away; for E would seem intuitively obvious to a person who believed the Principle of Sufficient Reason, but might lose all its intuitive perspicacity for one who comes to believe PSR is false.

This difficulty does not seem serious to me. It is historically true that formulation of E or of H is consequent upon an understanding of and interest in PSR; but this is irrelevant. The sense of E is not conferred by any belief in PSR, but through the conceptual interrelationship of its own parts; E was formulated, moreover, precisely because PSR seemed inadequate. But, it will be argued, explanation does not mean anything any more; explanation or accounting, as a fundamental, underived metaphysical relation, makes sense only if it is thought to be a primitive relationship which characterizes all things. What sense does it make to speak of a sufficient explanation of a given state of affairs, when the totality of actual states of affairs lacks a sufficient explanation? For one who holds the Principle of Sufficient Reason to be true, it makes sense to imagine that there is a sufficient explanation for a given event, since he thinks the explanations of single events can be traced back to a sufficient explanation of all events. But the whole heart of the concept of "sufficient explanation" has been torn out, it is argued, by the doctrine that there is no sufficient explanation for the totality of what is actual.

This unhappy consequence does not follow strictly from the facts at hand. It is true that the sufficiency of one fact as an explanation for another is not exactly as it was conceived by those who thought the chain of explanations would run unbroken to ultimate factors which would obtain regardless of circumstances. It is true that "sufficiency of explanation" has a somewhat different status in a world-view where E is the strongest general principle we are willing to employ. To say that one state of affairs is a "sufficient account" of another will have a precise sense only relative to some presupposed general relationship or theory which includes the events in question. But that relativity of the accounting relationship (which is to be described with respect to some general theory or in relation to some general doctrine of agency) in no way weakens the general claim that any contingent state of affairs is hetero-explicable; for while the particular accounting relationship between two states of affairs may very well come to be regarded as theory-relative, the accountability of the states of affairs will be prior and independent. Hence the alterations in the concept 'accounts for' that are required by our rejection of PSR will not vitiate our use of Principle E, although it cannot be denied that these alterations demand an analysis of the concept 'explains', and perhaps a revamping of the kind of enterprise the metaphysician pursues (an analysis we cannot undertake here).

While a direct analysis of 'explanation' and 'accounting' is required, we need not admit that in the meantime E has lost its intuitive plausibility. Just the contrary: barring the disclosure of some logical inconsistency in the structure of E, no analysis of the general relation of 'accounting', according to which a philosopher seeks the "accounting-for" or the "explanation-of" the actual states of the universe, can be considered successful if it does not render E more plausible than not. It is, of course, an open question whether those analyses of 'accounting' or 'explanation' which will make E intuitively obvious will be able to sustain the consequences that we have drawn from E and from similar principles. We cannot make it a necessary condition for an analysis of our basic concept that all our uses of it should be found consistent. Still, we have at present no reason for thinking E implausible, but rather every reason given us by the actual practice of theoretical science (both physical and philosophical) from the earliest times to our own, to think that the hypothesis "It is consistent to say that there is an actual and contingent state of affairs which is in principle inexplicable" is absurd. What could there be about any contingent state of affairs which would make it in principle inexplicable?

Suppose someone says that there could be a contingent state of affairs, "There is a cat on the mat," which is inexplicable. In virtue of *what* could it be inexplicable? By what would it differ from a similar state of affairs, "There is a cat on the mat," which *is* explicable in principle? We cannot make explicability a "first-level" property of anything, any more than we can make inexplicability a first-level property of anything. Thus, we noted earlier that the uncausability and unpreventability of the being of God is *not* the nature or essence of God, but is a consequence of His nature or essence—a nature or essence which cannot be discursively and completely formulated by human beings, though I think we can do much more than we have done to describe more fundamental attributes of God. In any case, we do not take God's existence as a *contingent* and *inexplicable* state of affairs.

Central to all that we have argued lies the principle that the logically contingent is hetero-explicable—a principle that is basic to the conceptual foundations of all theoretical sciences, which are not confined to constructive formalism, but purport to provide theoretical accounts of parts of the actual universe. Would it really be plausible, responsible, rational, or even sane for me to say "Modern relativistic general dynamic theory is not an adequate account of the behavior of the celestial systems because their movements are in principle inexplicable"? What could there be in the nature of such systems which would render them inexplicable? Whatever it might be—if it were even conceivable—it would, I say, render their states of affairs *beyond* the realm of the logically contingent. Hence, the intuitive plausibility of E, far from being weakened by our abandonment of PSR, becomes strengthened because its truth becomes a necessary condition for the adequacy of our concept of theoretical explanation or accounting. All these remarks are not, however, to be taken as a proposal that we ignore the questions as to the relationship between "explaining" or "accounting" as a scientific enterprise and the "ontological correlate" of this enterprise, or that we ignore the puzzle as to what kind of analysis is appropriate for the underived metaphysical relation 'accounts for' or 'explains', since we have already made it evident that a worthwhile "reductive" explication of the relation will probably be impossible.

A further note: The statement that any contingent but actual state of affairs may consistently be said to have an explanation or account

in some other
the princi'
possib'
a

ov
suff
nor a
exampl
And Prin
which acc
of affairs; bu
tent to say that
means that *if* the
would result wou

SUFFICIENCY THROUGH AC

Sufficiency in philosop
in another way from, bu
by Aristotle and his succes.
which we ultimately find a
and contingent, but as the gro
is actual and contingent. In the
seen as a consequence of His a-s
explains why every contingent sta
There is a ground for the accountabl
which has its being on its own accou
agency that *could*, by augmenting the
what is now actual, and could have done
degree by which we conceive the actual to

in some other contingent but actual state of affairs is not a denial of the principle demonstrated in Section 2 of this chapter: "It is not possible that there be some state of affairs, q, which accounts for the actuality of every contingent but actual state of affairs." It has been premised (a) that no contingent state of affairs can account for its own actuality and (b) that no necessary state of affairs can be *ex se* a sufficient account for any contingent one. Hence neither a necessary nor a contingent state of affairs could be a candidate for a counter-example to the principle above.

And Principle E does not entail that there can be some state of affairs which accounts for the actuality of *every* contingent but actual state of affairs; but only that for *any* contingent state of affairs, it is consistent to say that there is some state of affairs which accounts for it. This means that *if* the entirety of what is actual were accounted for, what would result would not be *this* possible world, but a possible world.

SUFFICIENCY THROUGH ACCOUNTABILITY

Sufficiency in philosophical accounts of the universe can be obtained in another way from, but one that is not alien to, that contemplated by Aristotle and his successors. God will appear, not as the ground in which we ultimately find a "sufficient reason" for whatever is actual and contingent, but as the ground for the *accountability* of whatever is actual and contingent. In the omnipotence of God (which is to be seen as a consequence of His a-*seity*), we will find that factor which explains why every contingent state of affairs is hetero-explicable. There is a ground for the accountability of the contingent, a ground which has its being on its own account and which is the necessary agency that *could*, by augmenting the actual, have accounted for what is now actual, and could have done so without regard to the degree by which we conceive the actual to have been augmented.

Conclusion

Attempting to provide the beginnings of an analytic reconstruction of natural theology, we have dealt with a variety of traditional questions, such as the arguments for the existence of God, the problem of evil, the relationship between God's universal causality and human freedom, the nature of omnipotence, the metaphysical dependency between God and the world, and the questions concerning the reasons for the creation of the world.

These considerations have led us to discuss, among other things, some relationships between proper names and logical modalities (Chapter II, applied in Chapter VI), the falsity of the Principle of Sufficient Reason (Chapters III and VII), its replacement by the Principle of Explicability (Chapters III and VII), and the nature of metaphysical dependence (Chapter VI).

What can we conclude about the feasibility of the whole enterprise of constructive philosophical theology? We can conclude that it is full of difficulties, but that these difficulties result not from the unintelligibility, inconsistency, or ineffability of our traditional Judaic-Christian conception of God, but rather from the multitude of essentially connected logical, metaphysical and epistemological problems which are nowhere near solution. For instance, we can appeal to no well-established theory about the relationship of logical modalities to "real" modalities (possibility and necessity); we have no fully satisfactory characterization of what is "inconsistent" to employ; and the early chapters were haunted by the lack of a proper analysis of the nature of "begging the question,"which would have clarified a number of points. In order to make even a beginning, we had to risk speculations about the nature of and uses of proper names, and about the nature of metaphysical dependence; we even had to speculate about the existence of a decision-method or method of assessment which would make philosophy a science, in order to have any clear idea about what our arguments would have to do in order to be good or successful. In a word, the construction of a plausible natural theology is to be slow and piecemeal; but the cause lies not as much in the nature of the theological subject matter as in the impoverished philosophical resources we are able to devote to it. What results we have attained surely illustrate that.

The cause of religion—even the cause of a rational and reflective approach to religion—will not suffer from the endless delay I anticipate. As has been remarked often in this book, the purpose of philosophical inquiry into constructive natural theology is purely theoretical; it is for the satisfaction of the intellect alone. Nothing is done with an apologetic outlook, or with a practical purpose of any sort. Those so-called believers who look to philosophy to buttress or perhaps replace their faith with a system of "established truths"are deluding themselves. No philosophical inquiry is terminating. Believers who are waiting and wanting to ground their faith in the achievements of philosophy are waiting for a train that does not stop here; it is their misfortune that so many of our predecessors apparently promised that it would.

Index